*View of Great Salt Lake from Bear River Valley
(U.S., Congress, Senate, Executive Documents No. 3,
32d Cong., spec. sess., Serial 608, 1851, opposite
p. 268).*

PATTERN and PROCESS

RESEARCH
in
HISTORICAL GEOGRAPHY

NATIONAL ARCHIVES CONFERENCES / VOLUME 9

Papers and Proceedings of the Conference on the
National Archives and Research in Historical Geography

SPONSORED BY THE NATIONAL ARCHIVES

AND RECORDS SERVICE

November 8-9, 1971
The National Archives Building / Washington, D.C.

PATTERN and PROCESS

RESEARCH
in
HISTORICAL GEOGRAPHY

---

edited by

RALPH E. EHRENBERG

HOWARD UNIVERSITY PRESS
WASHINGTON, D.C.
1975

Published by Howard University Press for the
National Archives Trust Fund Board
National Archives and Records Service
General Services Administration
Washington, D.C.

Library of Congress Cataloging in Publication Data

Conference on the National Archives and Research in Historical Geography, Washington, D.C., 1971.
Pattern and process.
(National Archives conferences; v. 9)
Bibliography: p.
Includes index.
1. United States—Historical geography—Congresses.   2. United States—Historical geography—Sources—Bibliography.   3. United States. National Archives.   I. Ehrenberg, Ralph E., 1937-   ed.   II. United States. National Archives and Records Service. III. Title.   IV. Series: United States. National Archives. Conference; v. 9.
E179.5.C58 1971   911'.73   74-23617
ISBN 0-88258-050-7

Contents

Exploration, Surveying, and Mapping

Transportation, Commerce, and Industry

Rural and Urban Settlement

Appendices

Foreword

Since 1967, the National Archives and Records Service has held a series of conferences for the exchange of ideas and information between archivists and researchers. These conferences are designed both to inform scholars about the wealth of useful research materials available in the National Archives and to provide an opportunity for researchers to suggest ways in which their use of these records could be facilitated.

The National Archives and Records Service, a part of the General Services Administration, administers the permanently valuable, noncurrent records of the federal government. These archival holdings date from the days of the Continental Congresses to the present.

Among the approximately one million cubic feet of records now constituting the National Archives of the United States are such significant documents as the Declaration of Independence, the Constitution, and the Bill of Rights. However, most of the archives, whether in the National Archives Building, the regional archives branches, or the presidential libraries, are less dramatic. They are preserved because of their continuing practical utility for the ordinary processes of government, for the establishment and protection of individual rights, and for their value in documenting our nation's history.

One goal of the National Archives staff is to explore and make more widely known these historical records. It is hoped that these conferences will be a positive act in that direction. The papers of each conference are published in the belief that this exchange of ideas and information should be preserved and made available in printed form.

Arthur F. Sampson
Administrator of General Services

Preface

This volume consists of papers prepared for the Conference on the National Archives and Research in Historical Geography which was held on November 8-9, 1971. The conference was the ninth in a series of semiannual conferences sponsored by the National Archives for the purpose of exploring topics of mutual interest to archivists and the scholarly community. As with earlier conferences, a central focus or theme was chosen that reflected important but largely untapped resources in the National Archives. Because of the massive impact the federal government has had on the past, and continues to have on the present and future, geography of the United States, it was decided that an appropriate conference theme would be historical geography.

A. Philip Muntz, former director of the Cartographic Archives Division, and Ralph E. Ehrenberg, present director, were codirectors of the conference. Mr. Ehrenberg is also the editor of this volume. Both Dr. Muntz and Mr. Ehrenberg have been active in the acquisition and preservation of documentary material of a geographic nature and the dissemination of this informtion to the scholarly community. This volume represents one of the means of this dissemination.

JAMES B. RHOADS
Archivist of the United States

Introduction

RALPH E. EHRENBERG

Archives and the study of geography have been closely associated throughout recorded time. The clay tablets on which the Sumerians scribed their geographical glossaries and city plans more than four thousand years ago comprised the earliest archives. During the Age of Reconnaissance much of the geographical knowledge of the known world was deposited in the archives of Seville. More recently, the rise of nation-states has contributed to the establishment of national archives that generally house documentary materials pertaining to a nation's geography.

One of the objectives of the Conference on the National Archives and Research in Historical Geography, which was held on November 8 and 9, 1971, was to make geographers more aware of this long and close relationship by examining in particular the relevant geographical resources stored in the National Archives of the United States. While a few historical geographers have examined the value of archival source material for particular topics or time periods, such as railroads or the colonial period, no comprehensive guide has yet been prepared. Realizing that the tremendous volume of documentary records located in the National Archives of the United States probably prohibits such an assessment for American geographers, the codirectors of this conference believed that an alternative was to encourage geographers to visit the National Archives and to examine for themselves the potential sources that are available. With the same thought in mind, a bibliography of finding aids to resources in the National Archives was also planned but, unfortunately, was not completed in time for the conference. This bibliography now appears as Appendix A to this volume. Additionally, ten resource papers, listed in Appendix B, describing the records of selected topics or regions were prepared by staff members and distributed during the conference. The response to these finding aids has been gratifying and several are now in their third printing.

Another objective of the conference was to provide for the first time a common forum for archivists and scholars interested in the historical geography of the United States. It was hoped that by an open exchange of information and ideas, both archivists and historical geographers might have a better understanding of each other's interests and research needs. To this end, a series of papers were presented by scholars, describing current research interests and to some extent the state of the art in 1971, and by archivists, describing the value and potential of the National Archives as a research center for historical geography.

The conference was opened by keynote addresses by James B. Rhoads, archivist of the United States, and Andrew Hill Clark, Finch Research Professor of Geography, University of Wisconsin. The keynote session was followed by a special session on black population and general sessions on exploration, surveying, and mapping; transportation, commerce, and industry; and rural and urban settlement. The general sessions were broad in scope to allow for coverage of a variety of subjects. Due to the length of time between presentation and publication the papers presented at the conference have undergone some rearrangement and editing, but their substance has not been altered. In a number of papers, bibliographies have been brought up to date.

A. Philip Muntz, formerly director of the Cartographic Archives Division, was codirector of the conference and to him must go most of the credit for its success. He not only conceived of the idea of a conference on historical geography but also was instrumental in planning the program and contacting many of the speakers. A program advisory committee composed of Gary S. Dunbar (University of California, Los Angeles), John Fraser Hart (University of Minnesota), and Robert D. Mitchell (University of Maryland), was particularly helpful in selecting speakers. Their guidance and assistance is gratefully acknowledged. Donald W. Meinig (Syracuse University), Wilbur Zelinsky (Pennsylvania State University), Lester J. Cappon (Newberry Library), Douglas R. McManis (Columbia University), and Edward T. Price, Jr. (University of Oregon) were responsible, as session chairmen, for an exceptionally well conducted and productive series of meetings.

Many members of the staff of the National Archives made important contributions. Dr. Rhoads and Edward G. Campbell, assistant archivist of the Office of the National Archives, made possible the conference and the publication of this volume by their active support and encouragement. John E. Byrne of the Educational Programs Office provided valuable logistical assistance prior to and during the conference. Thirteen professional archivists of the staff of the Office of the National Archives made the conference more meaningful by sharing their expert knowledge of pertinent records either as session commentators or by contributing resource papers. Their names can be found in the Biographical Sketches and in Appendix B. A special debt of gratitude is also owed to the entire staff of the Cartographic Archives Division for their valuable assistance, especially Patrick McLaughlin for a variety of duties; Charles Taylor and Gary Morgan for taking over some of my administrative duties during the conference and the preparation of this volume; and Linda Cullember, Ophelia Bowman, and Virginia Cooke for typing the manuscripts.

Finally, I am particularly grateful to Angela Wilk of the Publications Division for her capable assistance in editing the papers and for seeing the volume through the press.

Research on the Historical
Geography of the United States

Introduction

D. W. MEINIG

The Conference on the National Archives and Research in Historical Geography was an auspicious occasion for American historical geography. The great interest shown in this conference and the quality of the participants and papers marked a new stage in the development of historical geography. Even a few years ago, such an attendance or such a program could not have been assembled. I well recall Herman Friis lamenting not long ago the disparity between the enormous riches in the National Archives and the few geographers who showed much interest in them.

That number is still far too few, but the conference was recognition that a lively body of historical geography scholars had emerged. And it made one dare to hope that the gathering was portentous, for if it does produce, as intended, a much greater use of the geographical materials in the National Archives, we may at last be significantly under way with the grand task implicit but perilously underdeveloped in American geography—the description, analysis, and interpretation of the full course of our national history from the various perspectives of the geographer.

We have one great example well known to all historical geographers, Ralph H. Brown's *Historical Geography of the United States*. A splendid work by an exemplary scholar, it is one display of what a geographer can do to illuminate the American past. A glance at Brown's bibliography will show his heavy dependence upon a rich array of governmental records. But his study was not only a singular work in its time, it remains a lonely book on our shelves. It is twenty-three years since that volume appeared, and it has no companions of similar general intent.

This is not intended to suggest that we should all be writing books of the same scope, but only that together we should all be generating a much larger body of studies which would provide the foundation for a variety of geographical interpretations of America.

The National Archives contains the main raw materials for that foundation, and it will be built through the joint labors of archivists and geographers. The keynote speakers of the conference, James B. Rhoads, archivist of the United States, and Andrew Hill Clark, Finch Research Professor of Geography, University of Wisconsin, represented the two sides of this necessary collaboration.

The Role of the National Archives

JAMES B. RHOADS

The National Archives is recognized as one of the principal centers for historical research in the United States, although it is perhaps not so widely known for its considerable resources pertinent to geography, anthropology, sociology, economics, and allied disciplines. Through a series of scholarly conferences, of which the conference on historical geography was the ninth, we hope to make our holdings and services better known to workers in all the social sciences and, at the same time, to learn more about recent research trends, views on the uses and relative values of various kinds of federal documentation, and about ways in which the Archives can better fulfill its research functions.

The United States was quite late in establishing an archives. Numerous files of valuable records were lost to fires, floods, and other misfortunes during the nineteenth and early twentieth centuries, but after years of dedicated work by members of the American Historical Association, particularly through its Conference of Archivists and its Public Archives Commission, the federal records were inventoried and the National Archives Building, opened in 1935, was provided for housing and maintenance of these records. In the nearly four decades since its establishment, the Archives has extended and diversified its services. Now known as the National Archives and Records Service, (NARS), a component of the General Services Administration, this agency supervises the activities of the Archives here in Washington; the libraries of Presidents Hoover, Roosevelt, Truman, Eisenhower,

Kennedy, and Johnson; and the federal records centers. Of the latter, located in fifteen key cities across the country, eleven maintain records in their archives branches particularly pertinent to the history and historical geography of their respective regions.

Since 1935 the NARS staff has arranged and brought under basic control a vast body of records; has developed a system of archival theory and practice; has published and distributed a lengthy series of guides, catalogs, and lists of the records; has provided to scholars and the general public a wide variety of reference services; and has assisted the government in the development of efficient and economical paper-work management procedures. In 1969 we inaugurated *Prologue: The Journal of the National Archives,* a quarterly, scholarly publication that contains substantive historical articles, bibliographical essays pertaining to archival holdings and techniques, and news notes of interest to scholars concerned with primary sources; every issue of *Prologue* has included material potentially useful to historical geographers.

Geographers have been employed in the National Archives since 1937, when W. L. G. Joerg established the Division of Maps and Charts. During his fifteen-year tenure, Joerg built the division into one of the world's great map depositories. Now known as the Cartographic Archives Division, this office is staffed by geographers and historians with substantial geographic training. A separate focus of geographical research in this agency is the Center for Polar Archives, founded and directed by Herman Friis, another active and respected geographer.

In spite of our long-term affiliations with the geographic profession and an active program of describing and publicizing our holdings, we would like to encourage many more geographers to avail themselves of our resources than have appeared thus far. Countless books and articles have been based on the maps and other geographic sources in our files, but most of them have been basically historical and only peripherally geographical.

The value of the early General Land Office records and similar archival documents was recognized thirty years ago by Carl Sauer in a major statement on historical geography. Sauer said:

> The first step in the reconstruction of past stages of a culture area is the mastery of its written documents. The discovery of contemporaneous maps is the first thing hoped for, but rarely realized. We have, however, scarcely exploited the documentary possibilities in the United States of old land surveys as to notations on the character of vegetation and of "improvements" early in the period of settlement. There is a fair amount of valuable material in the Land Office plats and in the older records of land grants that give glimpses of the pioneer landscape. Factual data, precisely

localized, of enumerations of persons and goods, of land titles, assessments [and] production, lie neglected in various archives to await exploitation. ("Foreword to Historical Geography," in *Land and Life,* ed., John Leighly [Berkeley: University of California Press, 1963], p. 366.)

Although few recent methodological statements by geographers have dealt at length with the uses of archival documents, it is obvious that profitable use has been made of early state and provincial records. However, while researching regional and local topics, one may be surprised to find that a large percentage of the federal records documenting national policy do so within a decidedly geographical context. These files contain much historical material pertinent, and in some cases vital, to regional studies.

The federal records deal with an enormous variety of geographical and historical themes. Together with the Land Office records, files created during the nineteenth century by the Bureau of Indian Affairs and the Army Corps of Engineers are particularly significant. These agencies alone have bequeathed to today's scholars a graphic representation of the exploration and settlement of the United States westward from the thirteen original colonies and of the surveying and diminution of Indian lands and resettlement of the tribes.

In addition to the maps compiled through exploration and land survey, there are hundreds of thousands of historically valuable maps, charts, and aerial photographs created by agencies engaged in a variety of technical and administrative operations. Among these are the cartographic records of various bureaus of the Department of Agriculture, illustrating the changing patterns of agriculture and rural settlement in the United States; the State Department records, pertaining to the development of our national boundaries and the geography of the boundary areas; the Census Bureau and Federal Housing Authority records, showing urban growth and change; and the records created by the Post Office Department and certain branches of the army, showing the development of a national transportation and communications network during the nineteenth century. Many of these records are described in detail in published National Archives lists and inventories and in the various resource papers prepared by NARS staff members, listed in the appendixes of this volume.

I am dwelling on maps only because they are the most obvious archival sources for historical geography. It is axiomatic that any research in archives should exploit all documents pertinent to the topic; the reports, correspondence, and other textual documents held in the various records divisions at the Archives include much valuable statistical and descriptive data for historical geographers. Some of these holdings are discussed in this volume by representatives of several of these divisions. Additionally, early photographs and other graphic documents in the files of the Audiovisual Archives Division might furnish useful insights into cultural landscape patterns and processes during the nineteenth century.

I hope that the papers in this volume will serve as an encouragement to undertake more research into our holdings and to make inquiries about documents pertinent to your areas of interest. The staff of the Office of the National Archives welcomes written requests and often can furnish considerable assistance through correspondence alone. And for researchers who have the time and opportunity to visit the Archives personally, the staff will be pleased to make the records available for examination and furnish photocopies of selected items for a nominal fee. The agencies of origin maintain restrictions on the use of some twentieth-century files, relating principally to diplomacy and military and security operations, but almost all of the nineteenth-century records are free of restrictions.

In conclusion, I would like to call attention to two developments that should be of interest to historical geographers. First, for many years we have made available to the public printed facsimiles of significant historical documents from our holdings. Thus far, only one map has been issued, but we intend within the next few years to begin work on a series of facsimile folios of archival maps having exceptional historical and geographical importance. Second, in our finding aids publication program, we are now placing increased emphasis on lists, catalogs, and guides relating to specific historical themes and geographical regions. These will in no sense replace the lengthy series of inventories and preliminary inventories through which we have described the records of individual federal agencies. Rather they will augment them by providing the researcher subject-oriented descriptions and by demonstrating the organic and thematic relationships between archival record groups.

Geography, in company with the other social sciences and humanities, has witnessed the advent of dramatic new research approaches in recent years, utilizing statistical manipulation, model-building, and related devices. Continuing theoretical advances are important to the growth of any discipline. I feel safe in saying, however, that historical geographers, like historians, will never want to stray far from the primary documentary sources which, with fieldwork, form the basis of their vital empirical investigations. The job of the National Archives is to preserve those sources and make them available for research.

First Things First

ANDREW HILL CLARK

I warmly support the judgment of the archivist of the United States about the reliance that historical geographers should have on the kinds of primary sources likely to be found in archives. Indeed, that viewpoint explains the title of this paper. The word "archives," I am told, is derived ultimately from a Greek root meaning "in the first place" and although the derivative, *te archeia,* referred specifically to public or governmental records, the pristine root meaning seems even more appropriate in that archives now provide scholars with a wide variety of primary evidence of private as well as public origin.

Historical geographers use a wide variety of sources—holographic, printed, electronically recorded, photographic, artifactual, pedologic, biological, and chemical—and they should be as precise, as *primary,* as possible. In our utter dependence upon reliable primary evidence, we turn most often to archives and archivists for help.

Dr. Rhoads has suggested that archivists might like to know more about the nature of research interests of historical geographers, and he has been kind enough to invite suggestions on ways in which archivists might be more helpful to us. In this paper, the first theme will be addressed explicitly, the second theme, largely implicitly.

Capsule disquisitions on methodology inevitably become *pronunciamentos,* not reasoned arguments, but time forbids anything more. And it is important that archivists understand the needs of historical geographers. This is, of course, a personal statement and commits no one

9

else. Footnote references are given for those who will want to look into these matters further, but it is hard to suggest appropriate sources that are comprehensive, balanced, and brief. Individual statements tend to be strongly idiosyncratic,[1] and concensus reports of groups or symposia are usually even less useful. A recent Social Science Research Council publication,[2] prepared by a group of geographers, failed to come up with a balanced and judicious view of the nature and interests of geography. Notable was a deemphasis, or highly eclectic conception, of cultural geography and an almost complete absence of discussion of the interests and activities of historical geographers as such—hardly a negligible matter considering the growing number of individuals in this field.

Historical geographers are first of all geographers but, also, necessarily, kinds of historians, as are most archivists. Thus it may be most useful to discuss the purposes and activities of historical geographers largely by analogical references to the academic discipline of history.[3] This discussion will not apply to those of the cultural-ecological wing of historical geography who do not make extensive use of archives.[4] There are others who claim the name whose individual interests rarely bring them to the documentary sources; indeed, there appear to be some so theoretically or hypoempirically biased against archival information *per se* that they almost seem to look upon archives as establishments of intellectual ill-repute. But most geographers recognize that they are in constant need of the kinds of evidence of which archivists are the principal collectors, organizers, and curators.

As in any healthy academic discipline, geographers maintain a continuous dialogue as to methods and purposes. We, also, are often influenced by changes in fashion and new styles, which may lead to an undervaluing of solid work of the past not considered to be in the current mode. The intellectually therapeutic value of a regular house-cleaning to discard the superficial and the meretricious is indisputable, but we really must do better than in the past in preserving the best of our inheritance. It is clear that most of today's younger generation of geographers realizes this, even when, in perfect tune with their times, its members have been most excited about finding statistically expressible regularities in the locational aspects of phenomena or in staking a geographical claim to related theory or analytical procedures in one of the categorically defined physical, life, social, or behavioral sciences.[5] Whatever one's bias may be, these represent unexceptionable activities, and many historical geographers, and their peers among historians, are so engaged. Unhappily, a methodological vogue may be misconstrued as methodological essense, and such activities, in themselves, often fall short of reaching what should be our major and ultimate disciplinary goals. As one of my more imaginative and numerically skilled colleagues recently put it, "If we limit ourselves to the rigorous and productive delights of statistics and algebra, we shall not advance far beyond the chess-game tradition of Alice's journey on the far side of the looking-glass."[6] Let me hasten to add that there is heartening evidence that, during the past five years, there has been a substantial reevaluation of the claims or pretensions of some of geography's most voguish swingers.

Incidentally, this personal viewpoint is far from antagonistic to the computer-induced opportunities for many kinds of qualitative research. Wittingly, or unwittingly, geographers are behavioralists, much more interested in generalized man than in individual men, so to speak, and collective man often is most easily described, analyzed, and interpreted by statistical methods, if quantifiable evidence can be found.[7] In the fifties, before more sophisticated facilities were available, my seminar students used to sit over batteries of hand calculators doing correlation studies. Indeed, two decades earlier I had worked for many years as a statistician, often supervising the punching and Hollerith-machine processing of large quantities of cards. But only insurance companies and government census bureaus then thought the noise, size, maintenance, and concurrent expense of the cumbersome equipment worthwhile. Thus, if my strong espousal of quantitative work in the fifties changed to call for restraint in the sixties, it was not that my interest in collective man and in quantitative analysis of evidence, whenever such evidence was available, had decreased in the least. One must always use the means most likely to achieve one's sensible and appropriate goals. At the same time, on occasion I have vehemently rejected the preposterous proposition that we cannot make useful studies of the eighteenth, seventeenth, or earlier centuries because we do not have the kind of information available for the nineteenth or twentieth centuries. It is, of course, often more difficult and the product often less nearly definitive, but the results of tackling such challenging problems of research have attracted wide scholarly interest.[8]

From my scattered acquaintance with the philosophical and methodological, not to mention substantive, literature of history,[9] my conclusion as to what major scholarly purpose most historians see for their discipline is that it is a synthetic interpretation of changes of various kinds and scales, over variously defined periods of time, in ideas, cultures, economies, political entities, and much more, in all of their inextricable intertwinings. The definitive work on the revolutionary period

11

in America never will be written, but each new competent study by a socioeconomic, political, or any kind of historian—and, we hope, increasingly by historical geographers—creates the possibility of an improved interpretation and a more acceptable larger synthesis. This is not to see the ultimate purpose of the historian as the search for single keys to cosmological cultural understanding (as it seemed to Toynbee, Spengler, Sorokin, Marx, and Comte)[10] but, rather, ever-fuller interpretative descriptions of the past with whatever explanations seem valid and appropriate.

My view of the ultimate goal of geography and geographers is that it is the elucidation of the character of places and areas of the earth as that character reflects the interwoven phenomena of the world of man.[11] Any scholar trained to operate by a certain set of canons of logic or scientific method will be concerned with analyzing by those canons what is found, viewed inductively or deductively. Indeed, as we try to understand Annapolis, Atlanta, Chicago, California, Canada, the Islamic realm, or the tropics, we are aided by the generalizations and probabilistic models developed in past decades and we can always use more, improved models. But the ultimate synthesis cannot be arrived at only by procedures developed from a narrow expertise or programmed for a rigorous statistical methodology; it very much needs the broad training, experience, skill, and knowledge that can lead to a personal interpretative judgment. Subjective? Well, of course, it must be to a degree subjective, unless you believe that there is a calculus that can explain the island of New Guinea or the French Revolution.

Despite a substantial volume of excellent, widely useful studies in the "new" history of the postwar generation,[12] the new trends in history (and, to my point here, geography) often lure our apprentices, including some of the best, almost completely into the service of economics, sociology, and, sometimes, botany or geology, so that their direct contributions as geographers or historians may be negligible. Certainly, breadth of training is desirable and geographers have license as economists, statisticians, or geologists, for example, as far as they have competence and should follow their vision of truth wherever it leads. But an interest in the location or change through time of some phenomenon does not itself make a scholar a geographer or historian. Economic phenomena and plants, as such, must be the central concern of the economist and botanist. It is when the geographer or historian puts his hypothesis or model to work in a broader framework, ignoring disciplinary boundaries and labels, that he serves his own field more fully and directly. I confess that I am old-fashioned enough (I hope not to the point of simplicism) in my views to find the common use of the adjectives "historical," to refer to time, and "geographical," to refer to location, very useful, even when categories of phenomena described or discussed are very limited in scope. Moreover, I would insist that geography and geographers always are to be distinguished by an overriding concern with location, places, areas, regions, territories, or realms. But, withal, as I view the ultimate purposes of the scholarly efforts of geographers or historians, they are to produce synthetic interpretations as rigorous as the quality of their evidence, or the relevance and credibility of the hypotheses or generalizations employed allow, and always to a degree subjective, achieving this by a blend of scientific and humanistic training and skills. Whatever else it may be, historical and geographical interpretation remains, to an important degree, an art.[13]

This approach is perhaps the result, in part, of having been biased early, by philosopher Karl Popper, with a deep suspicion of historicism, that is, the conviction that historical prediction is the true aim of the social sciences and that "this end is attainable by discovering the 'rhythms' or 'patterns' or 'laws' or 'trends' that underlie the evolution of history."[14] If, ultimately, it may be possible to get a generally useful interpretation of Baltimore or the Chesapeake Bay hinterland at any time, or through any period of time, by something like a vastly expanded econometric analysis—which with Popper I am inclined to doubt—it is not possible now. Yet I regard efforts to make the fullest possible interpretations of such entities as fundamental geographical purposes. This is not to assign to geographers the impossible task implied by saying that they *must* be interested in *everything,* but it does mean that they *may* be interested in virtually *anything.* And yet their geographical bias will be evident in concern with locations, places, and areas; with comparisons, contrasts, and interconnections through terrestrial space; and with environmental or ecological circumstances in which human activities are carried on in a place or region.

Indeed, it is because of our deep and ancient ecological interests that we welcome so warmly the current popular concern with ecological balance and the problems of environmental deterioration. Moreover, we may ask the help of archivists in the study of such matters for earlier centuries. But I hope they do not share with all too many historians the semantic fallacy[15] that because of our deep interest in the natural environment, one may use "natural environment" and "geography" as synonyms. Despite every effort to eradicate the notion, I still find doctoral candidates in history, with minors in geography, writing in their dissertations about the "geography" of Maryland, Tasmania, or elsewhere, as if it meant no more than the rocks, the rain, the rivers, and the roses. Such a fixation easily leads to the conclusion that geographers are, or tend to be, environmental determinists and that historical geographers study the "significance," "influence," or "control" of nature in various kinds of changes in the human condition.[16] Yet, while I protest such a distorted view, I insist that we remain interested in any natural circumstances of the past and, particularly, in the perception that contemporaries had of those circumstances.[17] What was thought to be (of climate, vegetation, fauna, or soils, for example) often was more important to the making of decisions than actuality.

Earlier, I said that historical geographers considered themselves geographers first, and most of what has been discussed is applicable to all geographers, even though the analogies with history have been used constantly as vehicles. The corollary question is, "What may distinguish a historical geographer from other geographers?" Once again, a parallel from history is useful—the view of history in general, on the one hand, as compared with contemporary history or current events, on the other. Briefly, the more we are concerned with generations before our own and with processes of change through substantial periods of time, the more "historical" is our geography.

Turning to our demands on archivists, our interest is in collective man instead of individual men. Of course we are human and can easily be swayed by information on personal idiosyncrasies in the evidence we examine. But we would be less likely to go into the Clinton materials in the Clements[18] (perhaps trying to explain the general's cantankerous disposition which was a major British handicap in the War for Independence) than to be examining the kinds of sources used by Jackson Main,[19] although to different ends and, I suspect, different conclusions. To the degree that we remain geographers, rather than generalized theoretical behavioral scientists, we may have occasion to look at almost anything, and I hope that we will honor all artificial bounds to our curiosity by ignoring them. But there is little doubt that our main requests will be for such mundane things as census materials; assessor's and other tax records; evidence about land tenure, land alienation, and land transfer; buying, selling, and transfer of goods; employment; migration; records of baptisms, marriages, and deaths; church membership; newspaper circulation; tavern locations; and the like. The most noticeable difference between us and other historical students digging in the same files will be our concern for the quantity, quality, and integrity of the locational provenance of the information sought.[20] It will be much more pleasant (and useful) to be asked, when we present our credentials as geographers, in what places and times we are interested, than to be faced with a blank stare of incredulity before being directed to the natural history museum down the hall. Important, also, to many other kinds of historical research is where things are in relation to other things. I would hope that whenever archivists are about to decide against a locational index or cross-classification for any set of materials, they will think not only of geographers but, also, of an opportunity to protect their principal clientele against a species of the *Erewhon* fallacy, which assumes that where things are is of no special significance to what happens there.

In closing, I should like to refer to two present vogue or jargon words, "spatial" and "territoriality," to reveal a little more about geographers and their interests. The first has been used so much that, as Marvin Mikesell recently suggested, it is beginning to sound like an incantation.[21] If one finds a geographer using it constantly, he may not simply be trying to "snow" you—although that is by no means certain—but, as with the current fantastic overuse of "like" by the young, he may simply have slipped into lazy speech habits. Nevertheless, I would attribute its wide use to an overriding concern with the locational arrangements over the face of the earth of relevant phenomena of both nature and culture and with the significance of connections through terrestrial space between places. What is, rather tautologically, often referred to now as "spatial movement," as in migration patterns or the diffusion of things or ideas, has long been of great interest to geographers and may lead us to rather large samples of evidence from particular universes of phenomena.[22]

"Territoriality," also, may sound like jargon, but it expresses concerns that are of ancient geographical interest.[23] If, today, we could develop an effective research design to draw temporally changing boundaries between the hinterlands of Los Angeles or San Francisco, we might make a contribution to understanding the internal stresses that have been produced in California by the pulls of its two major nodes. New Jersey is perpetually cracked by the polarities of New York and Philadelphia, but it is not easy to find where the crack lies and, as a matter of historical concern, it clearly has migrated with time. Indeed, the outreach of any city, at any time, involves the examination, selection, and ordering in numerous ways of great varieties and amounts of information. A historical geographer might want to try to delineate the territorial changes in the zones of influence of Britain and Russia in the Middle East and Central Asia in the nineteenth century or of Britain and France in the Upper Ohio Valley between King George's War and the French and Indian War. We may try to determine the extent of relatively open land

15

east of the Mississippi at any time during the past four centuries and of how its territorial sway may have changed through time. And, of course, our attempted explanations will vary ·according to our several conceptions of what an explanation is and how it can be arrived at.[24]

There are many other areas of interest to historical geographers which I have not gone into in this paper.[25] We need far more discussion than we have had about the use of maps, more or less contemporary with the circumstances they depict[26] (e.g., the facsimile atlases, now becoming so common); about our special needs in terms of data storage and retrieval systems;[27] and about the possibility (and, if possible, the methods) of establishing generalizations about the perception of particular areas at particular times.[28] On the other hand, a great majority of Americans are urbanites today, and urban studies have absorbed a large amount of the time of contemporary social scientists, both as to training and later research. Needless to say, historical urban studies have my warm support, but I have wondered if that strong bias in terms of training might prove to be a hindrance to effective work on many largely rural societies and economies of the past. I thought of discussing approaches to research and exposition of the history of exploration, one of the areas where John K. Wright observed "history and geography meet."[29] That might have led naturally into discussions of scientific exploration, of scientists on the frontiers, and of the consequent extension of scientific knowledge.[30] I was even going to suggest that historical geographers be invited to courses in archival training, from time to time, to give lectures and that historical geographers try to persuade archivists to reciprocate.

In conclusion, I should observe that a consequence of emphasizing theory on the part of social or behavioral scientists has been the implication that we should deemphasize facts and, with that deemphasis, turn away from much of the meticulous training in their discovery, handling, and interpretation. This training, traditionally, has been associated with the best historical scholarship.[31] One can certainly sympathize with the objections of those who condemn the unselective amassing of facts and, in particular, the misguided efforts of any who waste priceless skill, time, and energy because they fail to realize that a good sample may tell quite as much as a whole universe. But, surely, this is no more than a statement of the obvious. The need for information and the integrity of whatever information is used remain of absolutely vital concern. Indeed, the ability to discover, evaluate, and make selective use of information is the fundamental basis of productive, scholarly activity. Once more, I insist on "First Things First," and nothing is more primary to historical geographers than complete, relevant information, whether we find it in field, library, or archive or whether it is obtained by direct or remote sensing.[32] Finally, I believe we must remember that archives are the richest sources of information available to historical geographers, and we depend heavily upon archivists to assist us in our search, analysis, and utilization of this data.

NOTES

1. There are, however, many of them. For example, Alan R. H. Baker, ed., *Progress in Historical Geography* (Devon: Newton Abbot, 1971); Andrew H. Clark et al., "Historical Geography," *American Geography Inventory and Prospect,* ed. Preston E. James and Clarence F. Jones (Syracuse: Syracuse University Press, 1954), pp. 70-105; H. C. Darby, "Historical Geography" *Approaches to History,* ed. H. P. R. Finberg (London: Routledge & Kegan Paul, 1962), pp. 127-56; Helmut Jäger, *Historische Geographie* (Braunschweig: Routledge & Kegan Paul, 1969); H. C. Prince, "Progress in Historical Geography," *Trends in Geography,* ed. Ronald U. Cooke and James H. Johnson (London: Pergamon Press, 1969); *idem,* "Real, Imagined and Abstract Worlds of the Past," *Progress in Geography,* International Reviews of Current Research Series, ed. Christopher Board et al. (London: Edward Arnold, 1971), 3: 1-86; Carl O. Sauer, "Foreword to Historical Geography," *Annals of the Association of American Geographers* 31 (1941): 1-24; and C. T. Smith, "Historical Geography: Current Trends and Prospects," *Frontiers in Geographical Teaching,* ed. Richard J. Chorley and Peter Haggett (London: Methuen & Co., 1965), pp. 118-43.
2. Social Science Research Council, *Geography,* Behavioral and Social Science Series, (Englewood Cliffs, N. J.: Prentice-Hall, 1970). See also, the review of this report by Marvin W. Mikesell in *Annals of the Association of American Geographers* 61 (1971): 408-11.
3. I do this, in good measure, because geographers face very much the same kind of methodological and epistemological problems as do historians. There is a brilliant, if somewhat erratic, discussion of a philosopher's epistemological approach to history in the preface to David H. Fischer's *Historians' Fallacies: Toward a Logic of Historical Thought* (New York: Harper & Row, 1970), p. xi. He points out that much of the argument of the epistemologists is not of much use to working historians for three reasons: (1) analytical philosophers of history are not much interested in such trivial problems as utility; (2) they have not been sufficiently empirical in their procedures; and (3) they characteristically have tried to analyze historical knowledge in terms of something else more familiar to them. He adds that most philosophers who attack the subject tend to try to force historians into a Procrustean bed, the rigid mold of a working formula called the "Deductive Model of Explanation." I find the analogy for geography very close. Perhaps it should be added that, despite the attraction of Fischer's "problem-solving" approach to historical research, he may give too little attention to the ultimate use of the solutions to the problems or the hypotheses those solutions generate as contributions to synthesized interpretations of broad patches of the past.
4. It is true, however, that many of the so-called Berkeley school of cultural

17

historical geographers (students of Carl Sauer and his associates, deeply imbued with Sauer's ecological interests) also have been first-rate archival scholars. I might name five, rather at random, with whose work I am most familiar: Marvin Mikesell, James Parsons, Frederick Simoons, Dan Stanislawski, and Robert West.

5. There has been, to say the least, a plethora of discussions in English of quantitative research in matters of geographical interest, especially since Richard J. Chorley and Peter Haggett took the lead with their trend-setting books: Haggett, *Locational Analysis in Human Geography* (London: Edward Arnold, 1965), and their jointly edited collection, *Models in Geography* (London: Methuen & Co., 1967). The principal English language journal specializing in work of this kind is *Geographical Analysis* of Columbus, Ohio, which began publication in 1969. Besides a broad range of articles, it reviews monographs in the field.

   Many have been caught up in the problem of identifying "purely geographical" problems or of developing purely geographical solutions to such problems. Put another way, it seems to have been assumed by many that "geography" can be equated with some identifiable (presumably Euclidean) geometry of the human condition and that its axioms and theorems constitute, or lead to, a set of "laws" which are the core of the discipline and establish its respectability among the sciences. I have found the most useful critique of such positions to be in the writings of Robert David Sack, especially in "Geography, Geometry and Explanation," *Annals of the Association of American Geographers* 62 (1972): 61-78; idem, "A Concept of Physical Space in Geography," *Geographical Analysis* 5 (1973): 16-34. The first of these has an extensive review of the core ideas of William Bunge's *Theoretical Geography* (Lund, Sweden: Royal University of Lund, 1966). Perhaps more explicit is his review of David Harvey's *Explanation in Geography* (London: Edward Arnold, 1969) in *Historical Methods Newsletter* 6 (1972): 68-72; and "The Spatial Separatist Theme in Geography," *Economic Geography* 50 (1974): 1-19.

6. George Dury, "Merely from Nervousness," *Area*, no. 4 (1970), pp. 29-32.

7. Ibid. Perhaps there is nothing in geographical literature as useful to historical geographers, however, as: (1) William O. Aydelotte, "Quantification in History," *American Historical Review* 71 (1966): 803-25; (2) Jerome M. Clubb and Howard Allen, "Computers and Historical Study," *The Journal of American History* 54 (1967): 599-607; and (3) Samuel P. Hays, "The Use of Archives for Statistical Inquiry" in *Prologue: The Journal of the National Archives* 1 (Winter 1969): 7-15, a bellwether of American quantitative historical research. But heavily quantitative historical studies themselves have a much longer pedigree, and there have been scores of them, especially since the Trempealeau County (Wisconsin) study of the late 1950s, inspired and directed by Merle E. Curti, *The Making of an American Community* (Stanford: Stanford University Press, 1959).

8. The problems of using a wide variety of source materials in British archives (largely accumulated for purposes of taxation, evaluation, and administration) into the fairly distant past are discussed with a wide variety of examples in Alan R. H. Baker, J. D. Hamshere, and J. Langston, eds.,

Geographical Interpretation of Historical Sources, Readings in Historical Geography (Devon: Newton Abbot, 1970).

9. It would be gratuitous for me to list readings in the philosophy and methodology of history here, but perhaps I should confess some of my favorites and, thus, my biases. A predilection for argument by example and for sprightly prose and organization suggests two very recent items (both now available in paperback): Fischer, *Historians' Fallacies,* and Robin W. Winks, ed., *The Historian as Detective* (New York: Harper & Row, 1969). In its own way as mildly outrageous and stimulating as Fischer is John H. Plumb, *The Death of History* (London: Macmillan & Co., 1969). From past generations my favorite readings came from Max Weber and Marc Bloch, and my most valued admonitions from Harold Innis, Carl Sauer, and John K. Wright.

10. It has been called to my attention that the fallaciousness of the arguments of those who offer us single keys to the secrets of the universe is in part mitigated by the stimuli, insights, or feedback illustrated in the almost countless attempts—with or without success—to demonstrate the wrongheadedness of the builders of the all-embracing explanatory models. Indeed, Sorokin and Marx demonstrated a strong empirical interest, skill, and achievement that will long stand as exemplary, despite the fragility of their explanatory structures.

11. Richard Hartshorne's *Perspective on the Nature of Geography,* Association of American Geographers, Monograph Series no. 1 (Chicago, 1959), gives what, to me, remains the very best capsulized characterization of the nature of geography as a scholarly discipline, "The scientific description of the earth as the world of man." The problems are evident in that he used a chapter to elucidate each key word.

12. One thinks at once of such scholars as Allan Bogue, Albert Fishlow, and William Parker, particularly Bogue's "United States: The New Political History," *Journal of Contemporary History* 3 (1968): 5-27.

13. John K. Wright, of blessed geographical memory, once called my attention to one of Marc Bloch's many wise observations: "Let us guard against stripping our science of its share of poetry. Let us also beware the inclination, which I have detected in some, to be ashamed of this poetic quality. It would be sheer folly to suppose that history, because it appeals strongly to the emotions, is less capable of satisfying the intellect" (*The Historian's Craft* [New York: Vintage Books, 1953], p. 8). The sentiment is directly applicable to geography. My own strong feelings were made explicit in "Praemia Geographiae: The Incidental Rewards of a Geographical Career," *Annals of the Association of American Geographers* 52 (1962): 229-41.

14. Karl Popper, *The Poverty of Historicism* (London: Routledge & Kegan Paul, 1957), p. 8. Other discussions which I have found useful include two items published in the same year: Isaiah Berlin, *Historical Inevitability,* The August Comte Memorial Trust Lecture no. 1 (New York, 1957); and William H. Dray, *Laws and Explanation in History* (London: Oxford University Press, 1957). On "laws," see also Sack, "Geography, Geometry and Explanation."

15. My indebtedness to Fischer, *Historians' Fallacies,* will be obvious to all

who know his work. Chapter 10 deals with fallacies of semantical distortion which can be avoided only by careful definition and discriminating usage.

16. One of the more sprightly discussions of the problem, perhaps especially relevant for historians who know Ellen Churchill Semple's *American History and Its Geographic Conditions* (1903; rev. ed., Boston: Clarence F. Jones, 1933), is John K. Wright's "Miss Semple's 'Influences of Geographic Environment;' Notes toward a Bibliography," *Geographical Review* 52 (1962): 346-51. The reference is, of course, to her *Influences of Geographic Environment: On the Basis of Ratzel's System of Anthropo-Geography* (New York: H. Holt and Co., 1911).

17. Perhaps the most useful recent comment by a historical geographer is H. Roy Merrens, "The Physical Environment of Early America: Images and Image-Makers in Colonial South Carolina," *Geographical Review* 59 (1969): 530-56.

18. The reference is borrowed from Winks, *The Historian as Detective*, and refers to William B. Wilcox, "The Psychiatrist, the Historian and General Clinton: The Excitement of Historical Research," *Michigan Quarterly Review* 6 (1967): 123-30.

19. Jackson T. Main, *The Social Structure of Revolutionary America* (Princeton: Princeton University Press, 1965). One of the more perceptive critical reviews I judge to be that of Bernard Bailyn in *American Historical Review* 71 (1966): 1432. See also Fischer, *Historians' Fallacies*, p. 72.

20. This is of central importance in all geographical interpretation of historical sources. See Baker, Hamshere, and Langston, *Geographical Interpretation*.

21. Mikesell's review in *Annals of the Association of American Geographers*. Precisely, Mikesell, in referring to the reiteration of the word "spatial" in the work referred to, remarked that the "collective effect is that of an incantation."

22. The principal innovator of research into the movement of artifacts and ideas through terrestrial space has been Torsten Hagerstrand of Lund, Sweden; see his 1953 study, published recently in English, *Innovation Diffusion as a Spatial Process* (Chicago: University of Chicago Press, 1967). I believe the most impressive American student to be Richard Morrill. See his "Waves of Spatial Diffusion," *Journal of Regional Science* 8 (1968). Peter R. Gould, *Spatial Diffusion*, Association of American Geographers, Commission on College Geography, Resource Paper no. 4 (Washington, D. C., 1969), has a brief but up-to-date bibliography.

23. A very recent discussion of the geographical interest in territoriality, which seemed to me first-rate on all counts, with an excellent up-to-date bibliography is Edward W. Soja, *The Political Organization of Space*, Association of American Geographers, Commission on College Geography, Resource Paper no. 8 (Washington, D. C., 1971).

24. See Sack, "Geography, Geometry and Explanation."

25. For example, the ideas suggested by John F. McDermott, ed., *Research Opportunities in American Cultural History* (Lexington: University Press of Kentucky, 1961), are most suggestive of themes which historical geographers will be following in one archive or another.

26. The most sophisticated approach perhaps ever taken to this problem is that being used by Lester J. Cappon and his associates in producing the *Atlas of*

Early American History. The first volume, covering the period of the American Revolution, is scheduled to appear in late 1975.

27. Clearly, there should be a substantial geographical input into the planning of such things as the joint project of the Interuniversity Consortium for Political Research, at Ann Arbor, and the Committee on Quantitative Data of the American Historical Association.

28. T. H. Saarinen, *Perception of Environment,* Association of American Geographers, Commission on College Geography, Resource Paper no. 5 (Washington, D.C., 1969), has a useful bibliography. One might also refer to Merrens, "Physical Environment of Early America"; David Lowenthal, ed., *Environmental Perception and Behavior,* University of Chicago, Department of Geography, Research Paper no. 109 (1967); Malcolm Lewis's many papers relating to nineteenth-century perception of the Great Plains, e.g., "William Gilpin and the Concept of the Great Plains Region," *Annals of the Association of American Geographers* 56 (1966): 33-51; and an intriguing item, R. M. Newcomb, "Environmental Perception and Its Fulfillment during Past Times in Northern Denmark," *Skriften Fra Geografisk Institut,* Ved Aarhus Universitet, no. 26 (Aarhus, 1969).

29. John K. Wright, "Where History and Geography Meet: Recent American Studies in the History of Exploration," *History of Exploration and Cartography,* Proceedings of the Eighth American Scientific Congress 9 (1940): 17-23.

30. It is salutary to remember that Pehr Kalm, Alexander von Humboldt, and Mungo Park were simply outstanding members of a very numerous, virtually ubiquitous, fraternity. For the United States one thinks, almost at random, of Colden, Cutler, Gray, Guyot, Hayden, Lyell, Michaux, Muhlenberg, Powell, Schoolcraft, and Wizlizenus. Fortunately, historical geographers like Herman Friis, Gary Dunbar, and John Warkentin have been setting the pace for us here. See Friis's discussion of the David Dale Owen Map of Wisconsin in *Prologue: The Journal of the National Archives* 1 (Winter 1969): 9-34, and for a sort of annotated bibliography of one variety of source, his footnotes to "Stephen H. Long's Unpublished Manuscript Map of the United States Compiled in 1820-22 (?)," *California Geographer* 8 (1967): 75-87. Dunbar has been working for some time on Lorin Blodget, and Warkentin has published his perceptive *Western Interior of Canada* (Toronto: McClelland and Stewart, 1964), about the explorers of that area. Another somewhat different species of visitor, but one of great interest to historical geographers, is described by Carl O. Sauer, "The Formative Years of Ratzel in the United States," *Annals of the Association of American Geographers* 61 (1971): 245-54. Friedrich Ratzel, then a young naturalist aged twenty-nine (who was to become one of the best known cultural geographers in the world at the turn of the century) spent two years in the United States, beginning in 1873, writing articles for the *Kölnische Zeitung.*

31. Prince, "Real, Imagined and Abstract," pp. 22-24.

32. See, for example, R. M. Newcomb, "An Example of the Applicability of Remote Sensing: Historical Geography," *Geoforum* 2 (1970): 89-92, which has a most useful and relevant bibliography on the point.

Afro-American Population

Patterns and Problems in the Historical Geography of the Afro-American Population of New Jersey, 1726-1860

PETER O. WACKER

Over two decades ago, in concluding a pioneering study, Wilbur Zelinsky referred to the population geography of the free Negro in antebellum times as "one of the more poorly charted areas of American historical geography."[1] Unfortunately, this statement remains all too true today, not only in regard to the historical geography of the free black population before the Civil War but for the total Afro-American population through time in the United States.[2] Moreover, with a few rather notable exceptions, geographers have engaged in far too little research concerning the historical geographies of the rich variety of other racial and cultural groups present in the United States. This, of course, possesses especial "relevance" today in the decade of the seventies, with the new black consciousness and the growing awareness of ethnic and cultural roots on the part of many other groups.

This paper will be concerned with only the black population and only with *outlining* some of the most salient patterns and problems in the historical geography of that population for the state of New Jersey from colonial times to the census of 1860. It is intended by this to demonstrate the wealth of data potentially available to geographers, which can and should be utilized to fill the lacunae in our knowledge of the

Portions of the research for this paper were supported by the John Simon Guggenheim Memorial Foundation, the New Jersey Historical Commission, and the Rutgers University Research Council. This aid, generally for two projects of wider scope, is acknowledged with much gratitude.

25

subject. Perhaps two conclusions this writer has drawn in regard to his sparse work in this area should be put forth at the beginning. The first is that it is an ironic fact that because of the status of Blacks through time in this country and because of their easy identification by skin color, more population data exist for the historical geography of the Afro-American population than for any other ethnic group. Colonial[3] and national censuses,[4] for example, identify Blacks but very, very rarely break the whites down as to origins or cultural affinities. The second conclusion is that there are enough data available to warrant the publication of several books on the subject by interested historical geographers. Histories, of course, abound and many more will and should be written, but very little of a spatial nature has been introduced into the voluminous literature on the past of black Americans.

Why choose New Jersey as the locale for research of this kind? Perhaps foremost is the fact that a stress on *Heimatkunde*[5] as a pedagogical device on this writer's part has involved both himself and his graduate and undergraduate students with readily accessible local primary materials. But the choice of New Jersey transcends the confines of pedagogy alone.

From early colonial times onward, New Jersey possessed great ethnic and cultural diversity in her population. By late colonial times, this diversity was probably the greatest of any of the Atlantic seaboard colonies. Many of the cultural groups possessed distinct regional concentrations, easily mapped and compared with other phenomena.[6]

New Jersey is also of special interest in regard to her population of African origin. The first census of the United States, taken in 1790, revealed that New Jersey led all northern states in the percentage of her population made up by Blacks (7.7 percent).[7] New Jersey also lagged far behind her neighbors north of the Mason and Dixon line in the abolition of slavery, not enacting a gradual abolition law until 1804.[8] A traveler from Connecticut passing through New Jersey in 1823 echoed a common northern view, calling the state "the land of slavery."[9] The census of 1860, for example, still listed eighteen superannuated slaves, officially termed "apprentices," residing in the state. Further, the distribution of Blacks in New Jersey, as well as their condition, varied significantly from region to region in the state through time. This, of course, makes a "changing geography" approach quite viable for the historical geographer. Last, but by all means not least, is that as European immigration began to swell after 1820, New Jersey cities, especially Newark, were the destination of many. The gradual abolition of slavery, in theory, allowed free Blacks to make the same choice, which some were able to do. Along with other northeastern states, New Jersey shared the processes concerned with urbanization, industrialization, and the revolutions in transportation, but in contrast with her sister northern states undergoing these processes, New Jersey possessed a relatively large, resident black population that, potentially, could have been vitally involved in these dynamic changes.

Before discussing the changing geography of New Jersey's black population, it is appropriate to consider the varied origins of that population. Negro slavery in the Middle Colonies appears to have been initiated by the Dutch West India Company in 1625 or 1626. These first Blacks were most likely taken from Spanish or Portuguese prizes.[10] Thus began an association between agricultural settlers of "Dutch" origin and Negro farm labor, which was to continue, even with the vast improvement in status of the Afro-American, well into the nineteenth century. That Blacks were most prized for their addition to the agricultural labor force can be seen in a report written in 1644 recommending the importation of more Blacks to the Dutch colonies because "Negroes would accomplish more work for their masters, and at less expense, than farm servants, who must be bribed to go thither by a great deal of money and promises."[11]

Subsequent migrations of Dutch farmers from New York to New Jersey, especially to Bergen, Somerset, Middlesex, and northern Monmouth counties (figure 1),[12] served to diffuse Afro-Americans within the state. As will be seen later, the most obvious gross positive correlations between the black population and other phenomena through 1860 are with (1) areas settled by the Dutch (figure 2),[13] (2) those areas of fertile agricultural soils which were settled early (figure 3),[14] and (3) the Inner Coastal Plain and Piedmont physiographic provinces (figure 4).[15] The major exception to the latter two correlations is that where a strong English Quaker population existed (figure 5), slavery was more slowly established, manumission more rapidly achieved, and an influx of free Blacks later encouraged.

Few reliable data exist on the origins of New Jersey's black population during the colonial period. New York, which furnished slaveholding settlers to New Jersey, imported slaves from Madagascar, the Guinea Coast, Angola, and the West Indies.[16] The only official data for New Jersey are for Perth Amboy in Middlesex County, beginning in 1686, with scattered entries through 1734.[17] The West Indies, Angola, and Madagascar were cited as places of origin. No official data exist for the

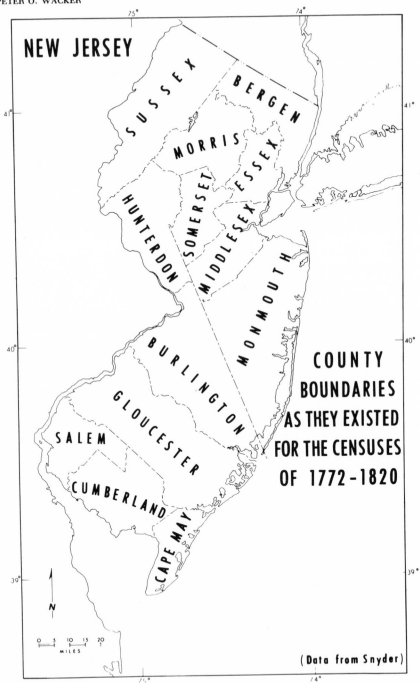

NEW JERSEY

SUSSEX

BERGEN

MORRIS

SOMERSET

ESSEX

HUNTERDON

MIDDLESEX

MONMOUTH

BURLINGTON

GLOUCESTER

SALEM

CUMBERLAND

CAPE MAY

COUNTY
BOUNDARIES
AS THEY EXISTED
FOR THE CENSUSES
OF 1772-1820

N

0 5 10 15 20
MILES

(Data from Snyder)

Fig. 1.

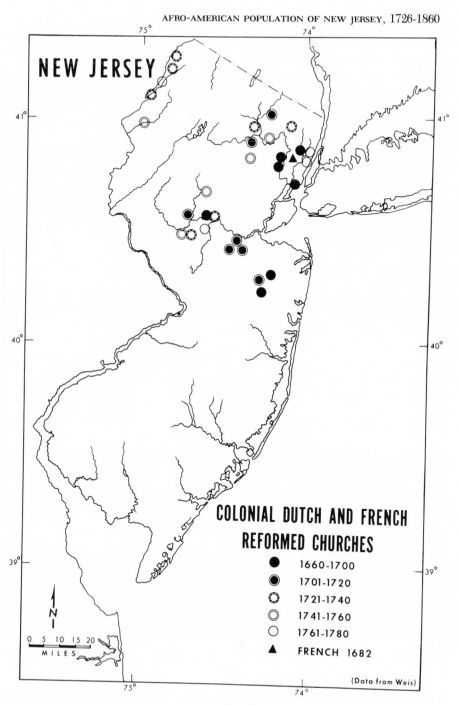

NEW JERSEY

COLONIAL DUTCH AND FRENCH
REFORMED CHURCHES

●   1660-1700
◉   1701-1720
◍   1721-1740
◎   1741-1760
○   1761-1780
▲   FRENCH 1682

(Data from Weis)

Fig. 2.

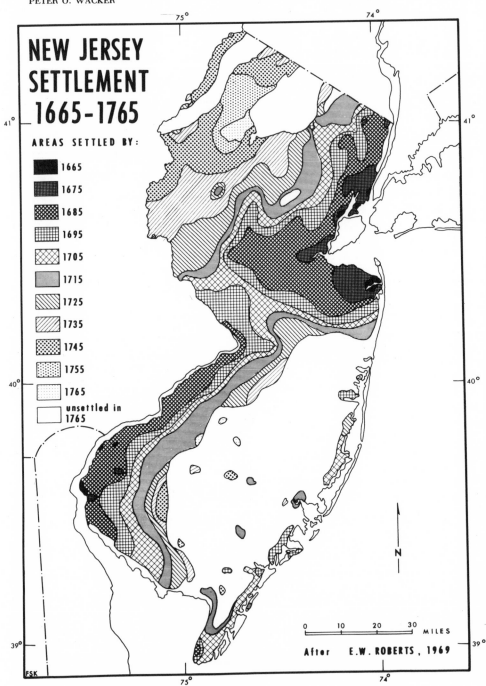

NEW JERSEY
SETTLEMENT
1665-1765

AREAS SETTLED BY:

- 1665
- 1675
- 1685
- 1695
- 1705
- 1715
- 1725
- 1735
- 1745
- 1755
- 1765
- unsettled in 1765

0 10 20 30 MILES

After E.W. ROBERTS, 1969

FSK

FIG. 3.

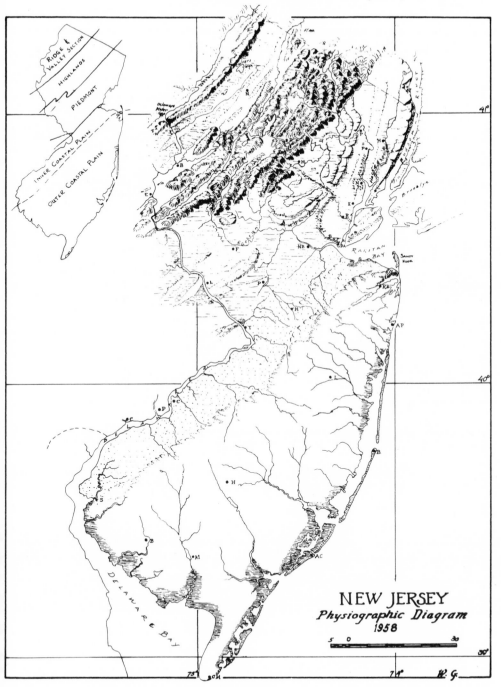

NEW JERSEY
Physiographic Diagram
1958

FIG. 4.

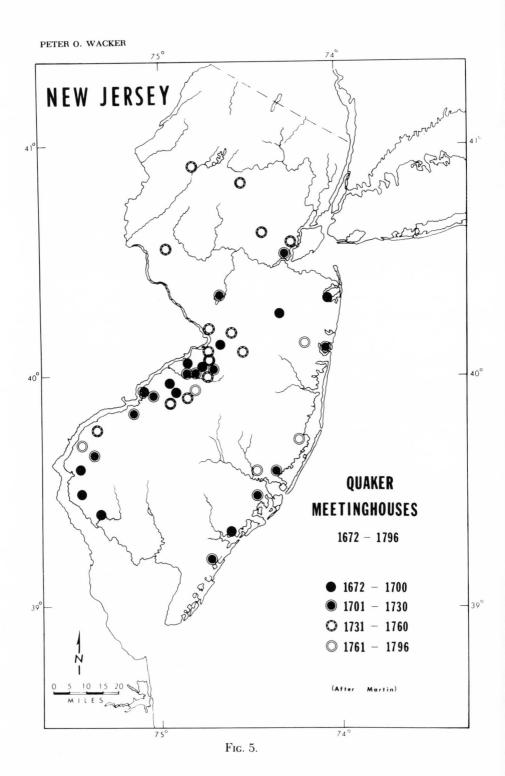

NEW JERSEY

QUAKER
MEETINGHOUSES

1672 — 1796

● 1672 — 1700
◉ 1701 — 1730
◎ 1731 — 1760
◯ 1761 — 1796

(After Martin)

0 5 10 15 20
MILES

N

Fig. 5.

TABLE 1

NEW JERSEY—CRUDE BIRTH AND DEATH RATES, PERCENTAGES OF NATURAL INCREASE, INCOMPLETE CENSUS OF 1772

County	Blacks			Whites		
	Birth Rate†	Death Rate†	Percentage of Natural Increase	Birth Rate†	Death Rate†	Percentage of Natural Increase
Sussex	45.61	21.05	2.46	33.43	6.93	2.65
Hunterdon	35.61	12.78	2.28	30.32	8.20	2.21
Burlington	28.72	12.31	1.64	26.46	9.44	1.70
Gloucester°	41.13	18.96	2.22	32.47	12.79	1.97
Salem	26.84	13.42	1.34	30.37	16.77	1.36
Cumberland	27.27	‡	2.73	31.33	14.75	1.66
Cape May	36.03	‡	3.60	21.84	10.92	1.09
Morris	46.32	35.42	1.09	31.96	7.96	2.40
Mean	35.61	15.69	1.99	30.43	10.05	2.04

°Waterford Township missing.
†Per thousand.
‡No deaths recorded.

West Jersey counties of Salem, Cape May, Gloucester, or Burlington, and, in 1726, Governor Burnet indicated that "there are few Negroes, if any imported in West Jersey."[18] Early census data bear this out.

Some suggestion of the ultimate sources of the Blacks continuing to be brought into the colony after 1734 may be had from newspaper advertisements and announcements of runaways. Sales of recently imported Blacks in the 1750s and 1760s were carried on from ships anchored off Cooper's Ferry in Gloucester County. Most of these Blacks were directly from West Africa. Runaways throughout the colony had quite diverse origins, indeed. Frank, who had absconded from Hanover in Morris County could speak "English, Dutch, Spanish and Danish."[19] Through at least 1780, many Blacks directly from West Africa are mentioned.[20]

Natural increase, of course, largely served to swell the Afro-American population in later years. The only official data on births and deaths for the black and white population covering a wide area occur in the incomplete census of 1772. A glance at the data on natural increase (births

33

TABLE 2

NEW JERSEY—AVERAGE ANNUAL PERCENTAGE OF POPULATION INCREASE OR DECREASE, BY COUNTY, 1726-1810

County	Nonwhites					
	1726-38	1738-45	1745-72°	1745-90	1790-1800	1800-10
Middlesex	5.5	10.68	. . .	1.46	2.53	.74
Essex	1.8	2.67	. . .	4.42	2.91	.98
Monmouth	4.27	5.32	. . .	2.59	.78	.17
Somerset	7.76	−7.59	. . .	10.46	.41	1.21
Bergen	5.32	−3.37	. . .	6.77	2.14	−.21
Burlington	2.79	3.62	2.59	2.04	1.61	.85
Hunterdon	4.61	15.72	5.11	4.99	1.66	.38
Gloucester	1.44	9.37	2.09†	3.64	3.26	3.58
Salem	1.89	.23	4.38‡	7.33‡	2.67	5.40
Cape May	. . .	3.40	4.20	4.40	1.48	.79
Morris	. . .	. . .	22.26§	26.16§	2.79	2.11
Cumberland	. . .	. . .	. . .	. . .	3.41	7.02
Sussex	. . .	. . .	. . .	. . .	2.19	2.12
Mean	4.52	2.24	4.91	4.62	1.86	1.11

°No returns for several counties.
†Waterford Township missing, 1772.
‡Including newly formed Cumberland County.
§Including newly formed Sussex County.

minus deaths) for the year 1772 (table 1), with the average annual percentage increase in the black population from 1745 to 1772 (table 2), will demonstrate that a substantial introduction of Blacks from elsewhere must have occurred. Also, the imbalance in the sexes, i.e., far more males than females, recorded for Afro-Americans through the colonial period indicates the premium placed on the introduction of black males to the labor supply (table 3).

Included in the black slave population were the products of mixed Indian, white, and Afro-American parentage. The reason for this was that children born to a slave mother retained her status.[21] There also seems to have been some miscegenation between free Blacks and Indians in the colonial period.[22] In the southwestern counties, especially, mulattoes are often mentioned in the newspapers as "servants"

TABLE 3

NEW JERSEY—MALES PER 100 FEMALES, BY COUNTY, 1726-1830

County	1726°	1738°	1745 (all)	1772°	1830 (all)
			Nonwhites		
Middlesex	123.28	145.96	121.96	No data	95.13
Essex	117.94	100.00	121.39	No data	91.14
Monmouth	188.88	153.26	132.90	No data	107.49
Somerset	131.25	145.71	130.20	No data	100.78
Bergen	142.97	126.10	159.91	No data	122.73
Burlington	136.50	154.02	118.27	137.42	103.54
Hunterdon	95.55	141.50	112.96	134.27	95.27
Gloucester	152.38	175.00	149.38	121.95†	116.29
Salem	136.84	101.78	92.78	133.33	121.29
Cape May	160.00‡	120.00‡	136.36‡	111.76	112.03
Morris	. . .	. . .	158.05‡	137.07	109.15
Cumberland	. . .	. . .	. . .	264.00‡	120.72
Sussex	. . .	. . .	. . .	136.23	100.00§
Mean	138.41	136.17	128.24	137.22	105.51

°Males over sixteen only.
†Waterford Township missing.
‡Fewer than one hundred persons.
§With Warren County.

instead of slaves. It is probable that many light-skinned mulatto run-aways were successful in passing as whites.[23]

In addition to importation, natural increase, and influx along with their owners migrating to New Jersey, spatial shifts in New Jersey's black population were in part due to successful flight on the part of some from one county or colony to another. In late colonial times, there is much evidence to show an influx of runaway or free Blacks to locations in the southwestern portion of the state.[24] During the Revolution, hundreds of slaves, especially from Bergen County, sought freedom behind British lines.[25]

Distributional data on New Jersey's Afro-American population by county first became available with the census of 1726 (figure 6). In that year the Negro population numbered 2,581. The distribution of Negroes

35

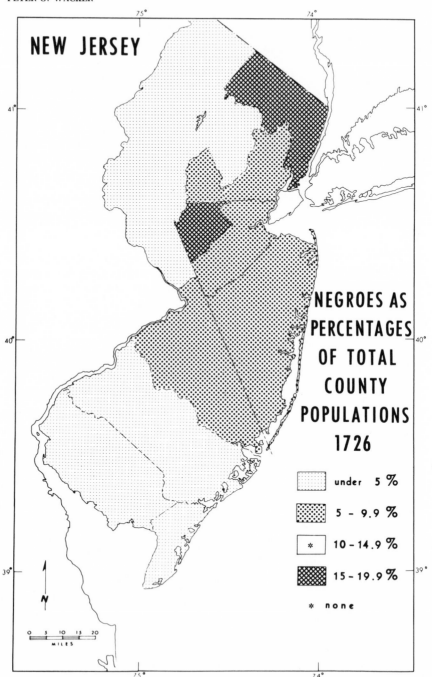

NEW JERSEY

NEGROES AS
PERCENTAGES
OF TOTAL
COUNTY
POPULATIONS
1726

under 5 %

5 - 9.9 %

10 - 14.9 %

15 - 19.9 %

* none

MILES

FIG. 6.

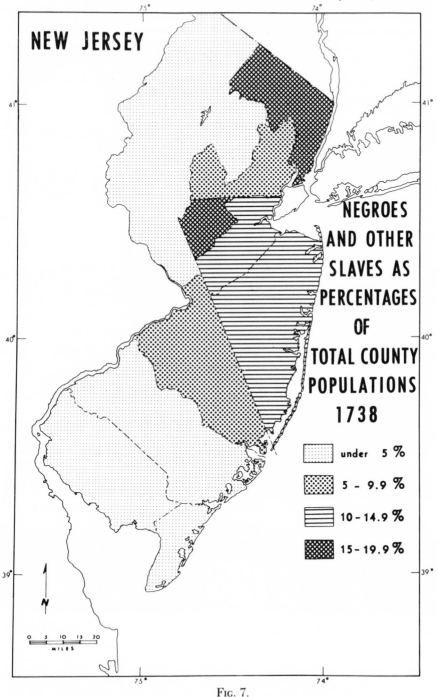

NEW JERSEY

NEGROES
AND OTHER
SLAVES AS
PERCENTAGES
OF
TOTAL COUNTY
POPULATIONS
1738

under 5 %

5 - 9.9 %

10 - 14.9 %

15 - 19.9 %

N

0 5 10 15 20
MILES

FIG. 7.

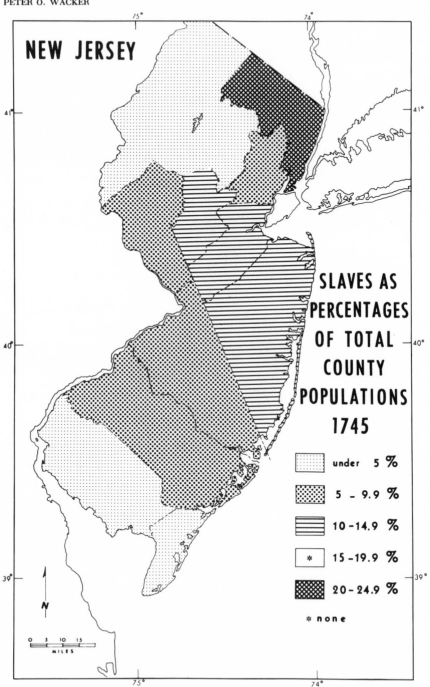

NEW JERSEY

SLAVES AS
PERCENTAGES
OF TOTAL
COUNTY
POPULATIONS
1745

under 5 %

5 - 9.9 %

10 -14.9 %

15 -19.9 %

20 - 24.9 %

N

0 5 10 15
MILES

FIG. 8.

TABLE 4

NEW JERSEY—AVERAGE ANNUAL PERCENTAGE OF POPULATION INCREASE
OR DECREASE, BY COUNTY, 1726-1810

			Whites			
County	1726-38	1738-45	1745-72°	1745-90	1790-1800	1800-10
Middlesex	1.25	8.28	. . .	2.56	1.08	1.47
Essex	4.31	1.42	. . .	3.37	2.49	1.73
Monmouth	1.85	6.04	. . .	2.08	1.87	1.26
Somerset	8.28	-3.32	. . .	5.71	.42	1.55
Bergen	4.23	-3.91	. . .	7.18	1.99	1.24
Burlington	2.20	4.31	3.49	3.79	1.91	1.64
Hunterdon	5.28	9.19	2.48	2.55	.46	1.65
Gloucester	4.00	.72	5.75†	6.41	2.01	2.19
Salem	4.08	2.41	2.19‡	3.74‡	1.30	.46
Cape May	3.92	2.58	1.67	2.50	1.95	1.91
Morris	. . .	. . .	13.48§	15.44§	.86	2.31
Cumberland	. . .	. . .	. . .	. . .	1.49	3.16
Sussex	. . .	. . .	. . .	. . .	1.54	1.32
Mean	3.58	4.72	4.52	4.43	1.46	1.64

°No returns for several counties.
†Waterford Township missing, 1772.
‡Including newly formed Cumberland County.
§Including newly formed Sussex County.

for 1726 reveals quite clearly the early dichotomy between East and West Jersey alluded to by Governor Burnet. East Jersey, consisting of the counties of Bergen, Essex, Middlesex, Monmouth, and Somerset, held 54.08 percent of the white population of the colony, but 74.20 percent of the slave population. Dutch-settled Bergen and Somerset counties led in the proportion of Blacks to whites.

Eleven years later the proportions for East and West Jersey remained about the same with, respectively, 53.18 percent of the whites and 77.14 percent of the Blacks located in East Jersey (figure 7). The proportion of Blacks in both Middlesex and Monmouth counties rose slightly from 1726.

The census of 1745 revealed a slightly altered pattern of distribution, with the newly formed county of Hunterdon as well as Gloucester County in West Jersey including more than 5 percent Blacks (figure 8).

39

Somerset County, expanded to include part of what had been Essex County, declined in both absolute and relative numbers of Blacks (table 2). Bergen County's black population also declined, but a larger decrease in the white population raised the percentage of Blacks in Bergen's total population (table 4). In the case of both Blacks and whites, the decreases in Bergen and Somerset can probably be attributed to the large influxes of Afro-Americans along with their white owners into Middlesex and Hunterdon counties, just as the extraordinarily low rate of increase in Salem County between 1738 and 1745 (table 2) was probably due to an exodus to nearby Gloucester, which grew rapidly during the period. Of course, the points of entry for imported slaves, Perth Amboy and Cooper's Ferry, probably served, in part, to create these differentials in growth for Middlesex and Gloucester counties. It might, also, be noted that the portion of Essex County joined to Somerset was characterized by a general absence of Blacks through the census of 1860.

The, unfortunately, incomplete census of 1772-73 that was not taken in the old counties of East Jersey, revealed some changes in the percentages of Blacks in West Jersey (figure 9). Gloucester County fell in her percentage of Blacks, while both Salem and Cape May emerged with more than 5 percent Negroes in their total populations. In both cases, this was due to a much more rapid rate of increase in the black population than in the white population (tables 2 and 4). In the case of Salem County, where the rate of natural increase among Blacks was only 1.34 percent for the year, even less than the 1.36 percent for whites, the increase had to be due to an influx of Blacks. Thus began the rural black population in the southwestern portion of the state, which has persisted to the present.

Statewide distributional data on the Afro-American population is again provided by the national census of 1790 (figure 1, table 5). This enumeration included the classification "slave" or "free" so that in order to understand changes in the distribution of Blacks, we must compare the slave classification of 1745 with the nonwhite category of 1790. When this is done, it can be seen that nonwhites fell in relative numbers in Bergen and Middlesex counties and rose in Somerset County. Bergen's decline, despite an enormous annual increase averaging 6.77 percent per year, was due to an even higher rate for whites, 7.18 percent per year (tables 2 and 4). In Middlesex, neither rate of increase was as impressive—1.46 percent for Blacks and 2.56 percent for whites—but the differential served to diminish the relative numbers of Blacks. Somerset County experienced the highest rate of increase in the Afro-Ameri-

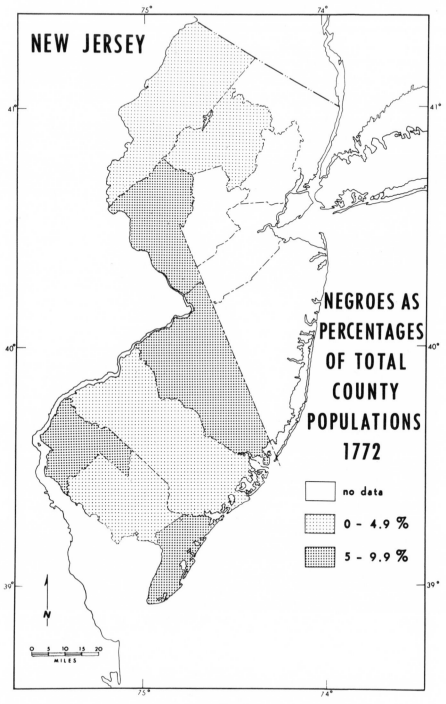

FIG. 9.

TABLE 5

New Jersey—Percentage Black and Percentage of All Blacks Free, by County, 1790 and 1800

| County | 1790 | | 1800 | |
	Percentage of Total Population	Percentage Free	Percentage of Total Population	Percentage Free
Middlesex	9.11	9.41	10.24	14.40
Essex	7.48	12.02	7.72	11.52
Monmouth	11.52	18.11	10.57	22.28
Somerset	15.91	7.51	15.90	8.59
Bergen	19.78	7.70	18.97	6.67
Burlington	4.55	72.48	4.45	80.38
Hunterdon	7.36	18.90	8.18	29.89
Gloucester	3.98	81.23	4.39	91.37
Salem	5.23	68.49	6.09	87.72
Cape May	6.02	9.03	5.81	44.94
Morris	4.21	7.01	4.93	11.43
Cumberland	3.12	53.48	3.63	78.32
Sussex	2.58	12.89	2.73	16.56
Mean	7.70	19.45	7.94	26.17

can population for any county with a large number of Blacks, 10.46 percent as the annual average for the forty-five-year period. The growth rate for whites was also substantial, 5.71 percent annually, well above natural increase alone.

Few changes occurred in the West Jersey counties in the distribution of Blacks between the censuses of 1772 and 1790. Burlington County fell in her percentage of Afro-Americans, largely because of a slightly greater annual increase in the white population.

The census of 1790, in listing Blacks as free or slave, provides a much clearer view of the contrast in the condition of Afro-Americans from section to section of the state (table 5). The Quaker-settled counties of old West Jersey, which had generally lagged early in the eighteenth century in the importation of slaves, were in the van at the end of that century in the manumission of Blacks.[26] Those East Jersey counties which had always held high absolute and relative numbers of Blacks, especially Bergen and Somerset, contained the smallest numbers of free Blacks in 1790. The 1790 distribution of free nonwhites again reveals the East-West Jersey dichotomy referred to earlier.

A somewhat finer focus is provided by the limited data by township contained in the 1790 census. Those townships immediately contiguous to strong Quaker Burlington County possessed relatively large percentages of free Blacks (figure 10); those having large New Jersey-Dutch populations possessed the largest absolute numbers of Blacks, with the smallest percentages of free Blacks (figure 11). The census of 1800 again reveals, essentially, the same patterns as that of a decade earlier, with manumission of Blacks proceeding at a rapid rate in the West Jersey counties but very slowly indeed in East Jersey (table 5).

Statewide data on a township unit basis became available in the census of 1810 (figure 12). Few surprises exist for anyone familiar with countywide data for 1790, 1800, or even much earlier. The Afro-American population was especially dense in Bergen and Somerset counties and was fairly evenly distributed on the better soils of the Inner Coastal Plain. The dot map also reveals the pronounced difference in status between the southwestern counties and the Dutch-settled areas. The picture is perhaps a little clearer when the percentages of Blacks in the various townships is plotted (figure 13). Four areas of especially dense Afro-American population stand out, three of them in East Jersey—eastern Bergen County; central Somerset, with some adjoining townships in Hunterdon and Middlesex; and northern Monmouth County. Rather isolated from the centers of black population elsewhere in the state is the cluster of Blacks in western Salem County.

Unfortunately, the census does not give us an age-sex breakdown for Afro-Americans at this time. In theory, those free individuals of working age should have been able to move to employment opportunities elsewhere if they were not to be found at home. Age-sex data do exist for the white population in 1810, and the wide disparities in such ratios suggest that substantial movements, probably almost entirely of white males, did occur (figure 14). This was probably over short distances, as townships with fewer males than females often adjoin those where the balance is quite different. Other than in West Windsor Township, where Princeton contained a relatively large number of young men as students, the surplus of young white males was where various industrial activities were taking place. Ironworking and lumbering in the Outer Coastal Plain show up especially clearly.[27] The fact that such concen-

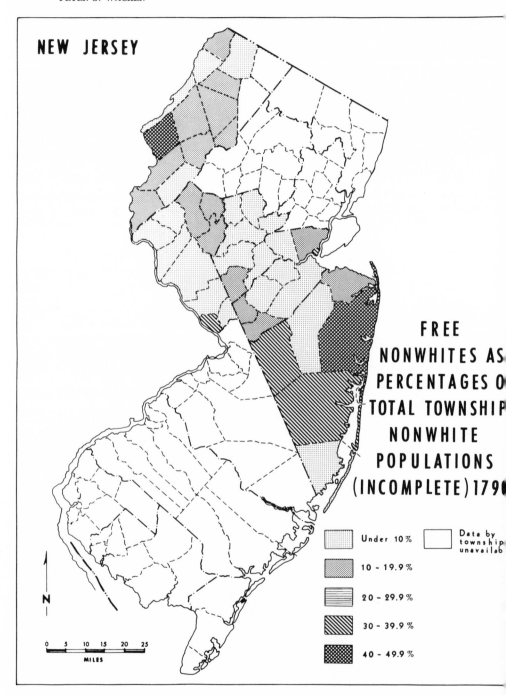

NEW JERSEY

FREE
NONWHITES AS
PERCENTAGES O
TOTAL TOWNSHIP
NONWHITE
POPULATIONS
(INCOMPLETE) 179(

Under 10 %

10 - 19.9 %

20 - 29.9 %

30 - 39.9 %

40 - 49.9 %

Data by
township
unavailab

N

0   5   10 15 20 25
MILES

FIG. 10.

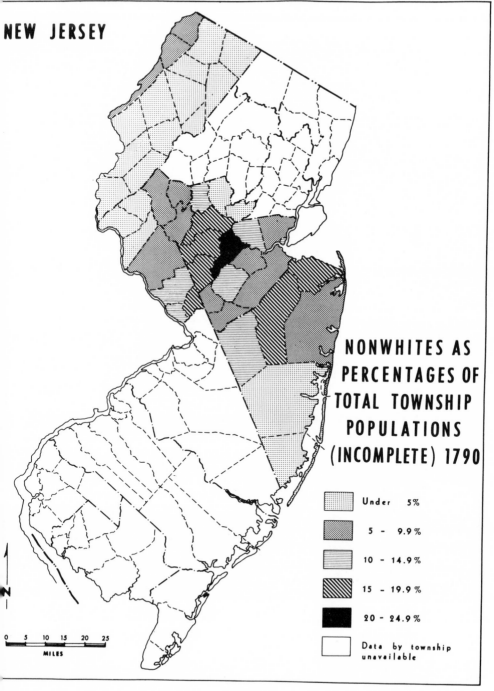

NEW JERSEY

NONWHITES AS
PERCENTAGES OF
TOTAL TOWNSHIP
POPULATIONS
(INCOMPLETE) 1790

Under 5%

5 - 9.9%

10 - 14.9%

15 - 19.9%

20 - 24.9%

Data by township
unavailable

0   5   10   15   20   25
MILES

FIG. 11.

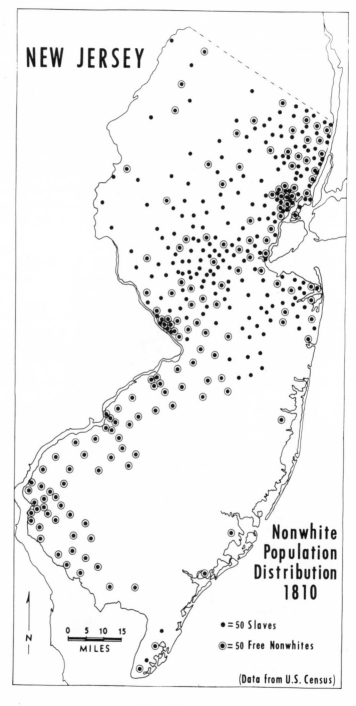

NEW JERSEY

Nonwhite
Population
Distribution
1810

0 5 10 15
MILES

N

●= 50 Slaves

◉= 50 Free Nonwhites

(Data from U.S. Census)

FIG. 12.

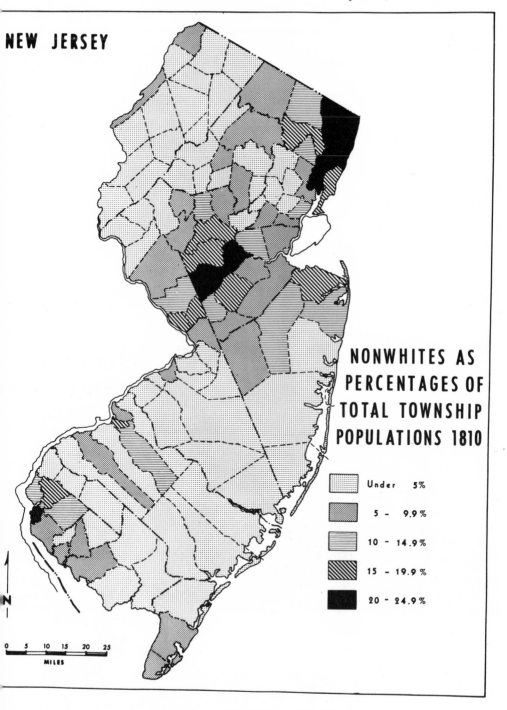

NONWHITES AS PERCENTAGES OF TOTAL TOWNSHIP POPULATIONS 1810

Under 5%

5 - 9.9%

10 - 14.9%

15 - 19.9%

20 - 24.9%

FIG. 13.

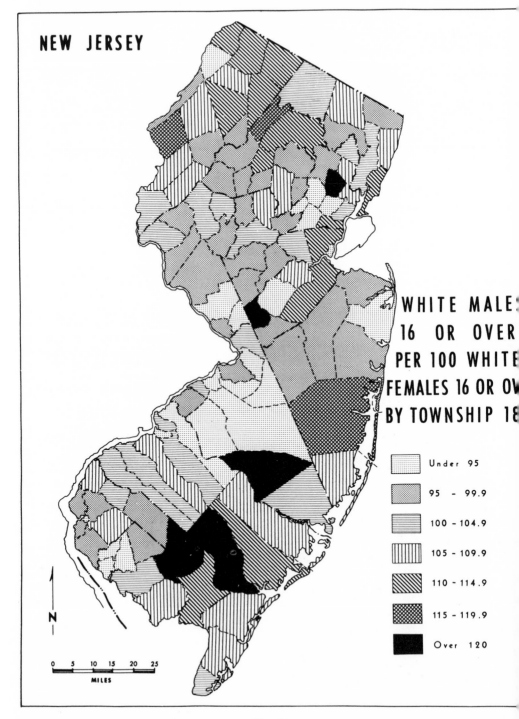

FIG. 14.

trations of white males and industrial activities do not seem to be related to black populations, slave or free, suggests that Afro-Americans were not thus involved.

Comparable age and sex data for both Blacks and whites became available in the census of 1830. The distribution of Afro-Americans by township, slave and free, looks very much like that of twenty years before (figure 15). A few more Negroes were in the Outer Coastal Plain, perhaps indicating a small migration to industries there. The clusters of Blacks at Newark and Trenton grew a bit. The numbers of slaves greatly diminished, but clusters still remained in those areas which had many slaves in 1810.

Comparing the 1830 map of the relative percentages of Afro-Americans by township (figure 16) with that of 1810, we find that although Blacks are still found in very much the same areas as before, their *relative* numbers have dramatically declined, except for the southwestern portion of the state.

The distribution of the ratios of males per 100 females is available by township for both whites and Blacks in the census of 1830. Several trends are discernible. One is the relatively small number of black males in urban places (figure 17). All of the townships containing urban places had less than 100 black males per 100 black females, often much less. In Newark Township, for example, the ratio was 72.91; Elizabeth, 87.32; North Brunswick, which included New Brunswick, 77.81; Trenton, 78.94; Burlington, 83.03; Newton Township, including Camden, 93.20; and Salem, 97.61. On the other hand, ratios of 100 or more characterized the rural townships surrounding these urban centers, and most rural townships had more black males than females. The most likely reason for these imbalances, of course, was the short-distance migration of black females to urban places offering employment as domestics, with black males either remaining in or moving to agricultural employment opportunities.[28]

The imbalance in sex ratios for Afro-Americans is especially striking when compared spatially with the same relationship for whites (figure 18). Some urban places had many fewer white males than females, but these were generally not those where industrialization was taking place, and the imbalance was not nearly as severe as it was with Blacks. Newark, well into its industrial growth, had a ratio of 105.08, for example. Further, the nonurban townships where white males were especially numerous were not, as with Blacks, just the agricultural areas. Especially large numbers of young white males were found in the townships bordering the route of the newly constructed Morris Canal.[29]

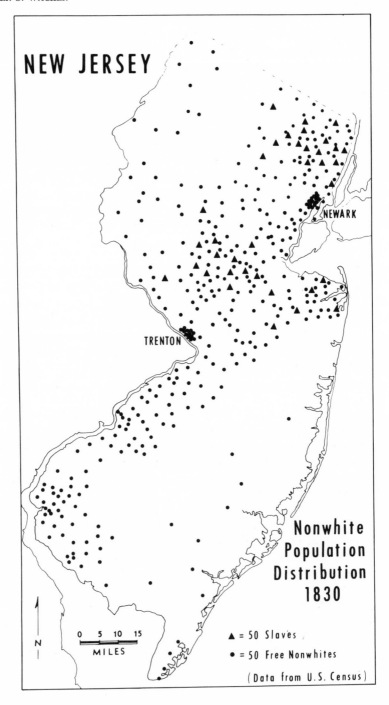

FIG. 15.

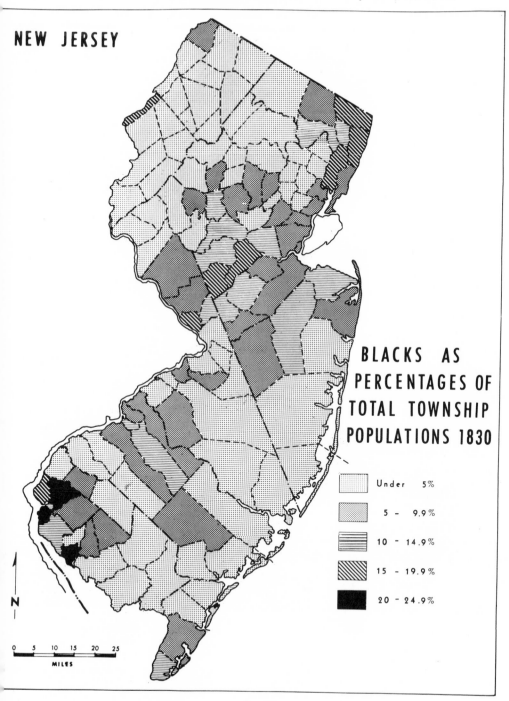

NEW JERSEY

BLACKS AS
PERCENTAGES OF
TOTAL TOWNSHIP
POPULATIONS 1830

Under 5%

5 - 9.9%

10 - 14.9%

15 - 19.9%

20 - 24.9%

N

0   5   10   15   20   25
MILES

FIG. 16.

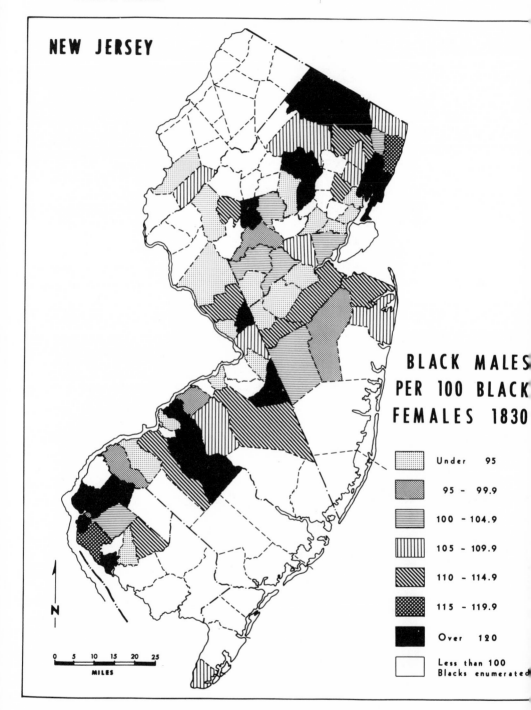

FIG. 17.

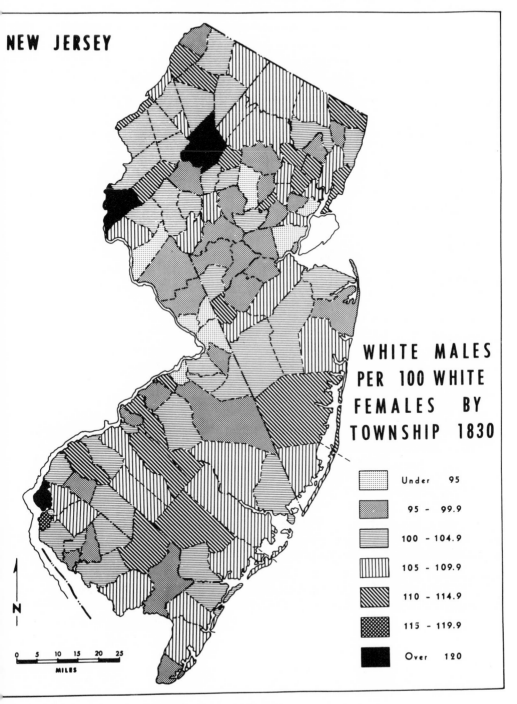

Fig. 18.

Ironworking and industrial areas in the Highlands and in the Outer Coastal Plain also harbored more white males than females but, generally, contained insignificant numbers of Blacks.[30]

By 1830 the number of white aliens, largely Irish, resident in New Jersey, was quite small (figure 19). Where such aliens were in residence, however, Afro-Americans were usually not present in large numbers. Job opportunities on the Morris Canal, in iron and other industries, which were denied Blacks, were obviously being taken up by the gentle tide of white foreigners.

It is logical to begin the end of this paper with some of the spatial patterns related to the movement of some Afro-Americans to the growing urban places of the day (figure 20). It should be emphasized, however, that even by 1860 this was a relatively minor current, and that from 1840 to 1860 the *relative percentages* of Blacks in urban places actually declined in the face of the tide of Irish and German immigration. However, it is in the cities, such as Newark, which was only 1.78 percent Black in 1860 that the roots of today's Afro-American residential and social patterns must be examined.[31]

The choice of Newark for such a study relies not only upon the well-known problems of that city's black population today, but also upon the facts that the city is and was the largest in the state and experienced the processes concerned with revolutionary changes in industry and transportation as well as the influx of substantial numbers of foreign-born whites after about 1830.[32] Newark's Afro-American population, at the time, was well established, often property owning, and free during this period and, thus, theoretically available for inclusion in the changes.[33] Therefore, Newark, rather than many other northern cities which did not possess significant black populations until World War I, is a logical case study for the roots of black ghettos.

A map of Newark's Afro-American population, based on Pierson's *Directory* of 1840, indicates no single black ghetto but rather scattered pockets of Blacks in and near the downtown area (figure 21).[34] The pattern based on the *Directory* of 1860 is much the same, but more intensive because of the larger number of Blacks listed (figure 22). Some clusters were formed or were overlooked by the *Directory* previously, and others seem to have disappeared. In any case, there is no single black ghetto but several neighborhoods with Blacks in residence.[35]

The *Directory* may also be of use in determining the occupations of those listed. An obvious shortcoming is that less than 20 percent of the black population was listed, and these were, presumably, the more stable and successful. In the 1840 *Directory*, 72 of 117 black males

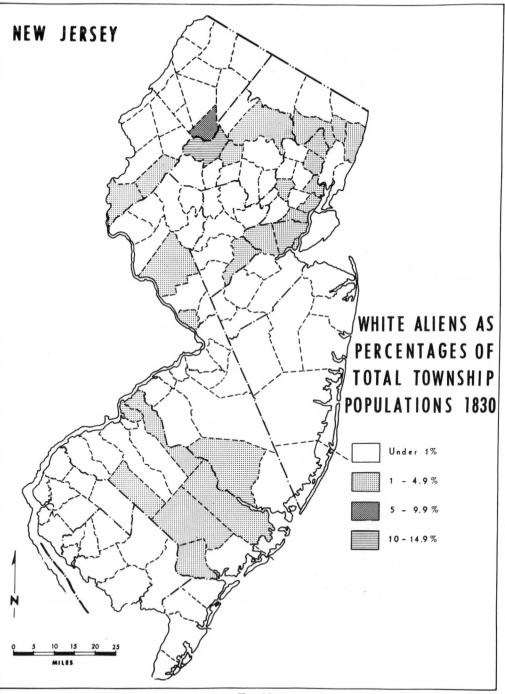

NEW JERSEY

WHITE ALIENS AS PERCENTAGES OF TOTAL TOWNSHIP POPULATIONS 1830

Under 1%

1 - 4.9 %

5 - 9.9 %

10 - 14.9 %

N

0   5   10   15   20   25
MILES

Fig. 19.

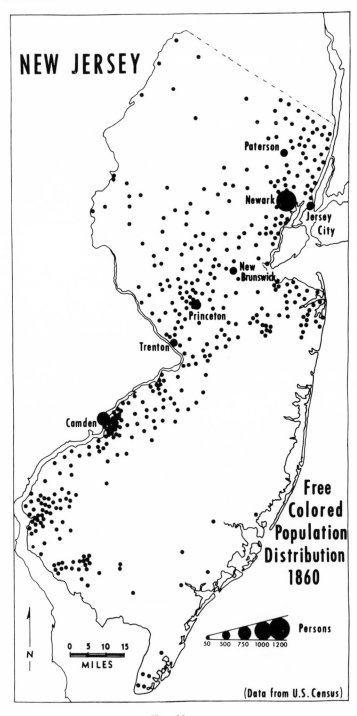

FIG. 20.

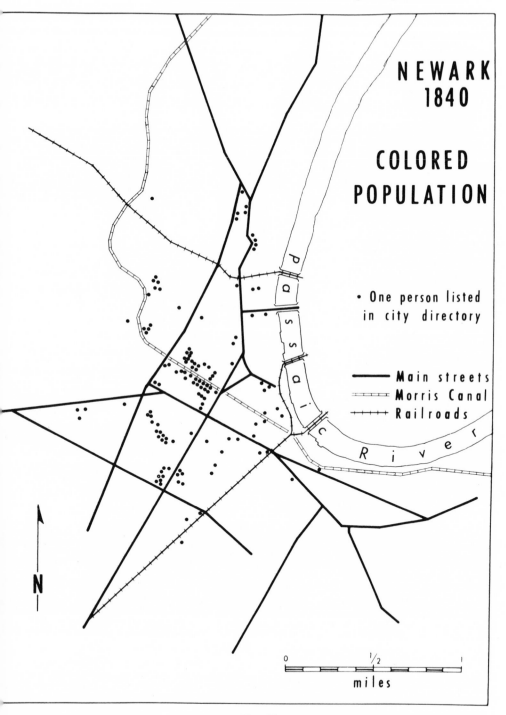

NEWARK
1840

COLORED
POPULATION

• One person listed
  in city directory

━━━ Main streets
╫╫╫ Morris Canal
┿┿┿ Railroads

N

0   ½   1
miles

FIG. 21.

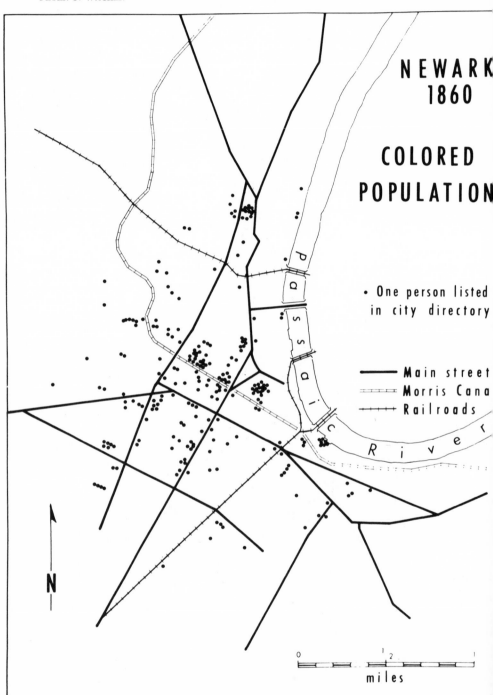

Fig. 22.

listed had no occupation indicated. Seventeen were termed laborers. Service occupations such as barber, waiter, coachman, and the like, accounted for 14. Only 8 were listed as artisans—blacksmiths and carpenters, largely. Three, apparently, were businessmen involved in a wood dealership, an eatinghouse, and a livery stable. None, except possibly a planemaker, appeared to be involved with the manufacturing industries, which were in such abundance in the city. Residence and occupation had no particular association. In 1860, 201 black males were listed. Almost half had no occupation indicated. Eleven admitted to being only laborers, while almost 30 percent were involved in personal services. The percentage of artisans also increased but the total number (fifteen) was not impressive. Twelve businesses, mostly small-scale, such as vegetable and oyster dealerships and restaurants, were listed. Eight were involved in professions including teaching and the clergy. Again, the data from the *Directory,* although suspect, do not indicate any real involvement in manufacturing.

The manuscript census of 1860 is especially valuable as a source of information on the spatial variation of Newark's social characteristics.[36] Although addresses are not given, data by ward divisions are available, including name, age, sex, race, place of birth, occupation, literacy, and ownership of real and personal property. The wealth of relatively accurate data available, along with exact knowledge of ward boundaries, makes possible the use of computer mapping, such as the SYMAP program of the Harvard Laboratory for Computer Graphics.[37] Several of these follow, with patterns covering the areas of arbitrarily decided 20 percent class intervals. These vary with the data.

The map of population density is based on 20 percent class intervals, between 4,944 and 44,898 persons per square mile (figure 23). The area of greatest density, with between 36,907.19 and 44,898.00 people per square mile, is located downtown, centering on the business district and its periphery. Zonal decreases occur, with the lowest densities on the outskirts of the city. In theory, this is as the situation should have been.

A map of the percentage of Afro-American heads of household, in the total number of all heads of household, reveals almost the same pattern (figure 24), but it must be remembered that very small percentages, divided into five 20 percent intervals, constitute the patterns. Thus, the areas of the densest concentration of Blacks contain only between 3.44 percent and 4.30 percent black heads of household. A quite visible departure from the zonal arrangement in the preceding map is the wide area in the eighth ward to the north possessing a black population.

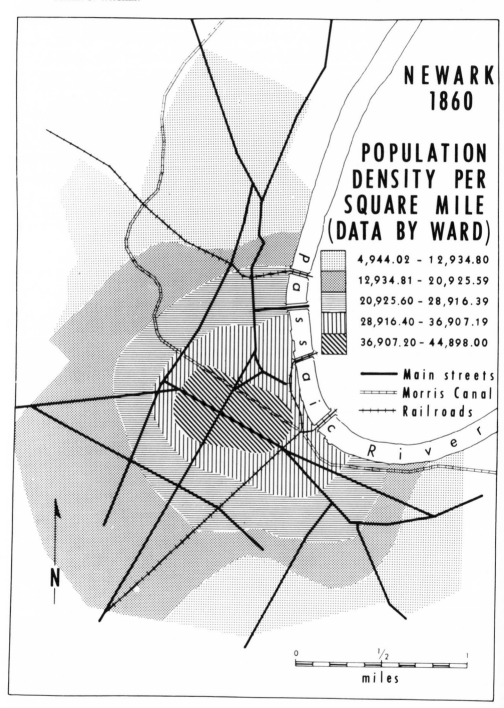

NEWARK
1860

POPULATION
DENSITY PER
SQUARE MILE
(DATA BY WARD)

4,944.02 - 12,934.80
12,934.81 - 20,925.59
20,925.60 - 28,916.39
28,916.40 - 36,907.19
36,907.20 - 44,898.00

Main streets
Morris Canal
Railroads

Passaic River

N

0   ½   1
miles

FIG. 23.

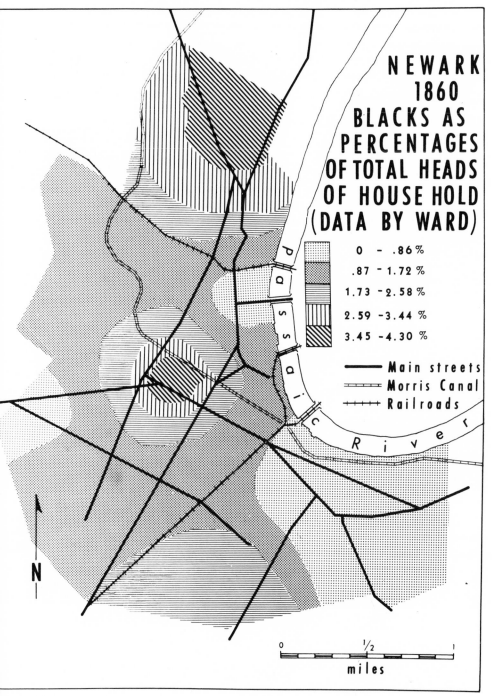

FIG. 24.

Some idea of the areal patterns of other ethnic and cultural groups may be ascertained with similar maps of the much larger Irish and German immigrant groups. These were, respectively, 21 percent and 26 percent of all families in Newark at the time. The most densely Irish areas, with from 30.92 percent to 37.40 percent Irish families, do not at all correlate with areas where there is a relatively large black population, and a zonal arrangement around the center of the city is not indicated (figure 25). Germans, who arrived decades later than the Irish also did not exhibit a zonal pattern (figure 26). A large part of the German population was far from the downtown area in the lightly populated and newly developed periphery. The highest class interval represented indicates a percentage of between 48.36 and 58.80, which does not truly portray what the manuscript census reveals—block after block of houses with a solidly German population in many areas. Those individuals not of German birth were the sons and daughters of those born in the German states. If there were any "ghettos" in Newark in 1860, they were German speaking.

The census of 1860, when perused block by block for the black population as well, reveals much the same pattern as that of Pierson's Newark *Directory*—small pockets of Blacks existing in white neighborhoods of mixed origin, generally near the central business district.

Data on employment, ownership of real property, household size, and literacy were compiled from the manuscript census for those wards with the largest Irish, German, and Afro-American populations. There is no way of telling whether these data are representative without sampling every ward, but I believe they are indicative of the general trends. Germans were generally employed in skilled trades and manufacturing. Few were unskilled laborers. Irish were employed in less skilled trades and manufacturing; almost 40 percent were unskilled laborers. The few Blacks sampled were almost all listed as laborers or involved in personal services. About a third of the German families were homeowners, while less than half as many Blacks or Irish were as fortunate. In the downtown ward where Blacks were most numerous, more of them, on a percentage basis, owned real estate (13.6 percent) than did the Irish where they were most numerous (11.97 percent). The Irish led in number of people per household and children per household, respectively, 8.93 and 5.16, followed by the Germans with 8.60 and 3.89, and the Blacks with only 7.88 and 3.30. Almost all children of school age attended school, but adult illiteracy rates varied considerably among the three groups. On the average, the black household held 1.68 adults who were illiterate, the Irish, .72, and the Germans were virtually all literate with only .02 illiterates per household.

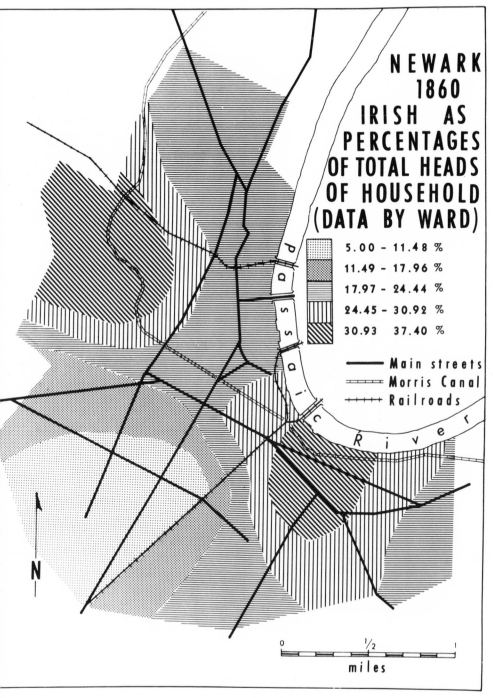

FIG. 25.

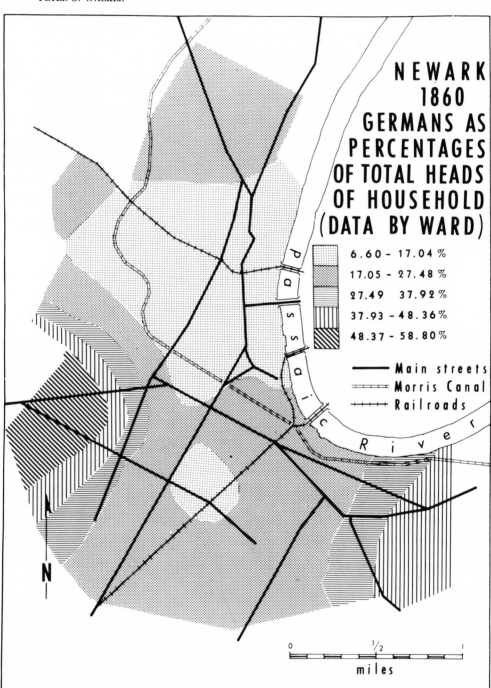

NEWARK
1860
GERMANS AS
PERCENTAGES
OF TOTAL HEADS
OF HOUSEHOLD
(DATA BY WARD)

6.60 – 17.04 %
17.05 – 27.48 %
27.49 37.92 %
37.93 – 48.36 %
48.37 – 58.80 %

Main streets
Morris Canal
Railroads

Passaic River

N

0   ½   1
miles

FIG. 26.

In concluding this paper, may this writer remind you that he promised only an *outline* of some of the most salient patterns and problems associated with the changing geography of New Jersey's Afro-American population. Many problems warranting additional investigation have, I trust, been implicit in this presentation. I hope I have whetted your appetites for far more knowledge in this general area. What is true for New Jersey is certainly true for other states and areas in the country.

Indeed, there is an abundance of manuscript materials awaiting detailed analysis which can provide some of the answers we seek. These exist especially in the form of tax lists and censuses. The tax lists, penetrating well into the eighteenth century, are especially valuable in regard to the associations between property ownership, slaveholding, and religious or ethnic affiliations.[38] A start in these materials has been made with the help of a well-known genealogist for selected townships in Somerset County at the beginning of the nineteenth century. Slaveholding in these areas was found to correlate better with the ownership of large farms than with Dutch origins, for example.[39] Similar investigations need to be carried out for other areas of the state, especially for the Dutch and Quaker-settled counties.

The manuscript censuses are especially valuable in ascertaining place of birth, property ownership, and occupations for Blacks. For instance, we have already seen that a surprisingly large percentage of Afro-Americans owned real estate in Newark. And the manuscript census materials of 1860 for widely scattered townships also suggests substantial real estate ownership on the part of Blacks (table 6). The data for Mannington Township, which is located in Salem County in the southwestern portion of New Jersey, are especially interesting because such large numbers of Blacks in residence there in 1860 were born outside the state. Those born in New Jersey were almost entirely born within the county. Almost 21 percent of the total Afro-American population had come from Maryland and about half as many originated in Delaware. Another surprise was that, in the case of fourteen of forty-eight real property owners, neither husband nor wife was born in New Jersey, so that their inheritance of the real property they held is doubtful. The area must have been a well-known haven for free Blacks.[40] One young black man residing there in 1860 had been born in Canada, and a child whose parents had been born in Maryland had himself been born in Massachusetts.

Newark, of course, is a case study *par excellence*. Much, much more can be done with even the manuscript census of 1860, especially with the application of computer mapping. As the Afro-American population

TABLE 6

SOME CHARACTERISTICS OF THE BLACK POPULATION OF NEW JERSEY HEADS OF HOUSEHOLD, SELECTED TOWNSHIPS, 1860

Township	N	Born in New Jersey	"Laborer" as Occupation	Real Estate Ownership
Mannington (Salem County)	159	61.01%	81.13%	30.82%
Princeton (Mercer County)	140	88.07	51.43	27.86
Hillsborough (Somerset County)	36	91.66	91.66	36.12

is such a very small proportion of the total population in 1860, however, work must continue with later censuses as well.

Obviously, the spatial data here presented needs "fleshing out" at some length—we have only a skeleton so far. A large part of the flesh can come from the manuscript sources mentioned. Often, however, official quantitative data do not exist and one must turn to sources such as contemporary newspapers, letters, and family papers. The latter exist for many white slaveowners but, unfortunately, few Blacks have deposited their family papers in archives.

Certainly, the nonquantitative data can be suggestive. Was there a decline in the level of skills possessed by Afro-Americans as manumission occurred, for example? Eighteenth-century newspaper advertisements of slaves for sale and announcements of runaways list many who were skilled millers, carpenters, and ironworkers. Few free Blacks with such skills appear in the 1860 census. The newspapers should also be instructive in regard to the barriers erected against black employment in the various manufacturing industries.[41]

In final conclusion, we might ask ourselves what the relevance of this scholarship is today. First of all, we have not had true *American* history because of the exclusion of many racial and ethnic groups from consideration. With this, I think we can all agree. In a similar vein, we cannot have true *American* historical geography until all groups, including Blacks, have been considered. Surely, there are enough data available for spatial analysis to warrant even a new subfield, if need be, that of Afro-American historical geography. Who will be the scholars? Certainly, this area should not be the exclusive domain of any one racial or ethnic group, but it would be my hope that at least some of the young black men and women now entering the field of geography would consider such scholarship. Black Americans have been, unfortunately, conspicuous by their absence from the general ranks of historical geographers. Perhaps some knowledge of the wealth of spatial data available dealing with their own collective past and begging for analysis will act as a stimulus for Blacks to end the imbalance in the approach to American historical geography as well as the racial imbalance in the ranks of the scholars concerned. Finally, just as historical geography, with its spatial orientation, has generally been a boon to those attempting to understand history, the historical geography of Afro-America should be a distinct asset to those wishing to fully understand the black experience in this country.

NOTES

1. "The Population Geography of the Free Negro in *Ante-Bellum* America," *Population Studies* 3 (1949): 401.
2. O. Fred Donaldson, "Geography and the Black American: The White Papers and the Invisible Man," *Journal of Geography* 70 (1971): 138-49.
3. Official colony-wide censuses for New Jersey began in 1726 and have been published in various places in the New Jersey Archives. The archives consist of two series: William A. Whitehead et al., eds., *Archives of the State of New Jersey: Documents Relating to the Colonial, Revolutionary, and Post Revolutionary History of the State of New Jersey*, 1st ser., 42 vols.; and William S. Stryker et al., eds., *Archives of the State of New Jersey: Documents Relating to the Revolutionary History of the State of New Jersey*, 2d ser., 5 vols. (These volumes will be cited hereafter as NJA, 1st ser., and NJA, 2d ser.)

    The census of 1726 (NJA, 1st ser., 5:164) was sent to the Lords of Trade by Governor Burnet May 9, 1727. Data were collected "by the Sheriffs of the severall Countys." The population was enumerated by race "White" and "Negroe" as well as by sex and by age—over and under sixteen. No Indians were mentioned, and the status of Blacks—slave or free—was not recorded. The census of 1737-38 (NJA, 1st ser., 6:244) was probably taken by order of Governor Lewis Morris, but those responsible for the enumeration were not mentioned. "Whites" and "Negroes and Other Slaves" were listed separately, as were males and females over and under sixteen. The "Other Slaves" category presumably referred to mulattoes and Indians. In calculating male-female ratios for the several counties, the result for Essex County was such as to cast some doubt on the published figures. Simple addition and comparison of the totals with the published totals at the ends of other columns revealed that an error of between 693 and 703 had been made in the white males above-sixteen column for Essex County. Subsequent calculations added the mean of these two figures, 698, to the Essex total in order to arrive at the ratios and percentages presented in the tables included in this paper. Although no errors of such magnitude have been found in the other censuses used, this example is noted in order to indicate the caution with which all censuses, especially those of colonial days, should be used.

The census of 1745 (NJA, 1st ser., 6:242-43) was taken at Governor Lewis Morris's behest. The figures were broken down by county for East and West Jersey. Males and females above and below sixteen were separated into "Slaves" and an unnamed category, presumably consisting of whites. In the unnamed category was a column listing "Quakers or Reputed Quakers," by county.

The census of 1772 (NJA, 1st ser., 10:452-53) was taken between July 1, 1771, and July 1, 1772. Governor William Franklin indicated that "he wanted to have an Account of the Number of Inhabitants of this Province distinguished into several Classes, and of the number of Births and Burials in the same for one Year: and to ask the Advice of the Council in what manner he could best obtain the said Accounts. Whereupon the Council advised His Excellency to cause a number of Blank Lists to be printed with the proper Heads and Titles and to Issue Orders to the Several Sheriffs to request the Assessors in their respective Districts to fill them up at the time of their going about to take the Rates and Assess the Taxes on the Inhabitants. And a List was made out accordingly" (NJA, 1st ser., 18: 284-85).

On September 9, 1772, the governor indicated that only one return, that from Windsor Township, Middlesex County, had been received by him. The governor attributed the lack of cooperation in the matter to several causes; "Some of the Assessors object to complying with the Request . . . because it is not required by them by Law; others, because of an absurd, superstitious Notion, which has long prevailed amongst the Vulgar, that numbering the People is sinful, and will be attended with fatal Consequences to the Country; and others, because they suspect the Ministry have directed the Measure, in order to answer some particular Purpose of theirs. . . . But the refusal of the largest Number is founded, I am told, on their Unwillingness to take any additional Trouble, where they are not to have an additional allowance." Franklin averred that it was "not even known to the Ministry that any such Thing is in Agitation" and that his reason for requesting the census was because "A Right Knowledge of the Number of Inhabitants, Dwelling-houses, Births and Burials, of a Country is a matter evidently of great Importance to the public Welfare; and is peculiarly necessary and proper to those, who are Members of the Legislature. I have taken some Pains, during my Residence in this Colony, to obtain this useful Piece of Knowledge, but the most intelligent Persons I could meet with, were as ignorant, in this respect, as myself."

By September 15, Franklin was able to report to the House of Representatives that returns from several of the assessors of Hunterdon County had reached him, along "with a Petition requesting a recompense for their extraordinary Trouble in taking the Lists. . . . As many of them were not made acquainted with my Request, until after they had been about their Townships to take the Rateables, and therefore had the Trouble of going about a second Time. . . ." He recommended their being given "some compensation, adequate to their Services." The House replied the next day that "as the Time of Assessing the Inhabitants by Law is passed, and there is now no Probability that a compleat List can be had this Year, that the Members of this House will, in their several Counties, countenance the Taking the Lists, proposed by his Excellency, at the Time of next assessing the Inhabitants, when the House hopes the Lists will not only be taken with Accuracy, but with less Expence and Trouble, both to the Assessors and the People, and, that when the Returns are completed, that the House will take the Matter into further Consideration" (NJA, 1st ser., 9:322-27).

That Franklin had been correct in his judgment that little accurate information on population numbers and characteristics existed since the census of 1745 can be seen in the fact that the assessor of Windsor Township in Middlesex County, "though one of the most intelligent Men in the County, assured the Governor, that he did not imagine there were so many People, by 500 in the Township, as he found on taking their Numbers and that about the Year 1733 There were not above 40 Farms in the Township, and now there are near 300" (NJA, 1st ser., 9:325). Windsor Township included Princeton and had been settled well before 1733 (figure 3) so that the rapid increase since 1733 was all the more noteworthy and even more characteristic of other areas (tables 2 and 4).

The census of 1772 was unusually comprehensive for a colonial enumeration, and it is most unfortunate that the East Jersey counties' returns (with the exception of Windsor Township) are missing. Data included the number of dwellings per county, white persons "of all Denominations" and "Negroes." The whites were broken down as to age (under sixteen, sixteen to fifty, fifty to eighty, and "80 upwards") and sex. Blacks were enumerated as to age—over and under sixteen—and as to sex. Marriages, births, and burials of whites were listed as well as the number of families moving into and out of the province. Births and burials were listed for the black population, but, unfortunately, not marriages or movement into or out of the colony.

It is uncertain as to how many Indians may have been enumerated with Afro-Americans in the early censuses. The census of 1726 lists only whites and Blacks but that of 1737 lists "Negroes and Other Slaves," and the census of 1745 lists slaves. There is no question about the fact that there were some Indian slaves in New Jersey during the colonial period and they are on occasion mentioned as runaways in the newspapers. By the middle of the eighteenth century, however, not more than a few hundred Indians, slave or free, remained in the colony. See Rudolph J. Vecoli, *The People of New Jersey* (Princeton: D. Van Nostrand Co., 1965), p. 51. The census of 1772 listed only whites and Negroes so it is unlikely that any Indians were included in the enumeration.

4. The various published national biennial censuses are listed and described in Henry J. Dubester, *Catalog of United States Census Publications, 1790-1945* (Washington, D.C.: Government Printing Office, 1950). The published censuses through 1860, used in this study, are listed on pp. 3-11. These censuses, unfortunately, are not at all uniform. Some break both whites and Blacks down as to age and sex, some do not. The lack or pres-

ence of such data is indicated in the text of this paper as well as on the maps accompanying the study. Data by township first became available in 1790, but on a limited basis until the census of 1810. Manuscript national censuses are available on microfilm from the National Archives and are listed in U.S., National Archives and Records Service, *Federal Population Censuses, 1790-1890: A Catalog of Microfilm Copies of the Schedules* (Washington D.C.: National Archives and Records Service, 1971). Manuscript censuses of New Jersey before 1830 are not available.

5. Daniel Jacobson first made this writer aware of the effectiveness of *Heimatkunde* in undergraduate instruction.

6. See, for example, American Council of Learned Societies, "Report of Committee on Linguistic and National Stocks in the Population of the United States," *Annual Report of the American Historical Association for the Year 1931* (Washington D.C.: Government Printing Office, 1932), 1: 396-97; and U.S., Department of Commerce, Bureau of the Census, *A Century of Population Growth from the First Census of the United States to the Twelfth, 1790-1900* (Washington D.C.: Government Printing Office, 1909), pp. 119-21. The former source is considerably more accurate than the latter in regard to the Swede-Finn population of Cape May County and the Dutch population of Monmouth County.

7. U.S., Department of Commerce, Bureau of the Census, *Negro Population 1790-1915* (Washington D.C.: Government Printing Office, 1918), p. 51.

8. Marion T. Wright, "New Jersey Laws and the Negro," *Journal of Negro History* 28 (1943): 176-77.

9. Henry S. Chandler, comp., "Peter Chandler: A Biographical Sketch and His Diary of a Business Trip in New York [i.e., New Jersey, 1823-1824]" (N.p.: For Private Circulation, 190_). p. 6.

10. Elizabeth Donnan, *Documents Illustrative of the Slave Trade to America* 3 (Washington D.C.: Carnegie Institute of Washington, 1932): 405.

11. E. B. O'Callaghan, ed., *Documents Relative to the Colonial History of New York* 1 (Albany: Weed, Parsons and Co., 1856): 154. The "Dutch" population included not only Hollanders but substantial numbers of Flemings, Walloons, Huguenots, Germans, Scandinavians, and others.

12. These county boundaries are from John P. Snyder, *The Story of New Jersey's Civil Boundaries, 1606-1968* (Trenton: Bureau of Geology and Topography, 1969), pp. 20-21. Changes in county boundaries occurred several times before 1772. For the censuses of 1726 and 1738, for example, the Salem and Cumberland counties of 1772 were included within Salem County. Hunterdon, Sussex, and part of Morris County were all included in the Hunterdon County of 1726-38. A large part of northern Somerset County was included in Essex County in 1726-38. The boundaries for the census of 1745 were the same as those for 1726-38 except that Hunterdon, Somerset, and Essex had assumed the boundaries they would have in 1772. Morris County encompassed what was Morris and Sussex in 1772. In 1769, the boundary question with New York was resolved, and New Jersey's border was moved southward. These changes should be readily apparent in viewing the maps based on the various censuses.

13. Seventeenth- and eighteenth-century church distributions often give the best possible idea of the areal concentrations of certain cultural groups. The data for figure 1 were drawn from Frederick L. Weis, *The Colonial Churches*

and the Colonial Clergy of the Middle and Southern Colonies, 1607-1776 (Lancaster, Mass.: Society of the Descendants of the Colonial Clergy, 1938).

14. Edward W. Roberts, "New Jersey Settlement: 1665-1765" (seminar paper, Department of Geography, Rutgers University, 1969).

15. "New Jersey: Physiographic Diagram," Department of Geography, Rutgers University, 1958.

16. O'Callaghan, Documents Relative, 1:580; 2:222; 4:446; 623, 816; 5:814.

17. Donnan, Documents Illustrative, 3:408-9, 510-12.

18. O'Callaghan, Documents Relative, 4:811.

19. NJA, 1st ser., 26:333.

20. In 1786 the legislature promulgated a law designed to prevent the importation of slaves who had been brought to the country since 1776. See Wright, "New Jersey Laws," p. 174.

21. Irving S. Kull, ed., New Jersey: A History 2 (New York: The American Historical Society, 1930): 724.

22. NJA, 2d ser., 2:189.

23. There are many indications of this in the newspapers of the day. For example, Lewis, a mulatto "servant man" from Burlington was described as having "grey Eyes, very much freckled" and as being "so white, that he hardly would be taken for a Mulattoe, only by his Hair" (NJA, 1st ser., 25:138).

24. For example, see NJA, 1st ser., 25:166, 272, 505. For a most interesting account of the origins of one long-lived community, see William Steward, Gouldtown, A Very Remarkable Settlement of Ancient Date (Philadelphia: J. B. Lippincott Co., 1913).

25. Michael P. Riccards, "Patriots and Plunderers: Confiscation of Loyalist Lands in New Jersey, 1776-1786," New Jersey History 86 (1968): 18.

26. The Quaker aversion to slavery and activity in regard to abolition and manumission is described succinctly in Henry S. Cooley, A Study of Slavery in New Jersey (Baltimore: Johns Hopkins Press, 1896), pp. 20-23.

27. No one good source exists for the economic geography of the state at about this time. An idea of the distribution of some economic activities by county can be obtained in Tench Coxe, A Statement of the Arts and Manufactures of the United States of America for the Year 1810 (Philadelphia: A. Cornman, 1814), pp. 39-43.

28. Peter O. Wacker, "The Changing Geography of the Black Population of New Jersey, 1810-1860: A Preliminary View," Proceedings of the Association of American Geographers 3 (1971): 176.

29. Richard F. Veit, The Old Canals of New Jersey: A Historical Geography (Little Falls, N.J.: New Jersey Geographical Press, 1963).

30. An excellent idea of the spatial nature of the state's economic activities during this period can be had by consulting Thomas F. Gordon, A Gazetteer of the State of New Jersey (Trenton: Daniel Fenton, 1834), pp. 92-266.

31. Wacker, "Changing Geography," p. 176.

32. John T. Cunningham, Newark (Newark: New Jersey Historical Society, 1966), p. 101.

33. "People of Color, Newark, 1821" (unpublished list of black taxpayers and real property owners extracted from tax ratable data), New Jersey Reference Division, Newark Public Library, Newark, N.J.

34. A large part of the data on Newark was gathered and analyzed by some of

this writer's graduate and undergraduate students as an optional project in partial fulfillment of the requirements for a course in the historical geography of the United States given in the spring of 1971. Our data came primarily from B. T. Pierson, *Directory of the City of Newark,* which began publication in 1835, and the manuscript census of 1860. The *Directory* has the advantage of pinpointing addresses but, by admission, sometimes gives erroneous information. Also, only about one in four of Newark's white population was listed and in the case of Blacks, only one in six. Additionally, almost only male Blacks were listed, while the censuses indicate an imbalance in the sex ratio during the period favoring female Blacks.

The base used for the various maps of Newark is an inset titled "City of Newark" in G. M. Hopkins, *Map of New Jersey, 1860* (Philadelphia: H. G. Bond, 1860).

35. Jay Bartner and Randall J. Burton, "Settlement Patterns of the Black Population of Newark in 1860" (undergraduate research paper, Department of Geography, Rutgers University, 1971).

36. Sophia G. Hinshalwood, "Newark in 1860: Selected Social Characteristics of Its German, Irish, and Black Populations" (seminar paper, Department of Geography, Rutgers University, 1971); and Walter F. Howard, "The 1860 Census of Newark, New Jersey: Some Observations concerning the Distribution of the Irish, German, and Black Heads of Household" (seminar paper, Department of Geography, Rutgers University, 1971).

37. I am indebted to Walter F. Howard for developing the computer maps.

38. New Jersey, Department of Education, Division of State Library, Archives and History Microfilm and Records Unit, Trenton, New Jersey, "County Tax Ratables, 1788-1822." Unfortunately, the tax ratable data are quite incomplete as to areal and temporal coverage.

39. Steven B. Frakt, "Patterns of Slave-Holding in Somerset County, New Jersey," (research paper, Department of Geography, Rutgers University, 1967). A copy of this study is on file in the Special Collections Division, Rutgers University Library.

40. Newspapers are replete with references to runaways from the South in the general area. For example, see Joseph S. Sickler, *The History of Salem County, New Jersey* (Salem, N.J.: Sunbeam Publishing Co., 1937), p. 221.

41. Wacker, "Changing Geography," p. 176.

Some Sources in the National Archives for Studies of Afro—American Population: Growth and Movement

ROBERT L. CLARKE

This discussion is, quite briefly, about some federal records in the National Archives that can be used to study the growth, movement, and distribution of black Americans. It does not include all possible kinds of records that contain information on this subject. Nor does it include what must be a most obvious source—the population schedules of the decennial census. Instead, this paper concerns various records that deal with subject matter or information very different from population in general, or the black population in particular, and shows how these records, in a tangential manner, contain information that might be useful in population studies.

The Records of the Continental and Confederation Congresses and the Constitutional Convention, which are part of Record Group 360, in the National Archives Building, are one example of such materials. These records are in the literary forms common to government (letters, memorandums, resolutions, reports, debates, and journals). In subject matter these records include the usual matters with which a government engaged in war would be expected to deal. In the normal conduct of its business, the congresses did not show any interest in the size or movement of the population. Nevertheless, they created records that might be useful in studying the black population of the era.

Early in the Revolutionary War the British began to try to entice slaves to join His Majesty's forces, and during the war numbers of Blacks went to the British lines. As the fighting ended and peace came, the British forces left and numbers of American Blacks went with them. The American government was concerned with slaves as property, and because most Blacks were, or were presumed to be, slaves, and thus property, both governments were concerned about their exodus as a loss of property. The British agreed to keep lists of Blacks they took, so that the records might form the basis for later claims for losses of slave property. These lists, in conjunction with other materials, may be a source for study of the black population of that time. Record Group 360 shows that about three thousand Negroes accompanied the British when they sailed from New York, and New York was not the only embarkation port. This number is a small percentage of the estimated black population, but the information on the lists may be useful for population studies.

These lists contain several kinds of information. They contain names (sometimes a given and a surname), ages and general descriptions— "stout fellow, ordinary wench." Perhaps more important for the historical geographer, the lists contain names of the former owners, former owners' homes or residences, and years in which the Blacks left the owners. It may be interesting to note that there are Blacks listed who had left owners in South Carolina, Virginia, New Jersey, New York, and Massachusetts, as well as some who had been born free in the "British Isles" (West Indies?). (Figure 1)

The knowledge that the ships were bound for, among other ports Canadian ones, means that these records, and some related ones in the National Archives, may be of some value in studying the black population of Canada. The evacuees, at least temporarily, added to that population.

Some of the ports listed as destinations on the British-prepared lists are Port Roseway, Halifax, Annapolis Royal, Fort Cumberland, and, perhaps most important, Saint John's. A map of the Saint John's River and the community of Saint John's, which is in the Records of Boundary and Claims Commissions and Arbitration, Record Group 76, shows three communities labeled "Negro Settlements." (Figure 2) It is quite possible that some of the evacuees joined or began these settlements. Evelyn B. Harvey used at least some of these rolls in writing her article, "The Negro Loyalist," which appeared in the September 1971 issue of the *Nova Scotia Historical Quarterly*.

There are other records growing out of the Revolutionary War that could be used to study the movement and distribution of the Negro population. Apparently, several thousand black men were among the colonial patriots who battled the British for the independence of their

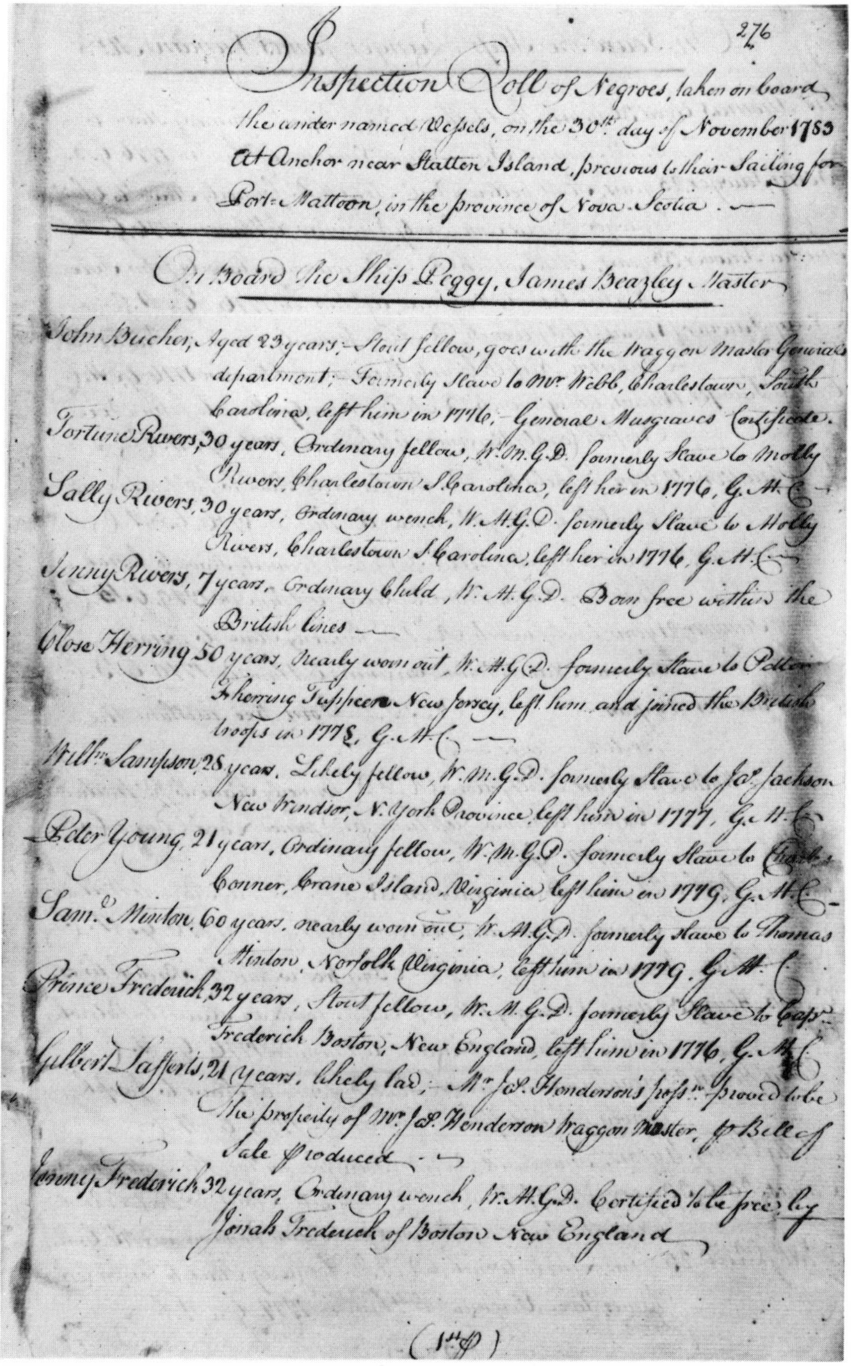

276

Inspection Roll of Negroes, taken on board the under named Vessels, on the 30th day of November 1783 At Anchor near Statten Island, previous to their Sailing for Port-Mattoon, in the province of Nova Scotia.

On Board the Ship Peggy, James Beazley Master

John Bucher, Aged 23 years,—Stout fellow, goes with the Waggon Master Generals department;—Formerly Slave to Mr Webb, Charlestown, South Carolina, left him in 1776.—General Musgraves Certificate.

Fortune Rivers, 30 years, Ordinary fellow, W. M. G. D. formerly Slave to Molly Rivers, Charlestown S. Carolina, left her in 1776, G. M. C.

Sally Rivers, 30 years, Ordinary wench, W. M. G. D. formerly Slave to Molly Rivers, Charlestown S. Carolina, left her in 1776, G. M. C.

Jenny Rivers, 7 years, Ordinary Child, W. M. G. D. Born free within the British lines—

Close Herring, 50 years, nearly worn out, W. M. G. D. formerly Slave to Peter Herring Tupper New Jersey, left him and joined the British troops in 1778, G. M. C.

Willm Sampson, 28 years, Likely fellow, W. M. G. D. formerly Slave to Jos Jackson New Windsor, N. York Province, left him in 1777, G. M. C.

Peter Young, 21 years, Ordinary fellow, W. M. G. D. formerly Slave to Charles Conner, Crane Island Virginia, left him in 1779, G. M. C.

Saml Minton, 60 years, nearly worn out, W. M. G. D. formerly Slave to Thomas Minton, Norfolk Virginia, left him in 1779, G. M. C.

Prince Frederick, 32 years, Stout fellow, W. M. G. D. formerly Slave to Capt. Frederick Boston, New England, left him in 1776, G. M. C.

Gilbert Jafferts, 21 years, likely lad, Mr Jos Henderson's pass, proved to be the property of Mr Jos Henderson Waggon Master, & Bill of Sale produced.

Jenny Frederick 32 years, Ordinary wench, W. M. G. D. Certified to be free by Jonah Frederick of Boston New England

(1st)

Fig. 1. *Inspection roll of Negroes on vessel "at Anchor near Staten Island," November 30, 1783.* (Records of the Continental and Confederation Congresses, National Archives Microfilm Publication M247, roll 66.)

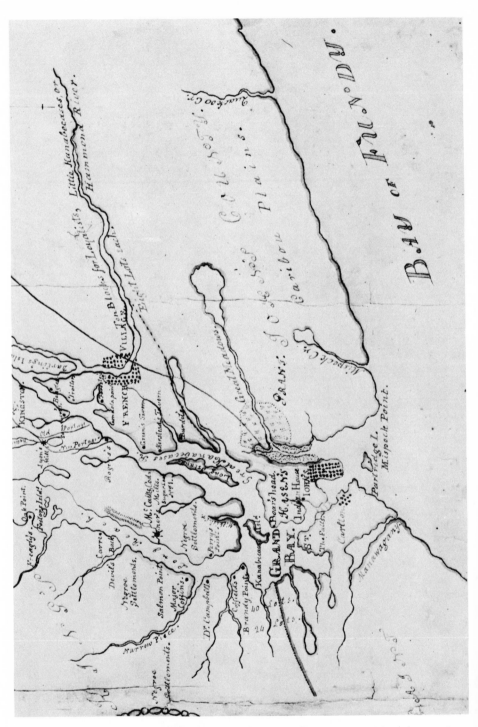

Fig. 2. *Map of Saint John's River and surrounding communities, August 1, 1812. (Records of Boundary and Claims Commissions and Arbitrations, Folder 1, Series 30, National Archives Building.)*

adopted land, and many of them, as veterans, joined their white comrades in seeking pensions from the government of the United States. Their applications are part of the Records of the Veterans Administration, Record Group 15, which is available as Microfilm M804 in the National Archives. Veterans' movements are sometimes revealed in aplications seeking to establish eligibility for a pension. Following are some examples of these entries: (1) Peter Jennings was born in Connecticut and enlisted in Rhode Island. After his discharge he was on a trade mission out of New York when he was shipwrecked in the Bahamas, where he probably lost his army discharge. In 1832, Peter Jennings, "a man of color," aged "eighty years, four months, and twenty-one days" and resident of Tennessee, applied for a pension. (2) William Stewart was born in Brunswick County, Virginia; he moved to North Carolina where he enlisted. Upon his discharge he lived in North Carolina for about twenty years and then moved to Pennsylvania where he had lived about twenty years when he applied for a pension. (3) Samuel Dunbar was born in Braintree, Massachusetts, and entered service there. When he was sixty-seven years old and applied for a pension, he was living in Lower Canada.

The pension applications of black veterans of the Civil War, also in Record Group 15, contain the same kind of information. Here the research is easier because the black Civil War soldier served in a segregated unit. A few examples are as follows: (1) Jane Johnson was the widow of Lee Johnson. Mrs. Johnson was born in Virginia as were her parents; she died in Louisiana. (2) Joseph Woodly was born in Washington, D. C. He secured a marriage license and married in New Orleans. (3) David Thompson was born in the District of Columbia, enlisted in New Orleans, and was discharged in Mississippi. In 1915 the Bureau of Pensions was writing to him at a St. Louis, Missouri, address. (4) Isaac Toops was born in Richmond before the war; he enlisted and was discharged in New Orleans.

The federal government has produced yet another kind of record that might be used to study the growth and distribution of the black population. When the framers of the Constitution gave the new government the power to lay and collect taxes, they also gave it the power to regulate foreign and domestic commerce. In its use of these powers, the government created Records of the Bureau of Customs, Record Group 36, from which various kinds of information can be obtained. For example, under the Constitution, the foreign traffic in slaves could not be prohibited before 1808. Figure 3 is the manifest of a ship arriving at Savannah from Place Goree on the West Coast of Africa on August 21,

1794, showing that it left with fifty-two captives but arrived minus three who died en route (figure 3). A study of such records might tell a good deal about the growth of the black population during these years. And it is interesting to speculate what a study of the same records might show even after the foreign slave trade became illegal.

The great increase in the slave population came after the end of the period of legal importation of Blacks from abroad. The change in the southern economy; the increase of cotton culture, with the spread of the plantation system; and the opening of new lands to the West (i.e., the Old West—Alabama and Mississippi) accompanied shifts in the black population. Part of this movement is reflected in the "slave manifests" of ships engaged in the coastal trade of the United States. A manifest for the port of New Orleans shows that this ship carried slaves from Baltimore on January 21, 1850, and was bound for New Orleans (figure 4). This manifest lists name (first and last), sex, age, height, and whether the slave was "Negro, Mulatto, or Person of Color." It lists both the person making the shipment and the person receiving it.

Manifests such as these and the other records described here might be used for a number of kinds of studies. The Revolutionary War materials could be useful for nineteenth-century population studies, since veterans of that war applied for pensions as late as 1850. Similarly, veterans of the Civil War, or their dependents, corresponded with the Bureau of Pensions as late as the 1920s. The foreign manifests could cast light on the growth of the black population in the late eighteenth century and, possibly, in the early nineteenth century. And the domestic slave manifests could tell a good deal about the movement of the slave population back to the Civil War.

Except for the foreign manifests, these records seem to offer another unique opportunity. Although there is a valid interest in the summary or aggregate, these totals might be misleading. For example, a known increase in the slave population in a given locality could lead to some conclusions about the birth rate among Blacks, but when these figures can be tested against other records of individuals, not *numbers* of individuals, a researcher might be able to discover the reasons behind the causes of the increase.

As the use of these federal records might cast light on some population trends among Blacks, there are, of course, other records that could be used for the same purpose. Obviously, I have not intended that this paper be a definitive one on this subject; I have intended only to suggest some federal records that hold promise for studies in the growth, movement, and distribution of Afro-Americans.

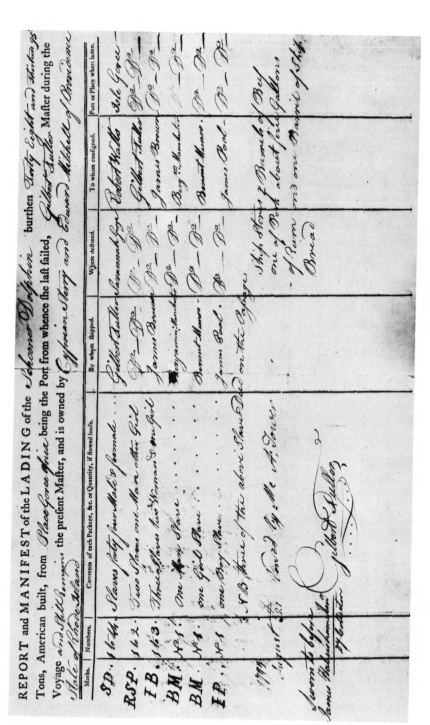

FIG. 3. *Manifest of ship arriving at Savannah from Place Goree, Africa, August 21, 1794. (Records of the Bureau of Customs, Foreign Incoming Manifests, National Archives Building.)*

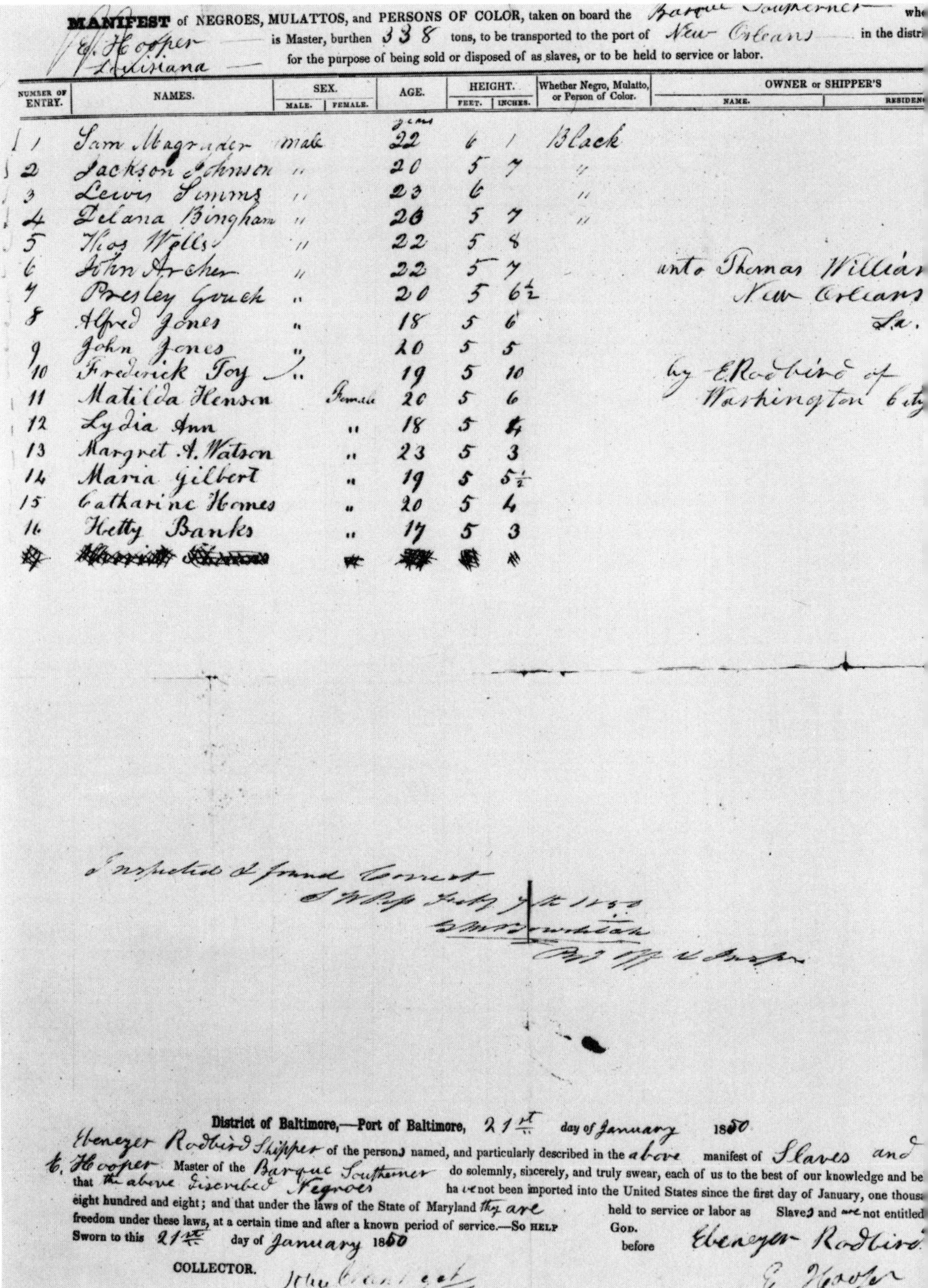

MANIFEST of NEGROES, MULATTOS, and PERSONS OF COLOR, taken on board the *Barque Southerner* whe_ *Jn. Hooper* _ is Master, burthen 338 tons, to be transported to the port of *New Orleans* _ in the distri_ *Louisiana* _ for the purpose of being sold or disposed of as slaves, or to be held to service or labor.

NUMBER OF ENTRY.	NAMES.	SEX.		AGE.	HEIGHT.		Whether Negro, Mulatto, or Person of Color.	OWNER or SHIPPER'S	
		MALE.	FEMALE.		FEET.	INCHES.		NAME.	RESIDEN_
1	Sam Magrader	male		22	6	1	Black		
2	Jackson Johnson	"		20	5	7	"		
3	Lewis Simms	"		23	6		"		
4	Delana Bingham	"		26	5	7	"		
5	Thos Wells	"		22	5	8			
6	John Archer	"		22	5	7		unto Thomas William_	
7	Presley Gouch	"		20	5	6½		New Orleans	
8	Alfred Jones	"		18	5	6		La.	
9	John Jones	"		20	5	5			
10	Frederick Toy	"		19	5	10		by E Rodbird of	
11	Matilda Henson		Female	20	5	6		Washington City	
12	Lydia Ann		"	18	5	4			
13	Margret A. Watson		"	23	5	3			
14	Maria Gilbert		"	19	5	5½			
15	Catharine Homes		"	20	5	4			
16	Hetty Banks		"	17	5	3			
~~17~~	~~Harriet Stokes~~	~~"~~		~~~~	~~~~	~~~~			

Inspected & found Correct
S W Riffs Secty Jany 7th 1850
~~ ~~
Riff Offr ~~ ~~

District of Baltimore,—Port of Baltimore, 21st day of January 1850.

Ebenezer Rodbird Shipper of the person_ named, and particularly described in the *above* manifest of *Slaves and* _ *E. Hooper* Master of the *Barque Southerner* do solemnly, sincerely, and truly swear, each of us to the best of our knowledge and be_ that *the above described Negroes* ha_ not been imported into the United States since the first day of January, one thousa_ eight hundred and eight; and that under the laws of the State of Maryland *they are* _ held to service or labor as Slave_ and _ not entitled freedom under these laws, at a certain time and after a known period of service.—So HELP GOD. Sworn to this 21st day of January 1850 before *Ebenezer Rodbird*

COLLECTOR. *John _____* *E Hooper*

FIG. 4. *Slave manifest of ship carrying slaves from Baltimore to New Orleans, January 21, 1850. (Records of Bureau of Customs, Slave Manifests, National Archives Building.)*

Discussion Summary

The discussion was conducted by *Wilbur Zelinsky, Department of Geography, Pennsylvania State University,* chairman of the session on Afro-American Population.

Jonathan Levine, editor of the Historical Methods Newsletter, University of Pittsburgh, began the discussion by asking *Peter Wacker, Department of Geography, Rutgers University,* whether or not he had examined family structure of the black population in Newark. Dr. Levine indicated that a similar study was in progress for Buffalo, New York. Dr. Wacker replied that his work has not yet reached that point.

Robert Clarke, specialist in Afro-American History, National Archives, was then asked if Civil and Revolutionary War pension records included any indication of race that would allow a researcher to make a random sample based upon race or would the researcher have to know in advance the name of a black person? Mr. Clarke pointed out that the records of the Revolutionary War and those of the Civil War are different. For the Revolutionary War, where Blacks did not serve in segregated units, "it becomes a matter of either starting with a name or searching through the records to try to identify the Blacks." He added that the latter method is very difficult and time-consuming.[1] But for the Civil War, where Blacks served in segregated units, one has only to determine which units were black units.[2] Then the researcher can get names from unit lists and use those names in checking through the pension application file.

Frank Innes, Department of Geography, McGill University, introduced the next topic of the discussion on fertility rates of Blacks. In a recent joint research project, Dr. Innes and Barry Higman, University of the West Indies, examined slave registrations in the West Indies dating from 1817 until emancipation in the 1830s. They observed that the Creole slave had a very low fertility rate, while "the newly imported slaves had relatively higher fertility rates in the slave period." Dr. Innis asked the speakers whether there was any similar evidence in the United States and whether there was any relationship between fertility rates and harshness of conditions of slavery among the Dutch in New Jersey.

81

Dr. Wacker commented that on the basis of the incomplete census of 1772, the fertility rate for Blacks was somewhat higher than for whites, but that this was also the case for the black death rate. "I think," he concluded, "if anything this probably bespeaks the harsh conditions not only in the Dutch-settled areas but in the frontier counties of that particular day." Mr. Clarke suggested that perhaps other causes than birth rate existed to explain the increase or decline of black population, such as the slave trade.

Charles Kovacik, Department of Geography, University of South Carolina, and Dr. Wacker continued with a general discussion concerning the problem of determining specific occupations from census data. A commentator from the floor pointed out that special instructions were issued in 1850-60 requiring census enumerators to distinquish between various occupations and that the word "laborer" ordinarily indicated a farm laborer. Dr. Wacker responded that many census enumerators did not follow these instructions and, in the case of city directories, the enumerators were often misled by incorrect information. In New Jersey, however, many census enumerators indicated occupation, particularly for whites; Blacks, however, "were seldom listed by specific occupation." Dr. Wacker also observed that laborers were quite mobile. Both the Newark directories and the manuscript censuses seem to indicate "that there was a tremendous turnover in both the black and white laboring population."

Carmen Delle Donne, Industrial and Social Branch, National Archives, turned the discussion to slaves in New Jersey immediately preceding the Civil War. He wondered why slave schedules were filled out for New Jersey in 1850 and 1860. Dr. Wacker pointed out that the sixteen or eighteen slaves listed as residing in New Jersey in the 1860 manuscript census were often very old—eighty to ninety years of age—and were living with free black families because there were legal and social advantages to remaining a slave in a free black family as opposed to being a free Black. A slave owner, he observed, had a responsibility to care for a slave, whereas a free Black of advanced age would not have received such care.

Peirce Lewis, Department of Geography, Pennsylvania State University, changed the discussion to the distribution of the black population in New Jersey and its relationship to underground railroad routes. Dr. Wacker observed that in the free black population of Mannington Township, located in the southwestern portion of the state, a large number of Blacks appeared to have been runaway slaves, particularly by 1860. "The rate of increase there, as I remember, is generally higher than the natural rate could be, and the influx seems to be from out of state." In answer to an inquiry by Dr. Lewis concerning the possibility of mapping the routes of the runaways by reference to census material, Dr. Wacker thought it would be very difficult due to the problem of scale.

Andrew Clark, Department of Geography, University of Wisconsin, concluded the discussion with the comment that a very rich source of information on Blacks, including maroons from Jamaica and the fairly substantial number of Blacks who migrated there from the United States during the War of 1812, could be found in the Colonial Office papers and in a variety of collections in the public archives of Nova Scotia.

NOTES

1. Since Mr. Clarke made these comments, the identification of black soldiers among the military records of the Revolutionary War has been made considerably easier by the publication of Special List no. 36, *List of Black Servicemen Compiled from the War Department Collection of Revolutionary War Records,* by Debra L. Newman (Washington, 1974).
2. A list of these units now appears in Special List no. 33, *Tabular Analysis of the Records of the U. S. Colored Troops and Their Predecessor Units in the National Archives of the United States,* by Joseph B. Ross (Washington, 1973).

Exploration, Surveying, and Mapping

La Florida Revealed: The De Brahm Surveys of British East Florida, 1765-1771

LOUIS De VORSEY, JR.

There can be no doubt that there has been a change of paradigm taking place within historical geography, as there has within the whole of geography, during recent years. One would hasten to agree, however, with Alan Baker who observed, "Trends within the discipline as a whole have not all been equally discernible within historical geography in particular."[1] Historical geography is, fortunately, endowed with what Baker termed "a long relaxation time." Exactly how historical geographers in this country will respond to the impulse toward behavioral, theoretical, and quantitative analyses, which appear to be shaping research in the human dimension of our discipline as a whole, remains for time to tell. Andrew Clark certainly struck an encouraging and optimistic note when he concluded his recent review of current research by North American historical geographers suggesting that "despite the upheaval in methodology that the quantifiers have generated in the social, historical, and natural sciences, historical geography may have gained more, and lost less, than many other traditional geographical fields of interest. Indeed it appears to be that the new methodologies are often peculiarly suitable to the study of the changing geographies of the past."[2]

It will not be the purpose of this paper, included as it is in the session on "Exploration, Surveying, and Mapping," to essay the probable directions or impacts of the new methodologies in historical geographic research. Rather, the focus here will be upon source materials, an element which will doubtless remain basic to that research regardless of

87

paradigmetric or methodologic change. Come what may, historical geographers cannot escape their traditional and intimate dependence on historical source materials. Nor can historical geographers escape the essential need to be fully aware of the exact nature of such source materials, their original intent and purposes as well as their inherent shortcomings and limitations. For these reasons, as well as the intrinsic scholarly challenges and rewards, practitioners of historical geography can be assured that studies concerned with the context and milieu of bodies of historical source material will remain worthy endeavors as the traditional empirical approach to their branch of the discipline gradually gives way to the more theoretical research approaches, which seem destined to develop and occupy center stage. Certainly, there was no lack of such studies in the historical geography sessions presented at the International Geographical Congress held in Montreal in 1972.[3] Brian Harley, himself an eminent historical geographer, was moved to conclude his recent review of the historical geography symposia presented at the Birmingham meeting of the Institute of British Geographers by suggesting that the "new" historical geography will require an increasing rather than a lessening attention to sources. In his words, "in historical geography . . . as models and quantification come of age, can we doubt, if we ever did, that the next round will lie with the sources? More than ever before, as the older disciplinary lines become blurred, our sensitive handling of traditional historical evidence is likely to determine the distinctiveness as well as the quality of our contribution."[4]

The body of source material under discussion here is the large corpus of historic-geographical materials produced by William Gerard De Brahm, Britain's first surveyor general of colonial East Florida. British East Florida was created as a new colony, following Spain's cession of peninsular Florida to the British Crown in return for Cuba on February 10, 1763. On that momentous day, Britain confirmed its control over virtually the whole of North America east of the Mississippi River. Included in this expanded overseas empire were the former French territories in Canada and the Mississippi valley, as well as the extensive Spanish mainland territory known as La Florida. These vast new domains had been only vaguely charted and superficially exploited by their original French and Spanish overlords, and to the British authorities they were *terrae incognitae* in the fullest sense of the term. Almost any British map showing Florida in the 1760s and early 1770s will exhibit gross errors in even the simple delineation of Florida's general outline. An engraved map by Emanuel Bowen, geographer to George II, can be taken as typical in this regard. Bowen prepared this handsome map in 1763 to illustrate the new territorial division of North America.[5] On this quasi-official map, the southern one-third of the Florida peninsula appears as a fragmented archipelago of large and small islands, separated by elongated sounds and large embayments. A symbolic spur of mountains can be traced south from the Appalachians to form a spine to the peninsula. A fanciful Saint Johns River is shown breaking this spine and flowing both to the north in its normal course and to the south to empty into the sea via at least two nonexistent southern distributaries. Such was the character of most British cartography attempting to show La Florida following its accretion to the North American empire of King George II. As one recent scholar has observed, "Actually, Florida remained an unknown and mysterious land to most Englishmen until several descriptions of the new colony were sent to Great Britain during the middle and late sixties."[6]

Royal advisors and administrators in London and America immediately felt the pressing need for accurate maps and geographic information as they began to grapple with the enormous task of organizing and developing Britain's vast new territorial acquisitions. In a communication to the king, composed early in 1764, the British Board of Trade admitted, "We find ourselves under the greatest difficulties arising from the want of exact surveys of these countries in America, many parts of which have never been surveyed at all and others so imperfectly that the charts and maps thereof are not to be depended upon."[7] The king's chief advisory panel further observed that "in this situation we are reduced to the necessity of making Representation to Your Majesty, founded upon little or no information, or of delaying the important service of settling these parts of Your Majesty's Dominions."[8] Such a state of affairs was clearly intolerable. The board concluded its communication with a recommendation "in the strongest manner that no time should be lost in obtaining accurate surveys of all Your Majesty's North American Dominions—but more especially of such parts as from their natural advantages require our immediate attention." Predictably, these last mentioned "parts" were designated as Atlantic Canada and East Florida, as the British now named the former Spanish possession of La Florida.

To help implement these much needed "accurate surveys," two new administrative units were created in America. The Potomac River was designated to separate the northern and southern survey districts. A surveyor general was appointed for each district and charged with the responsibility for conducting detailed geographical surveys. Named as the surveyor general for the Northern District was Captain Samuel Holland, the accomplished military engineer and cartographer then active in the Saint Lawrence valley.[9] To fill the southern surveyorship, the Board of Trade chose another accomplished engineer-cartographer with a military background and considerable local experience. He was William Gerard De Brahm, then serving as one of the two provincial surveyors general for the colony of Georgia.[10] In July 1764, De Brahm's commission as a joint surveyor general of Georgia was terminated and he was appointed surveyor general of the recently formed royal colony of East Florida and surveyor general of the newly created Southern District of North America.

Although a number of authorities have identified De Brahm as a native of Holland, the records clearly show that he was born in Koblenz, West Germany, on August 20, 1718.[11] His father, a member of the lesser nobility of the day, was a court musician in the service of the elector of Trier. Just where and how the young De Brahm, last of eight children, was educated is still to be determined. That he received an excellent training in languages (both classical and modern), mathematics, history, literature, biblical studies, and the burgeoning experimental sciences of the day, is amply proved by his later performance in British colonial America.

Florida historian Charles L. Mowat recognized De Brahm's multiple attainments and described him as "a man whose versatility of genius went beyond even that of the typical eighteenth-century dilettante, a surveyor, engineer, botanist, astronomer, meteorologist, student of ocean currents, alchemist, sociologist, historian, and mystical philosopher."[12] De Brahm wrote little concerning his childhood but did describe his father as "an admirer of natural philosophy," who was a devotee of alchemy, a pursuit far more common and respectable in the eighteenth century than at present.[13] It is not altogether surprising to find that the younger De Brahm maintained an active interest in alchemical research throughout his own long life.[14] Nor is it surprising, in view of the unsettled conditions that characterized central Europe during the first half of the eighteenth century, to discover that De Brahm found an outlet for his talents and energy in an army career. In the service of Emperor Charles VII, he saw action in eleven campaigns waged in Germany, Turkey, and France, under the commands of Prince Eugene and Counts Wallis and Seckendorf.[15]

In 1748, the thirty-year-old De Brahm resigned his commission as a "captain-engineer" in the imperial army and renounced the Roman Catholic faith. In his own words, he and his wife found themselves "persecuted and banished" from the Bavarian Palatinate as a result.[16] Like many other religious dissidents in war-torn southern Germany De Brahm was befriended by Samuel Urlsperger, senior pastor of the

Evangelical Ministry of Augsburg. Urlsperger was one of two foreign members of the predominately English "Board of Trustees for Establishing the Colony of Georgia in America." This group was actively promoting the youthful colony by encouraging and assisting groups of displaced German Protestants to relocate in Georgia. Through Urlsperger's good offices, De Brahm found himself in charge of a group of 156 German Protestants on their way to settle at Ebenezer, upstream on the Savannah River from Georgia's seat of government. The talented, young former imperial army officer had obviously made a very favorable impression on the influential Urlsperger, who paid his passage and freight to far off Ebenezer. Before departing Europe, De Brahm took care to have his last military commander, Count Seckendorf, prepare a testimonial attesting to his proficiency in the technical skills of military engineering and fortification design as well as his personal qualities of leadership and good moral character.[17]

These were the very qualities that were almost immediately perceived by the leaders of Georgia, Britain's southern frontier outpost, when De Brahm and his company of German immigrants arrived in 1751. James Habersham, who later acted as royal governor in the colony, wrote of De Brahm during December 1751 as follows: "The trustees, I believe, are not mistaken in Mr. von Brahm's abilities. He has been at a great deal of pains to view the country to fix on a settlement and has taken plans of all places he has visited, and I look upon him to be one of the most intelligent men I have ever met with, and will, I doubt not, make a very useful colonist."[18]

De Brahm's skill as a surveyor and cartographer, first alluded to by Habersham above, was quickly recognized and appreciated by his contemporaries in the colonial South. In the present period, a growing number of scholars working in historical cartography and geography have come to share this recognition and appreciation of his talents. William P. Cumming, author of the definitive study of the mapping of the colonial South, described De Brahm's first printed map of Georgia and South Carolina as "far superior to any cartographical work for the Southern District that had gone before."[19] Cumming further observes that "with De Brahm, we turn from the amateur to the professional, from the general outlines of the region to topographical accuracy."[20]

De Brahm was not content merely to survey the metes and bounds of a plot of land and draw a rough sketch or plat, which was the common practice of his day. Rather, he betrayed the essential qualities of a geographer in his approach to exploration and survey. This because he was inevitably concerned with the larger regional landscape complex of which his sketches and plats were parts. De Brahm's keen mind was

91

ever searching for broad patterns and interrelationships in nature. He observed and commented on regional variations in such patterns as those created by the landforms, soils, flora, fauna, climate, and human activities he encountered in his adopted American South. As early as March 24, 1752, he presented Georgia's government with "a map of that part of Georgia, which I have had an opportunity of Surveying since my arrival here: which I flatter myself will speak in my behalf and be more satisfactory and agreeable than anything I could say in a long and tedious letter."[21] Like the true geographer he was, De Brahm appreciated the eloquence of a well-constructed map.

It was not long before De Brahm's attainments and reputation attracted attention in neighboring South Carolina. James Glen, that colony's energetic governor, was deeply concerned with efforts aimed at improving Charleston's badly dilapidated fortifications. Glen invited De Brahm (who at this point substituted the Germanic prefix "von" in his surname with the adopted "De," which he retained until his death) to design a comprehensive defensive network of fortifications for his capital. In 1752, Britain's seaboard colonists were becoming increasingly fearful of French attack as tension with that power increased. The death of South Carolina's surveyor general during the summer of 1755, created a vacancy that Glen filled by issuing De Brahm an interim appointment to the post. These services, plus his important role in the construction of a fort in the heart of the Overhill Cherokee Indian coreland, in what is today the state of Tennessee, gave De Brahm excellent opportunities to travel over and survey much of South Carolina.[22] His incumbency in the post of surveyor general of the colony also insured him excellent access to the colony's cartographic and documentary archives.

In 1754, De Brahm and Henry Yonge were appointed as the first joint surveyors general of lands for the newly organized royal government of Georgia. Georgia's governor, like his counterpart in South Carolina, recognized De Brahm's standing as a military engineer and strategist and called upon him to draw up a comprehensive scheme of fortifications and outposts to provide a defense for the colony. The record clearly shows that William Gerard De Brahm quickly attained a position of considerable influence and leadership in both the youthful colony of Georgia and well-established South Carolina. He served as a military engineer, justice of the peace, cartographer, tax collector, and commissioner for the repair and construction of fortifications, in addition to his already mentioned roles as a provincial surveyor general. The concerned scholar of the present day may rest assured in the knowledge that De Brahm was a gentleman of considerable property, influence, and standing in both South Carolina and Georgia prior to his removal to East Florida, Britain's newest southern colony, in 1764.

His royal appointment to the newly created posts of surveyor general for the Southern District of North America and surveyor general of East Florida represented the highest form of contemporary recognition and approbation for De Brahm. He was to have cognizance over the surveying and mapping of "all His Majesty's territories on the Continent of North America which lye to the south of the Potomac River, and of a line drawn due west from the Head of the main branch of that River as far as His Majesty's Dominions extend."[23] Within this huge area, however, the Board of Trade placed first priority on "that part of East Florida which lyes to the South of St. Augustine, as far as the Cape of Florida." The surveyor general was to concentrate his immediate efforts to "the lands lying near the sea Coast of the great promontory [which] appear to their Lordships to be of the most pressing expediency, in order to accelerate the different Establishments which have been proposed to be made in that part of the country."[24] Figure 1 shows the extent to which De Brahm carried out this charge during the period from 1765 to 1771. He was ably assisted by a number of capable assistants and deputies, including Bernard Romans, Joseph Purcell, and Ferdinand De Brahm. These three went on to establish individual reputations as surveyors and mapmakers of note.[25] De Brahm and his assistants conducted numerous surveying expeditions by land, sea, and the Saint Johns River. From his Saint Augustine base, expeditions went forth as far south as the Florida Keys and along the Gulf Coast to Tampa Bay. Although his penetrations of the interior were frequently limited by threats of Indian attack, he managed to survey high up the Saint Marys River almost to its source in "Ackanphanoke" [Okefenokee] Swamp. Much of eastern Florida lying between the Saint Johns River and the Atlantic Ocean was explored and mapped as well.

Hurricanes, shipwrecks, attacks of fever, Indian problems, and official opposition all combined to make De Brahm's immense labors more arduous. In spite of these considerable drawbacks, his surveys were of the most meticulous and scientific character.[26] Frequent astronomic observations were taken on land to fix positions more accurately and determine the degree and direction of compass error in the areas surveyed. Astronomic fixes were also employed to obtain linear distances that were then compared with similar distances determined with a surveyor's chain over long and exhausting land traverses. In inaccessible locations, such as the Florida Keys, local baselines were established with the chain, and trigonometric techniques were utilized to complete the survey. A large number of detailed maps and charts

93

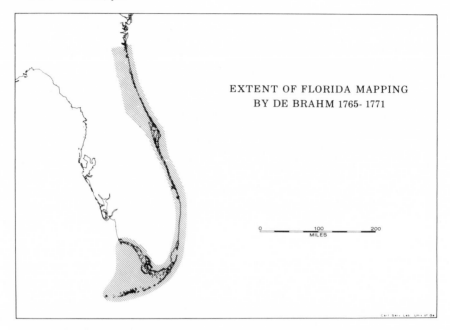

EXTENT OF FLORIDA MAPPING
BY DE BRAHM 1765- 1771

0   100   200
       MILES

FIG. 1. *Sketch map showing extent of De Brahm's mapping efforts in British East Florida, 1765-1771.*

were prepared by De Brahm and his deputies during the decade, which terminated with the outbreak of the American Revolution (figures 2 and 3).

In their instructions relating to the survey of Florida, the Lords of Trade provided De Brahm, by their own admission, with only "a rude sketch or outline."[27] He was told that precision and exactness were "required and expected," and that the latitudes and longitudes of the important places were to be determined by what they termed "just astronomical observations." Coasts and channels were to be sounded and water depths recorded along with any other information which could add to the safety of navigation.[28] De Brahm was further ordered to forward "observations and remarks" which would "tend to convey a clear and precise knowledge of the actual state of the country contained in the survey, its limits, extent, quantity of acres, principal rivers and harbours, the nature of its soil and produce, and in what points [it was] capable of improvement." Finally, the surveyor general was told to add "every information" which he thought might help the Lords of Trade in forming "a true judgement of the state of this im-

94

FIG. 2. *De Brahm's map of the Florida Keys area. (Reprinted, by permission, Trustees of the British Museum. Original map, Kings Mss. 211.)*

portant part of His Majesty's dominions." Clearly, De Brahm's task, as outlined in these instructions, was much more than a simple exercise in coastal charting. He was charged with the conduct of a comprehensive geographical reconnaissance in a distant and little known region for which only the crudest maps, if any, were available. All of this was to be accomplished on a total annual budget of £700.17.01. What was omitted from these instructions is, perhaps, more significant than what was included. One looks in vain, for example, for any mention of map scale. Moreover there is no detailed checklist of items to be mapped and reported upon. By present-day standards De Brahm was given an

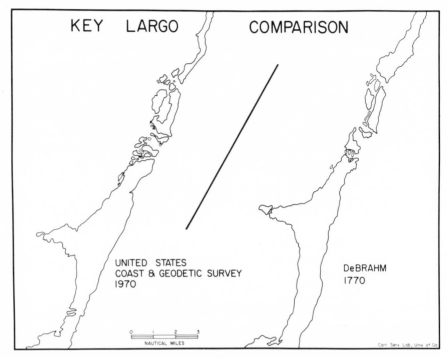

Fig. 3. *Comparison of De Brahm's outline of Key Largo with United States Coast and Geodetic Survey chart dated 1970.*

amazingly free hand in deciding how he should proceed in conducting the survey of Britain's new colony of East Florida.

How De Brahm proceeded to respond to this impressive charge is clearly stated in a communication he directed to the Lords of Trade in 1772.[29] In this he indicated that he was fully aware of both the privileges and perils involved in the execution of such a broad and loosely specified commission. He also mentioned that he was in some measure patterning his investigations along the lines of such well-recognized world travelers as Pierre Francois Xavier de Charlevoix, Antonio de Ulloa, and Louis Antoine de Bougainville. In his own words, De Brahm advised the Board of Trade that he had "intentionally set no bounds to my Historical Report, . . . which to improve I studied by copying after the best I knew who went before me upon similar Expedition[s]." He likened his final comprehensive report and maps to a "Table with a Variety of all things in several Courses, that each at the Table may meet with that he likes best." This analogy is an apt one since it is doubtful that anyone can come away from a reading of De Brahm's "Report of the General Survey in the Southern District of North America" without feeling at least temporary intellectual satiation. De Brahm provided a partial "menu" of what his final report included in the following extract, which he offered immediately after the report's title:

> Delivered to the Board of Trade and Plantations in three separate Returns, and Sections entering with the History of South Carolina and Georgia; then proceeding to the History of East Florida, and Surveys, containing in general of Said Provinces, the Climates, Beginnings, Boundaries, Figures, Contents, Cultures, Soils, Natural Products, Improvements, Navigable Streams, Rivers, Cities, Towns, Villages, Vapours, their Effect and Remedies, burning of Forrests, Winds, how to preserve Health, Pathology, Materia Medica, Diet, and Regimen, Ports, Bars, Numbers of Inhabitants, and Negroes, Exportation, Riches, Number of Trading Vessels, Cattle, Governments, Forces, Fortifications, of Fort Loudoun in particular; Indians and Apalachian Mountains, their Soil, Natural Produce, Air and Communications compiled from the Surveys, Voyages, Astronomical, Philosophical, and Chemical Observations and Experiments, Sea and Land Surveys of William Gerard de Brahm, His Majesty's Surveyor-General for the Southern District of North America.[30]

In the course of his six years of exploration and survey in East Florida, De Brahm prepared numerous maps and charts. These, along with his many lengthy letters and official "Report" to King George II, form an invaluable corpus of historical geographic source material describing Florida at a time when the relict features of Indian and Spanish occupation were still fresh in the landscape. To date, this corpus of source material had remained almost unused by scholars. It invites the attention of historical geographers and workers in other related disciplines.

It was, indeed, unfortunate that De Brahm was forced to prematurely terminate his surveys in order to personally appear in London to answer to charges of malfeasance that had been brought against him by Florida's hot-tempered governor, James Grant.[31] After a three-year delay the charges were dismissed, and De Brahm was exonerated and reinstated in his office with the vigorous support of the influential Lord Dartmouth. Even more unfortunate, however, was the fact that De Brahm's resumption of the Florida survey was permanently blocked upon his return to America by the outbreak of the Revolution in 1775. His survey ship, the *Cherokee,* was commandeered for military duties shortly after his arrival at Charleston, and his plans to continue with the mapping of Florida's Gulf Coast frustrated. It should be noted that De Brahm completed his last major scientific work during the period from 1775 to 1777, which saw him treated as a prisoner-at-large in South Carolina's center of revolutionary ferment. This is his 157-page manuscript titled "Continuation of the Atlantic Pilot," which is now found in a collection of the Houghton Library, Harvard University. In De Brahm's words, this lengthy manuscript describes "The Causes, Directions and Effects of Currents in the Atlantic Ocean. The Change of Magnetic Azimuth. The line of no variation, and weight of Atmosphere its excess and effect from Astronomical, and physical observations, made on a traject from Europe to America." As such it represents an almost unknown milestone in systematic eighteenth-century oceanographic research.[32]

The results of De Brahm's more than six years of surveying in Florida reached an influential contemporary audience as Britain pushed forward with schemes designed to populate and develop Florida. His work met with the personal approbation of George III, as well as his principal advisors and leaders of the eighteenth-century scientific community. Important aspects of De Brahm's Florida surveys reached broad audiences through his book titled *The Atlantic Pilot*.[33] This intriguing book of Florida sailing directions first appeared in English in 1772 and again, in French, in 1788. It is included in the revived Floridiana Facsimile Series, now being published by the University of Florida Press in conjunction with that state's observation of the National Bicentennial.[34] Although Bernard Romans scathingly criticized *The Atlantic Pilot* in his own *The Natural History of East and West Florida*, he did not hesitate to combine De Brahm's findings with his own in the 1797 volume, *A New and Enlarged Book of Sailing Directions*.[35] This was a considerable tribute since Romans, De Brahm's sometimes deputy, was one of the surveyor general's severest contemporary critics. During the Revolutionary War, many followed the events in the South with the aid of "A General Map of the Southern British Colonies in America," included in the widely circulated *American Military Pocket Atlas*.[36] This atlas, originally prepared for British army and naval officers, has recently been called the most popular atlas of the Revolution.[37] De Brahm's cartographic contributions are clearly recognized in the long title of this valuable atlas. Similarly, his hydrographic surveys along the southern American coasts were employed by Joseph Frederick Wallet Des Barres, famed author of the revolutionary era's cartographic opus magnum, *The Atlantic Neptune*.[38]

In the early decades of the nineteenth century, many authorities commented favorably on De Brahm's surveys of Florida. Among these were the famous surveyor, Andrew Ellicott, and the author of *Sketches, Historical and Topographical of the Floridas*, James Grant Forbes.[39] There is also evidence indicating that an original manuscript copy of De Brahm's official report and its included maps provided valuable information to government figures concerned with the development of Florida during the middle decades of the nineteenth century.[40] Floridian Buckingham Smith did much to make De Brahm's surveys available when early plans to drain the Everglades were under discussion. All things considered, it would appear that De Brahm's materials provided a degree of valuable background information as federal policy was formulated on questions concerning Florida's development during the decades following its purchase from Spain.

During the present century, De Brahm and his work slipped into a position of relative obscurity. H. Roy Merrens was largely correct in ascribing this condition to the relative inaccessibility of De Brahm's maps and manuscripts.[41] Added to inaccessibility of the materials themselves as a deterrent in their employment should be De Brahm's personal eccentricity.[42] His early flamboyance and pugnacity, coupled with his penchant for mystical writing in old age, has tended to discourage researchers from employing his materials in their historical studies.[43]

The recent publication of the full text and twenty-nine maps and sketches comprising De Brahm's lengthy official "Report" to King George III, covering the three southern colonies (South Carolina, Georgia, and East Florida), should do much to make his work known and accessible to a broad scholarly audience. So, too, should the lengthy biographical sketch and exhaustive notes and annotations accompanying the published report do much to remove the apprehensions of researchers who might otherwise be tempted to dismiss De Brahm as an eccentric mystic, a description which, it should be noted, would be entirely appropriate during most of the last two decades of his long life but far from that during his active tenure as the surveyor general for the Southern District of Britain's North American empire. During that tenure, La Florida was revealed as a viable, though challenging, arena for British colonizing schemes. Had the tides of eighteenth-century, great-power politics not swept Florida back to the control of Spain in 1783, there can be no doubt that De Brahm's reports, surveys, and maps would have played an immensely important part in charting the course of Florida's development. As they now exist in printed form and in American and English archives, they represent an invaluable and available trove of historical-geographical source material bearing on three of Britain's most southerly American colonies on the eve of the American Revolution. It remains now for historical geographers and others to exploit this trove, in both traditionally documented as well as quantified analyses and studies concerning the region's changing geography.

NOTES

1. Alan R. H. Baker, ed., *Progress in Historical Geography* (New York: John Wiley & Sons, 1972), p. 11.
2. Andrew H. Clark, "Historical Geography in North America," *Progress in Historical Geography,* ed. Alan R. H. Baker (New York: John Wiley & Sons, 1972), p. 143.
3. W. Peter Adams and Frederick M. Helleiner, eds., *International Geography 1972,* 2 vols. (Toronto and Buffalo: Toronto University Press, 1972), 1: 395-472.
4. John B. Harley, "Change in Historical Geography: A Qualitative Impression of Quantitative Methods," *Area* 5 (1973): 73.
5. Emanuel Bowen, *An Accurate Map of North America Describing and Distinguishing the British, Spanish, and French Dominions on This Great Continent. According to the Definitive Treaty Concluded at Paris 10 February 1763. . . .* (London: Robt. Sayer, 1763).
6. Robert L. Gold, *Borderland Empires in Transition: The Triple-Nation Transfer of Florida* (Carbondale and Edwardsville: Southern Illinois University Press, 1969), p. 17.
7. Great Britain, Public Record Office, Exchequer and Audit Department Records, AO 3-140.
8. Ibid.
9. Willis Chipman, "The Life and Times of Major Samuel Holland, Surveyor-General, 1764-1801," *Ontario Historical Society Papers and Records* 21 (1924): 11-90; John B. Harley, "Specifications for Military Surveys in British North America, 1750-75," *International Geography 1972,* ed. W. Peter Adams and Frederick M. Helleiner (Toronto and Buffalo: Toronto University Press, 1972), 1:424-25.
10. Louis De Vorsey, Jr., "William Gerard De Brahm: Eccentric Genius of Southeastern Geography," *Southeastern Geographer* 10 (April 1970): 21-29; idem, *De Brahm's Report of the General Survey in the Southern District of North America* (Columbia: University of South Carolina Press, 1971).
11. Baptismal Register of Saint Kastor's Church, Koblenz. Bistumsarchiv, Trier, West Germany (photographic copy in author's possession).
12. Charles L. Mowat, "That Odd Being De Brahm," *Florida Historical Quarterly* 20 (April 1942): 323.
13. Great Britain, Staffordshire County Record Office, Stafford, Dartmouth Manuscripts D1778 II 617.
14. Plowden C. J. Weston, nineteenth-century publisher of De Brahm's description of colonial South Carolina, observed: "I know nothing of De Brahm's life; but he lived within the memory of persons now alive, much addicted to alchemy, and wearing a long beard" (Plowden C. J. Weston, ed., *Documents Connected with the History of South Carolina* [London: Privately printed, 1856]).
15. Great Britain, Public Record Office, Exchequer and Audit Department Records, Claims, American Loyalists Series 2, AO 13-137, p. 126.
16. Ibid.
17. Great Britain, Public Record Office, Colonial Office Records, CO 5-374, p. 63. (Hereafter Colonial Office Records are indicated by the symbol CO.)

18. Allen D. Candler, ed., *The Colonial Records of the State of Georgia* 26 (Atlanta: Franklin Printing and Publishing Co., 1904-11): 319.
19. William P. Cumming, *The Southeast in Early Maps* (Chapel Hill: University of North Carolina Press, 1962), p. 54.
20. Ibid.
21. Candler, *Colonial Records*, pp. 347-48.
22. This was the ill-fated Fort Loudoun, located in Monroe County, Tennessee. For details on De Brahm's role in its construction, see De Vorsey, *De Brahm's Report*, pp. 18-24.
23. CO 324-17, unpaginated.
24. Ibid.
25. For a recent discussion of Bernard Romans, see Rembert W. Patrick's introduction to the facsimile reproduction of Romans's *A Concise Natural History of East and West Florida* (Gainesville, Fla.: University of Florida Press, 1962). A brief discussion of Joseph Purcell's career is included in Louis De Vorsey, Jr., "The Colonial Southeast on 'An Accurate General Map,'" *Southeastern Geographer* 6 (1966): 20-32. Ferdinand Joseph Sebastian De Brahm, son of De Brahm's eldest brother, had emigrated to Florida to serve as an assistant to his uncle. At least two of his maps are included in the papers of Sir Henry Clinton. These are listed in Christian Brun, *Guide to the Manuscript Maps in the William L. Clements Library* (Ann Arbor: University of Michigan Library, 1959), p. 92. For a brief biographical note on Ferdinand De Brahm, see Peter J. Guthorn, *American Maps and Map Makers of the Revolution* (Monmouth Beach, N.J.: Philip Freneau Press, 1966), p. 9.
26. For a discussion of the equipment employed in De Brahm's coastal surveys, see Louis De Vorsey, Jr., "Hydrography: A Note on the Equipage of Eighteenth-Century Survey Vessels," *Mariner's Mirror* 58 (May 1972): 173-77.
27. CO 324-17, unpaginated.
28. For a fuller discussion of De Brahm's hydrographic surveys, see Louis De Vorsey, Jr., "Eighteenth Century Hydrographic Surveys: A Source for the Reconstruction of Early Estuarine Environments," *Papers Given at Estuarine Geography Session, Annual Meeting, Association of American Geographers, April 18-21, 1971* (Washington: Office of Naval Research, 1971).
29. Great Britain, British Museum, Kings Manuscripts, Kings Mss. 210, p. 69-70.
30. Ibid., p. 3.
31. For accounts of the Grant-De Brahm feud, see Mowat, "That Odd Being De Brahm," pp. 331-35, and De Vorsey, *De Brahm's Report,* pp. 40-43.
32. Ralph H. Brown, it should be noted, drew attention to De Brahm's ocean-current research in his "The De Brahm Charts of the Atlantic Ocean, 1772-1776," *Geographical Review* 28 (January 1938): 124-32. It is unfortunate that most subsequent researchers interested in the Gulf Stream and Atlantic current systems have overlooked Brown's article as well as the pioneering nature of De Brahm's oceanographic research.
33. William Gerard De Brahm, *The Atlantic Pilot* (London: Printed for the author by T. Spilsbury, 1772).

34. Edited and with an introduction by Louis De Vorsey, Jr.
35. Bernard Romans, *A Concise Natural History of East and West Florida, a Facsimile Reproduction of the 1775 Edition with an Introduction by Rembert W. Patrick* (Gainesville: University of Florida Press, 1962); idem, *A New and Enlarged Book of Sailing Directions . . . Gulf and Windward Pilot . . . also the Additions of Captains W. G. De Brahm, Bishop, Hester, Archibald Dalzel, Esq., George Gauld, Esq., Lieut. Woodriffe and Other Experienced Navigators* (London: R. Laurie and J. Whittle, 1797).
36. *The American Military Pocket Atlas: Being an Approved Collection of Correct Maps, Both General and Particular, of the British Colonies. Especially Those Which Now Are, or Probably May Be the Theatre of War; Taken Principally from the Actual Surveys and Surveys and Judicious Observations of Engineers De Brahm and Romans; Cook, Jackson and Collet; Maj. Holland and Other Officers, Employed in His Majesty's Fleets and Armies* (London: Sayer and Bennett, 1776).
37. Peter J. Guthorn, *British Maps of the American Revolution* (Monmouth Beach, N.J.: Philip Freneau Press, 1972), p. 61.
38. For a review of Des Barres's colorful life, see G. N. D. Evans, *Uncommon Obdurate: The Several Public Careers of J. F. W. De Barres* (Salem, Mass.: Peabody Museum, 1969).
39. See *The Journal of Andrew Ellicott* (1803; facsimile reprint, Chicago: Quadrangle Books, 1962), p. 258; James Grant Forbes, *Sketches, Historical and Topographical, of the Floridas; More Particularly of East Florida* (New York: C. S. Van Winkle, 1821), p. 97.
40. See "Report of Buckingham Smith, Esq., June 1, 1848," U.S., Congress, Senate, *Senate Documents*, 30th Cong., 1st sess., Rep. Comm. no. 242, August 12, 1848, quoted in P. L. Phillips, *Notes on the Life and Works of Bernard Romans* (De Land, Fla.: Florida State Historical Society, 1924), pp. 15-17.
41. H. Roy Merrens, "The Physical Environment of Early America: Images and Image Makers in Colonial South Carolina," *Geographical Review* 59 (October 1969): 530-56.
42. Louis De Vorsey, Jr., "William Gerard De Brahm: Eccentric Genius of Southeastern Geography," *Southeastern Geographer* 10 (April 1970): 21-29.
43. Lawrence C. Wroth discussed his own serious doubts concerning the credibility of De Brahm as a source. Wroth knew of De Brahm first as the eccentric author of what he termed a "mathematico-mystical treatise," *The Apocalyptic Gnomon Points Out Eternity's Divisibility Related with Time Pointed at by Gnomon Siderealis* (Philadelphia: Francis Robert Baily, 1795). Only after a considerable amount of research did Wroth begin to discern De Brahm's true stature as a scientific surveyor. See Wroth, "The Bibliographical Way," *Colophon*, n.s. 3 (Spring 1938): 225-27. See De Vorsey, *De Brahm's Report*, p. 301, for a list of De Brahm's published works both scientific and mystical.

Thomas Jefferson and the Passage to India: A Pre-Exploratory Image

JOHN L. ALLEN

In the opening years of the nineteenth century, the idea of the Missouri River as the key to the riddle of the Northwest Passage dominated the geographical thoughts of those who desired the establishment of a water communication across North America. Foremost among these men who dreamed of a passage to India was Thomas Jefferson, owner of America's greatest collection of literature on the passage and the area through which it must run and the conceiver/sponsor of the Lewis and Clark Expedition.[1]

Jefferson's fascination with the water passage developed early in life. As a child of ten, he may have learned of the ambitions of some of his father's friends to send a party "in search of that river Missouri, if that be the right name of it, in order to discover whether it had any communication with the Pacific Ocean."[2] Exposure to such a concept may even have been Jefferson's lot in the classroom of James Maury's school for boys. Here, under Maury's tutelage, Jefferson quite probably acquired the principles of continental symmetry that were fundamental in his mentor's geographical thought. The eastern tributaries of the Mississippi had their sources near the navigable parts of the rivers that flowed to the Atlantic, Maury had written. It was only logical that the great river's western branches (particularly the Missouri) would "reach as far the other way, and make as near approaches to river emptying themselves into the . . . Pacific Ocean."[3] By sailing up a major western tributary of the Mississippi, "a short and easy communication" would be opened to the "Eastern Indies."

Map of North America from the Mississippi River to the Pacific by Nicholas King, 1803. (Lewis and Clark Map Collection, Geography and Map Division, Library of Congress.)

This conception, modified by increasing geographical knowledge of the western interior, conditioned Jefferson's image of the passage until after Lewis and Clark. In the years before he became president, the strength of the conception was reflected in Jefferson's repeated attempts to have the Missouri and its connections with Pacific-slope waters explored.[4] In 1793, at the time of the last of these attempts prior to the Lewis and Clark Expedition, Jefferson described the probable location of a route to the Pacific in a letter to the prospective transcontinental traveler, André Michaux: "As a channel of communication between these states and the Pacific ocean, the Missouri, so far as it extends, presents itself under circumstances of unquestioned preference. . . . It would seem by the latest maps as if a river called Oregan interlocked with the Missouri for a considerable distance, & entered the Pacific ocean, not far Southward of Nootka sound."[5]

This view of the passage was based on the geographical lore that Jefferson had collected over a period of twenty years prior to 1793, works which were, he wrote later, "a particularly useful species of reading."[6] But this data was not the only geographical information in Jefferson's possession at the time of the Lewis and Clark Expedition. In spite of the failure of the proposed Michaux journey, Jefferson had continued to gather lore on the geography and exploration of the trans-Mississippi West. His efforts intensified when he became president and recognized that his private interest in the discovery of a water route might receive official support.

During the first two years of his administration, Jefferson corresponded with scientists, frontier soldiers and settlers, government officials, and others, receiving from them current data on the West and speculation about a potential water route.[7] He also continued his purchases of published materials and obtained, before the end of 1802, Alexander Mackenzie's journals of his transcontinental travels and Aaron Arrowsmith's 1802 edition of the map of North America.[8] When Mackenzie's descriptions of the geography of the western regions and his statements about the proximity of the headwaters of the Missouri and Columbia were combined with Arrowsmith's cartographic representation, Jefferson developed an image of the probable water route that was more sophisticated than his earlier views.

This greater sophistication was evident in January 1803 when Jefferson presented, in a confidential message to Congress, his plans for a western expedition to discover the passage.[9] Mackenzie, he said, had crossed the continent in "a high latitude, through an infinite number of portages and lakes, shut up by ice through a long season." Such a route could not compete with the one the president now proposed—a route up the Missouri system, traversing "a moderate climate, offering according to the best accounts a continued navigation from its source, and possibly with a single portage from the Western Ocean."[10] The United States, Jefferson concluded, should make a concerted attempt to explore this route. Congress agreed and by the end of February had appropriated funds for what was to become the Lewis and Clark Expedition.[11]

With an expedition to the Pacific becoming an official reality, Jefferson began to organize his thoughts on the passage, and he and his secretary of the treasury, Albert Gallatin, commenced discussion on the reliability of contemporary maps, on the geography of the West, and on the objectives and suggested course of the forthcoming expedition.[12] Two major documents were shaped by these discussions: a list of instructions drafted by Jefferson and presented to Meriwether Lewis (Jefferson's private secretary and personal choice to lead the expedition) and a map of the trans-Mississippi West drawn by Nicholas King and, possibly, given to Lewis before his departure from Washington in July 1803.[13] In these two documents appear the elements which comprised Jefferson's image of the passage on the eve of the expedition.

"The object of your mission," the president instructed Lewis, "is to explore the Missouri river, & such principal stream of it, as by its course and communication with the waters of the Pacific ocean . . . may offer the most direct & practicable water communication across this continent for the purposes of commerce."[14] This had been the core of Jefferson's image for years. But in 1803 he knew, or thought he knew, a great deal more about the Missouri River, its connections with the Columbia, and the whole western interior than he had known earlier.

Jefferson had long recognized that the Missouri was the major river of the western interior, even larger, he had written, than the mighty Mississippi.[15] According to the most reliable of Jefferson's literary sources, the Missouri ran a course of well over two thousand miles from its source to its mouth.[16] The maps that were considered most trustworthy corroborated this information, placing the Missouri's source at approximately the 115th meridian. Not only was it lengthy, it was navigable, the president believed, "from its mouth to its source . . . for the largest pirogues,"[17] and Jefferson stated this opinion in his confidential message to Congress. But on this point Jefferson's increasingly refined geographical knowledge becomes evident. The majority of the rivers of the trans-Mississippi region could be utilized as transportation routes, the president wrote, and if the Missouri were a large, navigable stream, then it most probably had many tributary rivers which also could be used as commercial routes.[18]

One of Jefferson's latest items of information from the West reported that "many large navigable rivers discharged their waters" into the Missouri above the Mandan villages, the farthest penetration of the British and Louisiana fur trade toward the west.[19] It might have been this data which led Jefferson to include the phrase "the Missouri river, & such principal stream of it" in his orders to Lewis. It is a well-established historical fact that Jefferson had long considered the Missouri as the logical route to the Pacific. What is not so well known is that, by the middle of 1803, he was no longer thinking exclusively about the Missouri proper as the only direction a passage could take. One of the Missouri's tributaries might serve just as well.

To elaborate on this view and to lead to a deeper understanding of Jefferson's image, it is necessary to analyze the map mentioned in correspondence between Jefferson, Gallatin, and Lewis as the chart "to be completed" by Nicholas King.[20] This map (now among the Lewis and Clark manuscripts in the Geography and Maps Division of the Library of Congress) is basically a copy of the 1802 Arrowsmith map. But there are a number of differences between it and the Arrowsmith map which are significant.

On both maps the Missouri was formed by the junction of two major streams, which joined their waters just west of the Mandan villages. The northernmost of these flowed from around the 115th meridian and the 50th parallel, while the southern branch headed near the 113th meridian and the 46th parallel. On the Arrowsmith map, the northern branch was unnamed and the southern branch was called the "Missury." But on the King map, the *northern* river was labeled as the Missouri while the southern stream was named "Lesser Missouri." Was it this river that Jefferson was thinking of as that "principal stream" of the Missouri that might lead to the passage?

The Missouri proper, in Jefferson's view, was probably that river heading near the 50th parallel. Such information was presented on a map drawn by John Mitchell which was, Jefferson had written, "made with great care . . . and much nearer the truth" than many other maps of the time.[21] On both the King and Arrowsmith maps, this northern branch was shown heading near a source stream of the Columbia and, therefore, might have offered a chance for the passage. But in their correspondence, Jefferson and Gallatin had discussed the possible danger to the expedition should it come too near the establishments of the British above the 50th parallel. And in his instructions to Lewis,

Jefferson had specifically warned the future explorer away from "the Northern waters of the Missouri."[22] The president might well have been considering a route up the southern fork as the best American passage to the Pacific.

Such a route was provided for in Jefferson's possible image of the nature of the Missouri's source region, as illustrated by the King map. And here is the greatest difference between this map and every other contemporary chart. On other maps, a narrow range of mountains (the Stoney or Rocky mountains) was depicted as running in a continuous, unbroken chain from Canada to Mexico. But the King map showed this narrow range only as extending from the north to the 46th parallel. Beyond this southern terminus ran a long, unnamed river, flowing west from a source near the 107th meridian and joining the Columbia before it fell into the Pacific. The short version of the Rocky Mountains and the great southern branch of the Columbia appeared on no other map of the period. How is such an unusual cartographic representation to be explained?

Although it is true that virtually all period maps showed a continuous chain of mountains running the length of the continent, the abbreviated range of the King map did not necessarily controvert the geographical lore of the early nineteenth century.[23] The prominent American geographer, Jedediah Morse, had spoken of the range seen by the British in Canada as "terminating about the 47th deg. of latitude where a number of rivers arise and empty themselves into either the N. Pacific Ocean, into Hudson's bay, the waters which lie between them, or into the Atlantic Ocean."[24] Furthermore, Mackenzie himself had noted that he did not know how far south of his crossing the mountains extended, but that they became lower in altitude near the headwaters of the Missouri.[25] Peter Fidler, a fur trader from whom most of Arrowsmith's information was derived, reported that he had seen the "beginnings" of the range around the 46th parallel.[26] And although Arrowsmith drew a continuous chain to represent the Stoney Mountains, a legend on one of his maps described the area about the 46th parallel: "Hereabouts the mountains divide into several low ridges."

Unlike most people of his time, Jefferson had access to all this information. It may have been that he viewed the region near the 46th parallel as a broad upland or plateau area which did, as Morse (and Jonathan Carver before him) had stated, serve as a source area for the major western rivers. If so, then it would have been logical for him to assume that not only the southern branch of the Missouri but a southern branch of the Columbia as well had headwaters in this region. As in the case of the shortened mountain range, such a view was not precluded by the geographical knowledge of the time.

When he crossed the Stoney Mountains to Pacific drainage, Mackenzie reached a river which he and nearly everyone else later assumed was the Columbia. This contact was near the 55th parallel while, as has been noted, the sources of the Missouri's two major branches were much farther south. But in contemporary lore, Mackenzie's river (actually the Fraser and not the Columbia) was connected with the mighty river discovered by Robert Gray of the United States and surveyed for 100 miles inland by England's George Vancouver in 1792. Somewhere along the north-to-south course of the Columbia—between its source and the point where it turned west to the sea—there must be tributaries which had sources in the same range that gave rise to the Missouri. Mackenzie himself had pointed this out[27] and on both the King and Arrowsmith maps, one of these tributaries—the Great Lake River—appeared as a river heading just west of the headwaters of the northern branch of the Missouri. The King map alone showed the great conjectural southern branch of the Columbia opposite the sources of the Missouri's southern fork. But, like the other unusual features of the King map, this was reflected in Jefferson's possible image of the passage to the Pacific.

According to Jefferson's theories about the western interior, a region that gave rise to one river quite likely gave rise to others.[28] Consequently, the source region of the Missouri's southern branch was probably the source region for a stream of the Columbia system as well. Moreover, the same source area probably spawned the major rivers of the Southwest—the Colorado, Rio Grande, and mythical Rio des los Apostolos. In his instructions to Lewis, Jefferson said that connections might be had between the Missouri and the "Columbia, Oregan, Colorado, or any other river" of Pacific drainage.[29] He had specifically ordered Lewis to investigate this area between the Missouri and "the North river or Rio Bravo which runs into the gulph of Mexico, and the North river, or Rio Colorado which runs into the gulph of California" and to find out whether the "dividing grounds" between those rivers and the Missouri were "mountains or flat lands." This would seem to be good evidence that Jefferson's understanding of the western interior included the concept of a core source region for many western rivers near the southern terminus of the range drawn on the King map. It also indicates, rather conclusively, that the president was indeed visualizing a route up the southern, and not the northern, branch of the Missouri, since the sources of the latter were too far removed from any possible connection with southwestern streams.

What emerges from this is an image of the passage to India which, although not consistent with the physical realities of the western interior, did not contradict the knowledge in Jefferson's possession. As far as he knew, the source region of the southern Missouri and the southern Columbia might be a flat, level area—a plateau rather than a range of mountains. Through this plateau an American expedition might find an easy passage to India.

The final influence of Jefferson's possible image on the actual course of the Lewis and Clark Expedition was probably minimal. It is clear, however, that as late as the winter of 1804, the proposed course of travel worked out by the captains was determined by Jefferson's views. Distance and time estimates made by Clark during the period of preparation just before embarkation up the Missouri were based upon the assumption that the course to be followed west of the Mandans would be toward the source region at 113° West, 46° North—a course up the Missouri's southern branch.[30] But as the expedition proceeded up the Missouri in the summer of 1804, they learned much more than Jefferson had known (or speculated) about the Missouri and its tributaries. And during the winter of 1804-5, spent at the Mandan villages, in present-day central North Dakota, Lewis and Clark finalized a view of the Upper Missouri that caused them to discard the possibilities of a route up the southern branch of the Missouri as the shortest and quickest way to the Columbia.[31]

There were indeed two branches of the Missouri above the Mandans—just shown on the King and Arrowsmith maps. The northernmost of these was the Missouri itself. But it did not have a source near the 50th parallel, and it did not flow from the northwest as the King and Arrowsmith maps had shown. Instead, it had headwaters as far south as the 40th parallel and ran northeast for a considerable distance before turning east toward the Mandan villages. Somewhere along this southwest-to-northeast course would be found a portage to the Columbia—a portage across a range of mountains rather than through a plateau, but a short portage nevertheless.[32] This, then, was the proper route for the passage. But if the originally proposed route up the southern branch of the Missouri was rejected, the Jeffersonian image of the nature of that branch and its source region was not.

The southern branch was, of course, the Yellowstone. It came from a mountainous area far to the south, rather than a plateau.[33] But its headwaters lay in a region which spawned numerous major streams, just as Jefferson had envisaged. On maps drawn by Clark following the completion of the expedition, the Upper Yellowstone was shown in close proximity to the headwaters of the Rio Grande, Colorado, Arkansas, Platte, Snake, and a great, mythical southern branch of the Columbia called the Multnomah.[34]

For years this hypothetical arrangement of rivers confused the geography of the West. The misconception survived the wanderings of John Coulter and the mapping of George Drouillard.[35] It was furthered by Zebulon Pike, who proclaimed that the mountains of the Southwest formed "a grand reservoir of snows and fountains" from which mighty rivers flowed in several directions.[36] It was not until after the epic journeys of the Rocky Mountain fur trade that the myth of the core drainage region was erased from geographical lore. The hypothetical geography upon which Thomas Jefferson had based his hopes for the passage to India finally disappeared from the lore of the western interior. But Jefferson's image of the passage had been responsible for one of the world's greatest exploratory ventures. And the image shaped the nature of geographical thought about the American West for nearly half a century.

NOTES

1. A complete discussion of Jefferson's geographical knowledge and his role in planning the Lewis and Clark Expedition may be found in John L. Allen, "Geographical Images of the American Northwest, 1673 to 1806: an Historical Geosophy" (Ph.D. diss., Clark University, 1969), chap. 5.
2. Ann Maury, "The Letters of James Maury," *Memoirs of a Huguenot Family* (New York: G. P. Putnam's Sons, 1912), p. 391.
3. Maury, *Memoirs*, p. 388.
4. Jefferson made his first overtures to George Rogers Clark in 1783; in 1786 he tried to induce John Ledyard to make the journey; and in 1793, as a member of the American Philosophical Society, he prepared the instructions for André Michaux, a French botanist commissioned by the society to explore the Missouri. See Donald Jackson, ed., *Letters of the Lewis and Clark Expedition, with Related Documents* (Urbana: University of Illinois Press, 1962), pp. 654-69.
5. Jefferson to Michaux, 30 April 1793, Thomas Jefferson Papers, Manuscript Division, vol. 82, Library of Congress, Washington, D.C. Published in Jackson, *Letters*, pp. 669-72, and in Reuben Gold Thwaites, ed., *The Original Journals of the Lewis and Clark Expedition*, 8 vols. (New York: Dodd, Mead & Co., 1904), 7:202-4.
6. Julian Boyd, ed., *The Papers of Thomas Jefferson* (Princeton: Princeton University Press, 1950-65), 8:411.

7. Jefferson Papers, vols. 107-17.
8. Ibid., vol. 108, fol. 18750; vol. 132, fols. 22857, 22871.
9. Ibid., vol. 129, fols. 22204-8; Jackson, *Letters*, pp. 10-14; and Thwaites, *Original Journals*, 7:206-10.
10. This simple statement contains the three basic elements of Jefferson's overall image of the trans-Missouri West: the mildness of the climate, the navigability of the Missouri, and the single portage to Pacific-slope waters.
11. U.S., Senate, Congress, *Annals of the 7th-9th Congresses* 12 (1827): 103.
12. Jefferson Papers, vol. 130, fols. 22479, 22508; vol. 131, fols. 22582-83; and Jackson, *Letters*, pp. 27-28, 31-32, and 32-34.
13. Lewis's instructions are in the Jefferson Papers, vol. 132, fols. 22884-87, printed in Jackson, *Letters*, pp. 61-66. The original map can be seen in the Geography and Maps Division, Library of Congress. A partial description of the map is given in Annie H. Abel, "A New Lewis and Clark Map," *Geographical Review* 1 (1916): 329-45. The King map is not the "new Lewis and Clark map" which is the main subject of the article.
14. Jefferson Papers, vol. 132, fol. 22884.
15. Thomas Jefferson, *Notes on the State of Virginia* (London: John Stockdale, 1785), p. 10.
16. Cf. Antoine Simor le Page du Pratz, *History of Louisiana* (London: T. Becket, 1763), 1:38.
17. Jefferson Papers, vol. 108, fol. 18456.
18. This was a widely accepted notion in 1803. See John L. Allen, "Geographical Knowledge and American Images of the Louisiana Territory," *Western Historical Quarterly* 2 (1971): 151-70.
19. Thomas Jefferson, "Official Account of Louisiana," *Miscellaneous*, ed. Walter Lowrie and Walter Franklin, American State Papers (Washington, D.C.: Gales and Seaton, 1834), 1:350.
20. Jefferson Papers, vol. 132, fols. 22759-60; Jackson, *Letters*, pp.51-53.
21. Ibid., vol. 130, fol. 22508; Jackson, *Letters*, pp. 31-32.
22. These waters, Jefferson wrote, "have been ascertained to a considerable degree and are still in a course of ascertainment by English traders and travellers."
23. Allen, "Geographical Images," pp. 158-62.
24. Jedediah Morse, "The Shining Mountains," *The American Gazetteer* (Boston: Thomas and Andrews, 1803).
25. Alexander Mackenzie, *Voyages from Montreal . . . to the . . . Pacific Ocean*, reprint ed., 2 vols. (Toronto: Courier Press, 1911), 2:346.
26. Fidler's maps and reports were deposited in the collections of the Hudson's Bay Company in London. Arrowsmith had access to these collections and utilized, therefore, the most recent geographic data gathered by the British fur trade in the construction of his maps.
27. Mackenzie, *Voyages from Montreal*, 2:347.
28. The theoretical "pyramidal height-of-land" had been applied to North American geography since the middle of the eighteenth century. See Allen, "Geographical Images," pp. 159-60.
29. These words did not appear in the final "official" version of Jefferson's instructions. They did, however, appear in every preliminary or draft copy

and must have been known to Lewis. Elimination of this section from the released instructions might have been for political purposes.

30. Ernest Staples Osgood, ed., *The Field Notes of Captain William Clark, 1803-1805* (New Haven: Yale University Press, 1964), pp. 19-20.
31. Thwaites, *Original Journals*, 6:51-52.
32. Ibid., pp. 54-55.
33. Ibid., pp. 52-53.
34. The Multnomah was a misinterpreted version of the Willamette. The captains had seen the mouth of the Willamette but had not explored it thoroughly. Local Indians had described the river's course but when their descriptions were combined with the explorers' theoretical biases, the resultant image was a distorted one.
35. Both Coulter and Drouillard were members of the Lewis and Clark party who had returned to the Rocky Mountain region following the expedition. The route of Coulter's travels appeared on a map drawn by William Clark, ca. 1810, as a preliminary version of the map published with the first official journals of the expedition. See *History of the Expedition under the Command of Lewis and Clark* (Philadelphia: Bradford and Inskeep, 1814). A map drawn by Drouillard, ca. 1808, is in the manuscript collection of the Geography and Maps Division, Library of Congress.
36. William H. Goetzmann, *Exploration and Empire* (New York: Alfred Knopf, 1967), pp. 17-28.

The United States Land Survey as a Principle of Order

HILDEGARD BINDER JOHNSON

Whether we "do" historical geography from the past forward to the present or from the present backward to the past, we follow a linear orientation and depend upon documentary dating. Ralph H. Brown, for example, created *Mirror for Americans: Likeness of the Eastern Seaboard* by working from an earlier past to the year 1810.[1] Such chronological structure does not mean that our search for sources cannot benefit from the geographical reality of the present and, in fact, could be somewhat directed by questions presented by the naively given reality. Some ground observations, such as former field borders running in a straight line across river bottoms, terraces, and bluffs on both sides of the Whitewater Valley in southeastern Minnesota, motivated this observer to probe into the historical origins of a cadastral survey that helped to create the most extensive consistently formal agricultural landscape in the world. Clarence Glacken's observation that its "sight has been much more striking, dramatic, and worthy of study to foreigners than to Americans" pertains to the sight as viewed from an airplane.[2] In concurrence with Richard Neutra, who wrote that "our mind seems to be bent in processing the amorphous intake of the senses by means of a specific secretion of its own—namely order,"[3] it appears that the amorphous intake of the landscape by the American mind is strongly filtered through rectangular order. This paper will first focus on selected formal ingredients in the legislation since 1785 and then discuss a few operational aspects in the historical development of the survey as a principle of order.

114

ELEMENTS OF DESIGN

"An Ordinance for Ascertaining the Mode of Disposing of Lands in Western Territory in 1785" and "An Act Providing for the Sale of the Lands of the United States in the Territory Northwest of the River Ohio in 1796" created the township system of thirty-six square miles or sections, to be laid out on the nonvarying grid. The square formal aspect of the first plan, which legislated sale by square townships, was repeated in 1804 and 1832 when land of the public domain could be bought as square quarter sections and square quarter, quarter sections, or "forties," respectively.

The order, as legislated between 1785 and 1832, is very simple as to forms (square or rectangular), as to sizes (all are multiples of forty acres), and as to the nonvarying position of the two coordinates (namely, true north/south). Scholarly efforts to identify the originator of this plan reflect our general devotion to the causality principle but should be discouraged. "No man in particular was the originator," said an engineer in an address in 1908. "There is no great or original conception in the idea of the Indiana principal meridian with its base line.[4] Indeed, it behooves us to acknowledge that different peoples in different places and at different times can arrive at similar solutions independently of each other when facing similar problems. A wealth of evidence has been produced by humanists, anthropologists, and archeologists for the usage of the circle and the cross as pervasive forms in cultures for delineating pieces of the earth's surface for human usage. These forms have their roots in the human condition. The widely occurring use of the number of six for subdivisions may, also, be linked to the primary directions in space "natural" to humans, i.e., left to right, forward and backward, up and down.

Circles are not very useful for planning assignment of land over a large area, or, in the American case, planning the sale of large areas, since tangential circles do not yield a contiguous field. The hexagonal field, already of interest to Pappus of Alexandria, a Greek geometer in the late third century, A.D., lacks rectangularity and simple parallelism essential in such enterprises as weaving or brickmaking and convenient for plowing, assessing land for taxes, and subdividing land into lots. Thus, a field of squares, subdivided into squares (the simplest pattern to design), is the most efficient for many purposes. It is hard to resist the temptation to search for evidence of connections between the similarities of the thirty-six sections in our township system and the thirty-six tsubos in the Japanese jori system under which the fields of the Nara plain were redesigned in the seventh century. But the search has proved fruitless so far.

115

A plausible and simpler explanation of such similarities is the facility with which man can orientate himself toward north on the Northern Hemisphere and the inherent advantages for planning ideal schemes by grouping six-by-six or four-by-nine equal-sized squares. Common sense must acknowledge common man's ability to design a township plan, as the squatters did in Iowa, one of whom reported from Marion County in the 1830s as follows:

> The absence of section lines rendered it necessary to take the sun at noon and at evening as a guide by which to run these claim lines. So many steps each way counted three hundred and twenty acres, more or less the legal area of a claim. It may be readily supposed that these lines were far from correct, but they answered all the necessary claim purposes for it was understood among the settlers that when lands came to be surveyed and entered, all inequalities would be righted. Thus, if a surveyed line should happen to run between adjoining claims, cutting off more or less of one or the other, the fraction was to be added to whichever lot required equalizing, yet without robbing the one from which it was taken, for an equal amount would be added to it in some other place.[5] (Figure 1)

The design of order in the Ordinance of 1785 is very different from searching for orderliness or laws in nature. It reflects egalitarianism through geometry, characteristic of many colonization plans on paper. The stipulation of 1785 that out of every township four lots, numbered 8, 11, 26, and 29, shall be reserved for future sale by the United States has the symmetry so frequent on utopian plans (figure 2). Also, the adherence to true north yields the same advantage as a Mercator projection—lines that run straight up/down and left/right for longitude and latitude. It is not surprising then that the German pilot, who wrote in *Harper's* magazine in 1950 about the survey, praised the section lines as "just what a pilot wants a country to be—graph paper. You can head the airplane down a section line and check your compass. But you hardly need a compass. You simply draw your course on the map and see what angle it makes. Then you cross the sections at the same angle."[6]

The survey is a very efficient way to designate parcels for sale on a map. It was not expected that it would be possible to be totally exact, hence the ever-recurring phrase of "as near as may be" for the stipulated measurements and markers, be it in legislation or in the instructions to deputy surveyors from the surveyor general, throughout the nineteenth century.

From its inception the survey was designed to render the land as a flat surface, thus the repeated instructions for leveling the chain and plumbing the pins. The instructions in 1815 were that the level or

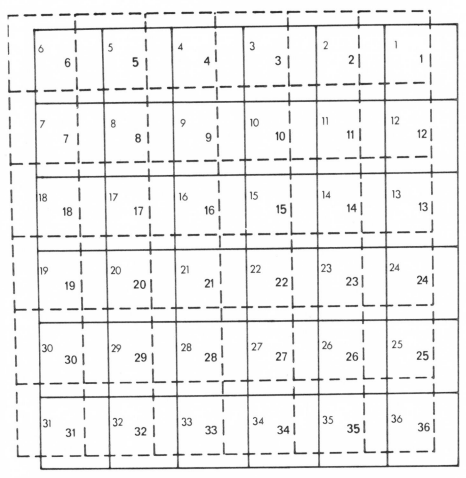

Fig. 1. *The squatter's township plan, adaptable to the surveyed township for determining legal claims.*

horizontal length of the chain must not be taken over the surface of the ground when it is hilly or uneven and that it may be necessary to shorten the chain to measure correctly. The General Instructions of 1855, which remained basic for surveying until 1910, told the surveyor: "The length of every line you run is to be ascertained by precise horizontal measurement, as nearly approximating to an air line as possible in practice on the earth's surface."[7]

To summarize: The survey derived from a flat surface concept, which

117

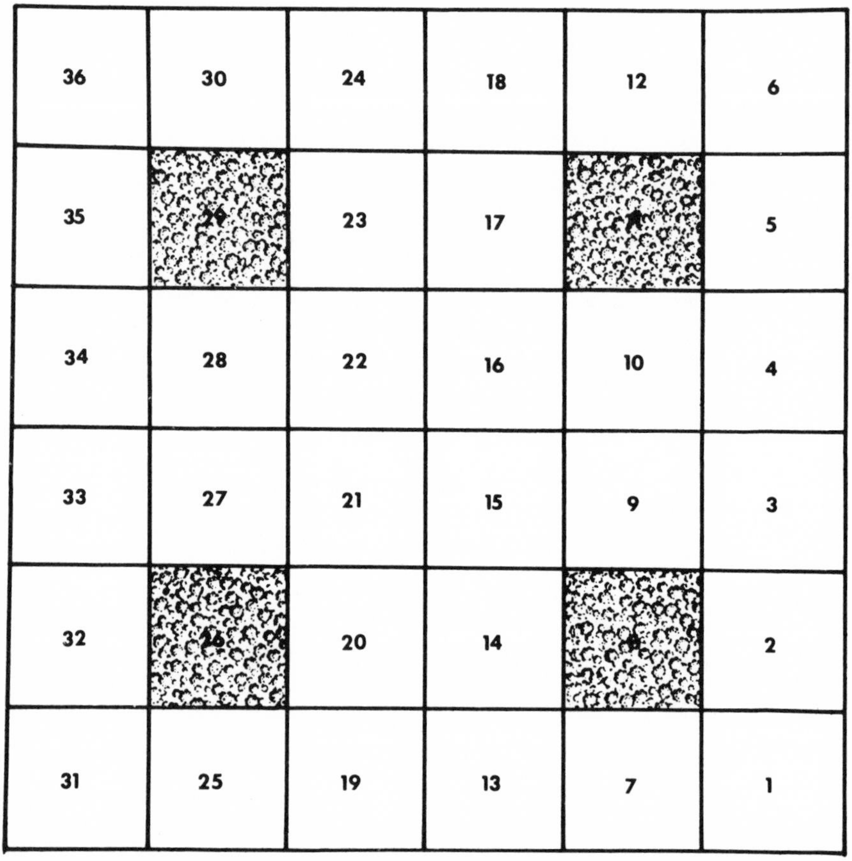

36	30	24	18	12	6
35	29	23	17	11	5
34	28	22	16	10	4
33	27	21	15	9	3
32	26	20	14	8	2
31	25	19	13	7	1

FIG. 2. *Four sections to be reserved for future sale with arrangement reminiscent of several utopian plans of the eighteenth century. Sections 8, 11, 26, and 29 have the same location under the original numbering system stipulated by the Ordinance of 1785 and under the numbering system of the Land Act of 1796, which began with Section 1 at the northeast corner, ending in Section 36 at the southeast corner.*

might well be called a model. Its straight lines were not novel; in fact, most boundaries, particularly after the invention of the compass, even in regions where we deal with so-called crooked boundary lines, are usually a series of short, straight lines. Excellent illustrations of the variety of field divisions and delineations of property and of field borders by straight lines in "Old World agriculture," often with an overall appearance of curves, sector divisions, or gores, are found in

118

the recently published *Atlas der Deutschen Agrarlandschaft*.[8] But these straight-lined borders do not result in consistently rectangular fields. The advantages of rectangularity and of parallelism for numbering blocks and streets for orientation and for the installation of one-way traffic systems in urban traffic everywhere are as obvious as the historical fact that the founding fathers could not envisage the extent to which the rectangular system was going to be applied. But distinctive to the American survey is the adherence to the nonvarying grid and the uninterrupted extension by addition of a closed system, literally expressed in uncounted instructions to "close" sections or townships at their corners. The quotation in praise of the system in an article of 1884, that "no other country possesses one so nearly perfect in theory as in practice,"[9] means saying the same as a fourth generation surveyor in West Saint Paul in 1971: "Any other system would create complications." Jackson Payson Treat praised the survey in 1905 as "a general system of disposition."[10] Half a century later Marion Clawson spoke of a system of disposal and emphasized the difficulties for good land use resulting from rigid boundaries.[11] The system's disregard for topography is probably its most widely recognized drawback. Hugh Bennett of the Soil Conservation Service made the contour a household word in America, largely by criticizing the "misinterpretation or violation of the ways of nature in undertaking to impose a straight-lined, square agriculture in a round country."[12] Modern criticism of monotonous city plats and suburban divisions rarely discerns the survey's role in the prevalence of grid-pattern towns in the United States.

OPERATIONAL ELEMENTS

Any cadastral system, be it jori, township, or Roman Centuriation, can become reality only by stipulating units of measurement. The act of 1785 specified details—such as marking trees—requiring that some descriptive notes be made by surveyors, that townships must contain thirty-six square miles, and that they be measured with a chain. Edmund Gunter invented the 66-foot-long chain in England in 1620. A denotation of this unit of measure is the mile, of 5,280 feet. The geographical mile which Jefferson had suggested in 1784, based on 1/90 of a degree at the equator, is 6,080.2 feet and is used by the United States Coast and Geodetic Survey. The area of 43,560 square feet is the sum of 10 square chains—66 x 66 x 10 equals 43,560—and 640 acres are a square mile. The square mile was, by 1832, sub-

119

TOWNSITES ENTERED (1855-1880) BY STATE AND SIZE IN DESCENDING ORDER

State	40-80 Acres	160 Acres	200-240 Acres	280 Acres	320-360 Acres	360-400 Acres	600-700 Acres	800-900 Acres	1,000-2,000 Acres	2,000-5,000 Acres
California	18	33	10	8	6	9	11	1	1	...
Utah	8	18	5	6	12	8	19	4	14	2
Kansas	7	25	5	6	43	4	4	...	...	...
Minnesota	2	7	2	10	8	1	...	...	...	...
Nebraska	...	3	1	3	21	1	...	...	...	...
Colorado	2	3	...	3	9	2	2	...	...	...
Montana	1	3	1	...	3	2	1	...	1	...
Nevada	8	3	...	...	1	...	1	...	1	...
Arizona	...	1	...	...	3	...	...	...	2	...
Idaho	...	...	...	2	...	2	2	...	...	...
Iowa	...	1	2	1	1	...	...	...	...	...
New Mexico	...	...	...	...	1	...	2	...	...	...
Oregon	2	1	...	...	...	...	...	...	...	...
Wisconsin	1	...	...	1	...	...	...	...	...	...
Washington	1	1	...	...	...	...	...	...	...	...
Wyoming	...	...	...	...	...	...	1	...	...	...
Dakota	...	...	1	...	...	...	...	...	...	...

(SOURCE: Thomas Donaldson, *The Public Domain* [Washington, D.C.: Government Printing Office, 1884], pp. 300-305.)

divided into 40 acres as the smallest unit by which the public domain could be transferred to other public and private ownership, until recently. The townsite acts of 1824, 1844, and 1867 specified grants for townsites in multiples of 40 acres, and an act of 1877 limited townsite grants to sizes of 2,560 acres. The only list of towns which originated with such townsite grants that seems available in print is in Donaldson's *Public Domain* (see table). Search in the National Archives would help to learn about those that could have been granted after 1880.[13] While large cities often did not incorporate sufficient land early enough for their development, many towns which remained small have incorporated too much land. In either case, statistical raw data are spatially derived from squares or rectangles to a large extent.

Platting or planning small towns by subdividing forty acres became "natural;" two successive divisions by two brought parcels down to five acres. Since any further division by two results in a fraction, two and a half acres, there are a great number of town and city blocks of five acres with five chains for the short side and ten chains for the long side minus the width of streets, usually sixty-six feet.[14] These proportions, derived from the survey, will be part of our environment for a long time since, over wide areas, lots, streets, and utilities became, by the middle of the twentieth century, "frozen" into the urban rural fringe when, in the process of development, subdivisions expanded by forties and sections.[15]

A system of the magnitude of the survey becomes reality not by one edict but by a historical process in which the rules, by being applied, generate forces of their own. One of the rules that was not legislated but established by practice is the correction line, necessary to reconcile the discrepancy between converging meridians on the earth and the straight north/south running meridians on the plats. Generally, in the nineteenth century, townships were surveyed first with reference to baselines and meridians, then sections. Posts were set at half-mile points, but interior quarter-section lines were not surveyed and mapped. The idea was to proceed systematically from east to west, and at auctions land was to be offered in an east-to-west sequence. However, the survey was executed "piecemeal," as a historian of the survey called it, and not only encountered legally valid land claims made prior to the survey, particularly in the South and as far north as Missouri, but, more importantly, the survey could be undertaken only after Indian cessions "obtained without any reference to the accommodation of the surveys," to quote from the annual report of 1850 by the surveyor general at Dubuque.[16] Thus, there is a historical sequence but no model system regarding the location and length of baselines and principal meridians. Some curious references to the coordinates in the system resulted in the historical process. For example, townships in Minnesota and North Dakota as far north as Canada refer to the baseline in Arkansas, the northernmost township at the Canadian border being Township 164 north (figure 3). When it was decided to make the parallel of forty-three degrees and thirty minutes north latitude the Iowa-Minnesota state boundary, the northernmost township in Iowa numbered 100 and almost coincided with this independently selected parallel. The two east-west lines differ by fifty yards at most, locally known as fractions. This is a case of truth being stranger than fiction, considering the irregularities in Missouri between the Arkansas baseline and the 100th township line.[17] On the other hand, in Dakota County, Minnesota, a county surveyor's office

121

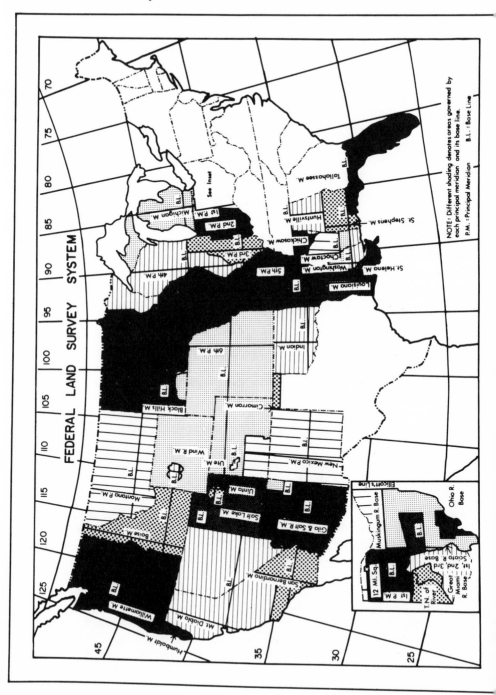

Fig. 3. *Distribution of the thirty-four principal meridians which govern the survey with the areas as they refer to the various meridians and baselines.*

was established with a full-time surveyor on January 1, 1972, because of particularly difficult conditions. Townships there were surveyed with reference to two baselines and two principal meridians—Township 115 is followed by Townships 27 and 28' bounded by the Minnesota and Mississippi rivers.

Selling proceeded just as piecemeal as surveying. After April 5, 1832, forty acres could be bought directly from the government by the man of modest means; they also were often sufficient to control an important site resource, such as waterfalls. A number of such millsites were claimed prior to Indian cessions in the Chippewa region of Wisconsin and are recorded by the surveyors on their original plats and field notes. The right of preemption and the credit system probably encouraged some people to claim more than a forty, by whatever means, with little regard for their ability to actually work the land. Still, the selection of forties by individual settlers helped to disperse small claims over a wider area.

Forty-acre units were most in demand according to the instructions of the Burlington Railroad Land Office, which emphatically asked its surveyors to examine the land they selected inside their sixteen-mile lieu limits by 40-acre tracts. Even when 80-, 120-, 160-, or over 160-acre holdings were contiguous, it did not mean contiguity inside the same section, or even in the same township. Quarter sections could and did take nineteen different forms as composites of four forties when settlers attempted to adjust their holding to the topography.[18] It does not take many quarter sections composed of forties or smaller tracts to make the assemblage of contiguous units of 160 or more acres difficult. Some forties became inaccessible forties and are still in the public domain, be it federal land or land held by the state. They can serve as a sort of commons for adjoining owners, as illustrated by an example in Becker County, Minnesota (figure 4). Winona County, settled in the 1850s, still had seven such forties of state land in 1959. The process of assembling forties by successive purchases over a period of years was encouraged by railroad land advertisements and state immigration pamphlets which told the settler to start with a forty and then acquire another and still another as his economic situation improved. Farmers still "round-out" their holdings by square forties, to use the vernacular. Forty-acre tracts exist only as entries on General Land Office plats, not on surveyors' maps, since the federal government could not undertake the surveying of forties because the expense would have been incalculable, according to the General Land Commissioner. Ownership and management patterns thus have the geometry

123

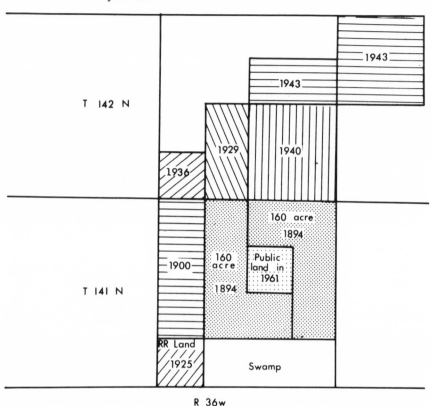

Fig. 4. *An example of a "forty" that became accessible to the adjoining owners only and was still in the public domain in 1961. Another farmer homesteaded in 1900 with 120 acres in Section 8, Township 141 N, Range 36 W. He added, between 1925 and 1943, 40, 80, 40, 160, 80, and 160 acres in Sections 8, 5, and 4. This farm has 680 acres in one contiguous piece.*

of the forty rather than that of square quarter sections or sections for their spatial components.

The idea of the so-called checkerboard pattern, i.e., alternating squares, appeared in the Ordinance of 1785 as follows: "The township or fractional part of a township No. 1 in the first range, shall be sold entire; and No. 2 in the same range, by lots; and thus in alternate order through the whole first range." In the nineteenth century, railroad grants designated odd- or even-numbered alternate sections of various width to either side. For example, the McGregor Western Railroad Company was to run in a westerly direction on or near the forty-third parallel of north latitude until it intersected the railroad from Sioux City to the Minnesota line and got "every alternate section designated by odd numbers for ten miles" on either side of the road, and the Cedar Rapids and Missouri River Railroad Company received the vacant, even-numbered sections from public lands not otherwise disposed of through congressional authorization in 1856. The idea of alternation reflects some understanding of hoped-for spatial interaction: alternate improved sections were to raise the value of the nonimproved sections in between.

Alternate holdings by public and private owners have led to great difficulties for good land-use management. For the slope of the eastern Sierra, Harold Haefner summarized it recently as follows: "This extremely complex and complicated ownership pattern cannot be explained rationally, only historically through variable federal land policies which did not originate locally but in far away Washington."[19] Not that irregular forms could not also lead to scatteration, but systematic spatial alteration, all other variables excluded, can be achieved most easily and with greatest disregard for topographic conditions when one simulates a checkerboard, "un jeu de dames" to quote a French investigator of the origins of homestead legislation.[20]

Another operational element is one of omission. The survey is very impressive from the air, not so much through the rectangular fields aligned along cardinal directions as through the quadratic grid of section roads which were not mentioned in the legislation. The Canadian survey is markedly different in that it stipulated roads, generally 100 links wide, for every other mile crossing township lines and every mile crossing range lines (figure 5). In the United States, section lines are generally public roads.[21] They developed historically. One can speculate that section lines, when they were measured during the summer, were visible for some time after a party of six men went through a wooded area retracing steps, marking witness trees, setting posts, and camping. In the prairie, monuments would have been conspicuous, at least for a while, and a trace from wagons would indicate the line. Usage and makeshift maintenance, often described in county histories, then established the section roads and frequently covered up the markers. However, obstacles were avoided, according to the vernacular saying that "the longest way around is the sweetest way home," and many section roads thus had curves, while others followed the section lines, more or less correctly surveyed. Later, at the discretion of the county commissioners, the maintenance of township roads was taken over by the county. While state and federal roads, with better engineering re-

N

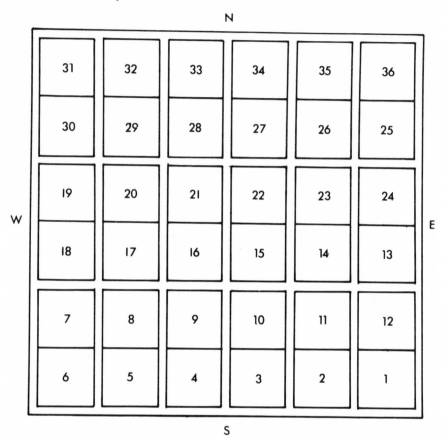

31	32	33	34	35	36
30	29	28	27	26	25
19	20	21	22	23	24
18	17	16	15	14	13
7	8	9	10	11	12
6	5	4	3	2	1

W   E

S

FIG. 5. *The Canadian survey, which made allowance for roads at 100 links (sixty-six feet) between sections.*

sources, became increasingly more level, many section roads became straighter and ran up- and downhill more consistently than initially, unless a high degree of dissection interrupted the section road pattern. The roads north and south from the aforementioned Minnesota/Iowa boundary are an example (figure 6). Thrower found that under the rectangular survey, fundamental survey lines coincided much more with public roads than in the unsystematic survey and that 90 percent of the survey lines are public roads.[22] For present purposes, planners consider Chisago County, Minnesota, about 50 percent overroaded with section roads. The lack of federally initiated provision for roads, coupled with

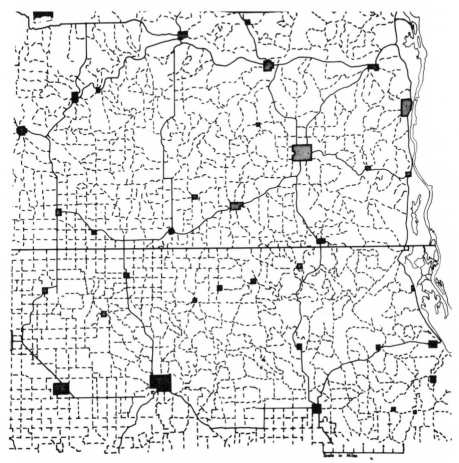

FIG. 6. *Road system along the Iowa/Minnesota boundary at 43° 30′ latitude north, reflecting the breakdown of the section road pattern in dissected country close to the Mississippi River.*

the settlement pattern of single farmsteads, again promoted dispersal which could have been reduced by other patterns equally systematic and with the same accessibility as the quadratic section road pattern. (Figure 7) The increased proximity of homes might have alleviated the isolation of a Per Hansa and his family in O. E. Rolvaag's *Giants in the Earth*. How accessibility by section roads facilitates outward expansion of the suburban fringe is easily observable from an airplane and has been schematized by Tunnard.[23]

127

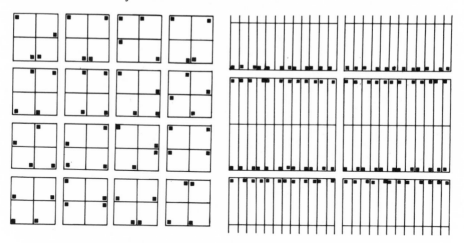

Fig. 7. *Diagram of a scheme* (right) *by which every farm would have 160 acres but with every other road unnecessary. Compare to the square section road pattern* (left), *which contributed to the dispersal of settlement and assumed that every farm would have access to the road and comprise a quarter section.*

CONCLUSION

It is noteworthy that the survey system, under which townships and counties tend to be rectangularly shaped spatial units, maintained itself in spite of great efforts by the chief of the Soil Conservation Service who, in the 1930s and 1940s, wanted soil conservation districts based on watersheds as natural regions. The districts became county-based districts for reasons of administration and political power with straight-lined boundaries for townships and property lines, resulting in a "conservation landscape" where contoured fields are set into frames patterned through the original plan. The persistence of section and property lines is actually acerbated by the abrupt ending of contoured fields which do not mesh along straight lines. We might also speculate that American geographers' zest for mapping county data over large areas, and particularly the Middle West, has been served by the system. For computer research, the forty-acre unit—dating back to 1832—was found most serviceable by John Borchert in 1970 when dealing with Minnesota, since this was the unit for which most data are available. Surveyors now can measure distance with an accuracy of $\pm$ (.01 feet + $\frac{distance}{100,000}$) i.e., less than an inch per mile. Nevertheless, according to the 1947 government *Manual of Surveying Instructions*, they must restore lost and obliterated corners. And by general rules, the record evidence is considered unchangeable after the United States passes title to land. This record evidence is the original field notes and plats, largely dating from the nineteenth century, and is available in the National Archives.

NOTES

1. Ralph H. Brown, *Mirror for Americans: Likeness of the Eastern Seaboard, 1810* (New York: American Geographical Society, 1943).
2. Editor's Note in Norman J. W. Thrower, *Original Survey and Land Subdivision* (Chicago: Rand McNally & Co., 1966), p. vi.
3. Richard Neutra, *Survival Through Design* (London: Oxford University Press, 1954), p. 123.
4. W. A. Truesdell, "The Rectangular System of Surveying," *Journal of the Association of Engineering Societies* 41 (November 1908): 207-30, 227.
5. Quoted from Roscoe L. Lokken, *Iowa Public Land Disposal* (Iowa City: State Historical Society of Iowa, 1942), p. 69.
6. Wolfgang Langewiesche, "The U.S.A. from the Air," *Harper's* 201 (October 1950): 179-98, 188. Another reference to "the mystique of geometry" in Iowa is Laurence Lafore, "In the Sticks," *Harper's* 243 (October 1971): 108-15, 109.
7. J. S. Dodds et al., *Original Instructions Governing Public Land Surveys of Iowa* (Ames: Iowa Engineering Society, 1943), p. 121.
8. Erich Otremba, ed., *Atlas der Deutschen Agrarlandschaft*, Issues 1-3 (Wiesbaden: Franz Steiner Verlag, 1962, 1965, 1969).
9. Charles Whittlesey, "Origin of the American System of Land Surveys," *Journal of the Association of Engineering Societies* 3 (September 1884): 275-80, 279.
10. Payson Jackson Treat, "Origin of the National Land System under the Confederation," *Annual Report of the American Historical Association*, 1905, pp. 233-39; p. 239: "We must award a liberal meed of praise to the members of the moribund Congress for devising a liberal system of disposition."
11. Marion Clawson, "How We Disposed of Most of Our Public Land," *Uncle Sam's Acres* (New York: Dodd, Mead & Co., 1951), chap. 3, pp. 42 ff. See, also, A. Allan Schmid, *Converting Land from Rural to Urban Uses* (Baltimore: Johns Hopkins Press, 1968), preface by Marion Clawson, p. v.
12. Hugh H. Bennett, "Land and People," *Soil Conservation* (September 1941), p. 74. One of the many examples of opposing straight-lined fields.
13. Thomas Donaldson, *The Public Domain* (Washington, D.C.: Government Printing Office, 1884). List of townsite and county seat acts up to June 30, 1880, pp. 298-99.
14. John R. Quay, "Use of Soil Surveys in Subdivision Design," *Soil Surveys and Land Use Planning*, ed. L. Y. Bartelli et al., Soil Science Society of America and American Society of Agronomy, 1966, chap. 8, p. 76, points to the relationship between the frequency of five-acre blocks and subdivision practices.

15. George S. Wehrwein, "The Rural-Urban Fringe," *Economic Geography* 18 (July 1942): 217-28; p. 228 uses the term "frozen."

16. Lowell O. Stewart, *Public Land Surveys* (Ames: Collegiate Press, 1935), p. 46. "The inviolable practice has been to survey no lands until the Indian title thereto was extinquished and the Indian occupancy terminated. Hence the surveys have followed in the track of the aboriginal cessions, and these cessions have been obtained without any reference to the accommodation of the surveys, and have been so limited in area and so various and ir-regular in figure as not to admit of the proper establishment of a basis for the surveys, which after much reflection, I believe would most properly have consisted in marking given parallels without reference to civil divi-sions, and at stated and equal distances establishing true meridians."

17. An example of an error in township exteriors for Township 33 N, Range 1 East, 5th Principal Meridian in Missouri is mapped in ibid., p. 45, fn. 16.

18. Hildegard Binder Johnson, "Rational and Ecological Aspects of the Quarter Section," *Geographical Review* 47, no. 3 (1957): 330-48.

19. Harold Haefner, *Höhenstufen, öffentliche Ländereien und private Land-nutzung auf der Ostseite der Sierra Nevada (U.S.A.)* (Zürich: Juris Druck Verlag, 1970), p. 108.

20. L. Vacher, *L'homestead aux États-Unis* (Paris: 1895), p. 39. "L'intersection des lignes tracées dans la direction des quatre points cardinaux, determine un premier réseau qui rappelle la disposition des casiers d'un jeu de dames."

21. Statutes for the laying out and maintenance of state, county, and township, i. e., section roads vary from state to state. See Frank Emerson Clark, *A Treatise on the Law of Surveying and Boundaries* (Indianapolis: Bobbs-Merrill Co., Inc., 1922), pp. 550-58. "The land was usually patented by the quarter section, but no reservation was made in Kansas for roads. The only reservation for roads by law was in the case of Oklahoma where the public highways, four rods wide between each section of land, were reserved by the Act of May 2, 1890 (43 USC 1095)." Information, gratefully acknowl-edged, by letter, November 10, 1971, from Clark L. Gumm, Division of Cadastral Survey.

22. Thrower, *Original Survey*, p. 93.

23. Christopher Tunnard and Boris Pushkarev, *Man-Made America: Chaos or Control?* (New Haven and London: Yale University Press, 1963), p. 81, shows diagrams of individual housesites along section roads and then the frontage completely built up as the "final problem stage."

Reflections on the American Rectangular Land Survey System

WILLIAM D. PATTISON

Nearly fifteen years ago, at a public meeting, Hildegard Johnson and I first exchanged opinions on the American Rectangular Land Survey System. This was shortly after the publication of her oft-cited study, "Rational and Ecological Aspects of the Quarter Section," in the *Geographical Review*[1] and not long before the completion of my doctoral dissertation.[2] In resuming this discussion, the term I will be applying to our shared subject is *rectilinear partitioning*.

One might think of this paper as being titled, "Rectilinear Partitioning in Early Federal Land Policy: An Interpretation." And my analysis of this subject will be one of function, feedback, and flow. I will consider the ironic reversal of meaning—functional meaning—that rectilinear partitioning underwent soon after its advent in official discussions of federal policy for the West. Then I will discuss a time of limited feedback from the field, when the defensibility of rectilinear partitioning, in its changed functional significance, was tested by the reality of its consequences. In conclusion, I will consider the next period, when expanded feedback tapped a source whose significance few, if any, persons had originally foreseen. Perhaps this final part will be of greatest interest, since it deals most directly with the principal question raised in the preceding paper, "United States Land Survey as a Principle of Order." The value of the function-feedback-flow approach should become most apparent here. In each part, I am offering a thesis for the guidance of future work.

WILLIAM D. PATTISON

IN A DREAM

In the beginning, the directive that land be divided "by lines to be run and marked due north and south and others crossing these at right angles" was an element (and by no means an unimportant element) in an ambitious attempt to realize a dream of democratic rationality for the American West. My first thesis is that this directive found its way into American national law, not so much because of its own appeal, as because it held promise to the mind of Thomas Jefferson and probably of Hugh Williamson for the furtherance of this dream. Three laws were projected almost simultaneously in the spring of 1784 by committees of the Continental Congress, chaired by Jefferson: a law on Indian affairs, a law on new state governments in the West, and a law on the allocation of land. One may say that the *rationality* of rectilinear partitioning, as found in the third law, lay principally in its capacity to produce a graduated fit—a fit of proposed states (and an Indian boundary) to the earth as a whole, a fit of a new minor civil division (the hundred) to the states, and a fit of proposed square-mile lots to the hundred.[3] One may, also, point to a new system for measuring length and area that began with the partitioning pattern, an American metric system featuring a "geographical" mile, whose decimality anticipated the French metric system by more than ten years.[4]

And what of democracy, the guarantees of which were far more secure in the Jeffersonian law on state governments of 1784 than in the celebrated Northwest Ordinance of 1787? The democratic principle is found in the dimensions of the units, which facilitated for persons of ordinary attainment the computation of area (a procedure further expedited by the decimal system). It is found again in the right-angled intersection of boundary lines. One is irresistably reminded of a somewhat later report by Jefferson where, in discussing measures of capacity (quarts, gallons, and so forth), he expressed himself in favor of box-like containers with walls meeting at right angles, in preference to cylindrical vessels. Justifying this preference, he wrote, "Cylindrical measures have the advantage of superior strength: but square ones have the greater advantage of enabling everyone, who has a rule in his pocket, to verify their contents by measuring them."[5] Similarly, rectilinear land boundaries made it possible for any settler, employing the most rudimentary means of measurement, to verify the contents of a land purchase.

132

PARTITIONING RECONSIDERED

The reaction of members of the Continental Congress to the Jeffersonian land law may be briefly summarized. At first, they overwhelmingly rejected it, and then, through the deliberations of a new committee and an ensuing lengthy floor debate, they reconstructed it. In a new law,[6] land division was disassociated from state boundaries, and the proposed American metric system was entirely excluded. Gone were the hundred, the geographical mile, and the decimal principle. Further, all trace of the southern system of land disposal, a permissive system of claim-first-and-survey-afterward that had been preserved in the Jeffersonian scheme, was now removed. But rectilinear partitioning—cardinally oriented rectilinear partitioning—survived. On the surface this was strange since, in its own right, the scheme had few friends. "Eccentric and objectionable," said one member.[7] Another spoke of "this formal and hitherto unheard of plan."[8] And George Washington predicted that lands would not be accepted in this form "to the end of time" by those persons acquainted with them.[9]

A second thesis explains the survival of this rectilinear partitioning. A reconceptualization had occurred, recognition that rectilinear partitioning, for all its oddity, could serve the *seller's* interest with peculiar effectiveness. One discovers, in the proceedings of Congress at the time, a view of land as a commodity, perhaps even as a mass-producible commodity.[10] When the directive for rectilinear partitioning was added to provisions for prior survey and for sale at public auction, as happened in the new law, the quondam facilitator of a dream of democratic rationality became a device in the service of government as vendor. (To be sure, the contrast was not total, because federal self-interest undoubtedly operated in the Jeffersonian measure and because democratic New England institutions, such as the township and reserved land for schools, were introduced into the reconstructed legislation, but, I would say, the diagnosis of a shift in function holds true.)

Two points were made by defenders of rectilinear partitioning in the new context, both of which support the thesis. The first was that it would minimize the expense of surveying, and the second that, given its unvarying regularity and simplicity, it would greatly reduce the probability of later boundary disputes, and, hence, one infers, would enhance the value of the land at auction.[11] There is the argument: cost minimization on the one hand and the prospect of price appreciation on the other—a persuasive combination to a government hard pressed for income and unusually reluctant to raise money by taxation.

Writing to Jefferson, who had departed for France shortly after submitting his committee's report, James Monroe said of the new law, "It deviates I believe essentially from [your ordinance]."[12] So it did.

FEEDBACK FROM SURVEY AND SALE

Madison was referring to the Land Ordinance of 1785, key provisions of which were later reenacted under the Constitution, in the Land Act of 1796.[13] To illustrate historically the three stages in figure 1, (1) rectilinear partitioning in the *law* of 1785 led to (2) the appearance of rectilinear partitioning as an act of *survey* in the rugged hill lands of eastern Ohio in the summers of 1786 and 1787 which in turn led to (3) the invocation of rectilinear partitioning as a condition of *sale* in New York City, in the fall of the latter year.[14] And again: (1) rectilinear partitioning in the *law* of 1796 led within a few years to (2) the appearance of rectilinear partitioning as a *survey*, spreading westward into present-day Indiana, which in turn led to (3) the imposition of rectilinear partitioning as a regulator of *sales* at four newly opened land offices, in the general vicinity of the survey sites.[15]

A further step in interpretation can be seen in the Limited Feedback System (figure 2). The reference here is, first, to the experience of surveyors as a source of revisionist influence on the law, and, second, to land office experiences as another source of influence. For example (see feedback from survey to law in figure 2), *surveyors* were unhappy with the true meridian rule in the *law* of 1785, and they obtained congressional release from it.[16] After enactment of the 1796 law, they were uncertain how to subdivide townships whose boundaries were either too long or too short, and Congress responded with an amending act that dealt with this special question.[17] From the "marketplace," as time went on (see feedback from sale to law in figure 2), came a fairly steady demand for reduction in the minimum size of the grid-given parcels that Congress would allow. And in successive acts, Congress yielded on this score, originally permitting purchase by section in some townships only, then in all townships, and later permitting sale in less-than-full-section quantities.[18]

Thus, negative feedback took effect. Concurrently, an acceptance of the general principle of rectilinear partitioning was building up. Congress, which was concerning itself less and less with income from land

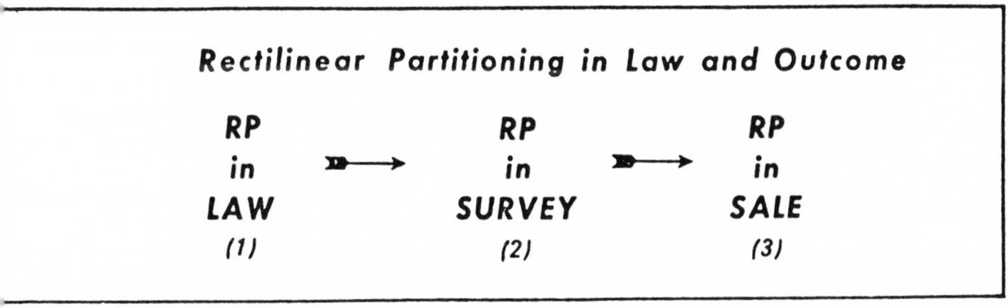

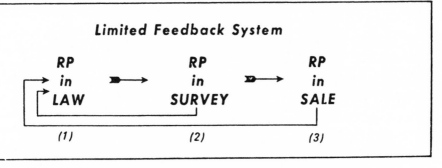

Rectilinear Partitioning in Law and Outcome

| RP in LAW (1) | → | RP in SURVEY (2) | → | RP in SALE (3) |

Fig. 1.

Limited Feedback System

| RP in LAW (1) | → | RP in SURVEY (2) | → | RP in SALE (3) |

Fig. 2.

conveyance, and more and more with keeping its production of property abreast of a rapidly moving frontier, was receiving positive feedback on the grid. Both in the field and in the land office, during the years after 1796, the pattern was winning, judged by both the old expectations of income yield and the new expectations of expedited turnover. This success supports my third thesis, that the establishment of rectilinear partitioning as a viable American institution may be attributed to the information system—the feedback system—shown in figure 2.

THE LANDSCAPE EFFECT

My fourth thesis is that the establishment of rectilinear partitioning occurred largely in innocence of its ultimate role as a determinant of landscape design. When was it fully realized in Washington that some-

135

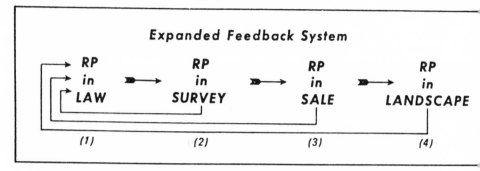

FIG. 3.

thing promulgated as a survey-and-sale program was inexorably generating a midcontinental macroarchitecture, a composition of roads, bridges, fields, fence lines, farmsteads, and central places, all deployed in a grand regularity of spacing and alignment? I, for one, do not feel confident of the answer, but let us hypothesize that by 1812, when the General Land Office was founded to exercise central authority over sales, the Expanded Feedback System shown in figure 3 had at least come into being.[19] Somewhere ahead lay the time when information from the geometrizing landscape would be taken seriously in discussions of land policy. But, by then, it was too late for relaxation, let alone rejection, of the partitioning scheme.

That macroarchitecture, with which we are all familiar and to which many geographers have felt a quite considerable attraction, emerged through an adaptive process (normally rather time consuming). Again and again in the wake of survey and sale, an original pioneer landscape, with roads following the easiest routes, gave way to a conforming landscape in which a new, rectified road network appeared, along with other obvious adjustments. Completion, or near completion, of the changeover produced the "county atlas image" of America, so capably examined in recent years by Norman Thrower.[20] I think of the process itself as coming under Fred Kniffen's concept of "initial occupance."[21]

It is a temptation to presume that the geometrized landscape, when achieved, was a fulfillment of the old Jeffersonian dream. The fourth thesis simply says, not so. I am convinced, mainly by Jefferson's correspondence, that he did not envision such a landscape effect. That he hoped to preprint jurisdictional bounds on the ground is unquestionable, as is his intent to fix permanently a network of very widely spaced reference lines for recordkeeping.[22] But I would suggest that his own experience with *property limits* in Virginia gave him little or no cause to expect that their western counterparts would prevail as long-term controls over the organization of roads and other physical features.[23]

To conclude, this paper will have served its purpose if its several leading propositions provoke debate or otherwise give structure to inquiry. The principles underlying them apply, I believe, not only to the present occasion—that of a dialogue between Professor Johnson and myself—but also in some measure to the enterprise of historical geography at large.

NOTES

1. Hildegard Binder Johnson, "Rational and Ecological Aspects of the Quarter Section: An Example from Minnesota," *Geographical Review* 47 (July 1957): 330-48.
2. William D. Pattison, *Beginnings of the American Rectangular Land Survey System, 1784-1800*, University of Chicago, Department of Geography, Research Paper no. 50 (1957).
3. For discussion of rectilinear partitioning in the context of the three laws, see ibid., pp. 3-67.
4. See section titled "The Geographical Mile" in William D. Pattison, "The Original Plan for an American Rectangular Land Survey," *Surveying and Mapping* 21 (September 1961): 342.
5. Thomas Jefferson, *Report of the Secretary of State, on the Subject of Establishing a Uniformity in the Weights, Measures, and Coins of the United States* (New York: N.p., 1790).
6. The full text of the new law (the Land Ordinance of 1785) appears, among other places, in Julian P. Boyd, ed., *The Papers of Thomas Jefferson* (Princeton, N.J.: Princeton University Press, 1950-), 7:140-47.
7. William Grayson of Virginia, who steered the new law to passage, feared that its provisions for prior survey and sale, quite as much as the partitioning design, would appear eccentric and objectionable. Grayson to George Washington, 15 April 1785, in Edmund C. Burnett, ed., *Letters of Members of the Continental Congress* (Washington, D.C.: Carnegie Institute of Washington, 1921-35), 8:96.
8. Richard Spaight to the governor of North Carolina, 5 June 1785, in Burnett, *Letters of Members*, p. 135.
9. Washington to Grayson, 22 August 1785, in John C. Fitzpatrick, ed., *The Writings of George Washington from the Original Manuscript Sources, 1745-1799* (Washington, D.C.: Government Printing Office, 1931-44), 28:234.

10. The congressional attitude toward land disposal is a theme of "The Land Ordinance of 1785," in Pattison, *Beginnings*, chap. 4, pp. 82-104.
11. Grayson to Washington, 15 April 1785, in Burnett, *Letters of Members*, pp. 95-96.
12. Monroe to Jefferson, 12 April 1785, in Stanislaus M. Hamilton, ed., *The Writings of James Monroe* (New York: G. P. Putnam's Sons, 1898-1903), 1:71.
13. The full text of the Land Act of 1796 appears, among other places, in Clarence E. Carter, ed., *The Territorial Papers of the United States* (Washington, D.C.: Government Printing Office, 1934-), 2:552-57.
14. These outcomes are covered in William D. Pattison, "The Survey of the Seven Ranges," *Ohio Historical Quarterly* 68 (April 1959): 115-40.
15. This sequence is accounted for in Pattison, *Beginnings*, pp. 185-204, 205, fn. 2.
16. Pattison, *Beginnings*, p. 132.
17. This provision for "overs and shorts" is quoted in C. E. Sherman, *Original Ohio Land Subdivisions*, Ohio Cooperative Topographic Survey Final Report (1925), 3:183-84. The earliest systematic instructions for implementing the provision may be found ibid., pp. 193-201.
18. For provisions on subdividing in laws of 1805, 1820, and 1932, see U.S., *Statutes at Large*, 2:313; 3:566; 4:503.
19. The significance of this date is that it marked the beginning of a three-year pause in westward expansion (because of the War of 1812), after which a vastly enlarged and accelerated survey program opened.
20. On the rectilinear macroarchitecture of a specimen area as of 1875, several decades after the time of the area's original survey, see Norman J. W. Thrower, *Original Survey and Land Subdivision: A Comparative Study of the Form and Effect of Contrasting Cadastral Surveys*, Association of American Geographers Monograph no. 4 (Chicago: Rand McNally & Co., 1966), pp. 82-85, 92-101, 112.
21. "By initial occupance . . . is meant the first post-pioneer, permanent settlement imprint" (Fred Kniffen, "Folk Housing: Key to Diffusion," *Annals of the Association of American Geographers* 55 [December 1965]: 551).
22. "Jurisdictional bounds on the ground" refers to the outlines of hundreds (or townships) and counties. "Widely spaced reference lines for record keeping" refers to the limits of Jeffersonian lots, occurring at intervals of one geographical mile.
23. Here I rely upon an unpublished memorandum by Carville Earle, Department of Geography, University of Maryland, Baltimore County, confirming the cross-property routing of roads in the country familiar to Jefferson. For Jefferson on the opening of new roads at variance with property boundaries, see Thomas Jefferson, *Notes on the State of Virginia*, ed. William Peden (Chapel Hill: University of North Carolina Press, 1955), pp. 136-37.

Original and Published Sources in Research in Historical Geography A Comparison

HERMAN R. FRIIS

Most historical geographers will agree that of all the branches into which geography is divided, historical geography is perhaps one of the most difficult, time-consuming, and taxing of one's patience. This is partly because the further back in time we project our study, the more difficult it is to find the sources. Correlatively, it is also difficult and often impossible to accurately and objectively appraise these sources for use, particularly if the only extant records are in published form.

Each mature and experienced researcher knows only too well that he must be continuously on guard against accepting as usable information all that is written, and, especially, that which is published. In short, he must know his sources. These sources normally are referred to as "original" and "published." The word "original" means, to most of us, the beginning, origin, first, initial, and earliest.[1] "Published," on the other hand, means to issue copies, by printing or other process, in multiple quantities for distribution.[2] A published item is normally derived from a unique "original."

Scholarly research requires both kinds of sources. Each of us who publishes the findings of his research for others to use has an obligation to identify the sources and to prove the veracity of the secondary or published source as well as that of the original. We could cite numerous examples to show that if we do not do this we may perpetuate errors of fact.

Some historical geographers in their research have carefully examined, appraised, and used the original records of public land surveys, official decennial censuses, land use, Indian land cessions, plats of survey of the public domain for initial settlement, and the distribution of original vegetation cover that are in the National Archives.[3] There are others who have researched railroad archives, state and local archives and libraries, and the private papers and official records in foreign archives and libraries.[4] These individuals are to be commended because this is fundamental research which requires infinite patience and maximum effort. It is research mainly in the original or an acknowledged primary source.

In keeping with the theme of the session on Exploration, Surveying, and Mapping, let us examine and compare the "original" and "published" versions of several representative examples pertaining to the American West that are in the National Archives.[5]

The first of the great government-sponsored exploring expeditions in the American West was authorized by President Thomas Jefferson in 1803, in order to find a satisfactory route across the newly acquired territory of the Louisiana Purchase. Meriwether Lewis and William Clark, leaders of the expedition, were the first to make known the vast extent and principal physiographic regions of the northwestern quadrant of the United States. Among their valuable cartographic contributions was a map of the United States, west of the Mississippi River, based on information made available to them while they wintered in the Mandan villages in the Great Bend of the Missouri River in 1804-5.[6] This map shows their concept of the American West before they undertook their epochal transect to the western ocean in 1805-6.

The map, drawn by William Clark, was sent down the Missouri River with other records of the expedition in the spring of 1805 and forwarded to President Jefferson.[7] Jefferson then sent it to Albert Gallatin, secretary of the treasury, who employed the competent Washington cartographer, Nicholas King, to make at least three copies of the map.[8] For some one hundred sixty-five years one of these copies (figure 1) has been filed among the official records of the War Department that now are in the National Archives.[9] The other copies accompanied Jefferson's message of February 19, 1806, to the Senate and the House of Representatives but are missing. We will not describe here the circumstances of the map's construction and the variant forms and versions that are found in other depositories. For these details I refer you to an article by Ralph Ehrenberg, who is making a study of King's geographical and cartographic contributions.[10]

This manuscript map was not reproduced for use in the official account of the expedition, edited for publication by Nicholas Biddle and

Paul Allen, published in Philadelphia in 1814.[11] Various editions and versions of this account were published prior to the so-called definitive work by the reputable scientist, Dr. Elliott Coues, in 1893, but, apparently, no faithfully accurate copy of the King map was reproduced with them prior to the one in the Coues edition. In this edition Coues notes, in part:

> This is the very map which was sent to the President, April 7, 1805, was transmitted by Jefferson to Congress in his message of February 19th, 1806, and was preserved in the archives of the War Department, but never published till Nov. 4th, 1887 [by Arnold Hague]. . . . As draughted by Nicholas King, 1806, this is the map which is repeatedly cited in the present edition [of Coues] as Lewis' map of 1806, it being so legended, as will be seen from the full-sized photographic facsimile, now first published.[12]

According to the note below the right bottom border of this map in Coues (figure 2), it is "reproduced from the original of the Lithotype Printing Company, 111 Nassau Street, N.Y."[13] The manuscript "original" King map (figure 1) measures 29⅝ by 40½ inches between neatlines, whereas the map in Coues measures 19⅞ by 28⅝ inches. Comparison of the two maps immediately reveals that Coues's map *is not*, as he says, a full-sized photographic facsimile. This is a misstatement which, incidentally, has been repeated by scholars, such as the historian, Reuben Gold Thwaites, who have cited Coues without checking the original.[14] The Coues map is an obvious inaccurate redrafting of the original. For example, the technique of rendering is strikingly different, as is the lettering and placement of information on the map.

Shortly after the summer of 1820, Stephen Harriman Long and his exploring expedition that traversed the vast expanses of the northern half of the Mississippi Valley returned to Washington and to Philadelphia.[15] The presumed official *Account* of this remarkable exploration was published in 1823 by Dr. Edwin James, scientist-historian of the expedition.[16] Between his return in 1820 and his departure on another exploring expedition in 1823, Major Long, with the able assistance of Lt. William H. Swift, compiled one of the most remarkable maps in the history of American cartography (figure 3). It is titled, "Map of the Country Situated Between the Meridian of Washington City and the Rocky Mountains exhibiting the route of the late Exploring Expedition commanded by Maj. Long, together with other recent surveys and explorations by himself and others. . . ." This manuscript original map is on a scale of thirty-six miles to an inch and measures 52½ by 46 inches between neatlines.

With the James edition of his *Account* is a printed map titled "Map

141

FIG. 1. "A Map of part of the Continent of North America, Between the 35th and 51st degrees of North Latitude, and extending from 89° Degrees of West Longitude to the Pacific Ocean. Compiled from the Authorities of the best informed travellers, by M. Lewis. . . . Copied by Nicholas King, 1806. Scale 50 miles to an Inch." Dimensions: 29⅜ by 40½ inches. Manuscript map in ink on paper. (Office of the Chief of Engineers, Headquarters Map Files, Ama 21, National Archives Building.)

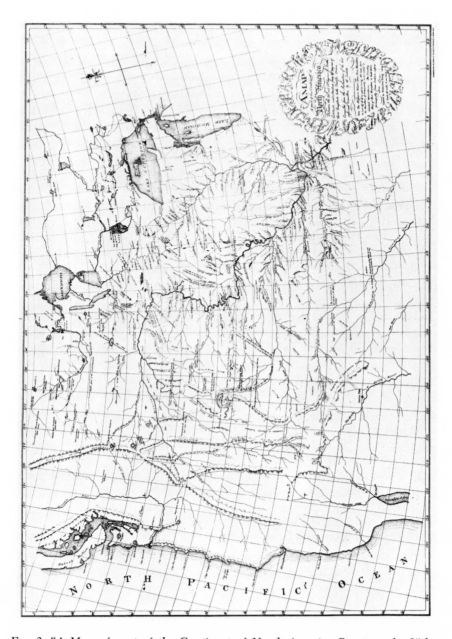

Fig. 2. "A Map of part of the Continent of North America Between the 35th and 51st degrees of North Latitude, and extending from 89° Degrees of West Longitude to the Pacific Ocean. Compiled from the Authorities of the best informed travellers, by M. Lewis. . . . Copied by Nicholas King 1806. Scale 50 miles to an Inch." Dimensions: 19⅞ by 28⅝ inches. Printed map on paper. (Elliott Coues, History of the Expedition under the Command of Lewis and Clark . . . , vol. 4 [New York: Francis P. Harper, 1893], pocket.)

of the Country Drained by the Mississippi." (Figure 4) It is on a scale of approximately sixty miles to an inch and measures 11-15/16 by 19-9/10 inches between neatlines. To my knowledge, the original Long map has never been published with an official government publication nor has it ever been published with any other printed account of the expedition. It is obvious that these two maps are cartographically quite different, yet there are striking similarities. The Long map includes a number of annotations about terrain, Indian population, and various cultural features, and it covers a much larger area of the United States. Scholars and others publishing in the field have not referred to the manuscript original, rather they have referred to and used with their publications the much reduced, redrafted, inadequate published version. For example, in the 1957 publication by Harlin M. Fuller and LeRoy R. Hafen of *The Journal of Captain John R. Bell, Official Journalist of the Stephen H. Long Expedition* . . . , is a copy of the published map with the notation that it was "prepared by Lieut. W. H. Swift and Major S. H. Long."[17] There appears to be no evidence that this published map was prepared by Swift and Long, though it appears to have been derived from it. What a pity these authors did not reproduce the Long and Swift manuscript original, figure 3. Similarly, Reuben Gold Thwaites in his edited reproduction of the James *Account* in his series of volumes on *Early Western Travels 1748-1846*, published in 1905, used only the printed map.[18]

Let us examine another form of presentation that requires continuous reference to and use of the original. The problems are pointed out by Donald Jackson and Mary Lee Spence, editors of the papers of *The Expeditions of John Charles Frémont*, volume 1, which was published in 1970. In this scholarly publication these editors show, by illustration (figures 5 and 6), that some of the letters signed as J. C. Frémont were indeed composed, signed, and posted by his wife, Jessica Benton Frémont, during his absence.[19] The letter in figure 5 was prepared and signed by Frémont; and the one in figure 6, bearing his name, was composed and signed by his wife. If the user of the printed, published version of the letter is not aware of this difference, and if the editor or publisher does not note this difference, the unwary searcher using the published version who does not compare them with the original will have been in error.

Landscape views and related kinds of illustrations are potentially an important source of visual or graphic information to historical geographers. But how reliable are they, and how certain can we be that they reflect the landscape or object viewed by the author of the original

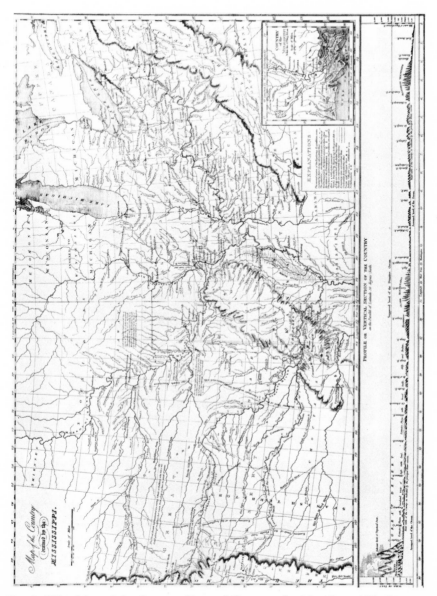

Fig. 3. "This Map of the Country Situated Between the Meridian of Washington City and the Rocky Mountains exhibiting the route of the late Exploring Expedition commanded by Maj. Long, together with recent surveys and explorations by himself and others is most respectfully inscribed, by his most obedient and humble servant S. H. Long, Major, U. S. Topl. Engineers . . . To the Hon. John C. Calhoun, Secy of War . . . Scale of Miles: 36 to an inch." Dimensions: 54½ by 48¾ inches (edge of map) and 52½ by 46 inches (neatline). Manuscript map in color and in ink on paper. (Office of the Chief of Engineers, Headquarters Map Files, U.S. 62, National Archives Building.)

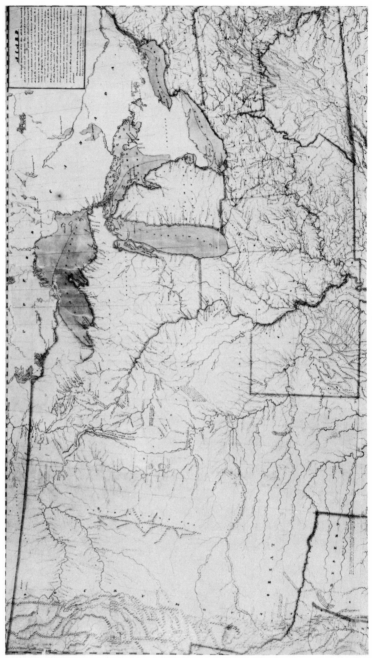

FIG. 4. *"Map of the Country drained by the Mississippi [River] . . . Prepared by Lieut. W. H. Swift and Major S. H. Long."* Scale: approximately one inch to sixty miles. Dimensions: 11-15/16 by 19-9/10 inches. Printed map on paper. (Reprinted, by permission of the publishers, The Arthur H. Clark Com-

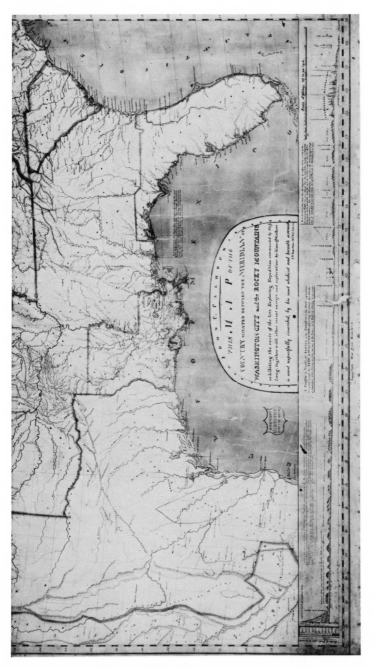

pany, from The Journal of Captain John R. Bell, Official Journalist for the Stephen H. Long Expedition to the Rocky Mountains, 1820, *by Harlin M. Fuller and LeRoy R. Hafen, vol. 6 [1957], map opposite p. 338, in LeRoy R. Hafen, ed.,* The Far West and the Rockies Historical Series, 1820-1875.)

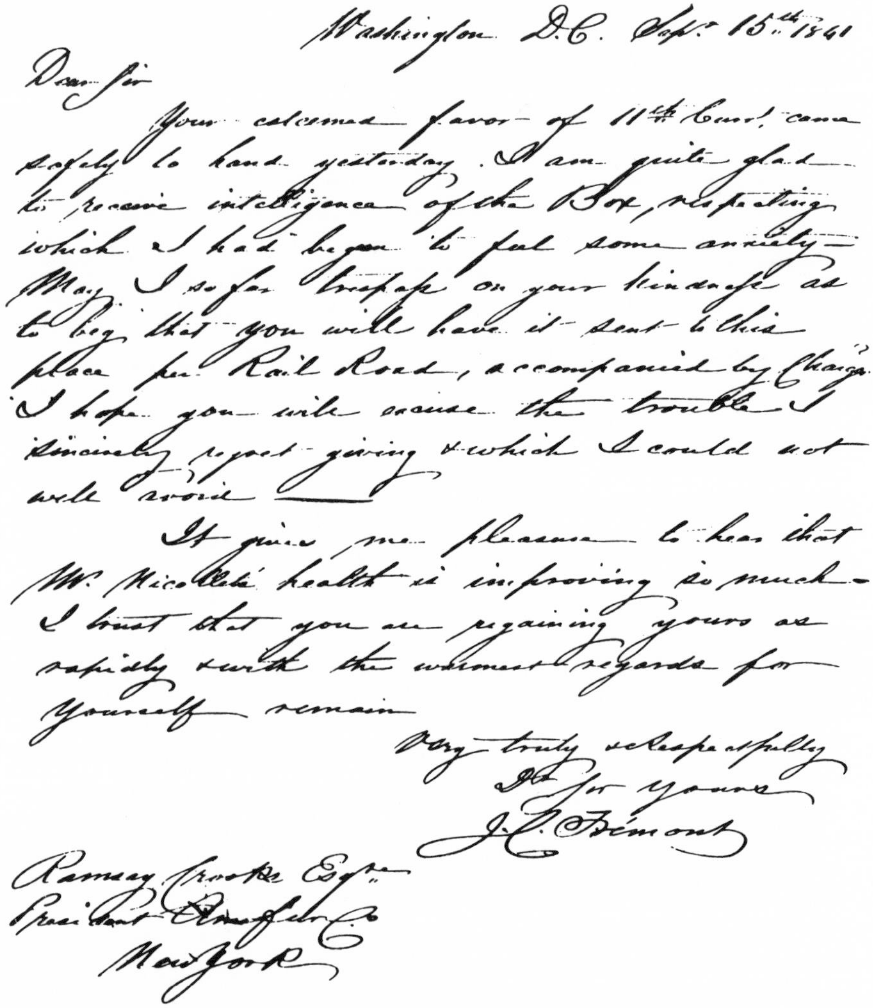

Washington D.C. Sept. 15th 1841

Dear Sir

Your esteemed favor of 11th Curt. came safely to hand yesterday. I am quite glad to receive intelligence of the Box, respecting which I had begun to feel some anxiety— May I so far trespass on your kindness as to beg that you will have it sent to this place per Rail Road, accompanied by Charges. I hope you will excuse the trouble I sincerely regret giving & which I could not well avoid.

It gives me pleasure to hear that Mr. Nicollet's health is improving so much— I trust that you are regaining yours as rapidly & with the warmest regards for yourself remain

Very truly & respectfully
Sir Yours
J. C. Frémont

Ramsay Crooks Esqre
President Am. Fur Co.
New York

A letter by Frémont, in his handwriting

FIG. 5. *Letter from J. C. Frémont to Ramsay Crooks, "Washington, D.C. Sept 15th 1841," identified as "A letter by Frémont, in his handwriting." (Reproduced, by permission of the publisher, University of Illinois Press, from* The Expeditions of John Charles Frémont, *vol. 1 [1970], p. xl, by Donald Jackson and Mary Lee Spence, eds.)*

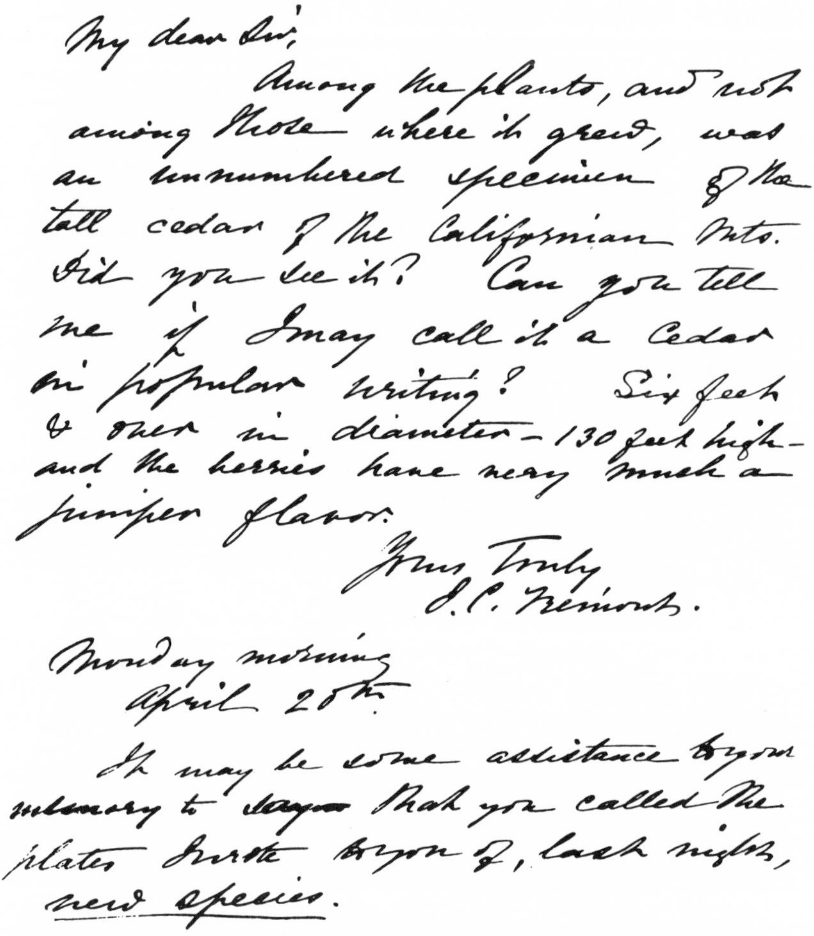

My dear Sir;

Among the plants, and not among those where it grew, was an unnumbered specimen of the tall cedar of the Californian Mts. Did you see it? Can you tell me if I may call it a Cedar in popular writing? Six feet & over in diameter - 130 feet high - and the berries have very much a juniper flavor.

Yours Truly
J. C. Frémont.

Monday morning
April 20th.

It may be some assistance to your memory to say that you called the plates I wrote to you of, last night, new species.

A letter by Frémont, in the handwriting of Jessie Benton Frémont

Fig. 6. *Letter from J. C. Frémont to* ____________________, *"Monday morning April 20th," identified as "A letter by Frémont, in the handwriting of Jesse Benton Frémont." (Reproduced, by permission of the publisher, University of Illinois Press, from* The Expeditions of John Charles Frémont, *vol. 1* [*1970*], *p. xli, by Donald Jackson and Mary Lee Spence, eds.)*

rather than the artistic talents of the lithographer or copy artist or, perhaps, the editor of the publication?

One of the most remarkable publications by the federal government during the mid-nineteenth century was the twelve-volume work comprising the official "Reports of Explorations and Surveys, to Ascertain the Most Practicable and Economical Route for a Railroad from the Mississippi River to the Pacific Ocean. Made under the Direction of the Secretary of War."[20] With these reports are exquisitely beautiful color lithographic plates of landscape sketches.[21] One of these (figure 7) appears with Lt. John G. Parke's printed report of his surveys in California in 1854-55.[22] It is titled, "Guadalupe Largo and San Luis Harbor [California]." With the original manuscript records in the National Archives are a few surviving original watercolor sketches prepared by the artists in the field with these expeditions for use by the lithographer in producing the lithographs. The original landscape view of "Guadalupe Largo and San Luis Harbor" (figure 8) was prepared by A. H. Campbell, artist-topographer, on the expedition.[23] Comparison of these two views reveals that the lithographer did, indeed, take many liberties with the original.

Frequently, official publications by the federal government are abbreviated or condensed versions of the original report, and they do not include the maps, landscape views, and related graphic materials accompanying the original.[24] This is understandable because the high cost of reproducing them is often prohibitive. The careful searcher may find, preserved with the original reports, these unpublished treasures of original information.[25] Unfortunately, many have been lost or were never returned to the government by the printers, engravers, and lithographers to whom they were sent for reproduction.

For example, in 1859 Capt. James Hervey Simpson commanded a topographical reconnaissance and mapping survey "across the Great Basin of the Territory of Utah for a direct wagon route from Camp Floyd, Utah, to Genoa in Carson Valley."[26] The routes of this reconnaissance are shown on a manuscript map compiled on a scale of one inch to approximately seventeen miles. This map was prepared for and published in the official report, which was not printed until 1876. However, this excellent report, a significant source of information on the geography of the region in 1859, does not include reproductions of the watercolor landscape views such as "Lake Bigler from the East (Sierra Nevada)" (figure 9) delineated by J. J. Young. Lake Bigler is in the foothills of Carson Valley shown in the far left or west on the map. There is a surprising volume of such original land-

Fig. 7. *"Guadalupe Largo & San Luis Harbor [California] . . . by A. H. Campbell . . . General Report, Plate 1 . . . ," ca. 1854. Dimensions: eleven by eight
inches. (John G. Parke, "Report of Explorations for Railroad Route from San
Francisco Bay to Los Angeles, California, West of the Coast Range . . . ,"*
Explorations and Surveys for a Railroad Route from the Mississippi River to
the Pacific Ocean *. . . , vol. 7 [Washington, D.C.: George W. Bowman, 1857].
The colored lithographic landscape sketch is opposite text page 1.)*

FIG. 8. *Guadalupe Largo and San Luis Harbor, California, presumably by Albert H. Campbell. Dimensions: six by nine inches. A watercolor sketch on paper. Probably the artist's original from which figure 7 was derived. (Office of the Secretary of the Interior, Pacific Railroad Surveys, General, Illustrations, National Archives Building.)*

Fig. 9. *"Lake Bigler from the East (Sierra Nevada). J. J. Young, del. Journal Plate IX."* Dimensions: 11⅜ by 23⅜ inches. Watercolor sketch on paper. *(Office of the Chief of Engineers, Headquarters Map Files, Misc. 120(5), National Archives Building.)*

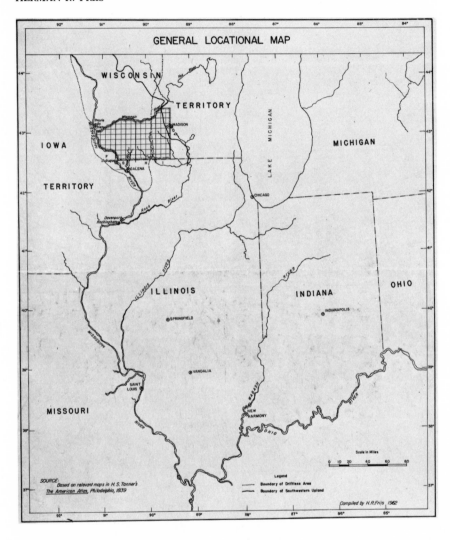

FIG. 10. "*General Locational Map* [*of Illinois, Wisconsin, Iowa, Michigan, Indiana, and Missouri showing place names and the area of Wisconsin covered by the Owen Survey in 1839*]. *Compiled by H. R. Friis 1962.*" *Scale: one inch to fifteen miles. Dimensions: 29⅝ by 26⅝ inches. Manuscript map in ink on paper. (National Archives Gift Collection of Materials Relating to Polar Regions, Papers of Herman R. Friis, National Archives Building.)*

154

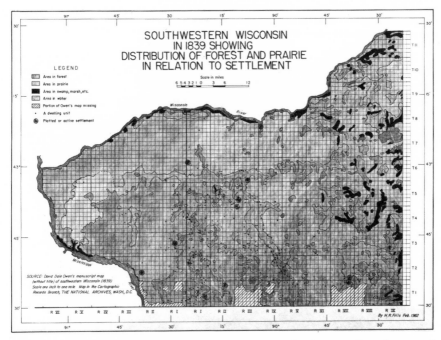

Fig. 11. "[*Map of*] *Southwestern Wisconsin in 1839 Showing Distribution of Forest and Prairie in Relation to Settlement. By H. R. Friis Feb. 1962.*" *Scale: one inch to four miles. Dimensions: 17¼ by 25¼ inches. Manuscript map in ink and color wash. (National Archives Gift Collection of Materials Relating to Polar Regions, Papers of Herman R. Friis, National Archives Building.)*

scape views, pencil sketches, edited lithographs, and similar graphic records that await the patient researcher.

The resources of the National Archives include a large number of manuscript records, such as manuscript maps and charts, that are unique; they have never been published and only rarely have they been examined by historical geographers. An example of how such a resource may be used in geographical research is that of the large, four-sheet manuscript map of southwestern Wisconsin, which as a unit measures sixty-eight by ninety-four inches. This map was discovered among the records of the United States Senate in the National Archives.[27] The area covered by the map is shown in figure 10. Research in the National Archives appears to prove that this manuscript original was compiled in 1840 in the General Land Office, on a scale of one mile to an inch from larger scale survey plats made in southwestern Wisconsin by Dr.

David Dale Owen, a geologist from New Harmony, Indiana, in the fall of 1839 for the General Land Office.[28] The large-scale plats appear to be missing from the official records of the General Land Office. Information shown on the recently (1962) compiled manuscript map (figure 11) is derived from the large-scale manuscript original map. It has been plotted in the precise location within each township as on the original. The result, in this case, is a map showing the distribution of dwelling units in relation to woodland and prairie as shown on the General Land Office map compiled from Owen's plats to accompany, but never published with, his report.

These few examples of original records in the National Archives are indicative of a treasure trove so vast, so pulsing with opportunity, that no one of us can comprehend the infinite potentialities of the resources. It defies our fondest imagination and should encourage our inquisitive sense to discover the "original" in preference to accepting on faith the "published" record.

NOTES

1. "Original" is defined as "a primary manuscript from which copies are made, . . . a work composed first hand . . . ," in Philip B. Gove, ed., *Webster's Third New International Dictionary of the English Language Unabridged*, s.v. "original."
2. The definition of "published" is "to produce for publication or allow to be issued for distribution or sale . . . ," ibid., s.v. "published."
3. Ralph H. Brown, *Mirror for Americans; Likeness of the Eastern Seaboard, 1810* (New York: American Geographical Society, 1943); idem, *Historical Geography of the United States* (New York: American Geographical Society, 1948); Herman R. Friis, *A Series of Population Maps of the Colonies and the United States, 1625-1790*, American Geographical Society Mimeographed and Offset Publication no. 3 (New York: 1940; rev. ed., 1968), pp. 1-46; Joseph A. Hazel, "Semimicrostudies of Counties from the Manuscripts of the Census of 1860," *The Professional Geographer* 17, no. 4 (Lawrence, Kans., 1965): 15-19; H. Roy Merrens, "Historical Geography and Early American History," *William and Mary Quarterly* 22 (1965): 529-48; idem, "Source Materials for the Geography of Colonial America," *The Professional Geographer* 15, no. 1 (1963): 8-11; William D. Pattison, "Use of the U. S. Public Land Survey Plats and Notes as Descriptive Sources," *The Professional Geographer* 8, no. 1 (1956): 10-14.
4. Douglas R. McManis, "English Evaluation of North American Iron during the Late Sixteenth and Early Seventeenth Centuries," *The Professional Geographer* 21, no. 2 (1969): 93-96; Donald W. Meinig, "Railroad Archives and the Historical Geographer," *The Professional Geographer* 7, no. 3

(1955): 7-10; Robert M. Newcomb, "The British Parish Church as a Repository of Landscape History," *The Professional Geographer* 18, no. 1 (1966): 3-4.
5. The primary depository of cartographic and related records of the United States government is the National Archives in Washington, D. C. Significantly, this large resource comprises the Cartographic Archives Division. The basic reference to these records is *Guide to Cartographic Records in the National Archives,* National Archives Publication no. 71-16 (1971): 1-444. In addition, inventories and special lists have been compiled for a number of the record groups. These are listed in *Cartographic Records in the National Archives,* General Information Leaflet no. 26 (Washington, D. C., 1973). For published articles on the history of surveying, mapping, and geographical exploration, as reflected in these records, see Martin P. Claussen and Herman R. Friis, *Descriptive Catalog of Maps Published by Congress, 1817-1843* (Washington, D.C.: Privately published, 1941); Ralph E. Ehrenberg, "Cartographic Records on the Red River Region in the National Archives," *Red River Valley Historian* 2 (1968): 5-7; idem, *Geographical Exploration and Mapping in the Nineteenth Century: A Survey of the Records in the National Archives,* Reference Information Paper no. 66 (1973), 22 pp.; Herman R. Friis, *A Catalog of an Exhibit Showing Federal Exploration of the American West before 1860,* National Archives Publication no. 64-6 (Washington, D. C., 1963), pp. 1-31; idem, "Highlights of the First Hundred Years of Surveying and Mapping and of Geographical Exploration of the United States by the Federal Government, 1775-1880," *Journal of the American Congress on Surveying and Mapping* 18, no. 2 (1958): 186-206; idem, "Highlights of the Geographical and Cartographical Contributions of Graduates of the U. S. Military Academy with a Specialization as Topographical Engineers prior to 1860," *Proceedings of the Eighth Annual Meeting of the New York-New Jersey Division of the Association of American Geographers* 1 (April 1968): 10-29; idem, "The Documents and Reports of the United States Congress: A Primary Source of Information on Travel in the West, 1783-1861," *Travelers on the Western Frontier,* ed. John F. McDermott (Urbana: University of Illinois Press, 1970), pp. 112-67; idem, "The Image of the American West at Mid-Century (1840-1860): A Product of Scientific Geographical Exploration by the United States Government," *The Frontier Re-examined,* ed. John F. McDermott (Urbana: University of Illinois Press, 1967), pp. 49-63.
6. The following are a few of the references to this map: Annie H. Abel, "A New Lewis and Clark Map," *The Geographical Review 1* (1916): 329-45; John L. Allen, "Lewis & Clark on the Upper Missouri. Decision at the Marias," *Montana, the Magazine of Western History* 21, no. 3 (1971): 2-17; Jesse S. Douglas, "Lewis Map of 1806," *The Journal of Military Affairs* 5 (1941): 68-72; Arnold Hague, "An Early Map of the Far West," *Science* 10, no. 248 (1887): 217-18; Donald Jackson, "A New Lewis and Clark Map," *Bulletin of the Missouri Historical Society* 17 (1961): 117-32; Samuel Latham Mitchill, "Lewis's Map of the Parts of North-America which Lie between the 35th and 51st Degrees of North Latitude from the Mississippi and the Upper Lakes to the North Pacific Ocean," *Medical Repository,* 2d hexade 3 (1806): 315-18.

7. Lewis to Jefferson, Fort Mandan, 7 April 1805, in Donald Jackson, ed., *Letters of the Lewis and Clark Expedition with Related Documents, 1783-1854* (Urbana: University of Illinois Press, 1962), p. 233.
8. Herman R. Friis, "Cartographic and Geographic Activities of the Lewis and Clark Expedition," *Journal of the Washington Academy of Sciences* 44 (1954): 348-49.
9. It was reproduced but to a considerably reduced scale in Hague, "An Early Map." It appears to have been in the map files of the Topographical Bureau of the War Department in 1818 or earlier, as it is recorded in a register of maps the bureau began about that date, probably by Isaac Roberdeau, a leading topographical engineer on the staff.
10. Ralph Ehrenberg, "Nicholas King: First Surveyor of the City of Washington, 1803-1812," *Records of the Columbia Historical Society* 69/70 (1971): 31-64.
11. Nicholas Biddle and Paul Allen, eds., *History of the Expedition under the Command of Captains Lewis and Clark . . . Performed during the Years 1804-5-6. By Order of the Government of the United States*, 2 vols. (Philadelphia: Bradford and Inskeep, 1814).
12. Elliott Coues, *History of the Expedition under the Command of Lewis and Clark . . . : A New Edition Faithfully Reprinted from the Only Authorized Edition of 1814 . . .* (New York: Francis P. Harper, 1893), 1:221.
13. Ibid., "Tracing Copy of the Original Map Forwarded by Meriwether Lewis to President Jefferson from Fort Mandan, April 7, 1805," vol. 4, pocket.
14. Reuben G. Thwaites, ed., *Original Journals of the Lewis and Clark Expedition, 1804-1806 . . .* (New York: Dodd, Mead & Co., 1904-5), 1:244; reproduced in the atlas volume.
15. Herman R. Friis, "Stephen H. Long's Unpublished Manuscript Map of the United States Compiled in 1820-1822(?)," *The California Geographer* 8 (1967): 75-88.
16. Edwin James, comp., *Account of an Expedition from Pittsburgh to the Rocky Mountains, Performed in the Years 1819 and 1820 . . . under the Command of Major Stephen H. Long . . .*, 2 vols. (Philadelphia: Carey & Lea, 1823). Reproduced in Thwaites, ed., *Early Western Travels 1748-1846*, vols. 14-17 (Cleveland: Arthur H. Clark Co., 1905).
17. Harlan M. Fuller and LeRoy R. Hafen, ed., "The Journal of Captain John R. Bell, Official Journalist for the Stephen H. Long Expedition to the Rocky Mountains, 1820," in *The Far West and Rockies Historical Series* 6 (Glendale, Calif.: Arthur H. Clark Co., 1957): 1-349.
18. Thwaites, *Early Western Travels*.
19. These are reproduced on pages xl and xli in Donald Jackson and Mary Lee Spence, eds., *The Expeditions of John Charles Frémont*, vol. 1 (Urbana: University of Illinois Press, 1970), travels from 1838 to 1844. For comments see p. xxxiii as follows:

    "Because Jessie B. Frémont wrote and signed many of her husband's letters, we have felt that there should be some indication of this to the reader. Our solution to the problem is set forth in the list of symbols."
20. *Reports of Explorations and Surveys, to Ascertain the Most Practicable and Economical Route for a Railroad from the Mississippi River to the Pacific Ocean. Made under the Direction of the Secretary of War, in 1853-56,*

U.S., Congress, Senate, *Executive Document* no. 78, 33d Cong., 2d sess., to 36th Cong., 2d sess., 1855-61. Many of the manuscript compilations of these reports and a few of the field survey maps are with the Records of the Office of the Secretary of the Interior, Record Group 48, in the National Archives. Not all of these were printed and included with the published volumes. Related materials can be found with the Records of the Office of the Chief of Engineers, Record Group 77, in the National Archives. (Hereafter records of the National Archives Building are indicated by the symbol NA. The symbol RG is used for record group.)

21. The provenance of these sketches is listed in Robert Taft, "The Pictorial Records of the Old West. 14. Illustrations of the Pacific Survey Reports," *Kansas Historical Quarterly* 19 (1951): 379-80.

22. "Routes in California . . . explored by Lieut. John G. Parke, Corps of Topographical Engineers in 1854 and 1855," in *Reports of Explorations and Surveys, . . . 1853-6 . . .*, vol. 7, U.S., Congress, Senate, *Executive Document No. 78*, 33d Cong., 2d sess., 1857, General Report Plate 1, pp. 1-42.

23. This watercolor and ink landscape view was received in the former Cartographic Records Division from Adolph Hoen of the A. Hoen Company, Lithographers in Baltimore, Maryland, in 1946. Hoen had been requested by W. L. G. Joerg, chief of the Cartographic Records Division in the National Archives, to search his archives for records of the Pacific Railroad Surveys because the company was responsible for the lithographic work done on some of the maps and illustrations in the 1850s. Hoen brought to the division in 1948 an envelope of perhaps a dozen manuscript and annotated lithographic proofs, including Campbell's "Guadalupe Largo and San Luis Harbor." The manuscript drawings apparently are those made by survey artists or artists in the Office of Explorations and Surveys of the War Department from pencil field sketches.

24. For details as to what was published and what was not published, see the Congressional Serial Set, particularly the journals, of each congress.

25. See, for example, in the Records of the Office of the Chief of Engineers, RG 77; Records of the United States House of Representatives, RG 233; and Records of the United States Senate, RG 46, NA.

26. James Hervey Simpson, *Report of Explorations across Great Basin of Utah for Direct Wagon-Route from Camp Floyd to Genoa in Carson Valley, in 1859* (Washington, D. C.: Government Printing Office, 1876). Simpson's manuscript report to Col. John A. Abert, chief of the Corps of Topographical Engineers, dated February 5, 1861 (Washington), is in the Records of the Office of the Chief of Engineers, RG 77, NA. Manuscript illustrations, maps, and profiles which were included with the report are filed as Misc. 120 and W 67 in the Records of the Office of the Chief of Engineers, RG 77, in the Cartographic Archives Division, NA.

27. It was received with a body of fugitive "oversize" records found in the Senate Office Building in 1938 and transferred to the then Division of Maps and Charts (currently the Cartographic Archives Division) in the National Archives. It is filed among the cartographic records of the Records of the United States Senate, RG 46, NA.

28. Herman R. Friis, "The David Dale Owen Map of Southwestern Wisconsin, 1839," *Prologue: The Journal of the National Archives* 1, no. 1 (Spring 1969): 9-28.

159

Discussion Summary

The discussion was conducted by *Lester J. Cappon, editor-in-chief, Atlas of Early American History, Newberry Library,* chairman of the session on Exploration, Surveying, and Mapping.

Hallock F. Raup, editor, The Professional Geographer, Department of Geography, Kent State University, began the discussion by inquiring why the twenty-five-mile square rather than the thirty-six-mile square was used as a township size in the Western Reserve. *William D. Pattison, Department of Geography, University of Chicago,* replied that it was due to "convenience of calculation. . . . You had an acreage figure that was a lot easier to handle, and the land company responsible for disposing of the land in the Western Reserve seemed to prefer it." Dr. Pattison added that many different township dimensions were suggested in the journals of Congress, with "representatives from New England and New York preferring seven miles to six." Dr. Raup then asked, "Where else have non-thirty-six-mile units been in use?" *Hildegard B. Johnson, Department of Geography, Macalester College,* replied that she did not know of any other square-mile units but that the *sitios* in Texas were square. Dr. Johnson also suggested that "the probability is pretty high" that some of the California mission tracts might be in the form of a square. *Herman Friis, Center for Polar Archives, National Archives,* recalled seeing a copy of a map of the Upper Ohio River prepared by Thomas Hutchins in the 1760s that showed an area divided into squares. Dr. Pattison identified the map as Henry Bouquet's plan for settlement.

Continuing the discussion, *Louis De Vorsey, Jr., Department of Geography, University of Georgia,* added that in the state of Georgia a system of rectangular survey was used for the original granted lands. These were square lots of land that were "given to a lucky winner at a state lottery." They ranged in size from 40-acre lots to 490-acre lots.[1] Following this answer, *Jeremiah Post, Map Collection, Free Library of Philadelphia,* pointed out that while the rural areas in Georgia followed a rectilinear system of land sale, the municipal boundaries are circular. "The assumption then," Mr. Post concluded, "is that land sale had nothing to do with municipalities." Dr. De Vorsey agreed and referred him to an article in the *Southeastern Geographer* by Howard Schretter on "Round Towns."[2] "The systems that I am alluding to," Dr. De Vorsey added, "follow the individual cessions of Indian lands to the state of Georgia. As a piece of land was acquired either through federal or state negotiations, or both, with Indian tribes, surveyors were sent in by the state to survey those large tracts of land in a rectangular fashion. . . . This was done prior to allowing any settlers on the land." These cadastral surveys and accompanying documents, according to Dr. De Vorsey, are now in the Georgia Surveyor General Department, located in the Archives and Records Building in Atlanta, Georgia.

Richard Randall, Rand McNally & Company, then turned the discussion to the impact that the rectilinear coordinate survey had on subsequent surveying and property ownership. In response, Dr. Pattison cited Paul Gates's *The Farmers' Age: Agriculture 1815-1860* as one work showing that litigation, fraud, and resurvey occurred despite the precautionary measure of rectilinear partitioning.[3] Dr. Pattison, however, questioned Gates's "sense of proportion in that regard. . . . There is no question that litigation was by no means entirely obviated by the adoption of the system. At the same time, there is no question that in comparable areas which were open to so-called indiscriminate survey, the litigation was incomparably greater. Norman Thrower's two model areas, I think, should satisfy everyone on that score."[4]

Dr. Johnson generally agreed but pointed out that it is a counterfactual argument. "We do not know what did not happen. . . . As for this problem of inaccuracy," Dr. Johnson continued, "I find some signs perturbing." As an example she cited the continual resurveying of Dakota County, Minnesota. "We seem to run into a human equation which seems to be very difficult to solve. Some people will not fight over as much as two or three feet. Some people will fight over two inches with a property line post. . . . This sort of line-minded accuracy," she observed, "is an idea that is not restricted to the United States but is basically a product of Western civilization that can be traced right back to John Locke, among others." Dr. Pattison added that "there was an early rule of law stating that the content of the parcel, as conveyed by the government, was legally final, whether it tallied or not, that is, whether or not the measured content tallied with the declared content. And to my best knowledge, that protected the government as vendor effectively from about 1804 onward despite the convergence problem."

Frank C. Innes, Department of Geography, McGill University, then inquired whether there was any evidence in the United States that an area was mapped before the actual survey had taken place. He noted that in Canada this was often the case, particularly in Quebec where the lots are long and narrow. As a result, people were often located on lots that turned out to be muskeg or sog rather than land. Dr. Pattison replied that this often occurred in the United States. And cited Dennis Jean's article on the same topic to illustrate a similar occurrence in Australia.[5]

Eldor Pederson, Department of Geography, George Washington University, continued the discussion of the land survey system by raising the issue of land speculation. He suggested that the land survey system developed in the form of the rectilinear grid to ease subdivision for land speculators. Dr. Pattison concurred to some extent saying that the "adoption of the design was done largely in recognition of its expediting effect on the land market." Dr. Johnson agreed that the rectangular land coordinate system made land speculation much easier because "you deal with 'easily described' parcels." But, she said, the same can be said of irregular parcels of land. Dr. Johnson did not agree, however, that the land survey system was developed specifically for land speculators. "That this was the intent," she concluded, "I consider almost impossible to say. At least I have never read that anybody intended to make speculation easy by the system."

Continuing the discussion about the motivation of the origin of the land survey system, *Kay I. Kitagawa, Department of Defense,* inquired whether there was "any documentary evidence that the adoption of the Ordinance of 1785 was motivated in part or was motivated in consideration of the difficulties of the metes and bounds system where the mapping of Maryland and Virginia, of which Jefferson was a native, had posed such confusion." Dr. Pattison quoted Hugh Williamson, who was on the committee for the land ordinance with Thomas Jefferson, as saying that "it will save us millions." Williamson, according to Dr. Pattison, also believed that the adoption of the rectilinear survey would prevent fraud, which he had observed in court in North Carolina.

William H. Wallace, Department of Geography, University of New Hampshire, then wondered if there was any connection between the adoption of the rectangular land survey system in the Old Northwest and the earlier experiences with rectangular systems in New England, "where many of the towns are rectangular, and range roads and rectangular lots were being used certainly by 1720." Dr. Pattison cited Amelia Clearly Ford's study, "a doctoral study under Frederick Jackson Turner early in the century," as one that shows "a very considerable and direct connection."[6] Dr. Pattison's own conclusion, on the other hand, was that "there was no connection in the original formation, that is, in the Jeffersonian draft. . . . But New Englanders recognized in that scheme something that resembled theirs sufficiently such that they could get behind it, as they did. . . . Curiously in 1796," Dr. Pattison concluded, "according to the record, no New Englanders came forward in support of its readoption. Instead, upstate New York Congressmen did." A commentator from the floor then asked whether some of these New Yorkers had migrated from New England bringing along their "New England point of view." Dr. Pattison suggested that may have been the case. "In addition, of course," he added, "they could have learned from the federal ordinance of, by then, eleven years earlier." *Walter W. Ristow, chief, Geography and Map Division, Library of Congress,* then pointed out that Simeon DeWitt, the first surveyor general of New York State and the surveyor "who was offered the job of head of the General Land Office prior to the time William Hutchins was given it, did use the rectangular survey for the Military Land Survey in Upper New York State."

John L. Allen, Department of Geography, University of Connecticut, closed the discussion of the rectangular land survey by suggesting that behavioral factors played an important, motivating role. "We have to look at the characters that were involved in . . . the committee of 1784, the nature of their thought about natural efficiency and this kind of thing, . . . particularly when you view people such as Jefferson and his colleagues." Dr. Allen continued, "They were eighteenth-century rationalists, I think, and nature was ordered, it was efficient, more or less, and an efficient system imposed upon nature was the best of all possible worlds. I think this may play somewhat of a role in the original creation of the Jeffersonian concept in 1784, with the proper division of states into equal units and names drawn from a number of different sources, and so forth."

Roger T. Trindell, Department of Geography, Mansfield State College, then changed the topic of discussion with a question directed to Dr. Allen concerning the role that John Ledyard played in Thomas Jefferson's image of the route to the West. Dr. Allen replied that Ledyard's role "was certainly a pretty minor one. . . . By the time Jefferson came in contact with Ledyard, which was in 1785-86, while Jefferson was minister to France, he had already developed pretty firm notions of some things, in the western part of the country, anyway. And he was at that time in the process of gathering maps, geographical literature that had been compiled by the French during their tenure in Louisiana." This was followed by a short exchange between Drs. Trindell and Allen concerning Jefferson's intention to commission Ledyard to lead an ex-

163

pedition to the West prior to the Lewis and Clark Expedition. Dr. Allen then briefly reviewed several attempts made by Jefferson to commission western expeditions. "The first offer which Jefferson made to anyone was made in 1783 to George Rogers Clark who for a number of reasons said that he could not undertake such an expedition. The brief, rather intermittent, contact with Ledyard while Jefferson was in France was really kind of a minor thing. The first serious attempt made was in 1793 under the auspices of the American Philosophical Society with André Michaux, who actually was commissioned by the American Philosophical Society, and subscription papers were drawn up to which a number of people donated, including Washington and Jefferson." Dr. Trindell then suggested that Ledyard also spent some time on an actual reconnaissance of the Pacific Northwest Coast and prepared a report for Jefferson. Dr. Allen concurred saying that Ledyard had accompanied Capt. James Cook on his last voyage when he charted the Pacific Coast of North America.[7]

Clinton R. Edwards, Department of Geography, University of Wisconsin-Milwaukee, pointed out that there was an additional factor that determined Jefferson's image of a possible passage to India. "This factor was the technology of the times, specifically that water carriage, not overland carriage, was looked to for the conveyance of passengers and cargo on the putative route through the continent, thus the emphasis on rivers and their routes. . . . I suspect," Dr. Edwards concluded, "that if land carriage had been thought to be the ideal way, Jefferson would perhaps have emphasized the avoidance of rivers, or at least river crossings, and would have sent Lewis and Clark in a wagon train across the country instead of up the Missouri in boats." Dr. Allen added that he believed Jefferson might also have been thinking about the possibility of extending a canal across the Continental Divide in order to connect the navigable Missouri and the navigable Columbia, "if the distance were small enough." A similar scheme to connect the headwaters of the Potomac and Ohio rivers had been contemplated as early as the 1780s by Jefferson.

Preston James, Department of Geography, Syracuse University, directed the last question of the discussion period to Dr. De Vorsey. Dr. James inquired how De Brahm could measure longitude in 1765 east and west of Saint Augustine. Dr. De Vorsey replied that De Brahm relied upon land traverse and by "sort of correcting his movements, observing his distances very carefully, and then correcting that for westward or an eastward distance." He also pointed out that De Brahm used a chronometer on his last voyage. Dr. James then asked if De

Brahm had any chronometers with him before the Cook expeditions; Dr. De Vorsey responded that none were mentioned in his journals until 1775.

NOTES

1. An excellent recent discussion on this system, as well as other land survey systems in the southeast, is Sam B. Hilliard, "An Introduction to Land Survey Systems in the Southeast," *West Georgia College Studies in the Social Sciences* 12 (June 1973): 1-15.
2. Howard A. Schretter, "Round Towns," *Southeastern Geographer* 3 (1963): 46-52.
3. Paul W. Gates, *The Farmers' Age: Agriculture 1815-1860* (New York: Holt, Rineland and Winston, 1960).
4. Norman J. W. Thrower, *Original Survey and Land Subdivision: A Comparative Study of the Form and Effect of Contrasting Cadastral Surveys* (Chicago: Association of American Geographers, 1966).
5. Dennis N. Jeans, "The Breakdown of Australia's First Rectangular Survey," *Australian Geographical Studies* 4 (1966): 119-28.
6. Amelia C. Ford, *Colonial Precedents of Our National Land System as It Existed in 1800.* University of Wisconsin Bulletin no. 352. (Madison: University of Wisconsin, 1910).
7. The report that John Ledyard prepared was *A Journal of Captain Cook's Last Voyage to the Pacific Ocean, in Quest of a North-West Passage, between Asia and America, Performed in the Years 1776, 1777, 1778, and 1779.* It was first printed in 1783 and reprinted in 1963 (Chicago: Quadrangle Books). An edited version by James Kenneth Munford was published by the Oregon State University Press at Corvallis in 1964.

Transportation, Commerce, and Industry

Persistence, Failure, and Mobility in the Inner City: Preliminary Notes

MARTYN J. BOWDEN

The levels of geographic mobility in America in the nineteenth century are barely credible. Frontier county studies disclose that only a quarter of the farm operators enumerated at the beginning of a decade were there at the end.[1] A lower persistence rate for the urban population was found in Rochester for the period 1849-59 (20 percent) and a slightly higher one in Poughkeepsie for 1850-60.[2] Higher levels of persistence were found in Northampton, Massachusetts, for 1850-60 and among the white population of Atlanta for 1870-80 (53 and 43 percent, respectively).[3] But persistence, as used in these urban contexts, fails to differentiate between stable (place persistent) establishments and establishments that move within the region, e.g., town or central district (regional persistent). In all four towns decennial rates of place persistence (residential stability) must have been less than 30 percent and in some cases below 20 percent.

Analysis of population mobility in metropolises has just begun. But the initial city directory studies of Thernstrom and Knights in Boston indicate "the incredible fluidity of the urban . . . population."[4] They find that in a city with a population of 448,000 in 1890, 789,000 individuals moved into the city between 1880 and 1890 and 693,000 moved out. Each year between 1880 and 1890 only 40 to 53 percent of the populace remained in the same residence and each year 27 to 39 percent changed locations within the city.[5] As in the frontier counties and the smaller towns, the decennial rate of place persistence in Boston must have been far below 30 percent.

The findings of Thernstrom and Knights, and certain of their assumptions about business mortality in the nineteenth century, prompted me to go back to the San Francisco directories that occupied me between 1961 and 1967. My objectives were to establish the rates of persistence, failure, and mobility of business establishments in the central district of a fast-growing metropolis (San Francisco) and to examine the effects of the inflow of newcomers and the relocation of established activities upon the expansion and locational shifts of the districts of the Inner City and, ultimately, upon the Central District as a whole.

In San Francisco the growth (expansion and locational change) of the Central District during 1846-1936 took place in five "bursts" of activity, focused on twenty-four years: 1850, 1851-54, 1866-72, 1907-11, and 1919-25, inclusive.[6] In each of the five stages there occurred among the nuclei of the Central District a sequence of locational shifts, beginning in the financial and apparel-shopping nuclei—the *core districts*— and spreading to the garment, medical services, household furnishing, civic, theater (live and moving picture), hotel, and other nuclei—the *peripheral district*.

During the years 1854-65, 1872-1907, 1911-18, and 1925-36, limited peripheral accretion and relative stability in location for the Central District and its constituent nuclei were the rule. Thus, for the eight decades for which I was able to collect data on the persistence, failure, mobility, and entry of establishments, three decades were characterized by "bursts" of growth—1865-75, 1905-15, and 1915-25—and five decades were characterized by locational stability of the Central District and its nuclei. Were the proportions of persistent and new establishments significantly different in the three decades of change compared to the five decades of stability? Which establishments initiated the locational changes of the nuclei within the Central District, the new entrants or the old establishments that relocated within the Central District? This paper presents some preliminary findings concerning the agents of locational change within the Central District.

Persistence is defined here as the survival of establishments in a delimited region (Central District) for ten years or more, and the *persistence rate* is a measure made in a particular year of the number of persistent activities present in the district during the preceding decade as a percentage of all establishments in the activity group. *Place-persistent* establishments are those that are locationally stable in the region during the preceding decade, and *regional-persistent* establishments are those that relocate within the region in the preceding decade.

Place-persistent establishments were few in most activity groups be-

170

fore 1875. Thereafter, in the periods of limited locational change of districts, until 1906, place-persistence rates were remarkably stable. This was true of activity groups experiencing marked increases in numbers as well as those that were not. The rates varied according to the mix of constituent establishments, being highest in activity groups composed exclusively of large establishments (e.g., theaters, 50-67 percent) and lowest in those composed exclusively of small establishments (e.g., medical services, 15 percent). Abrupt changes in place-persistence rates occurred in 1906-15 as a direct result of the total destruction of the Inner City. In this decade, most activities returning to the Inner City took advantage of the opportunity to relocate. By 1915-25, however, stable place-persistence rates were established at slightly higher levels than those current before the earthquake and fire.

Regional-persistent establishments were few before 1865, but in the next decade (one of marked locational change in the Central District) numbers and proportions of these establishments rose to a high peak. Thereafter, regional-persistence rates gradually declined to low points in 1896-1906. A high peak was recorded during the decade of marked locational change, 1906-15, and again rates fell off rapidly for most nuclei in the next two decades.

In the relatively fluid nuclei composed of small- to medium-sized establishments, regional-persistence rates were higher than place-persistence rates, even during stable periods (tables 1 and 2). Differences between the two rates were particularly marked in 1865-75 and 1906-15 (decades of major locational change in the Inner City as a whole). By contrast, it was only in these two decades that regional-persistence rates were higher than place-persistence rates in the more rigid nuclei composed of medium-sized and large establishments (tables 3 and 4), and in some of these nuclei the regional-persistent establishments were absent or rare.

Failure is taken here to be the disappearance of establishments from the city (as indicated by the city directory). It includes both business mortality and the seemingly insignificant movement of former Inner City activities to locations beyond the city's borders. The *failure rate* is the proportion of these establishments present in the Inner City at the beginning of a decade that had disappeared from the city by the end of it.

In the early decades, less than half of the establishments in most activity groups survived a decade in the Inner City. Thereafter, in the districts made up of small- and medium-sized establishments, the decennial failure rate appears to have been between 40 and 50 percent,

171

TABLE 1

PERSISTENCE, MOBILITY, FAILURE, AND ENTRY IN THE GARMENT ACTIVITY GROUP BY DECADE, 1854-1936

	1854 -65	1865 -75	1875 -85	1885 -96	1896 -1905	1905 -15	1915 -26	1926 -36
A. Total Number of Establishments Beginning of Decade	17°	122	125	142	130	164	214	291
B. Total Number of Establishments End of Decade	122	125(+1)	142(+4)	130(+2)	164(+1)	214	291(+2)	216
Place Persistence (% of B)	0	2	20†	22†	25	4	13†	23
Regional Persistence (% of B)	2	36†	31§	23†	21†	35	23†	22
Persistence (Subtotal)	2	37‡	49‡	43‡	45‡	39	35‡	45
Centripetal Mobility (% of B)	0	0	0	1	1	0	0	0
Emergence (% of B)	98	63	51	56	54	61	65	55
Entry (Subtotal)	98	63	51	57	55	61	65	55
Centrifugal Mobility (% of A)	0	0	0	0	0	1	2	0
Failure (% of A)	90	61	42	59	42	50	48	67
Entry: Persistence	98:2	63:37	51:49	57:43	55:45	61:39	65:35	55:45
Mobility: Stability	100:0	98:2	80:20	78:22	75:25	96:4	87:13	77:23

°The count of establishments is incomplete for 1854.
†One establishment had changed category by the end of the decade, i.e., became an establishment in a different activity group.
‡In the calculation of "persistence," establishments that changed category are not considered as part of the district at the end of the decade. The establishments are considered part of the district in the calculations of place and regional persistence.
§Three establishments changed category.

rising on occasion to 67 percent in decades that included severe depressions (1855-96 and 1926-36). The rate was more variable in nuclei composed of large establishments and in those with establishments of various sizes. In the theater district, for example, the decennial failure

TABLE 2

PERSISTENCE, FAILURE, AND ENTRY IN THE MEDICAL SERVICES
ACTIVITY GROUPS, PERCENTAGES BY DECADE, 1885-1936

	1885-96	1896-1905	1905-15	1915-26	1926-36
Place Persistence	12	13	4	15	24
Regional Persistence	16	16	25	24	20
Persistence	28	29	29	40	44
Centripetal Mobility	6	4	24	8	3
Emergence	66	67	47	52	53
Entry	72	71	71	60	56
Centrifugal Mobility	12	10	15	2	5
Failure	40	51	48	38	42
Entry: Persistence	72:28	71:29	71:29	60:40	56:44
Mobility: Stability	88:12	87:13	96:4	85:15	76:24

rate was between 50 and 75 percent in five decades and between 25 and 33 percent in three decades, whereas in the banking nucleus failure rates varied between 12 and 38 percent after the disastrous banking decade of 1875-85. The failure rate in the Inner City therefore, appears to have been between 40 and 50 percent, with low rates in 1875-85 and 1915-25 and high rates in the early and depression decades.

Of the six types of mobility affecting the Inner City, one is considered above—regional persistence, and two others—shifts of Inner City establishments to locations outside the city and the reverse movement—appear to be of limited significance for central-district growth. Two additional types are *centripetal mobility* (movement of establishments located in the Outer City at the beginning of a decade to an Inner City location ten years later) and *centrifugal mobility* (the movement in reverse). Both types were of some significance for nuclei on the edge of the Inner City, particularly between 1906 and 1915 (see tables 1 and 2).[7] Nevertheless, one of the surprising findings of the study is the limited scale of centrifugal and centripetal mobility detected so far.[8]

The sixth type of mobility is termed *emergence*—the creation of new establishments in the Inner City. Most establishments entering the Inner City are newly created, but it is practically impossible in direc-

173

TABLE 3

PERSISTENCE, FAILURE, MOBILITY, AND ENTRY IN THE THEATER ACTIVITY GROUP, SAN FRANCISCO, 1854-1936.

	All Theaters						Live Theaters			Movie Theaters		
	1854-65	1865-75	1875-85	1885-96	1896-1905	1905-15	1905-15	1915-25	1926-36	1905-15	1915-25	1926-36
A. Total Number Establishments Beginning of Decade	7	7	10	12	12	16	12	8	8	4	15	14
B. Total Number of Establishments End of Decade	7	10	12	12	16°	23	8	8	5	15	14	17
Place Persistence	28	20	50	67	37	0	0	75	80	0	71	53
Regional Persistence	0	10	8	0	0	21	37	0	0	13	0	6
Persistence	28	30	58	67	37	21	37	75	80	13	71	59
Emergence (Entry)	72	70	42	33	63	79	63	25	20	87	29	41
Failure	72	57	30	33	50	69	75	25	50	50	33	29

°Four movie theaters included

174

TABLE 4

PERSISTENCE, MOBILITY, FAILURE, AND ENTRY IN THE
BANKING ACTIVITY GROUP BY DECADE, 1854-1936

	1854 -65	1865 -75	1875 -85	1885 -96	1896 -1905	1905 -15	1915 -26	1926 -31
A. Total Number of Establishments Beginning of Decade	18	29	41	32	38	48	31	31
B. Total Number of Establishments at End of Decade	29	41	32	38	48	38†	31	19
Place Persistence	14	15	47	39	37	34	52	74
Regional Persistence	3	32	25	35	27	50	29	21
Persistence	17	47	72	74	64	84	81	95
Emergence (Entry)	83	53	28	26	36	16‡	19	5
Failure	73	35°	45	12	18	33°	19°	39°
Mobility: Stability	86:14	85:15	53:47	61:39	63:37	66:34	48:52	26:74

°Includes one or more mergers.
†Seven category changes were made at this point in time.
‡Includes one centripetally mobile establishment.

tory studies to distinguish these true emergents from the few establishments that enter the Inner City from outside the city's boundaries. Thus, both types of establishments are called here *emergents*. Emergents taken together with establishments moving into the Inner City from the Outer City are called *newcomers*. And the *entry rate* is the proportion of newcomers in an activity group in the Inner City. In general, the entry rate, like that of regional persistence, rose during periods of locational change of districts in the Inner City (tables 1 and 2).[9]

Comparing entry and persistence rates by decade, we find that in activity groups composed of small establishments, and, presumably in the Inner City as a whole, entry: place-persistence ratios and, in most cases, entry: regional-persistence ratios were higher than 3:1 in the first decade and, generally, more than 2:1 thereafter. By contrast, after 1875, in activity groups composed of large establishments and of establishments of various sizes, the ratios were far more variable, with newcomers frequently being outnumbered by both place-persistent and regional-persistent establishments.[10]

An indicator of the fluidity of the Central District is the decennial ratio comparing mobility (including emergence and regional persistence) and stability (place persistence). In activity groups composed of small establishments, the ratio of mobile to stable establishments was at least 4:1 in each decade between 1854 and 1936 and frequently much higher. And, in the early decades, the same was true of activity groups composed of large or variously sized establishments. Thereafter in these activity groups, however, the mobility component was generally much lower and more variable, the ratio ranging from 2:1 to 1:4. It seems probable, nevertheless, that in every decade, mobile establishments outnumbered stable ones by at least 3:1 in the Inner City.

In establishing the importance of newcomers as against persistent establishments in effecting locational changes, the garment district provides a fine case. Newcomers consistently outnumbered persistent establishments, and most of the establishments were small to medium-sized, particularly in the early decades. Furthermore, the locational shifts of the district were clear-cut in space and time: a marked lateral shift in the early 1850s, a leapfrogging in 1869-72 (figure 1), a lateral expansion, 1902-11 (figure 2), and a leapfrogging and dismemberment in the 1920s (figure 3).[11]

Patchy directory coverage in the early fifties made it difficult to establish the detailed sequence of entry of establishments into the focal area of the new nucleus. However, the few relocatees discovered there were overwhelmingly outnumbered by newcomers who were presumably responsible in the main for the displacement. The only occasion in which this was true was in the garment district.

The second major locational change, the leapfrogging of the district (1869-72), was started by the relocation of persistent establishments displaced by the rapidly expanding financial district (figure 1). And the locational shift of some well-established wholesalers from the section of the old garment district, threatened by the expanding financial district, consolidated the locational shift. Newcomers simply followed and filled out the frame of a new district established by regional-persistent establishments.

A similar sequence of events occurred after the turn of the century. Almost two-thirds of the garment establishments (132) in the Inner City in 1915 were newcomers, yet this analysis shows that the new district and the three nuclei to the west (figure 2) were essentially formed and re-formed by persistent establishments that returned

176

GARMENT DISTRICT:
LOCATIONAL CHANGES 1850-1875

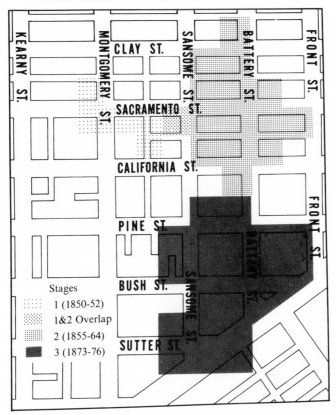

Fig. 1.

quickly after the fire. Eighty-two of these establishments persisted from 1905-15.

In the next decade another surge of newcomers entered the Inner City (187 of 291 establishments present in 1926), and, at the same time, the garment district was dismembered (figure 3). But, as in the two previous phases of growth and locational change, it was the displacement of a large number of medium-sized activities by the expanding office and financial districts that precipitated the break-up. Analysis of the sequent occupance of four key buildings in the new nuclei revealed that persistent activities both laid the groundwork for and affected the

177

GARMENT DISTRICT:
LOCATIONAL CHANGES 1906-1915

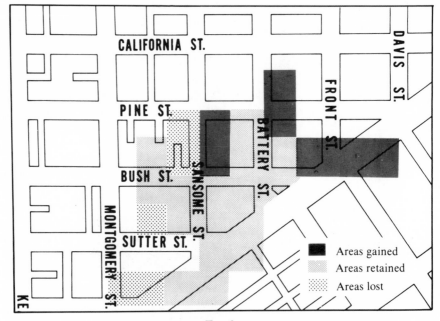

FIG. 2.

early occupance of these buildings. The proportion of newcomers to persistent establishments in these key buildings was very low in the early years of occupance and then began to rise rapidly. This suggests that the high proportions of newcomers in decades of locational change of districts in the Inner City were a consequence of the special opportunities created in such times.

To establish the representativeness of the recurrent sequence of events in the garment district, analysis was carried out for an activity group in which circumstances pointed to maximum instability and optimal conditions for the creation of new nuclei by the flood of newcomers to the Inner City.[12] This was the medical services activity group (1915-36). In this group, of which all establishments were small, there were three times as many newcomers as regional-persistent establishments in each decade between 1885 and 1936, and establishments that persisted in the same locale within the Inner City were very few (table 2).

178

GARMENT NUCLEI 1931

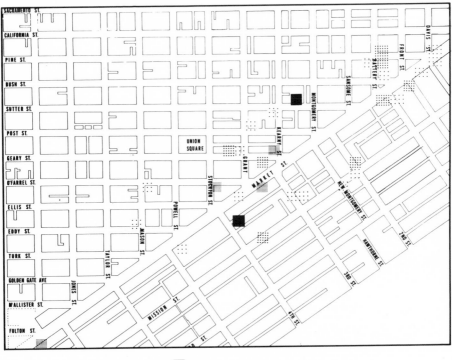

Grid-blocks divided into six groups based on Lorenz curve	■	1st	> 41-43	Number of establishments per grid-block
	■	2nd		
	▦	3rd	7-41	
	▥	4th	4-7	
	⣿	5th	2-4	

Lowest group not shown

FIG. 3.

After the complete exodus of medical service establishments from the Inner City after 1906, there were, by 1915, 1,100 medical service establishments in the Inner City, of which 800 were newcomers and 300 persistent. The medical nucleus, horizontally adjacent to the apparel-shopping district before the fire (1906), was relocated above it after the fire (figure 4), a locational shift made possible by the construction of a large number of tall, steel-framed buildings equipped with modern elevators. Analysis of the sequent occupance of buildings

179

MEDICAL ACTIVITIES 1905 & 1915

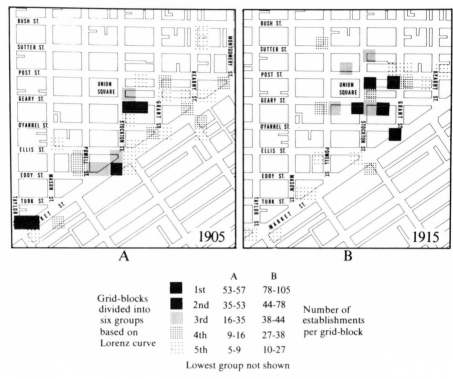

		A	B	
	1st	53-57	78-105	
Grid-blocks	2nd	35-53	44-78	
divided into				Number of
six groups	3rd	16-35	38-44	establishments
based on	4th	9-16	27-38	per grid-block
Lorenz curve	5th	5-9	10-27	

Lowest group not shown

Fig. 4.

opened before 1911 in the new nucleus reveals that the ratio of new-comers to persistent establishments in 1911 was higher than 8:3 (the district ratio in 1915) in all cases. This suggests that newcomers, half of which were establishments located in the Outer City before the fire, were instrumental in outlining the frame of the new nucleus and in establishing it.

Between 1915 and 1926, although both newcomers (940) and persist-ent establishments (620) were more numerous than in the previous decade, the entry-persistence ratio dropped from 8:3 to 3:2. In these circumstances, it was the persistent establishments that effected the marked lateral displacement and expansion of the medical nucleus in the twenties (figure 5). This conclusion is not equivocal, for analysis of the sequent occupance of the major buildings occupied in this move re-veals an entry-persistence ratio of less than 1:3 in the early years, grad-

CHANGES IN NUMBER OF
MEDICAL ACTIVITIES 1916-1931

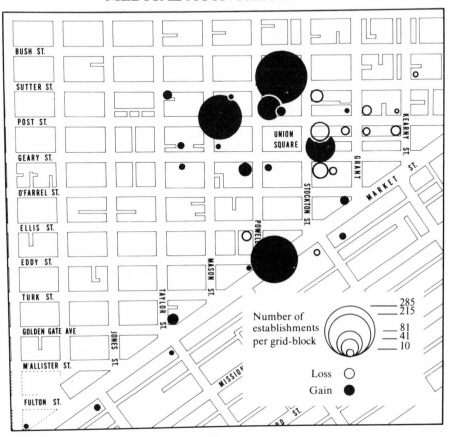

Fig. 5.

ually rising to 2:3 and 3:3. The very high proportions of persistent establishments relocating in the first phases of the change were, to a large extent, the consequence of mass displacement of medical establishments by the expanding department stores and apparel-shopping district (see table 5, which shows the succession of establishments in buildings that formed the core of the postfire medical nucleus). The sequence of events and the conditions existing before and after the locational shift were essentially the same as those in the garment district in 1865-1936.

181

TABLE 5

Changes in the Functional Structure of Three Buildings East of Union Square, 1921 and 1931

Number of Establishments

Type of Establishments	Howard Building (209 Post)		Whitney Building (133 Geary)		Schroth Building (240 Stockton)		Totals	
	1921	1931	1921	1931	1921	1931	1921	1931
Jewelry	5	13	14	30	0	1	19	44
Beauty Shops, etc.	0	4	4	23	0	14	4	41
Women's Apparel	4	11	6	9	0	1	10	21
Other Apparel	0	2	3	9	0	1	3	12
Others	1	2	2	4	0	2	3	8
Christian Science Practitioners	0	0	49	32	0	0	49	32
Medical	92	59	40	21	63	29	195	109
Breakdown of Medical Services								
Physicians and Surgeons	43	15	13	5	46	5	102	25
Dentists	39	32	17	6	17	15	73	53
Other Medical	10	12	10	10	0	9	20	31

These examples suggest that when the entry-persistence ratio was greater than 2:1 and the entry: regional-persistence ratio approached 3:1 in decades of Central District "bursts," newcomers may have been critical in effecting the change. But does this tentative generalization hold for activity groups composed exclusively of large establishments, e.g., the theater and moving-picture theater districts?

The theater district moved farther than any other district in the history of San Francisco's Inner City, expanding laterally in the mid-fifties, leapfrogging in the late sixties, leapfrogging again in the eighties, and splitting into live and moving-picture theater districts in lateral shifts made in the postfire era (figures 6 and 7).[13]

LOCATIONAL CHANGES
OF THEATER DISTRICT 1850-1875

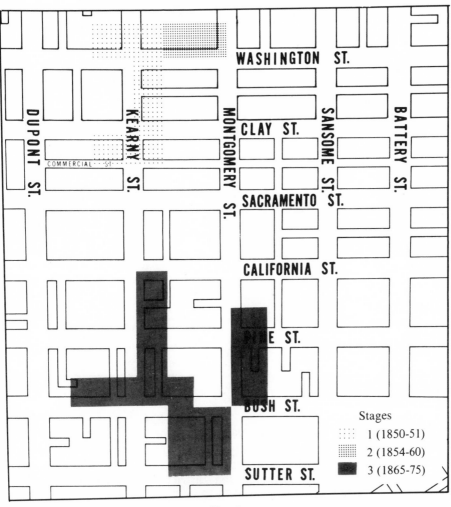

FIG. 6.

Newcomers were the most important agents in the first two locational shifts (figure 6). In both periods the entry-persistence ratio was well above 2:1 and entry: regional-persistence ratio was very much higher than 3:1 (table 3), the critical threshold levels suggested in the analysis of the medical and garment districts.

LOCATIONAL CHANGES
OF THEATER DISTRICT 1869-1906

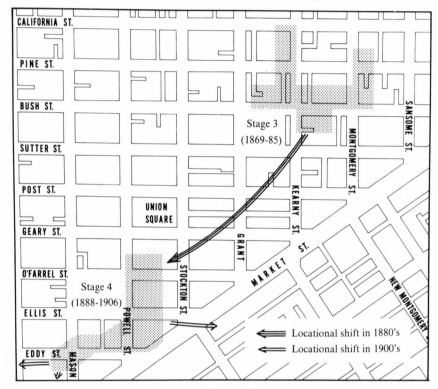

Fɪɢ. 7.

Newcomers also effected the leapfrogging of the theater district in the eighties, although the figures in table 3 would not seem to predict this. The lack of support is more apparent than real, however, because the remarkable changes in the theater district during 1880-90 are obscured by presenting the data for 1875-85 and 1885-96. In fact, between 1880 and 1890 there were five persistent establishments in the old (four) and new (one) theater nuclei, eleven newly emergent theaters in the new nucleus, and no theaters that relocated. Thus, both critical threshold ratios were surpassed in the decade of change.

The same thing happened in the decade after the fire. New establishments (mainly movie theaters)[14] outnumbered persistent establishments by 3.6:1. And it was essentially these new movie theaters (entry-persistence ratio in 1915 of 13:2) that effected the major locational change, i.e., two movie theater nuclei were established to the south and southwest of the small prefire concentration of movie theaters. The live theater nucleus was also displaced laterally to the north and east of its prefire position as a result of the locational acts of three regionally persistent and five emergent theaters. But this was a minor change compared to the leapfrogging of the movie nucleus which, in effect, split the formerly compact theater district into three discrete nuclei.[15]

On one occasion each in the early years of growth of the apparel-shopping and financial districts, newcomers greatly outnumbered persistent establishments and, as a consequence, were critical in both laying the groundwork and effecting the expansion and locational changes of both districts. For example, in the marked leapfrogging of the financial district,[16] well-established activities were responsible for the lateral expansion of the banking nucleus (and financial district) in the early fifties, but the marked leapfrogging of the financial district in the mid-sixties was effected largely by establishments new to the central district (table 4). Two rival financial centers (California Street and the Northeast, see table 6) comprised of new entrants grew up as discrete nuclei to the northeast and southeast of the existing financial district between 1854 and 1860. In the early sixties a further concentration of newcomers (see table 6 under California Street), particularly San Francisco's first sizable (commercial) banks, determined that the southeastern rival would become the new financial district. Of the banks in 1865, 85 percent had been created since 1854.

After 1870, however, as the range in size of the constituent establishments broadened, it was the decisions of the persistent medium-to-large and, later, large establishments (dominants) that became critical. In terms of expansion and locational change, the financial and apparel-shopping districts became, in effect, districts composed of large establishments, like the theater district. Only the dominants mattered. Large numbers of newcomers surged into the financial district throughout the nineteenth and early twentieth centuries, but they were almost exclusively small establishments that tended to cling to the district framed by the dominants.

The apparel-shopping activity group[17] is the most complex in the Inner City in terms of structure, growth, and locational change. In rapidly growing cities in the nineteenth century, there were in the Inner City at any point in time a main district, numerous rival nuclei (interceptors), and numerous nuclei that had been bypassed or discarded (in-

TABLE 6

Number of Banks in Three Sectors of
San Francisco, 1854-75

Year	California St.°	Upper Montgomery St.†	Northeast‡
1854	4	11	3
1858	3	4	4
1860	3	7	6
1865	9	9	5
1869	9	7	2
1875	13	8	0

°California Street between Battery and Kearny streets.
†Montgomery Street between Sacramento and Washington streets and including all four corners of both the Montgomery-Washington streets intersection and the Montgomery-Sacramento streets intersection.
‡The area northeast of upper Montgomery Street and north of California Street. It is bounded on the north by Pacific Street and on the east by Front Street.
Source: City directories.

cubators). A model of the development of the mature district (after 1870 in San Francisco) has been outlined elsewhere,[18] and it is perhaps sufficient to focus here on the main district before 1870.

In the early 1850s the apparel-shopping nucleus expanded and was displaced (figure 8). Again, patchy directory coverage for the early fifties made it difficult to establish whether displacement that occurred at this time was effected by newcomers or by persistent establishments relocating to the south. Nevertheless, relocations were very few, and, consequently, the greater part of the displacement must have been effected by the relatively large number of new establishments.

Between 1854 and 1865 a number of rival apparel-shopping centers developed as interceptors to the north and south of the established district, and in the middle and late sixties, the southern interceptor became the new apparel-shopping district. The effect of this was a leap-frogging of the district far to the south. Analysis has shown that the women's apparel shopping nucleus made the first locational change, followed by the men's clothing nucleus, and the jewelry cluster. The establishments instrumental in bringing about the first locational shift were small stores new to the Central District in the sixties, and medium-sized stores established before 1860 (figure 9). The former

LOCATIONAL CHANGES OF NUCLEI IN THE
APPAREL-SHOPPING DISTRICT 1850-1880

WOMEN'S APPAREL
SHOPPING NUCLEUS   JEWELRY CLUSTER

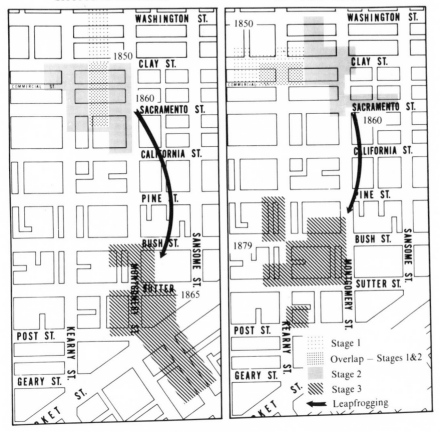

FIG. 8.

were very numerous and made it possible for a locational shift to take place to either the northern or the southern interceptor. The latter (medium-sized stores) were few in number, but by their selection of sites in the southern interceptor during the mid-sixties, they appeared to ensure that it would become the new women's apparel shopping district. These medium-sized stores were the embryonic department stores that would dominate the growth and locational shifts of the apparel-shopping district after 1870. In the sixties, however, some new-

187

RETAIL DRY GOODS AND CLOAK
& SUIT ESTABLISHMENTS 1858-1869

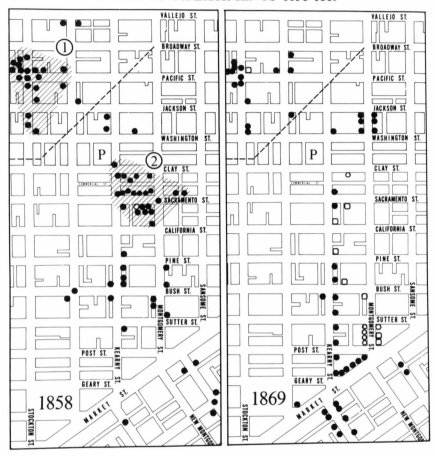

● Dry goods store   O Embryo department store
□ Cloak & suit store   ---- Approximate edge of Central District
① Upper Stockton St. area   P Portsmouth Square
② Sacramento St. women's apparel shopping nucleus

FIG. 9.

comers grew so rapidly to the status of embryonic department stores in the southern interceptor that it was becoming the new apparel-shopping nucleus without the embryonic department stores of the old nucleus. Hence, the entry of new establishments was perhaps more important than relocation of old ones in bringing about the leapfrogging of the apparel-shopping district in the late sixties.

By contrast, in the mid-seventies the rate of increase of new establishments dropped; well-established embryonic department stores were larger and more numerous than they had been in the sixties, and it was less likely that newcomers would grow rapidly enough to challenge these dominants. These large establishments effected the locational shift of the women's apparel shopping district in 1874-77 and in all subsequent phases of growth. In sum, in districts composed of establishments ranging in size from very small to very large, the only potentially critical newcomers were dominants. And as these were uncommon, the locational shifts of districts of this type were effected almost exclusively by large establishments that relocated within the Inner City (regionally persistent establishments).[19]

In conclusion, throughout the nineteenth century the decennial rates of place persistence of establishments in most districts in the San Francisco Central District were similar to the very low decennial rates of residential stability found by historians in both frontier counties and growing towns and cities. In every decade there were at least three times as many mobile as stable establishments in the Inner City. Between 1850 and 1936, in every year in the Central District's history, there were probably more *newcomers* than *persistent activities*. And in many activity groups, the ratio of newcomers to persistent activities was greater than two to one. This entry-persistence ratio was particularly high during periods of marked locational change of nuclei[20] in the Central District as a whole.

The locational effects of this flood of newcomers were, however, far fewer than their absolute numbers would suggest. Most newcomers were small and their chances of failure high. Even during the major bursts of locational change within the Inner City, newcomers tended to follow rather than lead locational shifts and to fill out the existing district rather than establish a rival center. The sharp upturn in the numbers of newcomers during periods of major locational change in many districts was not so much a cause of change as a consequence of the opening up of buildings in a new district already established by persistent activities that had shifted from the old district. This was particularly true in peripheral districts.[21]

Thus, in San Francisco newcomers effected major locational changes only in unusual circumstances, when certain critical threshold levels in the proportions of newcomers to persistent establishments were

189

crossed. In districts composed of small establishments, the thresholds were an entry: regional-persistence ratio approaching 3:1 and an entry-persistence ratio of 2:1. In districts composed of large establishments, the critical thresholds appeared to be lower: an entry-persistence ratio of 3:2 and (based on one clear case) an entry: regional-persistence ratio approaching 2:1. In districts in which the range in size of establishments widened through time the critical thresholds were, at first, those of districts composed of small establishments and, later (after 1870 in San Francisco), presumably those of districts composed of large establishments.[22] (In this latter situation, however, only the entry-persistence ratios of the dominants in the district would be significant.) When these critical thresholds were crossed, a new nucleus (nuclei) emerged and leapfrogging generally resulted, primarily because of the physical-morphological constraints placed upon the main (old) nucleus by contiguous districts.

Even in San Francisco, with its phases of very rapid growth and high entry rates, occasions when newcomers were critical in effecting locational changes were uncommon, particularly after the first two decades (1850-70). The great numbers of new establishments in the Inner City, particularly between 1870 and 1936, did little more than aid in laying the groundwork for change. Expansion and major locational changes of districts and of the Central District as a whole were outlined and effected by persistent and increasingly large establishments.

NOTES

1. James C. Malin, "The Turnover of Farm Population in Kansas," *Kansas Historical Quarterly* 4 (1935):339-72; Merle Curti et al., *The Making of an American Community* (Stanford: Stanford University Press, 1959), p. 68; Mildred Throne, "A Population Study of an Iowa County in 1850," *Iowa Journal of History* 57 (1959): 305-30; Peter J. Coleman, "Restless Grant County: Americans on the Move," *Wisconsin Magazine of History* 46 (1962): 16-20.

2. Blake McKelvey, *Rochester: The Flower City, 1855-1880* (Cambridge, Mass.: Harvard University Press, 1949), p. 3; and a computation made by Stephan Thernstrom and Peter R. Knights, "Men in Motion: Some Data and Speculations about Urban Population Mobility in Nineteenth-Century America," *Anonymous Americans*, ed. T. K. Hareven (Englewood Cliffs: Prentice-Hall, 1971), pp. 20-21, from data in Clyde Griffen, "Workers Divided: Social Mobility in Poughkeepsie, 1850-1880," *Nineteenth-Century Cities*, ed. Stephan Thernstrom and Richard Sennett (New Haven: Yale University Press, 1969), pp. 49-97.

3. Data computed by Thernstrom and Knights, "Men in Motion," from Richard J. Hopkins, "Occupational and Geographic Mobility in Atlanta, 1870-1890,"

Journal of Southern History 34 (1968): 200-213; and Robert Doherty, "Industrialization and Social Change: Northampton, Massachusetts, 1800-1860" (Paper prepared for Yale Conference on Nineteenth Century Cities, November 1968), cited in Thernstrom and Knights, "Men in Motion."
4. Thernstrom and Knights, "Men in Motion," p. 31.
5. Ibid., pp. 27-31.
6. Martyn J. Bowden, *The Dynamics of City Growth: An Historical Geography of the San Francisco Central District, 1850-1931,* (Ph.D. diss., University of California, Berkeley, 1967), pp. 266-69, 448-53, 478, 705-11.
7. In this decade, the total destruction of the Inner City scattered many Inner City establishments to the Outer City, where some remained, and later presented the opportunity for many activities located in the Outer City before the fire to move into new buildings constructed before 1915 in the Inner City.
8. Changes in the index of central tendency (the relative proportions of activities in the Inner and Outer cities) were primarily the result of changing numbers of failures and newcomers in the various activity groups.
9. The only major difference between the rates detected so far is in the medical services activity group (table 2).
10. It should be remembered that these decennial rates underestimate the total number of failures and entrants in each decade, simply because many establishments emerge and quickly fail without being caught at the cross-sectional dates, for example, 1865 and 1875. An underestimation of a smaller scale results from the fact that persistent establishments may survive eighteen years and yet be "caught" at the cross-sectional dates only once. In such a case, the establishment would appear as a newcomer and fail before being counted as a persistent establishment.
11. Bowden, *Dynamics of City Growth,* pp. 229-40, 405-15, 662-90.
12. Ibid., pp. 612-27.
13. Ibid., pp. 244-51, 424-37, 539-43.
14. Ibid., pp. 556-60.
15. Lateral expansion without displacement occurred in the twenties in the movie and live theater districts, and in both cases newcomers effected these minor locational changes. In neither of the districts, however, were critical threshold levels (ratios) approached (table 3), and this serves to point up the fact that locational changes are effected by newcomers even though threshold ratios are not attained. This is a frequent occurrence in districts composed of large establishments, for example the theater and hotel districts, in which relocation of establishments is rare, and practically all locational changes of the districts are effected by newcomers. Quite large blocks may be added to the theater and hotel districts by one or two newcomers such as the massive Palace Hotel and the large Grand Hotel added to the southern boundary of the hotel district in the 1870s. This is simply the filling out (lateral expansion without displacement) of a nucleus—a type of growth that occurred in the garment district between phases of major locational changes, as newcomers gradually filled out the district in the early 1860s and the mid-1870s. The only difference between this and the growth of the theater districts in the 1920s is one of scale—the size of the units constituting the activity group. In the garment

191

district the units are small and numerous and the extension of the district is gradual and often imperceptible, whereas in the theater district the units are few and large and accretion is infrequent and obvious in areal expression. The character of the activity group is such that these relatively minor locational changes (in the context of the theater district) become major changes when viewed in the context of nuclei made up of a large number of small establishments.

16. Bowden, *Dynamics of City Growth*, pp. 145-53, 179-203, 335-58, 479-94, 648-62.
17. Ibid., pp. 122-29, 204-29, 359-403, 494-528, 592-612.
18. Idem, "Growth of the Central Districts of Large Cities," (Paper presented at the Symposium on the New Urban History, Madison, Wisc., June 1970 [forthcoming volume of essays edited by L. Schnore]).
19. Further support for this conclusion is provided in Susan H. Kelly and Bruce L. LaRose, "The Growth and Movement of Manhattan's Central Business District as Indicated by Department Stores, 1860-1930," (Paper prepared for the Eighth Conference of the Eastern Historical Geography Association held at Briarcliff, N. Y., April 1974).
20. Martyn J. Bowden, "Downtown through Time: Delimitation, Expansion, and Internal Growth," *Economic Geography* 47 (1971): 130-31.
21. In these districts locational changes are frequently precipitated by external pressures, i.e., a large number of established activities, with competitive and complementary linkages, are forced to relocate in a short period of two or three years. These establishments tend to move together (leapfrogging) and in so doing create a new district or change the focus of the old one.
22. The critical thresholds for districts composed of large establishments were never crossed by the core districts in San Francisco after 1870.

Why Covered Bridges? Toward the Management of Historic Landscapes – The Case of Parke County, Indiana

JOHN A. JAKLE and
ROBERT L. JANISKEE

What historical geography is and what it is good for are obviously two very different questions. Most historical geographers would agree that we are primarily concerned with the description and analysis of past geographic distributions; many of us would further consider that our tasks should focus on identifying and understanding the processes of spatial distribution change. Some of us might encourage even more specific focus on past spatial behavior—the perceptual and decision-making aspects of locational choice in the historic past. But why are historical geographers so oriented? Of what value is our science—our art? Certainly all of us have our rationales. But certainly deep down we all believe that our expertise can somehow influence human perceptions and community decision making. Historical-geographical insights and viewpoints can lay the basis for better understanding our environment and our society as we plan for the future. In its geographical decision making, each generation determines the content of its geographical space and the spatial distribution of that content.

The authors wish to thank the participants of the Parke County Summer Field Course, conducted by the Department of Geography of the University of Illinois during the summer of 1970, for their assistance. The research experience, upon which this paper is in part based, was partially supported by the National Science Foundation and is reported upon in full in John A. Jakle et al., "The Potential for Historic Landscape Preservation in Parke County, Indiana" (discussion paper, Department of Geography, University of Illinois, Urbana, September 1971).

Most historical geographers feel strongly that full knowledge of past geographical conditions is vital to such determinations.

Yet historical geographers contribute relatively little of their expertise in decision-making councils. We do little to translate knowledge of past geographical conditions into real alternatives for environmental management today. Perhaps, as many critics have suggested, the lack of theoretically integrated research directly focused on immediate social problems has isolated historical geographers from problem-solving contexts. But beyond this it would also seem that too many historical geographers research and write primarily for one another's intellectual consumption and, thus, alienate themselves from the larger community. For many this latter state of affairs seems quite proper. But for others there seems to be an additional call. One additional step—to directly apply historical geography to immediate human problems—seems an all important goal. How can historical geographers of this persuasion proceed with their mission?

One direction (and we emphasize that it is one direction only) would be to further focus on the relic features of landscape as vital elements of today's and tomorrow's geographical environment. We are referring to landscape features that are in a contemporary sense anachronistic or rapidly approaching functional obsolescence. Relic landscape offers what might be termed a "counter-environmental" quality—a distinctiveness of place and time which counters the standardization of the emerging scene, the result of rapid and universal spatial reorganization with changing technology. It offers relief from the emerging sameness of place by providing varied environmental experiences historically derived and defined, and it serves to remind us of our environmental origins in less complicated technological times. In short, relic landscape constitutes a culturally defined recreational and educational resource with enduring, uniquely valuable, qualities. Historical geographers can and should move to more clearly define concepts of relic landscape as environmental resources to be managed toward the betterment of human life.

With these thoughts in mind, let us consider one American community that is capitalizing on the resource value of its relic landscape. Parke County, Indiana, has over the past fourteen years created a historic image of considerable touristic appeal predicated largely on the existence of its thirty-six covered bridges, the highest density of these bridges anywhere in the United States. Dubbing itself (in true American fashion) the "Covered Bridge Capital of the World," this community in western Indiana now attracts an estimated two hundred fifty thousand visitors a year. With the interest in covered bridges well developed, the community has begun to exploit the resource value of other relic forms in the landscape and to undertake historic landscape preservation on a relatively large scale. It is the purpose of this paper to briefly sketch the Parke County experience and to suggest ways and means by which historical geographers might better understand historic landscape preservation and encourage its development in rural communities that are endowed with relic landscape resources.

Parke County is an economically underdeveloped community characterized by a lack of manufacturing, a steady decline in agriculture, and a generally stagnant retail and wholesale sector. Amply demonstrating the county's lack of economic vigor is the fact that its current population of some fourteen thousand persons is less than its 1860 population. Against this background, community leaders began in the mid-1950s to search for ways and means to improve the community's economic posture. A "Long-Time Planning Committee" was formed under the auspices of the county's state agricultural extension agent as a "think tank" to review the spectrum of developmental alternatives, assign priorities, and stimulate action. Prominent among the alternatives considered was the fostering of an expanded visitor industry based on the newly discovered touristic appeal of the county's covered bridges.

To the chamber of commerce, the courthouse, and the newspaper editors had come a flood of requests for information concerning the history of the county's covered bridges and touring directions for finding them. Stimulated by a breed of covered-bridge enthusiasts—many loosely organized in covered-bridge associations at national, regional, state, and local levels—interest in covered bridges as a landscape curiosity had grown rapidly since World War II. At this point we can only speculate as to why covered bridges should appeal to Americans in search of antiquity. Like log cabins, old grist mills, and antique steam engines, covered bridges seem to have an almost mythical symbolic quality steeped in romance and nostalgia. Certainly, part of their appeal to tourists lies in the fact that they are readily accessible "drive-in" attractions. Caught up in an automobile-convenient age, Americans very easily fit covered bridges into their ongoing outdoor recreational *modus operandi*. In any case, outside interest in the bridges proved strong, and Parke County residents came to recognize the recreational utility of these relic landscape features. This change in resident landscape awareness triggered the first of several phases of historic landscape management in the county.

The initial phase consisted of small-scale and, generally, short-term developments undertaken by a few local individuals. Interestingly enough, the initial management attempts were quite geographic in an academic sense. A map of bridge locations was prepared for general distribution, and marked tourist routes linking the bridges were established. While this ostensibly benefited the entire county, it especially favored the residents of Rockville (the county seat) where the maps were distributed and the bridge tours started. In 1957, Rockville interests took further steps to attract tourists to the county seat by establishing a "farmers fair" for the sale of farm produce and handicrafts. With this action, the community entered a second developmental phase, characterized by further geographical centralization of activities (in order to achieve a "critical mass" in tourist promotion) and by a general trend toward larger scale operations.

The farmers fair was expanded to an annual ten-day event known as the Covered Bridge Festival, and, by 1964, attendance had grown to an estimated one hundred thousand visitors. Festival activities centered primarily on the courthouse square, where they were housed in large tents and temporary log and clapboard structures. But the success of the festival brought problems. So large an undertaking had it become that the loosely structured volunteer group, which had organized the festival on a year-to-year basis, proved inadequate. Organization of Parke County Incorporated in 1964, as a legal umbrella to encompass a wide spectrum of community development work (including industrial development) and to supervise the festival with a permanent staff, solved this problem. Henceforth, Rockville's development of Parke County's historic landscape resources would be integrally related to other economic development activities within a single institutional framework. Parke County Incorporated soon established a year-round tourist reception center and museum (in cooperation with the Parke County Historical Society), a second festival in the spring (developed around the theme of maple sugaring), and Billie Creek Village (a museum for the outdoor display of architecture).

Billie Creek Village is envisioned as a recreated middle western town of the 1880-1915 period. In a pleasant valley setting next to a covered bridge just outside Rockville, it already displays a general store, a doctor's office, a printing shop, a livery stable, a one-room schoolhouse, a log cabin, and the house of the county's only former state governor. All of the buildings are authentic, having been moved from original sites in the county. Present plans call for the addition of a grist mill, a church, a tavern, and other commercial buildings, as well as prominent examples of local nineteenth-century domestic architecture. A complete relic farmstead will be installed on an adjoining plot. Village development has been capitalized with profits from the Covered Bridge Festival, but an admission fee will be levied to defray the expense of an onsite permanent staff and to finance maintenance and improvements. The village will then not only be a year-round tourist attraction for the county, but will also provide space for many Covered Bridge Festival activities, thus relieving the overcrowded courthouse square.

A third developmental phase has seen an expansion and decentralization outward from Rockville to encompass the entire county. The idea of an annual festival has diffused to several other towns, including Rosedale and Mecca in the South and Montezuma in the West. The small towns of Bridgeton and Mansfield (each with their rare combinations of century-old grist mills, mill dams, and covered bridges) are now pursuing restoration and development schemes independent from the Rockville group. Within Parke County Incorporated, current thinking is also outward looking. Action has been taken to establish a bicycle path along an abandoned railroad connecting Rockville with Waveland in neighboring Montgomery County. The organization is also participating with four other counties in a west central Indiana economic development district. In addition, discussion has been generated regarding the historic restoration of Rockville's courthouse square to its late nineteenth-century image.

Thus, following an incipient awareness that covered bridges could lay the basis for a locally important visitor industry, the Parke County community has proceeded through several phases of historic landscape management toward a developmental spectrum encompassing outdoor museums, building restorations, and, now, even consideration of historic area preservation. Responsibility for the complex but important task of developing the full potential of the community's historic landscape resources is coming to rest largely in the hands of professional managers. Here, then, is a planning and decision-making context in which traditional historical-geographical expertise might be brought to bear with especially good effect. At the same time, an opportunity is offered for historical geographers to apply their science in new and innovative ways in order to derive information (of immediate value to historic landscape managers), evaluate it, and communicate it in a variety of readily comprehensible formats. We might, by way of example, explore the application of "user-perception" research to historic landscape management.

By user-perception research, we mean empirical studies directed toward a more complete understanding of the ways in which people comprehend (cognitively structure or "perceive") the landscape and its components. Underlying these studies are two basic premises: (1) landscape managers alter human perception and response when they engineer changes in the landscape, and (2) full knowledge of human landscape perception is vital to a landscape design process which seeks to maximize user benefits. Empirically derived user-perception data are thus offered as a rational alternative to the frequently unsupported assumptions about landscape perception which function implicitly in traditional landscape design. Employed in the context of historical landscape management, user-perception studies would systematically investigate the perceptions and responses that characterize contemporary man's encounters with the landscape of the authentic past and suggest specific means by which the recreational-educational component of these encounters can be enhanced through design. Fortunately, most existing user-perception research strategies and methods are easily adapted to the peculiar requirements of historical landscape perception studies. It remains for historical geographers to use (and improve) them to gain that more nearly complete understanding of visitor response to the historical landscape, which will enable us to contribute most effectively in the councils of historical landscape management. With this thought in mind, let us briefly examine a few user-perception research strategies and methods which may serve to get us started in that direction.

Perhaps no problem in historical landscape management is more basic than that of "taking stock" of landscape resources via some sort of inventory and appraisal. The problem essentially takes the form of the question, "Which landscape features and combinations of features are considered by visitors to have historical-recreational qualities and to what degree?" Values and preferences of this type can be determined by employing unidimensional psychometric testing and scaling devices of several varieties.[1] These simple procedures yield *numerical* (and if desired, ratio-relevant) ratings of landscape features that can be input directly to decision-making contexts in a readily comprehensible format without complicated (and thereby confusing) intermediate technical evaluation.

However, while knowledge of visitor landscape values and preferences is useful for many purposes, effective historical landscape management will, in the long run, be more dependent upon knowledge of *why* visitors respond to landscape as they do. We must, therefore, gain a more complete understanding of historical landscape comprehension as a multidimensional phenomenon in which evaluation is but one of many components. We must, in short, discover and explain the latent attributes of relic landscape which underlie and account for preference judgments. A major conceptual difficulty lies in reducing the inherent complexity of historical landscape comprehension to manageable proportions, while measurement problems center on the translation of highly subjective, emotional phenomena into meaningful qualitative and quantitative expressions. One possible solution is offered in the form of a psychological technique known as semantic differentiation.[2]

Semantic differentiation indexes the "meaning" of concepts (stimuli) by reference to their linguistic encoding.[3] Geographers and others have used this procedure to investigate the connotative dimensions of architecture, shopping centers, functional landscapes, environmental hazards, and so forth.[4] There are no serious impediments to the use of this highly generalizable technique in historical landscape user-perception research.

Offered by way of illustration is a preliminary user-perception study of the Parke County landscape we conducted in 1970. A sample of people who had visited Parke County were shown photographs of eight scenic and historic features found in the county—a covered bridge, a log cabin, an old wooden church, a large house of neoclassical design, and views of a highway, gravel road, stream, and farm pond. Visitors were asked to rate each of these features on a semantic differential. Analysis of these data revealed that visitors tended to judge the features along axes (or dimensions) of "beauty," "antiquity," and "pride." Also revealed was the extent to which each of the features conveyed these impressions—thus permitting objective comparison amongst them on the basis of these salient components of their meaning for visitors. A parallel study revealed that Parke County residents tended to judge the features along axes of a similar, but not identical, nature. We have tentatively dubbed these axes "friendliness," "uniqueness," and "pride." Thus, the results of this research not only show that historical landscape user-perception data can be generated by semantic differentiation, but also that visitor and resident landscape comprehension may be of a distinctly different nature. This latter finding lends support to the argument for empirically derived knowledge of visitor landscape comprehension and casts some suspicion on the assumptions that residents, acting in the capacity of landscape managers, are likely to make about visitor landscape perception.

In Parke County, an interesting experiment in historical management is progressing. Historical geographers should move to sow the seeds of similar experimentation elsewhere and to sustain experiments already underway through increased understanding of historic landscapes as a

199

part of the contemporary scene. Their expertise might be applied to awaken local communities to the existence of historic landscape resources through such familiar devices as maps and guidebooks and through the encouragement of activities such as establishing marked tourist routes. But, more importantly, at the later phases of landscape management, a more sophisticated social science capability might be applied. Recommended here is use and development of user-perception techniques applicable to defining and evaluating the subtleties of historic landscape cognition. Such effort would not only be predicated upon a sound theoretical base, given current user-perception research, but would be community problem focused. Historical geographers would be taking direct steps to translate their knowledge of the geographical past into meaningful alternatives of geographical decision making today.

NOTES

1. One method has respondents rate landscape features (or simulations of these features) on numerical scales of attractiveness. Cf. G. L. Peterson, "A Model of Preference: Quantitative Analysis of the Visual Appearance of Residential Neighborhoods," *Journal of Regional Science* 7 (1967): 19-32. Another method, the paired comparisons technique, requires respondents to make a series of binary choices among alternatives using an attractiveness criterion. Analysis of these data yields preference rankings on a ratio-relevant attractiveness scale. See A. L. Edwards, "The Method of Paired Comparisons," in *Techniques of Attitude Scale Construction* (New York: Appleton-Century-Crofts, 1957), pp. 19-52.

2. Charles E. Osgood, George J. Suci, and Percy H. Tannenbaum, *The Measurement of Meaning* (Urbana: University of Illinois Press, 1957). A representative, but certainly not inclusive, list of alternative strategies would include cognitive mapping, thematic apperception testing, multidimensional scaling, and attitude scaling. David Stea, "Environmental Perception and Cognition: Toward a Model for 'Mental Maps,'" in *Response to Environment*, Student Publication of the School of Design no. 18, ed., Gary J. Coates and Kenneth M. Moffett (Raleigh: North Carolina State University, 1969), pp. 64-75; H. A. Murray, *Thematic Apperception Test: Pictures and Manual* (Cambridge Mass.: Harvard University Press, 1943); John Sims and Thomas F. Saarinen, "Coping with Environmental Threat: Great Plains Farmers and the Sudden Storm," *Annals of the Association of American Geographers* 59 (1969): 677-86; Warren S. Torgerson, "Multidimensional Scaling," in *Theory and Methods of Scaling* (New York: Wiley, 1958), pp. 247-97; Edwards, "Method of Paired Comparisons;" and Myra R. Schiff, "Some Theoretical Aspects of Attitudes and Perception," *Natural Hazards Research*, University of Toronto, Department of Geography Working Paper no. 15 (1970).

3. The logic and method of semantic differentiation derives from the notion that every concept (e.g., log cabin) has a meaning which is made evident by the manner in which a representative sample of people describe it (e.g., interesting, old, unusual, humble, honest). The measurement instrument, termed a semantic differential, consists of a series of bipolar (opposed in meaning) adjective scales on which respondents rate concepts according to the extent of their association with one or the other adjectives in each pair. In the example that follows, a hypothetical respondent has rated the concept covered bridge "very interesting," "slightly passive," "quite old," "quite valuable," and so forth.

COVERED BRIDGE

interesting	x							dull
passive			x					active
old			x					new
worthless						x		valuable
•								•
•								•
•								•
strong		x						weak

The specific adjective pairs used in any given semantic differential will depend upon the concepts at issue and will normally be determined by a pretest of an extensive list. Data analysis is accomplished by a factor analytic technique that identifies the major axes (or dimensions) along which the concepts are judged to exist and expresses the meaning of each concept in terms of its location on each of the axes. This has the desired effect of reducing the inherent complexity of concept meaning to a number of simple components and permits comparison amongst them on the basis of *salient* differences and similarities in meaning. See Osgood, Suci, and Tannenbaum, *Measurement of Meaning.*

4. David Canter, "An Intergroup Comparison of Connative Dimensions in Architecture," *Environment and Behavior* 1 (1969): 37-48; Roger Downs, "The Cognitive Structure of an Urban Shopping Center," *Environment and Behavior* 2 (1970): 13-39; Joseph Sonnenfeld, "Equivalence and Distortion of the Perceptual Environment," *Environment and Behavior* 1 (1969): 83-99; and Stephen Golant and Ian Burton, "A Semantic Differential Experiment in the Interpretation and Grouping of Environmental Hazards," *Geographical Analysis* 2 (1970): 120-34.

Antebellum Interregional Trade
The Mississippi River as an Example

SAM B. HILLIARD

Regional self-sufficiency and interregional trade have been major themes in the study of nineteenth-century development in the United States. Discussion over such matters has filled innumerable pages of literature of the era and provided notable entertainment at associational meetings.[1] Briefly stated, the arguments center around the major regions —the East, West, and South—and their relative dependence upon each other for agricultural commodities, services, and manufactured goods. Recognized since antebellum times, this strong regional interdependence was reiterated by historians early in the twentieth century, and has become an integral part of economic history lore. One of the better summaries was written by Louis B. Schmidt in the 1930s:

> The rise of internal commerce after 1815 made possible a territorial division of labor between the three great sections of the Union—the West, the South, and the East. The markets which were developed for various products opened the way for the division of labor in regions where it had been practically unknown before. Each section tended to devote itself more exclusively to the production of those commodities for which it was best able to provide. There was fostered a mutual economic dependence between sections and the establishment of predominant types of industry in each which were in turn dependent on foreign commerce. The South was thereby enabled to devote itself in particular to the production of a few plantation staples contributing a large and growing surplus for the foreign markets and depending on the West for a large part of its food supply and on the East for the bulk of its manufactured goods and very largely for the conduct of its commerce and banking. The East was devoted

chiefly to manufacturing and commerce, supplying the products of its industries as well as the imports and much of the capital for the West and the South while it became to an increasing extent dependent on the food and the fibers of these two sections. The West became a surplus grain-and-livestock producing kingdom, supplying the growing deficits of the South and East.[2] (Figure 1)

Although Dr. Schmidt's interpretation is overly simplistic, leaving much room for criticism, it does outline a major theme in southern history. Moreover, his conclusion was based upon the considerable evidence of a large interregional food trade, much of which moved along the Mississippi River. A number of trade routes connected the major regions but three were especially important—the Hudson-Mohawk lowland, the coastwise Gulf-Atlantic route, and the Mississippi waterway—with the latter being most important in connecting the South and West. Even a casual glance at the physical arrangement of the eastern United States reveals the striking dominance of the Mississippi River. Majestic in its own right, its importance was magnified when augmented by the flowage of the major tributaries. Given the importance of waterborne commerce in the seventeenth and eighteenth centuries, it is no wonder that nineteenth-century visionaries waxed eloquent over the possibilities. New Orleans was lauded as the "natural" outlet for western produce, and its proponents foresaw that the "bounty" of half the nation would ride on the father of waters.

The presence of the Mississippi River system undoubtedly influenced economic activity in both the West and the Gulf South throughout the antebellum period. During the first third of the nineteenth century, it served as the major outlet for an otherwise isolated agricultural region and helped to make possible the growth and specialization of agriculture and industry in other parts of the country. In the last two or three decades before the Civil War, the Mississippi route was displaced by the northern water routes as the most important outlet for western goods, but the downriver traffic remained important until after the war. The Mississippi River system also had profound effects upon food supply in the South. Not always willing to produce foodstuffs in sufficient quantities to feed its own population, parts of the South depended upon western goods to make up any existing food deficiencies.[3]

A number of factors make a detailed assessment of the Mississippi River trade difficult. First, data on foodstuffs moving downriver are incomplete and probably inaccurate. Variation in container sizes and types (barrels, tierces, hogsheads, boxes, sacks) resulted in inaccuracy, and methods of compiling data must have resulted in underestimates

Interregional Trade

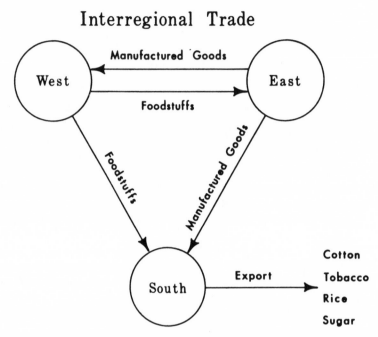

FIG. 1. *Cartogram of hypothetical interregional trade.*

in some cases and duplication in others. Another factor is that there is virtually no reliable information on river trade that trickled off into towns and plantations along the river upstream from New Orleans. Despite these inadequacies, there are enough data to substantiate an important river trade and to stimulate curiosity.[4]

An inventory of items moving onto New Orleans wharves during the second third of the nineteenth century reveals a wide assortment of goods (table 1). Not only did the city act as an entrepôt for southern-produced cotton and sugar, but through it was funneled much of the commercial output of the entire Mississippi-Ohio-Missouri-Tennessee watershed. It must have been an impressive sight—wharves and warehouses filled with every conceivable item of trade. One reporter commented: "Here is a boat stowed with apples . . . cider, cheese, potatoes, butter, chickens, lard. . . . Flour from Virginia and Ohio . . . cotton from Arkansas and Mississippi, lumber from Tennessee, whiskey from Missouri, tobacco from Kentucky. . . . Pork without end, as if Ohio had emptied its lap at the door of New Orleans. Flour by the thousand barrels. . . ."[5]

TABLE 1

Nonfood Items that Moved into New Orleans
from Upriver

Bagging	Glass	Oil
Bale rope	Gun powder	linseed
Beeswax	Hemp	castor
Buffalo robes	Hides	bear
Cigars	Horns	Skins, deer
Cotton	Hay	Skins, bear
Candles	Iron	Shot
Coal	Lime	Soap
Flaxseed	Leather	Shingles
Furs	Lead	Tallow
Feathers	Oats	Tobacco
Gin		Tow
		Twine

Foodstuffs were especially important, and thousands of tons moved into the port (table 2). Potatoes, flour, wheat, corn, meal, pork, beef, apples, whiskey, butter, cheese, onions, and cider made up the list. A casual count in the records published in *DeBow's Review* reveals some fifty items arriving in the city from the interior, with twenty-three of these being some type of food. A portion of the foodstuffs were exported almost immediately either to foreign ports or to cities in the eastern United States, while the remainder was used to fill hungry stomachs in the South. A portion (probably much more than we realize) lay there to spoil. The city itself had a tremendous appetite and its markets were huge. Even the usually critical Mrs. Trollope described them in 1827 as ". . . handsome and well supplied."[6]

While the variety was impressive, a number of items were outstanding. The most important were the meats and cereals such as corn, wheat, flour, meal, pork, bacon, and beef. Borne on flatboats, keelboats, barges, and steamboats, these foods (as well as some live animals) moved downriver in large quantities throughout the first half of the century. In absolute figures the Mississippi trade maintained itself quite well through the years, but as facilities along the Great Lakes-Saint Lawrence-Mohawk routeway improved, an increasing proportion of the western produce was siphoned away and its importance relative to the

TABLE 2

Food Items that Moved into New Orleans
from Upriver

Ale	Dried fruit	Potatoes
Apples	Flour	Pork
Beans	Gin	Porter
Brandy	Lard	Sugar
Butter	Meal	Venison hams
Beef	Molasses	Vinegar
Corn	Onions	Whiskey
Cheese	Pecans	Wheat
Cider	Pickles	

eastern route declined. This was true of most of the food trade, though there was variation from one item to another. Receipts of pork and beef, for example, suffered a decline in absolute amounts after a peak in the early 1850s. Receipts of wheat flour, on the other hand, showed an overall increase up to the late 1850s. Since much of the discussion about West-South trade has centered on the southern foodstuff trade, it seems appropriate to concentrate on the more important foods that moved into the South. In this case we shall deal with pork, beef, corn, and wheat.

Of greatest concern to the student of southern agriculture was the downriver movement of pork. The movement of pork into New Orleans began in the early part of the century as the packing industry, centered in Cincinnati, began to market surpluses. This trade increased from about twenty thousand tons in 1840 to a high of nearly one hundred thousand tons at midcentury, after which it declined to less than sixty thousand tons by 1860 (figure 2).

The beef trade of New Orleans suffered considerably from competition of other routes out of the West. In 1840, New Orleans received a modest one thousand tons of beef but the trade surged upward reaching a peak of about six thousand tons, with one year approaching ten thousand tons in the early 1850s, after which they declined to about four thousand tons annually (figure 3).

A considerable quantity of corn and meal moved into New Orleans each year, but the immense corn crops produced throughout the re-

Pork Trade

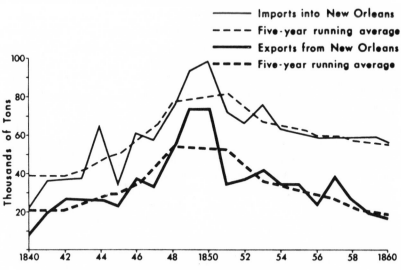

FIG. 2. *Pork trade of New Orleans.*

Beef Trade

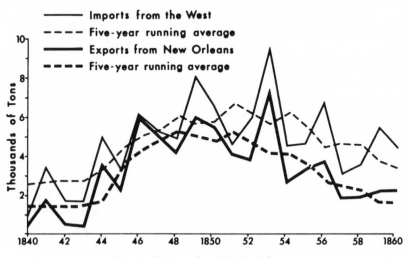

FIG. 3. *Beef trade of New Orleans.*

mainder of the South as well as the sizable crops grown in northern Louisiana, tended to limit the regional demand for corn. New Orleans and other urban areas consumed fair quantities but, except in bad crop years, the trade was much less important than either the wheat or pork trade. Imports of corn into New Orleans increased from a little over one million bushels in 1840 to about four million in 1846. A peak of nearly eight million bushels was reached around 1847, after which the annual trade decreased and leveled off at about three million bushels during the late 1840s (figure 4).

The movement of wheat and flour into New Orleans was quite erratic. The amounts received fluctuated widely from year to year, but unlike some commodities, wheat and flour imports continued to rise through the two decades. Based on five-year running averages, the imports were around two and a half million bushels in 1840 but were better than seven million by the end of the decade. A peak was reached during 1847-48 and a secondary high occurred during the early 1850s but, on the whole, the trend was upward (figure 5).

In addition to the regular river trade connecting New Orleans with the West was the local trade carried on upstream from New Orleans. Both itinerant traders and western farmers floated boats and rafts downriver and peddled their wares among the small villages and plantations along the rivers. A recent study of the western grain trade recognizes this local trade and estimates that it was very large, though little evidence is offered to substantiate the assertion.[7] Undoubtedly, the larger river towns such as Memphis, Vicksburg, Natchez, and Baton Rouge absorbed some provisions before they reached New Orleans, but data on this trade are rare and often difficult to interpret. For example, exports from Cincinnati give figures for "downriver ports," other than New Orleans, but do not specify the ports. Furthermore, Cincinnati was not the only center shipping foodstuffs south so the picture is somewhat hazy. On the whole, this writer believes the local trade in major foodstuffs carried on by farmers and bargemen along the stream above New Orleans was a relatively minor part of the total New Orleans trade. For one thing, it is difficult to demonstrate a large demand along the river. The only item greatly lacking was wheat, and one suspects that wheat deficits were not made up fully by imports but that southerners simply consumed considerably less than the national average. Furthermore, it is probable that planters along the river relied less on local bargemen than upon New Orleans factors for their supply. That such a situation should exist is puzzling, yet the advantages of trading with New Orleans merchants apparently offset any attractions the barge traffic offered.

Corn and Meal Trade

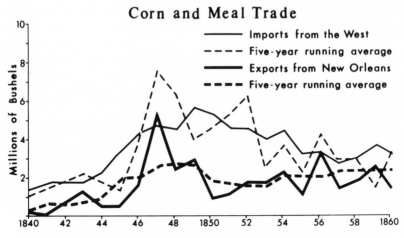

FIG. 4. *Corn and meal trade of New Orleans.*

Wheat Trade

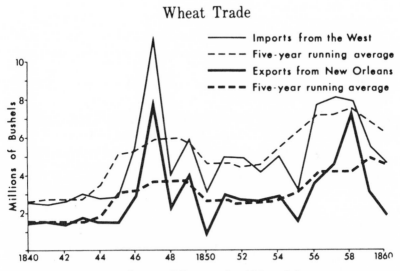

FIG. 5. *Wheat and flour trade of New Orleans.*

More than likely this resulted from the existence of a very active group of factors and merchants in New Orleans. Often handling the accounts of numerous planters in the interior, such businessmen were in a position to offer a wider range of goods and services and, thus, push out bargemen or local merchants who might have operated in places like Vicksburg or Natchez. This is not to say that the local river trade was nonexistent. It may have been much more important in trading perishable commodities (namely, potatoes, apples, cider, butter, cheese, and other fruits and vegetables) than was New Orleans. Where available, such items found a welcome market as evidenced by the Natchez newspaper that reported: "Apples and Irish potatoes are good things. We have had good things in Natchez for the last week . . . potatoes, with drawn butter and eggs; and apples raw, and apple dumplings, and apple pies, and baked apples, and roast potatoes, and potatoes boiled, and hash with potatoes in it . . . and sundry other fresh articles, for which we are annually indebted to the father of rivers, and one of his elder boys."[8]

On the whole, the local trade must have become relatively less important toward the end of the antebellum period. Most of the trade during the early years was borne by flatboats making it easier to do peddling between landings. Moreover, the trade sphere of New Orleans appears to have been much less well developed during the early years. The high cost of keelboating limited the amount of goods reshipped upriver, thus the local buyer looked to the bargeman for his produce.

One question that emerges from these data is the ultimate destination of foodstuffs moving downriver and its importance to the respective regions. In the case of pork, we must consider that quantity of meat that remained in the area for local use. Of the twenty thousand tons that moved into New Orleans in 1840, more than half moved through the city to other ports. However, this proportion did not remain constant. By the end of the period almost two-thirds of the pork was retained for local consumption. There were marked annual fluctuations, but the five-year running average shows an unmistakable increase (figure 2).

There were four major users of pork left in New Orleans: (1) the urban population of the city itself, (2) planters and other inhabitants of Louisiana outside New Orleans in which case pork moved into the city and then was sold to consumers located upriver or on streams and bayous in Lower Louisiana, (3) ships and steamboats plying the port of New Orleans whose crews needed provisions, and (4) plantations and towns along the Mississippi River and its tributaries within the state of Mississippi. Based on my own calculation of production and consumption, the deficit of Louisiana has been estimated at a little less than ten thousand tons in 1840 and 1850, and about twenty-one thousand tons by 1860.[9] However, these figures are based on data for the entire state including a number of high-production counties in northern Louisiana whose surplus hogs probably did not enter the commercial trade. Considering only the southern portion of the state and counties bordering the Mississippi River, the pork deficit was somewhat higher, approximately twelve thousand tons in 1840 and almost thirty thousand tons by 1860.

A substantial, though unknown, quantity of meat moved upriver from New Orleans into Mississippi. Mississippi had a high production potential in 1840, but it decreased steadily during the next two decades. Moreover, the number of deficient counties along the river increased. Based on the need within these deficient counties, Mississippi's needs were around one thousand tons in 1840, two thousand in 1850, and possibly four thousand in 1860.

The pork needed for provisioning ships is unknown, but certainly it was not insignificant. From 1851 and 1856 the number of vessels calling at New Orleans varied from about one thousand nine hundred fifty to about two thousand three hundred fifty (not including steamboats).[10] If each of these vessels took only one ton of pork (they probably took several tons), ships' provisions alone would have amounted to around two thousand tons or nearly 10 percent of the amount that remained in the city around 1850. If the steamboat trade is added, the figure easily could be doubled.

The uses outlined above appear to account for the greater part of the pork left in New Orleans. We must note, however, that additional pork may have moved into New Orleans but went unreported, and some pork probably trickled into the areas upriver from New Orleans, but we can only guess as to the scale of such a trade.

The trade in beef was comparatively less important than that of pork. Southerners simply were not beefeaters and this, together with the relatively large number of southern cattle, obviated the need for imports. However, despite this apparent surfeit of animals throughout the South, some beef and cattle moved down the Mississippi into New Orleans and the surrounding areas. The beef trade in New Orleans increased from about one thousand to over four thousand tons during the two decades, with a peak of around nine thousand tons in the early 1850s. Of the quantity that moved into New Orleans from upriver, a portion was exported, but a substantial proportion remained within the city for local use. This amount fluctuated from eight hundred to around

211

twelve hundred tons during the 1840-50 decade, after which it increased steadily until, by the late 1850s, a little over two thousand tons remained within the city each year. During some years it exceeded this amount, but the five-year running averages indicate a relatively steady but increasing quantity (figure 3).

Determining the ultimate use of this beef presents a different problem than was the case with pork. The huge Louisiana market for pork certainly was directly related to the virtual absence of hogs in southern Louisiana, a fact which was not true of the cattle industry. In fact, the Louisiana and Mississippi herders could have supplied the New Orleans market easily had their cattle been depended upon exclusively. However, it appears that herder-owned cattle suffered in comparison to the readily available (and presumably better quality) beef out of the West.

While the quantity of beef left for use in New Orleans increased during the last decade of the antebellum period, it remained relatively small compared to potential beef production in Louisiana and Lower Mississippi. Further, when one considers the needs of consumers in New Orleans and the demand for beef as a provision for ships and steamboats, little of the riverborne beef was left for resale to Louisiana planters or for shipment upriver into Mississippi. Approximately twelve hundred tons were left in New Orleans annually during the 1840s, and during the 1850s this increased to around two thousand tons. Even so, with a population of some one hundred seventy-five thousand in Orleans Parish, this would have amounted to only twenty-three pounds per capita in 1860. Not only could the city have consumed all the meat that moved downriver, it probably required additional beef from the Louisiana herds. Of course, there was some local barge trade along the river above the city, but compared to New Orleans, upstate Louisiana and Mississippi probably constituted minor markets.

Imports of corn into New Orleans increased from a little over one million bushels in 1840 to about three million in the late 1850s, with peaks of nearly eight million bushels in 1847 and six million in 1852. After that the trade remained between two and four million bushels. Annual exports followed imports closely during most years, with the amount remaining in the city varying from one to two million bushels. The only exception was during the early 1850s when the amount retained in the city tripled. As was the case with beef, the needs of the Crescent City accounted for most of the corn that remained in the city. Louisiana certainly did not have the trouble growing corn that it encountered in pork production (figure 4).

As noted earlier, the amount of corn left in New Orleans varied from one to about four million bushels annually during the three years for which we have production records. Although impressive in absolute number, these figures are not large considering the mouths to be fed in and around New Orleans, except for the years 1850-52 when unusually large quantities were left in the city. Nor does this include the consumption by plantations located outside Orleans Parish but near enough to purchase directly from within the city. Consequently, we must conclude that the corn that moved into New Orleans wharves was either exported from the city or consumed within or near it.

Turning to the last major item—wheat—we find that the amount of wheat left in New Orleans varied from about one to four million bushels during the two decades, with the peak years being 1846-57. During most other years it fluctuated between one and two million bushels (figure 5). Assuming a consumption rate of two bushels per capita (approximately half the national average), Louisiana had a potential deficiency of about six hundred thousand bushels in 1840, eight hundred thousand bushels in 1850, and better than a million in 1860. Mississippi's needs were about four hundred thousand in 1840, eight hundred thousand in 1850, and about seven hundred thousand in 1860. Together, they came close to accounting for the downriver trade. Moreover, we must consider the distinct possibility that urban dwellers consumed more wheat than rural southerners, expecially if it was readily available at a reasonable rate. Additionally, the large numbers of French inhabitants surely led to a high consumption of wheat flow in Lower Louisiana. Even today, there is an unmistakable love for pastries and wheat breads that is distinctly different from that of the Anglo-South.

As stated previously, there were other trade routes linking the West, East, and South. This paper deals only with the Mississippi River trade during the two decades immediately preceding the Civil War, yet its importance to the total West-South food trade lends strength to the conclusions that emerge. In absolute figures the Mississippi River food trade was impressive. It involved thousands of tons of provisions, much of which was exported, but significant quantities remained in New Orleans. Traditionally, this trade has been cited as evidence of interdependence between the food-producing West and the plantation South, yet when we consider the large demand *outside* the rural plantation system, it is difficult to visualize the river trade as a response to plantation food deficits. A more realistic view is to look upon the river trade as a response to urban and overseas markets, for together they greatly overshadowed the meager demands of the rural South.

213

NOTES

1. For a summary of the controversy, see R. L. Andreano, *New Views of American Economic Development* (Cambridge, Mass.: Schenkman Publishing Co., 1965), pp. 187-224. More recent works include Sam B. Hilliard, *Hog Meat and Hoecake: Food Supply in the Old South, 1840-1860* (Carbondale: Southern Illinois University Press, 1972); William K. Hutchinson and Samuel H. Williamson, "The Self-Sufficiency of the Antebellum South: Estimates of the Food Supply," *Journal of Economic History* 31 (September 1971): 591-612; and William N. Parker, ed., "The Structure of the Cotton Economy of the Antebellum South," *Agricultural History* 44 (January 1970).
2. Louis B. Schmidt, "Internal Commerce and the Development of the National Economy before 1860," *Journal of Political Economy* 47 (December 1939): 820.
3. Ibid.; Isaac Lippincott, "Internal Trade of the United States 1700-1860," *Washington University Studies* 4 (October 1916): 63-150; R. B. Way, "The Commerce of the Lower Mississippi in the Period 1830-1860," *Proceedings of the Mississippi Valley Historical Association* 5 (1918-21): 57-68; Albert L. Kohlmeier, *The Old Northwest as the Keystone of the Arch of American Federal Union* (Bloomington: Principia Press, 1938); and John G. Clark, *Grain Trade of the Old Northwest* (Urbana and London: University of Illinois Press, 1966).
4. Data on the Mississippi may be found in a number of places. The most comprehensive is William F. Switzler, *Report on the Inland Commerce of the United States*, U.S., Congress, Senate, 50th Cong., 1st sess., 1888, No. 6, pt. 2. Other sources are the various issues of *DeBow's Review* and *Hunt's Merchant's Magazine* and many of the southern agricultural periodicals.
5. James D. B. DeBow, *The Industrial Resources, Statistics, Etc. of the United States* (New York: D. Appleton and Co., 1854), 2:137-38.
6. Francis M. Trollope, *Domestic Manners of the Americans* (London: Whitaker, Treacher, and Co. 1832), 1:8.
7. Clark, *Grain Trade*, pp. 47-49.
8. Ulrich B. Phillips, ed., *Plantation and Frontier Documents: 1649-1863*, Documentary History of American Industrial Society, vols. 1 and 2 (Cleveland: Arthur H. Clark Co., 1909), 1:181-82.
9. For detail on the method of calculation see Hilliard, *Hog Meat and Hoecake*, pp. 102-6.
10. *DeBow's Review* (1854), 17:623; ibid. (1857), 23:374.

Archives and the Design
of Transportation Research

FRANKLIN W. BURCH

The word "design" in the title of this paper should be taken in a very general sense. It does not mean the design of controlled experiments or surveys nor the ways in which contemporary transportation needs and circumstances are stimulating a kind of applied humanities. Computation and simulation are not the keys to all social wisdom, and I shall not mention counterfactual research or postdictive studies, interesting though they are. This discussion is rather about some relationships, very simple and perhaps painfully obvious ones, between records and research. Although too much has been made of supposed communications gaps, there is a distance between the usual initial positions of archivists and researchers—between the directions in which they usually first look —that is, between the activities of the federal government that lead to the creation of records and the development of fields of knowledge.

The historic program roles of the federal government in transportation, as investor, engineer, regulator, and operator in what is less and less a private enterprise field, have been carried on by a number of agencies. The following litany of National Archives record group titles for civilian agencies alone (many of which are now defunct or part of the Department of Transportation), conveys well the range of activity in this area: the Alaska Railroad, Federal Aviation Administration, Civil Aeronautics Board, Federal Coordinator of Transportation, Office of Defense Transportation, Federal Highway Administrator, Inland Waterways Corporation, Interstate Commerce Commission, Bureau of

Marine Inspection and Navigation, Maritime Administration, Federal Maritime Commission, United States Maritime Commission, Maritime Labor Board, Bureau of Public Roads, Commissioner of Railroads, Federal Railroad Administration, United States Railroad Administration, Railroad Retirement Board, Saint Lawrence Seaway Development Corporation, Shipbuilding Stabilization Committee, War Shipping Administration, United States Shipping Board, Transportation and Communications Service, United States Travel Service, and Urban Mass Transit Administration.

Any researcher using the records of these agencies would probably also use the related records of higher executive, legislative, and judicial organizations in other record groups. There is still another world of transportation records in the National Aeronautics and Space Administration and the major components of defense agencies.

Historically, the term "internal improvements" connoted a constant interplay between private enterprise and national, state, and local governments until nearly the end of the nineteenth century. Thus, the archives of state and local governments are indeed at the grassroots of transportation research, in a political and in an area sense. In the future, some states may find all their transportation planning data on university computers. The archives of major private transportation corporations are slowly being opened, and it would be good to have a list of what can be used by researchers. There are, for example, 9,500 linear feet of Northern Pacific Railroad records, covering the years from the 1860s to the 1950s now available for use, with the permission of the Burlington Northern, at the Minnesota Historical Society.

Transportation has always been recognized and historically evaluated in its nation-building role. It is now often the first stage of complex locational and regional analyses. We have looked to historical geographers to explain our patterns of response, particularly since 1915, when C. J. Galpin observed in his survey of rural patterns of movement that the automobile made the farmer a "free lance," no longer tied to the nearest small settlement.[1] In recent years, as farmers left the land, commuting areas became the basis of economic regions and urban districts, while more and more of our social problems have focused on the automobile. Commodity and passenger flow studies have been incorporated into broader studies of transportation as an interacting element in networks, patterns, migration, markets, and accessibility. Now, theoretical debates about what is unique in geography take a tangible form when neighborhoods protest freeway locations. Regardless of the mode of transportation, from a public policy standpoint people seem to be spending an inordinate amount of time spinning their wheels. And that spinning is producing an almost unimaginable quantity of documentation.

How transportation research in geography has changed in recent decades is indicated in the summary publications of the National Academy of Sciences/National Research Council Committee on Geography and the National Academy of Sciences/Social Science Research Council Behavioral and Social Sciences Survey. The historical geographer is, I think, too simply dealt with in the NAS/NRC publication, *The Science of Geography*. It is suggested there that the historical (and regional) geographer "can make himself indispensable if he understands the direction in which the generalizing clusters are headed and relates his work closely to their growing edges."[2] There is a large area for comment around that big "if."

Of more direct concern is the fact that the current participation of geographers, both official and academic, in transportation policy and planning studies is giving them an earlier and a better idea than in the past of what records are available and what records are being created. But it matters not to an archivist if historical geographers see their work as part of natural science, social science, behavioral science, the humanities, or as standing alone. In methodological warfare, the archivist should be a neutral, but not a naive neutral.

Those of us who have withstood the lure of studies claiming the power to predict find an element of liberation in directly confronting sources not of our own creation. As an antidote to methodological over-sophistication and scholarship based merely on shifting the position of the observer, it is salutary exercise from time to time to think about the elementary distinctions between the techniques that one needs to use sources and the methods that tell one what evidence there is and what it means. Historical geography today is in an extremely strong position in this respect because of the versatility of its attack along empirical, behavioral, and theoretical lines. These three realms of historical geography, which use sources in somewhat different ways, are very well delineated by Hugh C. Prince in his article, "Real, Imagined and Abstract Worlds of the Past."[3]

It is certainly true that much research in geography can be and has been done using only published sources. Of course, published sources may also be archival sources, and, in fact, government publications have presented one of the most difficult appraisal and retention problems for archivists. The Interstate Commerce Commission's waybill statistical sample, begun in 1946, is a classic example of how much research on transporation a single source can support. The Interstate Commerce Commission issues about twenty-two publications, mostly annually, for the statistical series created on the basis of the 1 percent waybill sample from Class I railroads.

Many geography departments or their university libraries are now systematically acquiring source material published on microfilm. Available through the National Archives, for example, are 1,348 rolls of microfilm of the annual reports of common carriers to the ICC for the years 1888-1914. Geographers apparently have not used the Department of State diplomatic and consular dispatches very much or the Department of the Navy series of letters. Many of these are also on microfilm and are a fine source for a variety of studies, including those analyzing American perceptions of foreign areas and culture, to say nothing of foreign trade and logistics.

Historical geographers skillfully and systematically use maps, aerial photos, and statistics. And the objective of this publication is to highlight the challenge that lies in the hundreds of unpublished archival series of correspondence, administrative hearings, policy/planning studies, memorandums, program subject files, agency legislative, legal, and intergovernmental records, technical survey data, and budget records, many of which have an intricate network of central and field office copies.

Before discussing access to those series, two books deserve mention. One general published research tool, which contains much that I think all archivists would like all researchers to know, is *Government Publications and Their Use* by Lawrence F. Schmeckebier and Roy B. Eastin.[4] It is somewhat uneven in its coverage, but there is substantial and essential information, a "taken-for-granted-that-you-know-it" kind of information, in the chapters on catalogs and indexes, bibliographies, classification, congressional publications, constitutions, laws, court decisions, administrative regulations, presidential papers, and departmental operations. A critical use of easily accessible published sources while planning archival work makes possible a more intelligent and economical use of unpublished archival sources. The other book, which any scholar whose work will require systematic and frequent use of records in the National Archives should master at an early stage of his career, is titled, *Modern Archives, Principles and Techniques*, by the late T. R. Schellenberg.[5] Aside from its status as perhaps the only classic American contribution to the lasting body of archival writings, Schellenberg's elaboration of principles and techniques represented much of what was, and I think still is, common practice and operating assumptions of the National Archives. The book delineates, in fewer pages than any other book, the minimum areas of mutual understanding for staff archivists and visiting researchers.

Researchers are justifiably impatient to begin, whether or not their formal training has fitted them for archival research. Books like Schmeckebier's and Schellenberg's are not within the direct institutional responsibility of the National Archives but guides, inventories, and other finding aids for the records are. Now available for researchers is the long-awaited guide to cartographic records. Next, I hope, will be the publication of the still longer awaited new general guide to the National Archives. All archival finding aids, regardless of national origins, constitute a fascinating and a fairly well-defined genre. They provide a stimulus for ideas and planning research strategies and tactics, aside from the practicalities of their primary purposes. Every practitioner in a historical field needs that kind of help in his continuing intellectual battles between what is worth knowing and what can be known.

It is possible that archivists have allowed their responsibility for the physical order of records in a frugal archival economy to overly influence the format of their finding aids. Perennial problems arise between the researcher's usual subject-oriented requests and the archivist's organizationally or functionally arranged records. Since the publication in 1948 of a reference information paper on transportation records, the National Archives has not published a subject-oriented guide on transportation. It is too simple merely to say that it should have or should not have. A researcher can easily survey the published and unpublished inventories for the record groups of the principal transportation agencies, although these do not contain all the records that may be considered to relate to transportation. It is debatable whether or not finding aids that are subject-oriented in their primary or secondary classifications are of greater continuing usefulness than other kinds of aids. After initial explorations, it would seem that origin, time, and place are as useful arrangements as subject. It has taken the potentialities of computers to bring about a new look at the handling of the raw material of archival series descriptions. But I assume that there is agreement that no computer-based technology can supply exhaustive sets of research options for the use of records.

All these relationships between research and records are, of course, evident to anyone who pursues a study very far. A few years ago, initial research in the construction period of the Alaska Railroad, 1914-23—for which the archival sources were voluminous—led me to seek answers to questions about the preceding period, beginning in 1898, when private railroads were interested in Alaska. Aside from the White Pass and Yukon records, there were few corporate records extant. An analysis of railroads as found on published maps of Alaska would never excite a geographer, but the right-of-way maps filed in the General Land Office, reflecting dreams, plans, fraud, and track laid, probably would. My study of Alaska's railroad frontier between 1898 and 1915 became focused on the relations between federal development policy and private enterprise. These relations were amply documented (more on one side than the other) in at least fifteen record groups in the National Archives, in the private papers of three major federal administrators in the Library of Congress, in the records of continuous congressional hearings on Alaskan bills, and, from the standpoint of international competition, in the Public Archives of Canada. A guide to Alaskan records in the National Archives was then underway, but even the location of Alaska material proved difficult, wonderfully reflecting how widely dispersed were Alaskan interests among federal agencies. I did what any researcher should do—asked the help of the staff archivists who knew the records.

In the course of the study, the developing segments of what are now called resource management policies were revealed in the records of bureaucratic actions and reactions underlying the politics of the early conservation movement and the Progressive Era. Evaluations of these sources, asking why, and searching for structures of understanding and explanation, led to the research topics then being developed by others in historical geography and economics, which led back again to more searching in the records. Among other things, source evaluation made clear that environmental perception was as important to Alaskan decisions as any kind of environmental determinism, and that federal scientific agencies were strongly influenced by unexamined cultural values in developing natural resource management policies.

No one really believes, I hope, that to use an official record means to adopt an official view. After several cycles of neglect, it is easier now to appreciate the consequences of ignoring, for example, military history because we dislike war. It remains to be seen whether or not the current fashion for deprecating government and bureaucracy will lead to something more productive in administrative history. Using administrative history, for which the National Archives should be a center, to manage intellectually the vast scope of federal governmental activity offers few elements that can be converted into parlor games. A landmark as obvious as the creation in 1966 of the Department of Transportation has large influences on related records systems throughout government, and, therefore, on what needs to be known for the later selection and research uses of the archival portions of those records systems.

We are, today, at the end of about three decades of continuing efforts to reshape the transportation roles of national, state, and local governments, and no one thinks that job is complete. The expansion of federal activity in transportation fields in recent decades and the ways in which geographers and other scholars are studying transportation illustrate why both archivists and researchers must know more about each other's work as it progresses. Much of this exchange happens easily, every day. So I am not suggesting that what F. M. Cornford said about books and the young applies to archives and researchers. "The best way to protect the young from books," said Cornford, "is, first, to make sure that they shall be so dry as to offer no temptation; and, second, to store them in such a way that no one can find them without several years' training."[6] Archivists can study published works and see how sources have been used, but they generally lose contact with the ways that research and writing skills are taught in academic settings. Several years ago a study was begun to determine the ways in which original documentary source materials are used in the training of historians. The published results of the study testify primarily to the disarray in that field. It is puzzling to read that for graduate students in history "having to employ unknown research methods to find material often results in apprehensiveness and frustration."[7]

Archivists and researchers will continue to insist that the meaning of sources requires an understanding of the organization that produced them, its purpose, and its relation to others. It is always noted that archives result from activity, thus the words "organic," "system," and "process" are used to characterize them. There is a tendency, however, not to evaluate archival series in relation to the processes that produced them but only to extract from them items to be treated as discrete, unrelated documents. The diversity and quantity of archival series in the National Archives call for the continued development of a new archival heuristic—something more from the institution than the best finding aid so far produced, and something more from research methodologies than the outmoded search strategies of getting all the facts from all the documents on a subject. It seems to me that the archivist still has no clearcut role in a soundly supported division of labor to take the place of the one on which the old scientific history developed, that is, the division between the analytical work of critical scholars in external criticism and the work of historians in synthesis.

It is perhaps not sufficiently understood that what an archival institution does in designating some records for retention and ordering the destruction of others is analogous, on a large, indeterminate scale, to stages of a research process. The process is usually associated with the work of a single scholar and now, increasingly, with teams using computer-based data. But an archival institution creates and makes available for research a selected body of source material, "new" at least in the sense that the mass of records of which it was a part has been, or will be, destroyed. We have not really come to terms with the fact that what will be retained is now subject more to deliberate choice than to chance, nor with the problems resulting from the fact that many archival selection criteria must be of a methodological rather than a substantive nature.

Geographers have found quantitative data in archives difficult to use because of its partial character, its noncomparability, and the absence of common-unit area designators. Those considerations have turned geographers back to the improved design of their own field survey techniques and to continuing efforts to influence governmental data-gathering and statistical activities.

Contemporary issues have thus far focused public attention on our vast quantities of records, on the protection of privacy, and on computer applications. Almost totally ignored in the public media are the more basic decision structures for records creation, destruction, and retention. Archival appraisal theory and practice reflect, perhaps better than anything else, the direction in which an institution is moving. Although every researcher need not know the structure of law, rules, procedures, theory, facts, conclusions, and human and physical resources that assist or constrain the selection of records of archival value in an institutionalized decision-making process, professional organizations should insure that at least some of their active members are engaged in what might be termed "archives watching."

Although the study of historical geography has been well served by the National Archives, it is a temptation to think that they do order these things better in France. For example, an oral examination in the historical geography of France remains part of the entrance requirements of the École des Chartes, the French national school for medievalists, archivists, and librarians. Perhaps the most continually useful academic curriculum for a public archivist in this country remains a concentration in political history, which brings together constitutional, legal, diplomatic, military, and administrative history, with side dashes of political philosophy. The training of an archivist, whatever his formal education, is best done in a master and apprentice relationship, not as professor and student. As in other fields, what an archivist does on the job is far more important than what he has previously studied.

For the National Archives as an institution, a guided development of staff specialists in the disposition and research uses of records of the larger clusters of governmental activity is now more than ever necessary. This publication should provide incentives. The desirable pattern of archival competences should not be one that sees historians temporarily employed as archivists assisting historical geographers, for example, because they all have some common interest in history. It should be a pattern in which archivists, by being active scholars throughout their unique domain of public archives, are able to respond and contribute to the needs of all research disciplines, regardless of what records are used or why.

NOTES

1. C. J. Galpin, *The Social Anatomy of an Agricultural Community,* University of Wisconsin Agricultural Experiment Station Research Bulletin no. 34 (May 1915), p. 34.
2. *The Science of Geography,* Report of the Ad Hoc Committee on Geography, Earth Sciences Division, National Academy of Sciences/National Research Council Publication no. 1277 (Washington, D. C., 1965), p. 61
3. Hugh C. Prince, "Real, Imagined and Abstract Worlds of the Past," *Progress in Geography,* International Reviews of Current Research Series, ed. Christopher Board et al. (London: Edward Arnold, 1971), 3:1-86.
4. Lawrence F. Schmeckebier and Roy B. Eastin, *Government Publications and Their Use,* 2d ed. rev. (Washington, D. C.: Brookings Institution, 1969).
5. T. R. Schellenberg, *Modern Archives, Principles and Techniques* (Chicago: University of Chicago Press, 1956).
6. F. M. Cornford, *Microcosmographia Academica, Being a Guide for the Young Academic Politician,* 8th ed. (London: Bowes & Bowes, 1970), p. 11.
7. Walter Rundell, Jr., *In Pursuit of American History, Research and Training in the United States* (Norman: University of Oklahoma Press, 1970), p. 240.

Selected Materials in the National Archives Relating to Commerce and Industry

MEYER H. FISHBEIN

Researchers in the National Archives may well wonder how the members of the staff achieve the status of "expert" in various subject areas. Most of the specialists acquire their knowledge about particular topics, mainly in the field of United States history, through academic studies. After their appointment to the National Archives, they are assigned custodial responsibilities for records of agencies that are important generators of sources for these topics. As the experience of archivists broadens so does the area of their archival responsibility. A few, like me many years ago, are assigned records of certain related agencies and then steer their studies to the relevant topics.

My first assignment in the National Archives was as a laborer shelving records of the National Recovery Administration. Adjacent to my work area were the records of the Commerce and Labor Departments, the Interstate Commerce Commission, the Federal Trade Commission, and the Reconstruction Finance Corporation. Understandably, my earliest impression was that virtually all records in this institution related to commerce and industry. After many months, I learned that a great quantity of records dealt with such minor topics as military and diplomatic affairs, legislation, land management, and the administration of justice.

Industrial geography helped me rise above the laboring class when, soon after my appointment, I found for Leon Henderson, then the director of the Office of Price Administration, a set of NRA maps showing distribution zones for several industries. Many years later I used the NRA records for a study of the trucking industry, one of more than six hundred fifty industries that were covered by codes of fair competition. Each of these industries is represented by NRA documentation about its business leaders, location, trade associations, production, distributive channels, trade practices, manpower, working conditions, costs, prices, and other quantitative and qualitative data. This detailed information about the American economy between the world wars was gathered by an agency created by an unconstitutional act, the National Industrial Recovery Act. The Supreme Court declared, in the famous "sick chicken" case, that the act was in violation of Article I, Section 1, of the Constitution.

Federal programs relating to commerce and industry, like all legislative, judicial, and executive activities, are derived from the Constitution. Section 1, to which I referred, delegated all legislative power to Congress. The House of Representatives and the Senate have produced and received millions of documents relating to commerce and industry as by-products of the legislative process. Those of greatest research value have been in the custody of congressional committees. Each congressional committee usually transfers its records to the Archives within six years. Records of investigative committees, like those dealing with air- and surface-mail contracts (1933-35), the munitions industry (1934-46), and petroleum (1945-46) are rich sources for commercial data.

Skip a few lines in the Constitution and read that the House of Representatives is apportioned on the basis of population. To determine this apportionment the Constitution provides for an enumeration "within three years after the first Meeting of The Congress of the United States, and within every subsequent Term of ten Years." We have no evidence that the delegates to the Constitutional Convention foresaw a relationship between this provision and American commerce and industry, but, as we know, the constitutional powers have been expanded far beyond the original intent of these delegates.

The census of 1790 identified free white males over and under sixteen, thus providing a source for determining potential military manpower. Since then, of course, the census has expanded to provide sources for social and economic indicators. When Congress was considering legislation for the second census, it received a memorial from the Connecticut Academy of Arts and Sciences requesting inquiries on "the progress and decline of occupations." The American Philosophical Society petitioned for data on "the causes which influence life and health in these states, . . . the conditions and vocations of our fellow citizens," and the number of persons in the learned professions, fine arts, banking, insurance, commerce, handicrafts, and agriculture. These memorials got nowhere.

For the 1810 census the law authorized the collection of data on manufactures (kind, quantity, and value of production). A fragment of these raw data appear in the population schedules for that year. In 1820 the census of manufactures added the location of the establishment; the kind, quantity, and cost of the raw materials used; the number of men, women, boys, and girls employed; amount of capital invested; and the annual wages and contingent expenses. Twenty-one volumes of schedules of returns of this census are here in the National Archives and microfilm copies are available for sale.

In 1830 there was no census of manufactures. But in 1832 there was a census of certain manufactures in certain states. The Treasury Department conducted this census to gather data for tariff legislation, a hot issue of the time. The authority derives, I presume, from Article I, Section 8: "The Congress shall have Power to collect Taxes, Duties, Imposts and Excises." The original schedules for this enumeration were transferred to Congress with the summary published report and are now among the files of the Twenty-second Congress.

In 1840 the industrial census resumed, taking in mines, agriculture, commerce, manufactures, and schools. From then on, the scope of the special censuses has progressively broadened. The Archives is obtaining microfilm copies of the censuses of manufactures for the period 1850-80 because the Census Bureau distributed the original schedules to state institutions in 1919.

Most of the powers delegated to Congress under Section 8, in addition to the taxing power, generated large quantities of records relating to economic enterprises. The Treasury Department's records on taxes and duties include assessment books for income taxes levied against business for the period 1862 to 1915. These books contain information on production and income for the company and the taxes paid by individual businessmen. Customs records date from the establishment of the federal government and include considerable documentation about imports and exports, including many impost books and cargo manifests. Customhouse records are being transferred to our regional archives.

The income provided from taxes and duties were "to provide for the national defense and general welfare." The latter was the presumed justification for the NRA and numerous other agencies whose constitutional basis has been questioned. The courts have interpreted the defense powers quite broadly. Emergency control over our economy, including the recent price and wage freeze, is justified by war powers. The "war" emergency agencies from World War I to the present acquired and created voluminous records that may, subject to restrictions to protect business secrets, provide researchers with primary sources for American industries and, within these industries, thousands of firms.

The Department of Defense and its predecessors has had close relations with suppliers of goods and services. While most of the related records are disposable, a considerable quantity of materials remain in archival storage. These papers show how the army and navy carried out their responsibilities. The armed forces also provided their own goods and services. Records of armories and shipyards show the industrial process better than most business archives. The navy has been one of the largest industrial establishments in the nation.

Power "to regulate Commerce with foreign Nations, and among the several States, and with the Indian Tribes" generated other foreign trade records of the Treasury and Commerce Departments, case files of the Interstate Commerce and Federal Trade Commissions, and records on Indian trade in the Bureau of Indian Affairs. Let me illustrate by a few details about the ICC records. The index to the docketed cases shows the names of places and carriers and the commodities carried. The case files dealing with rates, the expansion and contraction of railroads, time zones, and other matters include petitions and statements from almost every community in the country on their transportation facilities and needs. Many also include maps, reports, affidavits, and other supporting evidence. One case, for 1887, documents the movement of immigrants from the port of entry. Others deal with the relationships among several means of transportation and the transportation problems in many industries.

Another ICC series of interest is the valuation case files. These were created under a 1913 act of Congress which required each common carrier to submit a considerable volume of documentation in order to establish a basis of initial valuation of its property. Some of these case files extend into the 1930s and contain detailed information about the carriers and their predecessors. Other records on our transportation system, with excellent resources for historical geographers, were created as by-products of the power "to establish Post Offices and Post Roads."

The types of records that I have mentioned raise important problems for archivists. We must choose which records are useful for research on important topics and therefore deserve preservation at the public expense. As director of the Records Appraisal Staff of the National Archives, it is my responsibility to oversee decisions on the retention and disposal of records. The complexity of this problem can be understood by referring to one file—the tariffs submitted to the ICC. The 1887 Interstate Commerce Act required every interstate carrier to file with the ICC copies of schedules "showing the rates and fares and charges for the transportation of passengers and property." This section created records showing the transportation rates for persons and/or goods moving interstate by rail, motor, water, or pipeline. The ICC says that it has no further use for the tariffs twenty years after the dates of their cancellation. Thus, my staff's problem is to determine whether the individual tariffs have value to researchers after the twenty years. There are on hand millions of individual tariffs; there were, in fact, two million on file with the ICC at the turn of the century. Last year the ICC received 305,000 tariff publications for filing.

We recognize residual research values of the tariffs for studies of transportation costs. Some researchers are certainly familiar with the monograph by Robert Fogel of the social costs of railroads at the latter part of the century and his counterfactual analysis of costs had there been no railroads. These tariffs were one of Fogel's primary sources.

We doubt that all tariffs need to be retained for this type of research. Therefore, a sampling of about three thousand cubic feet has been earmarked for retention. Most of these are for rail carriers, with smaller quantities for water and motor carriers, pipelines, freight forwarders, and express companies. We gave considerable thought to the sampling scheme. The sample is now at the Washington National Records Center.

Three thousand feet are still a lot of records. They represent a problem not solved but in abeyance. We have instructed the Washington National Records Center to keep a log of all research use made of these tariffs to determine whether they do, in fact, deserve preservation.

What authorizes us to make decisions on retention or disposal? I am not really certain but believe we will have to stand on Article IV, Section 3, Clause 2: "The Congress shall have Power to dispose of and make all needful Rules and Regulations respecting the Territory or other Property belonging to the United States." Congress, in its infinite wisdom, decided to delegate to the National Archives problems of disposal of records. Researchers will deliver the final judgment on our decisions. We save the records for them. Unless our potential market demands the files we retain, we are needlessly burdening taxpayers.

Discussion Summary

The discussion was conducted by *Douglas R. McManis, Department of Geography, Columbia University,* chairman of the session on Transportation, Commerce, and Industry.

Joel Sobel, Department of Geography, University of Minnesota, began the discussion by asking *Sam B. Hilliard, Department of Geography, Louisiana State University,* how he was able to differentiate northwestern produce in New Orleans from all other produce. Dr. Hilliard pointed out that although it is difficult to differentiate on a year-by-year basis for every item, data are available from *DeBow's Review,* United States government documents, and *Hunt's Merchant's Magazine.* As an example, he cited that for trade across Lake Pontchartrain, the destinations would be given for items such as cotton, sugar, and similar items. In other cases, Dr. Hilliard concluded, "You assume that certain goods had to come from the Old Northwest. For example, many of the foodstuffs simply were not produced in sufficient quantities in the Deep South for there to have been much of a trade."

John Brush, Geography Department, Rutgers University, then turned the discussion to that aspect of the study by *Martyn J. Bowden, Graduate School of Geography, Clark University,* concerning the classification of business units in the central business district and the differing impact that large establishments (partnerships or corporations) have on the frequency of changes as opposed to small establishments (individual establishments or single entrepreneurs). Dr. Brush pointed out that the majority of business turnovers, defined by entrance and disappearance of firms or entrepreneurs, would probably consist of small establishments, and that this type of turnover could distort the researcher's conclusions because it would appear as a large statistic even though the total volume of business in relation to the large establishments was small. Dr. Bowden acknowledged that many of the business establishments were small, particularly new businesses. Many of these were marginal and did not last very long. "That's why," he continued, "the failure rates are appreciably higher in the districts made up of very small establishments, . . . whereas in the districts composed of very large establishments, the failure rates tend to fall off quite markedly after the first two or three decades."

In spite of this trend, Dr. Bowden argued, it was the very large corporate establishments (or dominants) that were in essence "the locational decision makers, and the others (the smaller establishments) tended to follow." As an example, Dr. Bowden briefly reviewed the financial district of San Francisco, where the failure rate was very high. "In terms of developing a theory of central district growth," he concluded, "this means . . . that in certain districts we can simply forget this vast number of activities coming in. In terms of locational theory we are really concerned with the location decision making of these few critical activities that are the dominants in the districts." Only in districts "that are almost entirely composed of activities of similar size or where the range of the size is not great," such as during the initial period of development, do small, new businesses have an impact on locational change in central business districts.

Peirce F. Lewis, Department of Geography, Pennsylvania State University, then turned the discussion to the topic of historic landscapes as a resource. Dr. Lewis directed his first question to the problem of retention of the authenticity of past landscapes in an emerging contemporary landscape. *John A. Jakle, Department of Geography, University of Illinois,* agreed that it is a basic problem and that every community must solve this problem by itself. "However," Dr. Jakle continued, "before some sort of a resource management can be launched, there has to be a recognition that there is a resource. A case in point is Parke County. Although certain elements in the community were moving ahead in preserving covered bridges, establishing festivals, and creating museums, other sectors of the community were oblivious to historic content in the landscape. For example, the comprehensive land-use plan which emerged some two years ago for both the town and the county of Rockville had no recognition that there could be or should be such a thing as historic district zoning. Subsequently, there has been a recognition that since covered bridges occur along streams, and since timber also tends to predominate along streams, the zone which had been created and entitled 'Forest District' could also be used to encompass something which they are now calling 'Forest and Recreation Districts.' " Dr. Lewis then observed that "if we're going to leave it to each individual community, they are not going to learn it in time. . . . It would seem to me that if historical geographers have anything to say about landscape, we'd better say it in a way that more than just one town can understand." This led to Dr. Lewis's second point, that all landscapes are historic, not just those landscapes designated historic landscapes. As an example, Dr. Lewis cited David Lowenthal's article, "The American Way of History" [*Columbia Alumni*, Forum 9, no. 3 (1966), pp. 27-32] in which the author "remarks that Americans view historic landscapes as having picket fences around them, 'History, admission $1.00, children $.50.' Outside, no history."

Michael P. Conzen, Geography Department, Boston University, continued the discussion on historic landscapes. In his first point, Dr. Conzen made a plea for the preservation of the historic landscape, "whether it's urban or rural, . . . for the community as a whole in terms of its ordinary daily life rather than just in terms of the short periods which [tourists] spend on vacation." He then cited Europe as a place where "there is a far more widespread appreciation of the visual landscape as a day-to-day phenomenon and also as an ongoing expression of one's cultural heritage." Europeans, he continued, are more aware of "place identification and the relationship between individuals to their places." In his second point, Dr. Conzen observed that the term "preservation" had too narrow a connotation, derived from its association with museums. "We have to be wary of the term 'preservation' because this implies a rather museum-like approach to the artifacts and areas that we designate for . . . historic consideration. . . . I think that it would appeal to the community as a whole much more if we thought of modern uses for old structures. Certainly, in an urban context, there's a tremendous opportunity for this sort of thing." Dr. Jakle agreed on both points and added, "Suffice to say that tourism happens to be the way in which the Parke County community has discovered, or at least has initially discovered, relic features on the landscape. And it's around tourism that the initial efforts are evolving. I'm very much concerned to see other avenues pursued, and I agree with you. Management of historic landscape should not be simply to create tourist attractions. That's just one alternative."

Charles E. Lee, director, South Carolina Department of Archives and History and *Historic Preservation Liaison Office for South Carolina,* concurred with Dr. Jakle "that historic preservation as tourist attractions is something to be deplored." He also reminded the conferees that there are means available by which interested parties can enter the preservation field. "The National Historic Preservation Act of October 15, 1966, sets up a state preservation liaison officer in each one of the fifty-five states and territories. He is charged with making [an] inventory of the historic sites within his territory or state, and he is also charged with making a statewide historic preservation plan. This is done with funds from the National Park Service of the Department of the Interior. Each state has a review board, which must have an architect, a historian, and an archeologist. It says nothing about historical geographers, but it behooves you to find out who in your state is the state historic preservation liaison officer and to get in touch with him if you do want to help us control the environment." Dr. Lee concluded, "Similarly, you have the recreation program and statewide recreation plans. This is also under the Department of the Interior—the Land-Water Conservation Act, I think it's called. And these two activities go on together. So you do have a way to enter into this kind of environmental planning, and, indeed, you should and you must."

Rural and Urban Settlement

Settlement of the
Colonial Atlantic Seaboard

H. ROY MERRENS

The following paper differs from most of the others in this collection because it neither discusses nor is based on *national* archives. Instead, it focuses upon two topics. The first part of the paper makes several points about the study of early America and about *pre*national archival resources. The second part is concerned with a couple of long-recognized settlement patterns, in order to exemplify research opportunities on topics of basic importance, and to offer several conclusions about research on colonial settlements.

In any consideration of research in American historical geography, it is imperative that some attention be given to the period that the papers in this collection do so little justice to. Of the fifteen or so substantive papers being presented in this volume, only two and a half focus on the colonial period. Obviously, this underrepresentation of the colonial era is entirely appropriate here, because the resources of concern in this volume are the archives that comprise the materials that tell the story of the United States *after* its establishment as a nation, and what is collected by the National Archives and Records Service does not really embrace the documentary legacy of the earlier lengthy colonial experience. But it is worth emphasizing that the bias in favor of the national experience is not merely a specialized and quite legitimate concern of this conference, but is, in fact, a long-standing, basic, and unfortunate feature of historical geography in the United States.

About a quarter of a century ago, Carl Bridenbaugh, one of the most prolific of colonial historians, drew attention to an identical bias in American history in an article he wrote for the *American Historical Review* entitled "The Neglected First Half of American History."[1] That the time span of the colonial era constitutes almost one-half the duration of American experience on the continent is an obvious, but perhaps easily overlooked, point, as impressive to the historical geographer as it is to the historian. That the period has been neglected by historians is equally evident. Whether the subject matter of texts, monographs, and journal articles or the framework of curriculums in universities is taken as a measure of attention, the neglect is not much less marked now than it was when Bridenbaugh's statement appeared in 1948.

Historical geographers have long neglected the era. In 1958, Donald Meinig presented a statement in which he contrasted the significance of the period with the scant attention geographers accorded it.[2] The situation has changed a little since then, but not very much. My own preoccupation with the colonial period dates from the late 1950s. During the 1960s, a few other historical geographers began to give the period their concentrated attention.[3] Symptomatic of this interest and commitment was the republication by the American Geographical Society in 1968 of an earlier study of colonial population by Herman Friis.[4] His study was both pioneering in direction (because it was the first detailed presentation or analysis of the distribution of an element in the geography of colonial America) and of basic importance in subject matter (because it is safe to assume that, for students of the colonial scene, an awareness of how many colonists there were and where they were is of fundamental importance).

The neglect of the geography of colonial America is easier to understand than the neglect of its history. Given the small number of American geographers who have committed themselves to historical geography, and the fact that in the past a high proportion of historical geographers have located themselves and their work in the West and Midwest, it is not surprising that the geography of the eastern seaboard during the colonial era has received so little attention. Ralph Brown, an influential scholar in American historical geography, and still the only one who has attempted to write a textbook survey of the field in one volume, wrote an ingenious and imaginative account of the eastern seaboard.[5] But in this account he used 1790 as his starting point and he insisted that the geography of the preceding decades and centuries could not be reconstructed. Then, too, the enthusiastic interest in early American origins that might otherwise have led American geographers to immerse themselves in the colonial era would understandably have faltered when confronted by the apparent lack of familiar tools with which to execute such studies. For those trained to engage in productive field work, it is at least disconcerting to discover that work in the field is really not too directly relevant to studies of most facets of the geography of the seventeenth- and eighteenth-century seaboard. Consternation is compounded by the lack of another traditional tool—for the period prior to 1790, there is no comprehensive, systematically arranged body of quantitative data. And the source materials that are available to geographers who wish to concern themselves with colonial America are incomplete, heterogeneous, generally nonquantitative, sometimes difficult to locate, and invariably time-consuming when finally found and put to use.

I have drawn attention to these source materials elsewhere,[6] on more than one occasion, and a few of us have made substantial use of them. But by and large historical geographers still seem to be largely unaware of these materials. Unfortunately, there is no single depository of colonial archives equivalent to the National Archives, with a concentrated mass of basic primary sources gathered together under one roof and placed at our disposal by sympathetic, scholarly archivists. Instead, the basic materials reside scattered in perhaps twenty or thirty archival depositories located up and down the length of the Atlantic seaboard as well as in the interior and on the Pacific coast, sometimes even in private collections guarded by remarkably unsympathetic custodians loathe to place them at anybody's disposal. But the important point is that a mass of invaluable materials has survived, that it remains substantially unexploited by geographers, and that the lack of awareness of these archival resources is a pathetic commentary upon our interest in the prenational centuries and, incidentally, testimony to our reluctance to tackle first things first. A recent instance of this ignorance was inadvertently provided by the author of a perceptive analysis of the geography of wholesaling. In a volume which focused upon America and which adopted an avowedly historical approach, the author completely ignored the massive and voluminous wealth of extant colonial mercantile records and even went so far as to assert, quite dogmatically, that detailed colonial business records have not survived.[7] And this is only the most recent example of a persistently nescient approach to colonial archives.

Happily, this lament can be concluded on a less doleful note. Several years have elapsed since these comments were first put together for the Conference on the National Archives and Research in Historical Geography, and during that time two major studies of the changing geography of portions of the colonial seaboard have appeared, one by James Lemon and the other by Carville Earle.[8] Both are based upon the perceptive analysis of colonial archival sources. Both make substantial contributions to our understanding of the colonial scene. And in doing so, these studies provide exemplary illustrations of the kind of work that can be done on the neglected first half of American historical geography.

In the second and final part of this paper, the prospects for research in the geography of the colonial era will be exemplified by spotlighting a few of the things that we know and some of the things we do not know about settlement patterns of the colonial Atlantic seaboard. The various types of settlements created by colonists included manors and metropolitan centers, crossroad towns and courthouse marketplaces, hamlets clustered around village greens, and isolated farms dispersed about the countryside. To identify the regional variety in settlement patterns and to understand its changing distribution constitutes a major challenge for the geographer of the colonial seaboard. Of the various types of *rural* settlement, the two that scholars have made most of are the New England town and the southern plantation.

It is perhaps appropriate to single out the New England town first because the study of this venerable stereotype has entered a new phase and now, more than ever, cries out for attention by geographers. The origins of the New England town, viewed simultaneously as a form of settlement and as a set of institutions, were debated by historians for just about a century, from the mid-1860s to the mid-1960s. The debate seems to have been launched in a paper by Joel Parker, which appeared in the 1866 *Proceedings of the Massachusetts Historical Society*,[9] although it was the next major contribution to the debate, a paper read by Herbert B. Adams in 1881 on "The Germanic Origin of New England Towns," that is better known and is regarded as the seminal study.[10] A few years later, Charles M. Andrews challenged Adams's view of New England towns as exemplifications of the continuity of the Germanic village community and the unity of Teutonic history.[11] The debate went on and on, marked, perhaps, by increasingly less illustrious contributions. Few geographers expressed interest in the debate, and the few who did (such as, F. G. Morris, Edna Scofield, and Glenn Trewartha)[12] contributed little because they resorted to what were really commentaries on the studies of historians rather than presenting original studies of their own. These commentaries were inevitably superficial or static, or both, because their authors lacked first-hand familiarity with the available source materials.

The debate came to some sort of stalemate with the publication in

1963 of Sumner C. Powell's rigorous analysis *Puritan Village: The Formation of a New England Town.*[13] Powell's study did not settle many issues, but it did suggest that the previous attention to origins was perhaps misplaced. In the first paragraph of his concluding chapter, Powell expressed a point of view that few reviewers seem to have taken note of. He stated that:

> The historical debate on "the origin" of a type of social and political structure called "the New England town" is probably not over, but the question itself may be superficial today. We can now realize that there were multiple origins and many distinct early towns, and that all of these towns and their relationships need careful examination.[14]

One paragraph later, he qualified his point of view:

> If the question of the origin seems superficial, the investigation of the change, transition, and stability of English local institutions across the Atlantic ocean in the seventeenth century is not.[15]

While I accept Powell's emphasis on the analysis of change and his devaluation of the search for origins, I prefer to regard the concern with the genesis of the towns as being premature rather than superficial. It was premature because much more needs to be known about the qualities of the settlements themselves—their distribution, function, and gradual transformation—so that we will have a more soundly based understanding of the identity of the phenomenon whose origins we seek to understand.

The appreciation of regional variety and temporal variations among settlement forms in New England has been blurred rather than sharpened by long-continued and widespread acceptance of the stereotype of a New England colonial town, comprising a close cluster of houses, neatly disposed around a village green and in turn surrounded by fields and meadows. Enough has been substantiated about particular places in colonial New England to suggest that this model is of limited utility. Thus, in the earliest New England colony, such settlements were not characteristically compact, according to a recent study of farms and villages in seventeenth-century Plymouth.[16] Wethersfield, a seventeenth-century Connecticut village, first studied by Andrews and, subsequently, much cited by both geographers and historians as a typical example of a New England settlement, by no means accords well with the construct.[17] In eighteenth-century Rhode Island, the Narragansett plantations were apparently the most distinctive form of settlement.[18] And in New England as a whole, during the eighteenth century, settlement in isolated farmsteads seems to have been widespread. Evidently, then, the model was crudely formulated and failed to take into account regional and temporal variations.

About the time that Powell's study appeared, there began to appear also the preliminary results of a new approach to the study of settlements in colonial New England, centering around the intensive analysis of particular changing communities. In 1968, Bumsted and Lemon reviewed the first fruits of this new scholarship in the journal *Social History*,[19] and the June 1971 issue of the *American Historical Review* contains an essay by Rhys Isaac that evaluates four major monographs, all published in 1970 and all dealing with New England communities.[20] There are several other such studies by historians and no doubt more will be forthcoming. But the opportunities for geographical research on settlement in colonial New England are large and virtually unexplored. Hopefully, geographers will not leave the study of these places entirely to historians or resort to their past habit of simply providing a geographical commentary on the studies of historians. Colonial New England affords an intricate variety of settlement types awaiting study and source materials that are, in general, more voluminous, more informative, and more quantitative than the materials for other parts of the seaboard.

The other common model of colonial rural settlement is the southern slave plantation. If this was not the most widespread form of southern settlement, it was certainly the most dramatic. During the eighteenth century, it was characterized by broad acres, by large numbers of slaves, and by residences that tended to become grander and larger with each succeeding generation. A disproportionately large number of the most renowned plantations are Virginia houses, of which Nomini Hall is one of the most celebrated because it was the home of Robert Carter and was described in some detail in 1774 by the scholar who served as tutor to the Carter children.[21] Perched conspicuously on a hill, the main residence of Nomini Hall was eminently visible in the surrounding countryside. Two stories high, with many windows, a portico, five stacks of chimneys, and built of bricks covered with white mortar, it was presumably as elegant as any and more pretentious than many.

But as a model of southern settlement types, Nomini Hall, or indeed any of the imposing Virginia plantations, is of limited utility. This is, first, because there was a substantial degree of changing regional variety within the southern colonies, fostered particularly by differing emphases in crops, livestock, and forest products and by contrasts in duration of settlement; second, because plantations of all kinds, whether conforming closely to the model or not, comprised only a minority of southern forms of settlement, and the array of settlements established by the majority constitute equally important, if less readily identifiable, agencies of change; and, third, because the acceptance of a static model, based more or less exclusively upon a few renowned late eighteenth-century Virginia estates, has deflected attention from plantations as a spatially varying system of production and settlement whose origins are virtually unstudied. We do not even know where the system came from, whether it came from Mediterranean Europe (as one historian has suggested)[22] by way of African islands, South America, and the West Indies to the mainland in South Carolina, or from the English plantations in Ulster directly to Virginia, or whether both paths of diffusion were pertinent to the American development. But, as with the New England town, it might be more appropriate to identify the regionally variant and changing versions before we launch into a full-scale search for the origins of plantations.

Deficiencies of these and other models of colonial settlement need not be labored here. The point is that the formulation and acceptance of models was premature insofar as it has hindered, rather than facilitated, both presentation and investigation and to the extent that it came before there was a mass of substantial empirical data on regional and temporal variations in settlement forms and functions.

Future investigation may reveal the apparent diversity of settlement types along the colonial seaboard to be more apparent than real. In an earlier study of colonial North Carolina, I suggested that some of the supposedly rural settlements were actually performing urban functions.[23] But the role of itinerant merchants and country stores, the prevalence of decentralized merchandising, the fact that at least two components of trade (the physical movement of goods and the transactional process) may have taken place through different networks and that the locus of one was not necessarily the locus of the other, and the existence of ephemeral urban trading places—all of these features of trade of one kind or another complicate the relationship between colonial urban and rural settlements, on the one hand, and economic development, on the other, and force us to analyze the colonial settlement scene in the context of colonial commerce and the economic networks of that era.[24] The kind of work recently begun by historical demographers, economic historians, and historical sociologists will lead ultimately to the construction of more viable models of settlement, and one hopes that the small band of historical geographers professing a commitment to the colonial era will increase, and that they will focus upon the study of settlement during the first and more neglected centuries. Meanwhile, the recent recognition of the more or less dispersed nature of settlement in Plymouth, juxtaposed with the longer recognized form of settlement in Jamestown, serves as just one useful reminder that traditional contrasting models of settlement in New England and in the southern colonies are misleading and even, conceivably, in need of reversing in some respects.

NOTES

1. *American Historical Review* 53 (April 1948): 506-17.
2. "The American Colonial Era: A Geographic Commentary," *Proceedings of the Royal Geographical Society of Australasia, South Australian Branch* 59 (December 1958): 1-22.
3. I have discussed the results of this attention elsewhere. See H. Roy Merrens, "Historical Geography and Early American History," *William and Mary Quarterly*, 3d ser. 22 (October 1965): 529-48.
4. Herman R. Friis, *A Series of Population Maps of the Colonies and the United States, 1625-1790*, American Geographical Society, Mimeographed and Offset Publication no. 3, rev. (New York, 1968).
5. Ralph H. Brown, *Mirror for Americans: Likeness of the Eastern Seaboard, 1810* (New York: American Geographical Society, 1943).
6. I have briefly reviewed elsewhere the kinds of source materials that are available. See H. Roy Merrens, "Source Materials for the Geography of Colonial America," *Professional Geographer* 15 (January 1963): 8-11.
7. James E. Vance, Jr., *The Merchant's World: The Geography of Wholesaling* (Englewood Cliffs, N. J.: Prentice-Hall, 1970), p. 13.
8. The study by Lemon is titled *The Best Poor Man's Country: A Geographical Study of Early Southeastern Pennsylvania* (Baltimore, Md.: Johns Hopkins University Press, 1972). Earle's study is titled *The Evolution of a Tidewater Settlement System: All Hallow's Parish, Maryland, 1650-1783*, and it will shortly be published in the University of Chicago Department of Geography Research Paper series.
9. "The Origin, Organization, and Influence of the Towns of New England," *Proceedings of the Massachusetts Historical Society* 60 (January 1866): 14-65.
10. The study by Adams was read in 1881, first printed in 1882, and then presented as item number 2 on pages 45-78 of the first volume in the series of Johns Hopkins University Studies in Historical and Political Science, titled *Local Institutions* (Baltimore, Md., 1883).
11. *The River Towns of Connecticut: A Study of Wethersfield, Hartford and Windsor*, Johns Hopkins University Studies in Historical and Political Science, 7th ser., vols. 7, 8, 9 (Baltimore, Md., 1889).
12. F. Grave Morris, "Some Aspects of Rural Settlements of New England in Colonial Times," *London Essays in Geography*, ed. L. Dudley Stamp and S. W. Wooldridge (Cambridge, Mass.: Harvard University Press, 1951), pp. 219-27; Edna Scofield, "The Origin of Settlement Patterns in Rural New

England," *Geographical Review* 28 (October 1938): 652-63; Glenn T. Trewartha, "Types of Rural Settlement in Colonial America," *Geographical Review* 36 (October 1946): 568-96.

13. Originally published in 1963, Powell's book was republished two years later as an Anchor Book (Garden City, N. Y.).

14. Ibid. (1965 ed.), p. 178.

15. Ibid.

16. Darrett B. Rutman, *Husbandman of Plymouth: Farms and Villages in the Old Colony, 1620-1692* (Boston: Beacon Press for Plimouth Plantation, 1967), pp. 23-24.

17. Andrews, *River Towns of Connecticut*. Several authors have subsequently made much use of the study of Wethersfield and even reproduced Andrews's map of the town. But only one scholar has noted the crucial omission of a scale on the map that Andrews presented. See Anthony N. B. Garvan, *Architecture and Town Planning in Colonial Connecticut* (New Haven, Conn.: Yale University Press, 1951), p. 56. In any event, Wethersfield really bore little resemblance to a compact or nucleated settlement; as Andrews himself noted in the original study (p. 43), it was actually a double settlement, and each of the two parts was linear in form.

18. Although there is no satisfactory geographical study of these plantations, a number of historians have accorded them some attention. See, for example, William D. Miller, "The Narragansett Planters," *Proceedings of the American Antiquarian Society*, n.s. 43, pt. 1 (April 1933): 49-115.

19. J. M. Bumsted and J. T. Lemon, "New Approaches in Early American Studies: The Local Community in New England," *Histoire Sociale*, no. 2 (November 1968), pp. 98-112.

20. Rhys Isaac, "Order and Growth, Authority and Meaning in Colonial New England," *American Historical Review* 76 (June 1971): 728-37.

21. The details that follow are taken from Hunter D. Farish, ed., *Journal and Letters of Philip Vickers Fithian, 1773-1774: A Plantation Tutor of the Old Dominion* (Charlottesville: University Press of Virginia, 1968).

22. Robert L. Reynolds, "The Mediterranean Frontiers, 1000-1400," in *The Frontier in Perspective*, ed. Walker D. Wyman and Clifton B. Kroeber (Madison: University of Wisconsin Press, 1957), p. 31. See also the suggestive comments by the same historian in his book *Europe Emerges: Transition Toward an Industrial World-Wide Society, 600-1750* (Madison: University of Wisconsin Press, 1961), pp. 318-19, 433, 495-96.

23. See chap. 7, on "Urban Settlements and Decentralized Trade," in my *Colonial North Carolina in the Eighteenth Century: A Study in Historical Geography* (Chapel Hill: University of North Carolina Press, 1964), pp. 142-72.

24. Working with a historian, I have attempted some steps in this direction recently. See Joseph A. Ernst and H. Roy Merrens, " 'Camden's Turrets Pierce the Skies!': The Urban Process in the Southern Colonies," *William and Mary Quarterly*, 3d ser. 30 (October 1973): 549-79; Ernst and Merrens, "The South Carolina Economy of the Middle Eighteenth Century: A View from Philadelphia," *West Georgia College Studies in the Social Sciences* 12 (June 1973): 17-30.

Vegetational Perception and Choice of Settlement Site in Frontier Texas

TERRY G. JORDAN

There is a concept ingrained in the thinking of many historians and historical geographers that grasslands were shunned as settlement sites by American pioneers, that early settlers preferred to remain in forested areas and moved into prairies only after wooded districts were occupied. In particular, the practice of prairie avoidance has been attributed to *southern* Anglo-Americans. This idea has appeared in the writings of such noted historians as Frederick Jackson Turner, Ray Allen Billington, Percy Bidwell, and John Falconer, and they were joined by the well-known geographers Carl Sauer and Harlan Barrows. Among the few challenging this view, the most prominent has been Merle Prunty.[1]

Certainly the greatest champion of the concept of grasslands as hostile and forbidding was the late historian Walter Prescott Webb, whose book *The Great Plains* has been read and admired by historians and geographers alike.[2] The Webbian view is of an American culture shaped and nurtured in the shade of the dense eastern forests, a culture whose bearers ventured only reluctantly and late into unforested areas. Webb demarcated a line that supposedly divided the forested East from the prairies and plains of the West. In Texas, Webb's line left about one-third of the state on the forested side. Pioneers crossing this line, armed and equipped with the tools, ideas, and institutions which had served

Research funds for this study were provided by the Faculty Research Committee of North Texas State University, Denton.

them so long and so well in the woods that lay behind them, supposedly met with failure in the grasslands until they adapted to the new environment. This theme forms the central thesis of Webb's *Great Plains.*

It is here suggested that the view of Webb and the other scholars mentioned, while possessing some measure of validity in a general overview of the West as a whole, distorts the actual state of affairs concerning the settlement of a very sizable part of Texas by Anglo-Americans in the nineteenth century. Furthermore, the generally held belief that prairies as such were avoided represents a serious misreading of pioneer preferences. It is argued, first of all, that the vegetational pattern encountered by Anglo-American pioneers in Texas was far more complicated than the simple dichotomy of forested East and treeless West. The failure to recognize this complexity greatly distorts the vegetational reality upon which Texas pioneers based their decisions in choosing settlement sites. Second, I propose that the early Anglo-Texans, rather than being repelled by grasslands, were quite favorably inclined toward them and actually sought out prairies as places to settle, so long as timber was also available in the vicinity.

There is, of course, no sharp line which divides closed forest from open grassland in Texas. At best, Webb was sacrificing a large measure of reality upon the altar of generalization in proposing such a line. In reality, small areas of grassland were scattered throughout most parts of the eastern United States, particularly in the eastern part of Texas. Most vegetation maps presently available for the area of the United States are less than useless for analyses of settlement process, both because of their small scale and the emphasis placed on "potential" or "natural" rather than actual vegetation. I could list almost countless nineteenth-century accounts that describe grass-covered areas in East Texas. These accounts reveal a veritable Polynesia composed of hundreds and thousands of small prairies strewn across the portion of Texas which lay east of Webb's suggested grassland/forest borderline, east of the forest-prairie line on every vegetation map of the United States I have seen. There are about two hundred surviving place names containing the word "prairie" in East Texas (figure 1).

Included were several distinct types of prairie. Certainly the most common was the small interfluvial type, situated in the rolling uplands between the various rivers and creeks. Also numerous were *bottom* prairies, found adjacent to major streams such as the Colorado, Brazos, Red, and Trinity rivers. Much of the Colorado River bottom below the city of Austin was prairie, including one of some thousands of acres in extent.[3] In this category, too, were the so-called Brazos River

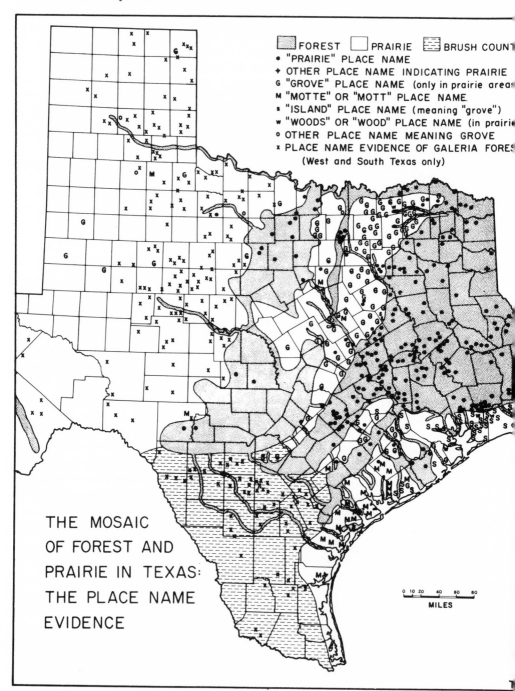

FIG. 1. *Place names suggest a very complex mixture of forest and prairie in Texas. In reality, the complexity was even greater than is indicated by the place names.*

weed prairies, where a rank growth of weeds reached a height of ten to fifteen feet and in which, unlike most prairies, no sod was present.[4] Perhaps also best considered a variety of bottom prairie were the cane-brakes, which lined many of the streams of East Texas. At least thirty streams in the eastern part of Texas bear the name Caney Creek.[5]

Obviously, then, there was a considerable amount of land in eastern Texas that was grass covered. Prairies were well known to the Anglo-American pioneers who settled eastern Texas, and they had been known to their fathers and grandfathers before them in states farther east.

Conversely, much of central and western Texas was well supplied with woodland. Especially noteworthy were the Cross Timbers, two belts of forest which stretched across north-central Texas from the Red River south to about the Brazos. Even in those portions of Texas domi-nated by grassland, timber generally was present in the form of iso-lated groves, sometimes also called "islands" or "mottes." Further-more, most stream courses were paralleled by narrow *galeria* forests, even far into West Texas. Names such as Palo Duro in the Panhandle area, Hackberry Draw in the trans-Pecos country, and Wood Hollow in the Big Bend area, indicate the presence of timber even in far western Texas (figure 1).

Perhaps the best measure of how far west the techniques associated with the forest culture were able to spread in Texas without undue inconvenience or modification is the areal extent of what has been called the "log culture complex." This refers to the dominant use in the pioneer stage of logs for building houses, sheds, churches, jails, and other structures. A survey of accounts from the nineteenth century, coupled with field observation, reveals that the log-culture complex spread intact at least *two hundred miles* west of Webb's line in Texas, reaching and in places even surpassing the 100th meridian (figure 2). Furthermore, some log buildings were erected still farther west, in areas such as the Panhandle, though it cannot be claimed that the use of logs was ever dominant there. The place name "House Log Creek" appears in the Texas Panhandle.

It is best, then, to regard the greater part of Texas as a broad zone of vegetational transition between forest and prairie, a zone in which both grassland and woodland were mixed together in an intricate mosaic. Just as prairies were not alien to the earliest pioneers of East Texas, so forests were present to comfort settlers in much of the west-ern part of the state. The vanguard of the Anglo-Texan frontier did not suddenly encounter a new and different vegetational environment

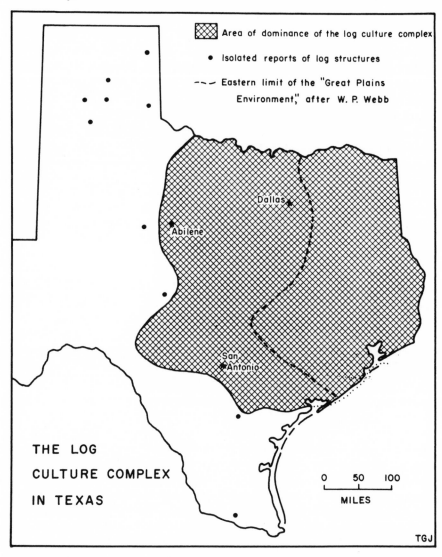

Fig. 2. *The use of log structures continued far into Webb's "Great Plains Environment," suggesting that ample timber was available across most of Texas. Even in the Panhandle, log cabins were found.*

in central Texas. Rather, throughout most of the state, the pioneer was called upon to evaluate an environment that offered both forest and prairie.

In making this evaluation, the East Texas pioneer found some obvious advantages in choosing prairie sites. The backbreaking task of forest clearance could be avoided by using the prairies for crops and pasture, and the pioneer farmer did not have to work for years with axe to obtain sizable fields and grazing areas. Nor were the first settlers who entered Texas from the East unaccustomed to using the small prairies. The fringes of Kentucky barrens were being occupied as early as the 1790s,[6] and it is quite apparent that grassy areas were often sought out as the most desirable settlement sites in many eastern states, as long as woodland was adjacent. Pioneers preferred to situate their holdings so as to include both grassland and forest, thereby combining the advantages of both vegetational types.

I am proposing that the early Anglo-Texans also behaved in this manner when selecting places to settle, and that the vegetational pattern allowed them to continue the practice of combining prairie and forest across most of the state. Webb's thesis is applicable only to the areas where timber was completely absent, and it is erroneous to claim that grassy areas as such were avoided. Indeed, as I will try to show, the settlers in eastern Texas consistently sought out prairies.

Many contemporary observers noted both the advantages of settlement on mixed forest-prairie sites and the response of the pioneers to these advantages. Writing in 1835, one writer stated that most Texas landholders owned both woodland and prairie, and that "the cultivation of prairie land requires less capital in the outset, and is more profitable in the end, than the cultivation of the [forested] bottoms".[7] Mary Austin Holley, author of two books about Texas in the 1830s, lauded prairies as potential cropland, referring to them as "fertile fields already cleared by the hand of nature." The settler, she added, "in locating himself selects the rich lands of the prairies, where he has no clearing to do and no other preparation . . . than that of turning the fertile loam."[8] A Britisher, William Bollaert, noted that "in the majority of locations, clearing the land is not necessary, for on the edges of the 'timbers' the farmer is immediately rewarded." Moreover, he added, "in the 'bottoms' and in woody country which extends from river to river, there are patches of open land sufficiently large for plantations and farms."[9]

The earliest Anglo-American colonization in Texas occurred along the south bank of the Red River in far northeastern Texas, beginning about 1814 or 1815 (figure 3). An American visiting these settlements in 1819 observed that the pioneers had occupied a bottom prairie near the river, which by the crops of corn and cotton appeared to be exceedingly fertile.[10] Both Jonesborough and Pecan Point, the two earliest Red River communities, were adjacent to bottom prairies which bore their names.

A similar preference was manifested quite early in the Austin Colony in south-central Texas, where American settlers began occupying lands in 1821 (figure 3). San Felipe, the capital of the colony, was itself situated on a prairie bluff overlooking the Brazos, with forest at hand, and many colonists there chose to farm grassland. At least as early as 1828, a Mr. Cummins who settled near San Felipe had laid out fields in the prairie, and he gave a strong recommendation to this practice.[11] One of the most sought-after areas in the Austin Colony, even before 1825, was the so-called Bay Prairie, a sizable section of the Coastal Prairie extending inland from the Gulf of Mexico shore. A certain Elisha Flowers, a colonist in the Bay Prairie, wrote to the founder of the colony, Stephen F. Austin, in 1826, informing him that he was plowing land in the prairie.[12] Nearby were other small prairies, scattered through the belt of bottom timbers which stretched between the lower Brazos and Colorado rivers, and these, too, were sought out by early settlers.[13] Generally, they were given the name of the family that claimed them, as in the case of Bailey's Prairie and Chance's Prairie near the mouth of the Brazos River, both of which commemorate members of Austin's original 300 colonists.[14] A Mr. Bailey, the same for whom the prairie was named, had fifty or sixty acres of prairie cultivated by 1831, with his house situated on the edge of the adjacent woods. Mr. McNeil, a plantation owner in the same area, lived in a house on the verge of a grove, with his fields and pasture in the prairie.[15] Stephen F. Austin himself agreed that prairie cultivation was best, writing in 1831 that many areas were "checkered off into small prairies and woodland tracts, thus presenting to the farmer large fields of rich lands cleared by the hand of nature and ready for the plough."[16]

Elsewhere in the Austin Colony, William Rabb raised the first crops in what is now Fayette County in Rabb's Prairie, situated in the Colorado River bottoms, while nearby, in another bottom prairie, a Mr. Moore was "turning over the previously unbroken sod" near the town of La Grange, early in 1831.[17] One of the oldest settlements near the Texas capital city of Austin was on the Webber's Prairie, colonized in 1839.[18] Near Bastrop, just downstream from Austin, pioneers planted

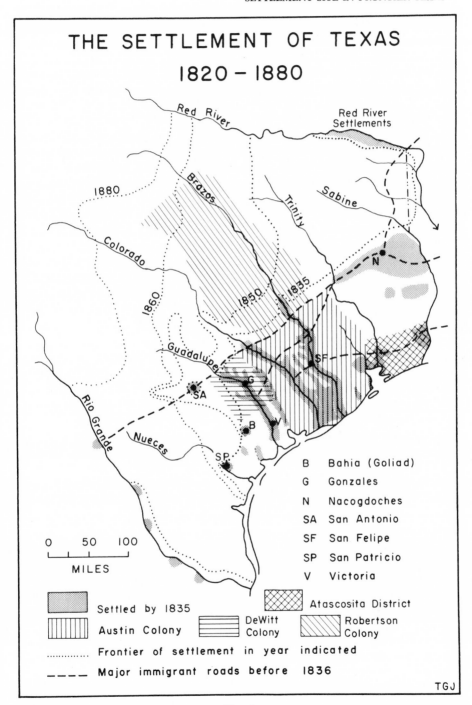

THE SETTLEMENT OF TEXAS
1820 – 1880

B   Bahia (Goliad)
G   Gonzales
N   Nacogdoches
SA San Antonio
SF San Felipe
SP San Patricio
V   Victoria

0   50   100
MILES

Settled by 1835
Austin Colony
DeWitt Colony
Atascosita District
Robertson Colony
Frontier of settlement in year indicated
Major immigrant roads before 1836

TGJ

Fig. 3.

crops in Wood's Prairie in about 1830, and others were settled on nearby Craft's Prairie and Hemphill's Prairie, both in the Colorado River bottoms, by 1836.[19]

Settlers in that portion of the Austin Colony which lay east of the Brazos River, near the present city of Houston, also sought out the prairies. A certain Jared Groce established a plantation on Wallace Prairie in southern Grimes County in the 1820s, placing large cotton fields in the grassland, while Jesse Grimes settled on nearby Grimes Prairie in 1827 and began cattle ranching. In adjacent Montgomery County, the traveler Gustav Dresel noted in 1839 that "there were approximately ten farmers living in and about the Montgomery prairie."[20]

Most prized of all lands in the Austin Colony were the canelands found along some of the stream courses. The cane was, according to one settler, "a certain indicator of the best soil," and it could be cleared by the simple expedient of setting a fire.[21] An early settler, Daniel Shipman, planted corn, pumpkins, and turnips in a burned-out canebrake near the Brazos River in Austin County as early as 1824, and some of the wealthiest planters of the Austin Colony located in the canebrakes along various streams near the coast in the 1820s.[22]

Pioneers in other parts of eastern Texas apparently chose settlement sites in much the same manner as their contemporaries in the Red River settlements and the Austin Colony. The small prairies which were strewn along the Old Spanish Road from the Sabine River to the Trinity River attracted immigrant farmers at a very early date. Two travelers passing through the area near the Louisiana border in 1835 wrote of a certain settler "who is settled on a fine tract of rich land, a part of which is prairie, and of the very best quality."[23] A decade later, another traveler noted that corn was being raised in the sandy prairies just west of Nacogdoches on the Old Spanish Road[24] (figure 3). In the pine forests of nearby Cherokee County, the settlement of Bean's Prairie was established in 1839 by Peter Ellis Bean, one of the early Texas pioneers.

Prairies fringed by woods were also sought out in the Robertson Colony, which lay on either side of the Brazos River upstream from the Austin Colony, in the central portion of Texas (figure 3). The most prized lands in that part of the state were the previously mentioned Brazos weed prairies, strung like beads on a necklace along the river bottoms through three counties. The weed prairies were attractive to settlers not only because of their legendary fertility, but also because no troublesome sod was present. It is believed that the weed prairies were former Indian agricultural clearings, abandoned only shortly before the coming of white settlers. The pioneer farmer simply burned off the weeds and planted his crops. One observer, in 1837, reported that the Robertson colonists who had planted in the weed prairies at the falls of the Brazos obtained fifty bushels of corn from each acre.[25] One of the earliest communities to be established in the Robertson Colony was Jones Prairie, founded in 1833 in one of the Milam County weed prairies.[26]

The only problem of any consequence associated with farming prairies in areas where timber was abundant was that of breaking the sod for initial planting, a practice described as early as 1833. To perform this task efficiently, the settler needed no fewer than four oxen and a strong plow that would cut at least fourteen inches deep. The breaking was best performed in summer, followed by cross-plowing and harrowing in early spring. A pioneer in the Blackland Prairie of southeastern Denton County used four yoke of cattle for breaking in 1851, having earlier bought a Carey turning plow, a large wooden instrument equipped with a steel point.[27] Some settlers resorted to a variety of simpler practices. A crude preliminary plowing, followed by use of an ordinary woodsman's axe to chop seed holes, sufficed to gain an initial corn crop.[28] In any case, many, if not most, settlers apparently felt that breaking sod was a lot easier than clearing trees. Indeed, in some areas the original forest-prairie pattern was apparently never greatly disturbed, with little agricultural clearing having been done to the present day (figure 4). For the fortunate few who claimed weed prairies or canebrakes, all that was needed was the application of fire, that most ancient of man's tools.

One certain indicator of the importance of prairies to early settlers in eastern Texas was their practice, observed in even the earliest years of colonization, of regularly setting fire to the grasslands. This practice, perhaps inherited from the Indians, supposedly destroyed weeds and dead grass, so as to make room for the new grass.[29] In addition, the fire removed all bushes and young trees, thereby preserving the prairie from encroachment by the forest. For the Anglo-American, prairie burning assured ample forage for his herds of cattle. That the settlers took the trouble to fire the prairies in their vicinity underlines the importance of the grasslands to them as ready-made pastures for livestock. The universality of the practice suggests the consistency with which the pioneers throughout Texas valued prairies.

To conclude, then, both prairie and forest were present over most of the portion of Texas settled by Anglo-Americans, offering the colo-

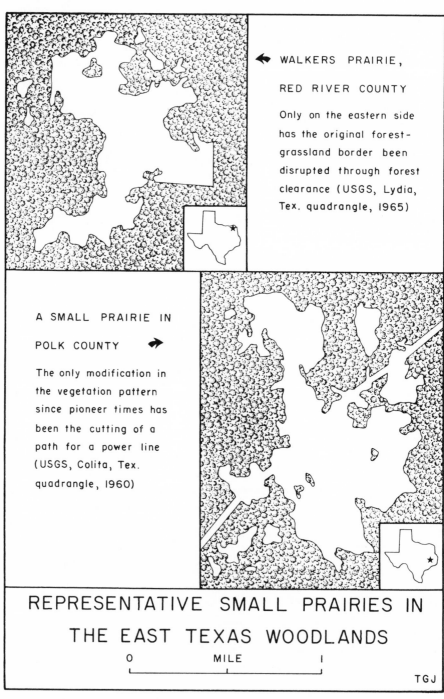

WALKERS PRAIRIE,
RED RIVER COUNTY

Only on the eastern side
has the original forest-
grassland border been
disrupted through forest
clearance (USGS, Lydia,
Tex. quadrangle, 1965)

A SMALL PRAIRIE IN

POLK COUNTY

The only modification in
the vegetation pattern
since pioneer times has
been the cutting of a
path for a power line
(USGS, Colita, Tex.
quadrangle, 1960)

REPRESENTATIVE SMALL PRAIRIES IN
THE EAST TEXAS WOODLANDS

0   MILE   1

TGJ

FIG. 4. *These small prairies are typical of hundreds scattered through eastern Texas. The relatively undisturbed outlines suggest that settlers in these areas did little clearing of the forest.*

nists the advantages of both types of vegetation. The pioneers utilized the forests for building materials and fuel, while locating fields and pastures in the prairies. Apparently, nearly all pioneers preferred such mixed vegetational settlement sites and took them as long as they were available. Preference for such sites was exhibited by immigrant southerners of variant economic status, from the humblest backwoodsmen to the wealthiest planters. With remarkable consistency, the earliest Anglo-American colonies in all parts of eastern Texas were situated adjacent to or in small prairies, and often they bore place names with a "Prairie" suffix. It is not too much to say that the course of pioneer settlement in eastern Texas was in part *guided* by the distribution of prairies. Similarly, pioneers in the grasslands of western Texas a generation or two later almost always settled by groves of timber or galeria forests. Consequently, it was the latecomers who settled either the closed forests, where no prairies were present, or the open grasslands, devoid of timber. Not one single contemporary record of any kind was found that suggested antiprairie sentiment on the part of Texan pioneers, and it is quite incorrect to view the southern frontiersman as a prairie-avoider.

NOTES

1. Frederick Jackson Turner, *The Frontier in American History,* 3d ed. (New York: Henry Holt, 1958), pp. 134-36; Ray A. Billington, *Westward Expansion, a History of the American Frontier,* 2d ed. (New York: Macmillan Co., 1960), pp. 294-96; Percy W. Bidwell and John I. Falconer, *History of Agriculture in the Northern United States, 1620-1860* (Washington, D.C.: Carnegie Institution, 1925), p. 158; Carl O. Sauer, *Geography of the Upper Illinois Valley and History of Development,* Illinois State Geological Survey Bulletin no. 27 (Urbana, 1916), p. 150; and Harlan H. Barrows, *Geography of the Middle Illinois Valley,* Illinois State Geological Survey Bulletin no. 15 (Urbana, 1910), p. 66. For the opposing view, see: Merle C. Prunty, "Some Geographic Views of the Role of Fire in Settlement Processes in the South," *Proceedings of the Fourth Annual Tall Timbers Fire Ecology Conference,* 1965, pp. 161-68; Terry G. Jordan, "Between the Forest and the Prairie," *Agricultural History* 38 (1964): 205-16; and Bernard C. Peters, "Pioneer Evaluation of the Kalamazoo County Landscape," *Michigan Academician* 3, no. 2 (1970): 15-25.
2. Walter Prescott Webb, *The Great Plains* (Boston: McGinn & Co., 1931).
3. George W. Bonnell, *Topographical Description of Texas . . .* (Austin: Clark, Wing, & Brown, 1840), pp. 60, 61; William Kennedy, *Texas: The Rise, Progress, and Prospects of the Republic of Texas* (1841; reprint ed., Ft. Worth: Molyneaux, 1925), p. 157; *Texas in 1840, or the Emigrant's Guide to the New Republic . . .* (New York: W. W. Allen, 1840), p. 51.

4. J. DeCordova, *Texas: Her Resources and Her Public Men* (Philadelphia: E. Crozet, 1858), p. 284; Kennedy, *Texas* (1925), p. 149.

5. Walter Prescott Webb and H. Bailey Carroll, eds., *The Handbook of Texas* (Austin: Texas State Historical Association, 1952), 1:289-90.

6. Carl O. Sauer, *Geography of the Pennyroyal*, Kentucky State Geological Survey, 6th ser. 25 (Frankfort, 1927): 134, 135.

7. David B. Edward, *The History of Texas; or, the Emigrant's, Farmer's, and Politician's Guide to the Character, Climate, Soil and Productions of that Country* . . . (Cincinnati: J. A. James, 1836), p. 63.

8. Mary Austin Holley, *Texas: Observations, Historical, Geographical and Descriptive, in a Series of Letters* . . . (Baltimore: Armstrong & Plaskitt, 1833), pp. 45, 52, 63, 65.

9. William Bollaert, *William Bollaert's Texas*, ed. W. Eugene Hollon and Ruth Lapham Butler (Norman: University of Oklahoma Press, 1956), p. 116.

10. Thomas Nuttall, *A Journal of Travels into the Arkansa Territory, during the Year 1819* . . . (Philadelphia: Thomas Palmer, 1821), reprinted in vol. 13 of Reuben G. Thwaites, ed., *Early Western Travels 1748-1846* (Cleveland: Arthur H. Clark Co., 1905), p. 221.

11. J. C. Clopper, "J. C. Clopper's Journal and Book of Memoranda for 1828," *Texas State Historical Association Quarterly* 13 (1909-10): 64; William F. Gray, *From Virginia to Texas, 1835, Diary of Col. Wm. F. Gray* . . . (Houston: Gray, Dillage & Co., 1909), p. 110.

12. Eugene C. Barker, ed., *The Austin Papers*, in *Annual Report of the American Historical Association, 1919*, vol. 2, pt. 2 (Washington, D.C.: Government Printing Office, 1924), pp. 1231, 1549.

13. Andrew P. McCormick, *Scotch-Irish in Ireland and in America* . . . (New Orleans: Printed by author, 1897), pp. 106, 112.

14. James Briton Bailey, a North Carolinian who settled Bailey's Prairie in 1821, and Samuel Chance, a Georgian who arrived in 1824; Webb and Carroll, *Handbook of Texas*, 1:95, 329.

15. *A Visit to Texas: Being the Journal of a Traveller through Those Parts Most Interesting to American Settlers.* . . . (New York: Goodrich & Wiley, 1834), pp. 39, 47, 64. See, also, Eugene C. Barker, ed., *The Austin Papers*, in *Annual Report of the American Historical Association, 1922* (Washington, D.C.: Government Printing Office, 1928), p. 349.

16. Stephen F. Austin, "Descriptions of Texas by Stephen F. Austin," ed. E. C. Barker, *Southwestern Historical Quarterly* 28 (1924): 108.

17. George W. Smyth, "Autobiography of George W. Smyth," ed. W. Allen, *Southwestern Historical Quarterly* 36 (1932-33): 204; Webb and Carroll, *Handbook of Texas*, 2:428.

18. Bollaert, *William Bollaert's Texas*, p. 190.

19. John H. Jenkins, *Recollections of Early Texas*, ed. John H. Jenkins III (Austin: University of Texas Press, 1958), pp. 11, 48; Annie D. Pickrell, *Pioneer Women in Texas* (Austin: E. L. Steck, 1929), pp. 186, 285.

20. Gustav Dresel, *Houston Journal, Adventures in North America and Texas, 1837-1841*, ed. and trans. Max Freund (Austin: University of Texas Press, 1954), pp. 72, 80; Webb and Carroll, *Handbook of Texas*, 1:738, 752-53.

21. Holley, *Texas: Observations*, pp. 50-51.

22. Daniel Shipman, Frontier Life . . ., *58 Years in Texas* (N.p., 1879), pp. 32-33; *A Visit to Texas*, p. 71.
23. Joshua James and Alexander McCrae, *A Journal of a Tour in Texas* . . . (Wilmington, N.C.: T. Loring, 1835), p. 6.
24. A. W. Moore, "A Reconnaissance in Texas in 1846," *Southwestern Historical Quarterly* 30 (1927): 254.
25. Z. N. Morrell, *Flowers and Fruits from the Wilderness; or, Thirty-Six Years in Texas and Two Winters in Honduras* (Boston: Gould & Lincoln, 1873), p. 62.
26. Webb and Carroll, *Handbook of Texas*, 1:928.
27. Detlef Dunt, *Reise nach Texas, nebst Nachrichten von diesem Lande* . . . (Bremen: Carl W. Wiehe, 1834), p. 137; DeCordova, *Texas: Her Resources*, p. 24; E. F. Bates, *History and Reminiscences of Denton County* (Denton: McNitzky Co., 1918), p. 302.
28. For a description of this technique as used by southern immigrants in the prairies of southern Michigan in the 1830s, see N. M. Thomas, "Reminiscences," *Historical Collections, Michigan Pioneer and Historical Society* 28 (1900): 534.
29. Bollaert, *William Bollaert's Texas*, pp. 74-75. See also Prunty, "Some Geographic Views," pp. 161-68; and, for special reference to Texas, V. W. Lehmann, "Fire in the Range of Attwater's Prairie Chicken," *Proceedings of the Fourth Annual Tall Timbers Fire Ecology Conference*, 1965, pp. 131-38.

Some Locational Implications of the Ethnic Division of Labor in Mid-Nineteenth-Century American Cities

DAVID WARD

Over the past decade investigations of nineteenth-century cities have exhibited two complementary developments.[1] Firstly, there has been an increased use of city directories, manuscript census schedules, and other sources, which make it possible to examine parsimonious segments of urban society by reference to a representative sample of individuals, households, social or ethnic groups, or firms. Secondly, there have been efforts to apply, retrospectively, some of the generalizations of the social sciences about modern society to conditions in nineteenth-century cities. These approaches are particularly appropriate for investigations of the ancestry and development of the highly differentiated social geography of mid-twentieth-century American cities.[2]

Some elements of the current residential pattern are of quite recent origin, but others were unquestionably evident by the turn of the nineteenth century, for it was during the first two decades of the present century that the first idealized representations of the arrangement of social groups and land uses within cities were formulated.[3] The appropriateness of these idealized descriptions of the social and economic geographies of American cities to conditions in the early and middle decades of the nineteenth century remains an open question. The neglect of this issue is perhaps not surprising, for very few North American cities attained a large size until quite late in the nineteenth century, and the processes of land-use specialization and residential differentiation are hard to detect in small or newly established settlements or, for that matter, in settlements experiencing extremely rapid growth and change. Under these circumstances, initially established patterns were quickly obliterated by the unprecedented pace of urban expansion. Until the recent increase in the use of manuscript census schedules, reconstructions of the distributions of people and activities within the cities were based upon the fragmentary and subjective documentation of contemporary descriptions and the highly aggregated statistical information of published state and federal censuses. These sources tend to mute any potential or actual differences between mid- and late nineteenth-century cities. Recent research based upon manuscript census schedules has, however, concentrated upon population persistence and turnover and social mobility. And although this work has revealed rather strikingly high rates of population turnover in a wide variety of settlements, their social geographic implications have remained largely unexplored.[4]

One obvious implication of population turnover of interest to urban geographers is the cumulative effect of high rates of residential mobility and intercity migration on the degree and level of residential differentiation within cities. Did high rates of turnover inhibit the formation of ethnic or social areas or did this process simply result in the movement of individuals from similar types of neighborhoods in different cities and have no major influence upon the process of residential differentiation? Certainly, there is some evidence which suggests that in those eastern American cities that housed substantial populations by the time of the Civil War, the degree of both land-use specialization and of residential differentiation was far less than in these same cities at the turn of the century.[5] These differences may be earlier and later stages of an urban pattern founded upon similar social and economic processes or, alternatively, they may represent the contrasting results of quite different processes. The resolution of this question will require much detailed empirical work on a wide variety of aspects of urban life. This paper proposes to examine only one aspect of this problem in one city, namely, the ethnic division of labor in New York City in 1860. The over- and underrepresentation of particular immigrant groups in different occupations was one of several influences which tended to encourage both the central concentration of foreign immigrants and the separation of one group from another at the turn of the century. An exploration of the locational implications of the ethnic division of labor at an earlier period might reveal, therefore, the kind or degree of differences between American cities at the middle and at the turn of the nineteenth century.

DAVID WARD

THE LATE NINETEENTH-CENTURY PATTERN

One of the most prominent aspects of the idealized descriptions of American cities at the turn of the century was the effect of the increased concentration and specialization of urban employment in central urban locations. The actual and potential expansion of commercial and industrial premises "blighted" the adjacent residential areas and encouraged socially mobile families to take advantage of the growing suburban residential choices made possible by the improvement and expansion of local transport facilities. Once vacated, housing near the central business district was subdivided into tenements for low-income people and suffered neglect in the face of imminent demolition. Since there were often unanticipated delays in the encroachment of industry and business and since the expansion of the central business district was not evenly distributed about its margins, old housing was demolished to make way for higher density, low-rent accommodations which might survive for several decades. The interrelationships between residential and nonresidential land uses on the edge of the central business district thus provided by far the largest supply of cheap housing for newly arrived immigrants. The central business district also provided the largest single source of unskilled employment, and pedestrian accessibility to these uncertain jobs may have been highly valued. Certainly, many immigrant families were dependent upon the wages of several rather than one member of the household, and the multiplication of modest, commuter carfares would have strained the resources of low-income families. Residence in relatively central quarters also would have minimized to some degree the journey-to-work problems of families constantly faced with under- or unemployment or the need to hold several jobs at once. This predicament resulted in frequent changes in the location of an unskilled immigrant's job.

These considerations of housing supply and of accessibility to employment suggest why, in general, low-income immigrants concentrated in central urban locations. But at a more specific level, these same considerations also account for the tendency of different ethnic groups to cluster in different parts of the central residential zone. The ethnic division of labor—whereby, for example, Russian-Jewish immigrants were overrepresented in the ready-made clothing industry and Italian immigrants in the distribution of fresh fruits and vegetables—compounded the effects of group consciousness and encouraged the concentration of these groups on those margins of the central business district where their preferred occupations were located.[6] Under these circumstances, ethnic residential areas and adjacent sections of the central business district were complementary rather than competitive land uses. The social problems of these central residential quarters were the result of the selective outward movement of socially mobile immigrants rather than of the blighting effects of business expansion. Indeed, most revisions of the idealized descriptions of American cities at the turn of the century have attempted to incorporate the effects of directional bias in the suburban movement of different ethnic and socioeconomic groups, of the greatly increased role of family life-cycle changes, and of the corresponding decline in the role of the journey-to-work in residential relocation.[7] Although the effects of selective social mobility and residential relocation of original ethnic quarters in the twentieth century have been elaborated,[8] the ancestry of the original central immigrant quarters has remained less clear.

THE MID-NINETEENTH-CENTURY PATTERN

The conditions which made possible the concentration of immigrants in central urban locations were certainly not present in American cities before the Civil War, and perhaps not until the seventies was the largest supply of cheap housing and unskilled jobs to be found in central urban locations. In the absence of an extensive and rapid system of local transportation, the incentive for people of moderate means to abandon dwellings conveniently located near commercial facilities of the city was not high. Even if the incentive had been higher, the rate of upward social mobility was much too low to release a supply of vacated housing equal to the demands of newly arrived immigrants. Without relatively even and high rates of upward social mobility, and assuming an increase in population density, the processes of "invasion and succession" or of "filtration" could scarcely have provided a supply of centrally located housing large enough to house immigrant populations, which soon accounted for half or more of many urban populations. Quite apart from this disequilibrium between supply and demand, because of the extraordinary rapid growth of the urban populations, almost all urban residents, irrespective of social status or economic condition, were seeking housing that had only recently been constructed.

Some of the basic assumptions of the idealized models of American cities at the turn of the century are clearly inappropriate to describe conditions during the middle decades of the nineteenth century. It is, therefore, possible that these different conditions supported a distinctive kind and degree of residential differentiation. On the basis of evidence from a limited number of cities, it is possible to suggest that

261

there was probably a considerable intermixing of occupational and ethnic groups during the first generation of large-scale foreign immigration into eastern American cities.[9] In Philadelphia and New York, there were ghetto-like concentrations of Irish and German immigrants in congested central quarters and well-established exclusive residential districts occupied by the native-born well-to-do. But large numbers of American, Irish, German, and other foreign-born groups also lived interspersed with one another. There existed, of course, a great deal of small-scale clustering of social or ethnic groups and well-defined social "gradients" or "cliffs" between streets and alleys. Somewhat larger concentrations of poor immigrants lived in "shantytowns" on the edge of the built-up area or on poorly drained land avoided by earlier physical expansions to the city. Nevertheless, the scale and extent of concentration by ethnicity, social status, or economic condition was decidedly limited. At a time when differences in rank and status may have been more emphatically defined and more readily accepted than later in the century, the need to confirm social position by residing in a district appropriate to that position may have had only a limited influence upon the emerging social geography of the mid-nineteenth-century city.

This interspersal of groups and intermixture of occupations in the period before the Civil War is perhaps surprising in view of the correspondence of the occupational distributions of Irish and German immigrants and their children and of Americans of native parentage with three broadly defined socioeconomic categories.[10] The Irish dominated employment in general laboring and domestic service; the Germans, some craft industries and the food trades; and native-born Americans, the professions and business. In short, class and ethnic origin should have reinforced one another if either exerted a pronounced influence on the process of residential differentiation. But the residential choices of immigrants were restricted not only by the limited availability of housing but also by the dispersed pattern of employment opportunities. Some activities were indeed already concentrated in central urban locations but many craft industries were spread throughout the city. Those which became dependent upon workshops near or within the central business district continued to "put-out" some segments of the production process.[11] Until the recruitment and deployment of general laboring by the contracting industries was formally organized from central labor markets, residence in peripheral urban locations may well have been more convenient for immigrants seeking day-labor jobs. Also, in the middle decades of the century, far larger numbers of domestic servants lived in or near the dwellings of their employers, and this practice accounted for the presence of size-able foreign-born populations within affluent residential districts.

IMPLICATIONS OF THE ETHNIC DIVISION OF LABOR

Since many employment sources and opportunities for immigrants were spread throughout the city, the ethnic division of labor would thus tend to encourage the intermixing rather than the concentration of ethnic groups. Without question, immigrants who preferred to live amongst their compatriots would be prepared to walk considerable distances to obtain employment, but the greater opportunities available elsewhere may have encouraged some to settle in ethnically less-homogenous sections of the city. Specifically, since the overrepresenta-tion of one ethnic group in one set of occupations resulted in the under-representation of other groups in the same occupations, opportunities for employment for one ethnic group may well have been greatest in areas where another group was predominant. On the other hand, the tendency for a majority group to patronize and support their compa-triots in their own residential quarters would restrict these oppor-tunities. The greatest opportunities for the surplus labor of an ethnic group in a particular occupation may, therefore, have occurred in newly developing sections of the city where no one particular group had yet established a dominance. Since foreign immigrant groups were rarely present in all cities in similar proportions, the locational implica-tions of the ethnic division of labor, in the last analysis, would be dependent upon the relative contributions of different immigrants to the population of a particular city. Clearly, in those cities overwhelmingly dominated by one ethnic group, the ethnic division of labor would be so weakly developed that any locational implications would be of minor consequence.

Most of these suggestions require rather careful empirical verifica-tion in a wide variety of cities. On the basis of data on a sample of households extracted from the 1860 manuscript census schedules for New York City, however, it is possible to provide a crude indication of the locational implications of the ethnic division of labor before both the development of the mass use of local transportation and the cen-tralization of most urban employment opportunities. (See figure) For the purpose of illustration, four occupational categories—two in which Irish households were overrepresented in relation to the city population as a whole and two in which German households were prominent—were

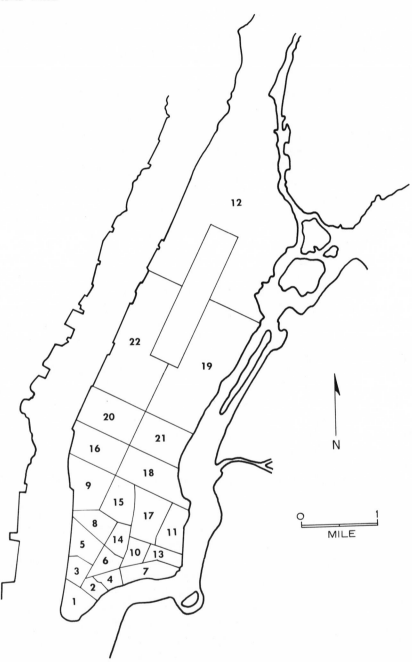

New York City wards: 1860.

selected for comparative analysis. Irish households, which accounted for about a quarter of the total for the city, were overrepresented in both general laboring and domestic service, while Germans, who formed about 16 percent of the city's households, were well represented in food production and distribution and some craft industries (table 1). Indices which express the relationship between the contribution of an ethnic group to the total employed population and its contribution to a particular occupation were computed to express the over- and underrepresentation of Irish and German households in the four selected occupational groups. The first index (table 2) describes the proportion of Irish and German households employed in the selected occupations in relation to the proportions of the total population of each ward employed in the same occupations. Wards were also assigned an ethnic status on the basis of the above-average presence of a particular group in each ward.

The first index reveals that the overrepresentation of Irish employment in laboring and domestic service was greatest in districts occupied by high proportions of German or native-American households (table 2). German employment in crafts and the food trades was prominent both in native American and in ethnically mixed and peripherally located wards. In spite of the interpretive difficulties encountered when reaggregating household data by areal units with the irregular areas and variable populations, there was a tendency for Irish and German employment in occupations in which the two groups were prominent to be proportionately greatest in those areas in which the overrepresented group was a minority of the total population of the ward. This complementarity of the occupational characteristics of different ethnic groups was, however, far from simple. For example, German craftsmen and food traders were prominent in native districts and in mixed areas, but the more diminutive presence of Germans in these occupations in Irish districts was influenced by the relative sizes of these two leading immigrant groups and the degree of their dominance in the selected occupations. Whereas the Irish households accounted for 80 percent of the total employment in laboring and 76 percent of that in domestic service, the smaller number of German households provided 54 percent of employment in the food trades and only 39 percent of that in crafts (table 1). The Irish, however, accounted for 42 percent of craft employment, absolutely more than the Germans, and 35 percent of those in the food trades. In spite of their relative underrepresentation in these occupations, the Irish provided for their own needs in those areas where they predominated (table 2).

The above observations refer to the distribution of proportionate

265

TABLE 1

A. Irish and German Employment in Selected Occupations: New York City, 1860

	Total Population	Irish Households		German Households	
		%	Index	%	Index
Laborers	11.4	15.9	1.3	6.1	0.5
Domestic Servants	16.2	21.6	1.4	12.1	0.8
Food Traders	4.7	2.9	0.6	8.9	1.9
Craftsmen	17.6	13.1	0.7	24.4	1.3

B. Contribution of Irish and German Born to Selected Occupations: New York City, 1860

	Irish Households		German Households	
	%	Index	%	Index
Laborers	79.9	1.4	15.1	0.5
Domestic Servants	76.4	1.3	21.1	0.7
Food Traders	35.3	0.6	53.6	1.9
Craftsmen	42.6	0.8	39.2	1.3
All Employed	57.3	. . .	28.2	. . .

overrepresentation of two groups in four occupations in relation to the total employment in these occupations in each ward. Since the occupational overrepresentation of both groups tended to be greatest in areas where the group in question was a minority in an area dominated by another group or by no single group, this measure gives no indication of absolute distribution of occupational representation. The second index (table 3) refers to the proportionate distribution of group employment in relation to the city as a whole and, therefore, allows for substantial variations in the total population of the wards. With some exceptions, the greatest absolute levels of occupational overrepresentation occurred in mixed and newly settled areas where no one group had established a local dominance. The exceptions all occurred in some, but not all, of the wards in which the overrepresented group was itself

266

TABLE 2

RELATIVE OVER- AND UNDERREPRESENTATION OF IRISH AND GERMAN
HOUSEHOLDS IN SELECTED OCCUPATIONS: NEW YORK CITY, 1860

Ward	Ethnic Character	Irish Households		German Households	
		Laborers	Dom. Svts.	Crafts	Food Trades
All Wards		1.3	1.4	1.3	1.9
1	Irish	1.2	1.1	1.7	1.8
2	Irish	1.2	1.1	1.0	1.3
3	Irish	1.0	1.2	1.4	1.1
4	Irish	1.2	1.1	0.9	1.4
5	Mixed	1.1	1.1	1.3	1.4
6	Irish	1.3	1.0	1.5	1.5
7	Mixed	1.3	1.2	1.2	3.0
8	Native	1.2	1.2	1.4	1.8
9	Native	1.7	1.6	1.5	2.3
10	German	2.7	1.8	1.1	1.3
11	German	1.9	1.6	1.1	1.5
12	Mixed	1.4	1.1	1.6	2.1
13	Mixed	1.8	1.5	1.0	2.4
14	Irish	1.1	0.9	1.3	1.4
15	Native	1.0	1.2	1.8	2.9
16	Native	1.3	1.2	1.6	2.3
17	German	1.5	1.6	1.3	1.3
18	Mixed	1.2	1.1	1.5	2.5
19	Mixed	1.5	1.3	1.8	2.5
20	Mixed	1.4	1.4	1.4	2.0
21	Mixed	1.3	1.2	1.3	2.6
22	Mixed	1.6	1.4	1.1	1.9
Average		79.9%	76.4%	39.2%	53.6%

extremely prominent. Spearman rank correlations of the distribution of the two groups within the city and the distribution of the contribution of each group to the four selected occupations were extremely low (table 3), suggesting that the ethnic division of labor was most pronounced in areas where the representation of a group was low or moderate. High correlations would presumably have occurred had the occupational overrepresentation varied in direct proportion to the contributions of the two groups to the total populations of each ward.

TABLE 3

Absolute Over- and Underrepresentation of Irish and German Households in Selected Occupations: New York City, 1860

Ward	Ethnic Character	Irish Households		German Households	
		Laborers	Dom. Svts.	Crafts	Food Trades
1	Irish	2.3	0.8	0.6	0.8
2	Irish	0.6	1.3	0.7	0.4
3	Irish	0.9	1.5	0.6	0.7
4	Irish	0.7	0.4	0.7	0.6
5	Mixed	1.2	0.9	0.7	0.9
6	Irish	1.2	0.9	1.0	0.7
7	Mixed	1.1	0.6	0.9	1.5
8	Native	0.8	0.8	1.0	0.9
9	Native	0.5	1.1	1.1	1.4
10	German	0.7	0.7	1.2	0.8
11	German	1.3	0.4	1.2	1.2
12	Mixed	2.3	1.0	0.8	0.5
13	Mixed	1.2	0.5	1.1	1.0
14	Irish	0.7	0.9	1.1	0.5
15	Native	0.2	1.6	0.5	0.7
16	Native	0.9	1.1	0.9	0.8
17	German	0.8	0.8	1.3	0.9
18	Mixed	0.7	1.6	0.6	1.0
19	Mixed	2.0	0.8	1.1	1.2
20	Mixed	1.1	0.9	1.0	1.0
21	Mixed	0.7	1.6	0.6	1.3
22	Mixed	1.5	0.7	0.8	1.3
Spearman Rank Correlations		.29	.39	.32	.21

The ethnic division of labor was a striking feature of the occupational structure of New York City during the first generation of Irish and German settlement. But it would appear that the occupational overrepresentation of Irish and German households in that city in 1860 was not highly concentrated in those districts where the overrepresented group was numerically or proportionately dominant. Certainly, the ethnic division of labor did not add greatly to the somewhat limited ethnic and socioeconomic differentiation of neighborhoods, and the mid-nineteenth-century city may well be more precisely defined in terms of complex patterns of interspersal of occupational and ethnic groups rather than as a mosaic of well-defined social areas. To be sure, most cities had areas defined by the affluence or extreme poverty of their residents, but the social identification of areas occupied by people in between these extremes of wealth was unclear, both on the ground and in the minds of contemporary social observers.

It must be emphasized, however, that in New York City, Irish and German households each represented substantial segments of the total labor force, but the effects of the predominance of Irish households have been noted. In cities with different proportionate representations of ethnic groups, the locational effects of the ethnic division of labor may well be quite different. In Philadelphia, the situation was similar to that in New York, but in Boston, where the German population was extremely small, the degree of ethnic and occupational clustering also was quite limited.[12] In Milwaukee, where Germans were the majority group, rather higher levels of residential differentiation have been noted.[13] These differences may record very basic differences in the ability of Irish and German immigrants to engross a section of the city or, alternatively, the somewhat different situation with respect to the housing market in a frontier city where large numbers of immigrants arrived during the period of initial settlement. In contrast, recent research on Omaha at the turn of the century suggests that the degree of concentration of ethnic groups in this newly settled city was not as high as in eastern cities at the same time.[14]

Comparative observations inferred from case studies need rather careful evaluation, however, for unless they are based upon a uniform metric, our observations may record only differences in the defining statistical parameters. In spite of the lack of truly comparative studies, it is clear that the emergence of an ethnically or occupationally defined social pattern and, more particularly, the central concentration of foreign immigrants by the end of the century, involved a rather complicated rearrangement of ethnic groups, which may itself have varied according to both the size and diversity of the immigrant population and the age and size of the city at the time of the first major immigrant influx.

NOTES

1. For example, see Stephan Thernstrom and Richard Sennett, eds., *Nineteenth Century Cities: Essays in the New Urban History* (New Haven: Yale University Press, 1969).
2. Peter G. Goheen, *Victorian Toronto, 1850-1900; Pattern and Process of*

Growth, University of Chicago, Department of Geography Research Paper no. 127 (Chicago: University of Chicago Press, 1970).

3. For example, Richard M. Hurd, *Principles of City Land Values,* New York Real Estate Record Association (1903); and Edward W. Burgess, "The Growth of the City," in Robert E. Park, ed., *The City* (Chicago: University of Chicago Press, 1925), pp. 47-62.

4. Stephan Thernstrom, *Poverty and Progress, Social Mobility in a Nineteenth Century City* (Cambridge, Mass.: Harvard University Press, 1964); Peter R. Knights, *The Plain People of Boston* (New York: Oxford University Press, 1972); and Howard P. Chudacoff, *Mobile Americans: Residential and Social Mobility in Omaha, 1880-1920* (New York: Oxford University Press, 1972).

5. Sam Bass Warner, Jr., *The Private City, Philadelphia in Three Periods of Its Growth* (Philadelphia: University of Pennsylvania Press, 1968); and David Ward, *The Internal Spatial Differentiation of Immigrant Residential Districts,* Northwestern University, Department of Geography Special Publication no. 3 (1970), pp. 24-42.

6. David Ward, "The Emergence of Central Immigrant Ghettoes in American Cities: 1840-1920," *Annals of the Association of American Geographers* 58 (1968): 343-59.

7. Duncan W. G. Timms, *The Urban Mosaic: Towards a Theory of Residential Differentiation* (Cambridge: Cambridge University Press, 1971).

8. Stanley Lieberson, *Ethnic Patterns in American Cities* (Glencoe, Ill.: Free Press, 1963).

9. Warner, *Private City;* and Ward, *Internal Spatial Differentiation.*

10. Robert Ernst, *Immigrant Life in New York City, 1825-1863* (New York: Columbia University Press, 1949), pp. 61-98; and Clyde Griffen, "Workers Divided: The Effect of Craft and Ethnic Differences in Poughkeepsie, New York, 1850-1880," in Thernstrom and Sennett, *Nineteenth Century Cities,* pp. 49-97.

11. For example, Jesse Pope, *The Clothing Industry of New York* (Columbia, Mo.: E. W. Stephens, 1905).

12. Warner, *Private City,* and Oscar Handlin, *Boston's Immigrants, A Study in Acculturation* (Cambridge, Mass.: Harvard University Press, 1959).

13. Kathleen N. Conzen, "The German Athens: Milwaukee and the Accommodation of Its Immigrants, 1856-1860," 2 vols. (Ph.D. diss., Department of History, University of Wisconsin, Madison, 1972).

14. Chudacoff, *Mobile Americans.*

Bonanza Towns
Urban Planning on the
Western Mining Frontier

JOHN W. REPS

The discovery of gold in California in 1848 dramatically sped the pace of settlement and the development of civil government in the American West. So rapid was the increase in California's population that it was admitted directly into the union in 1850 without passing through the intermediate stage of territorial organization. A decade later mining rushes in Nevada and Colorado, followed by those in Montana, Idaho, and South Dakota, added population to the mountainous West and resulted in the creation of additional territorial and then state governments.

Hundreds of towns developed in the mining regions. In California they occupied sites along the mother lode stretching from Mormon Bar northward through Sonora, Columbia, Jackson, Coloma, Grass Valley, and Downieville to Rich Bar. Across the Sierras the principal Nevada gold and silver towns included Gold Hill, Silver City, and Virginia City in the hills north of the Carson River valley as well as Aurora and Austin to the south and east.

The Colorado mining settlements could be found in such places as Central City, Blackhawk, Idaho Springs, Georgetown, Cripple Creek, and Leadville. In Montana there were Virginia City, Bannack, and

This paper is based on three chapters of a forthcoming book dealing with the history of urban planning and development in the American West. Research was made possible by a grant from The Amon Carter Museum of Western Art, Fort Worth, Texas. Only a few of the illustrations used by the author in presenting his paper at the conference have been reproduced herein.

Helena, along with the copper town of Butte. Deadwood, Lead, Crook City, and Galena were the chief mining towns in the Black Hills of South Dakota. Idaho, Utah, Wyoming, Arizona, New Mexico, and even Oregon and Washington, had their mining camps as well. Tombstone, Silver City, Orofino, Quartzsite, Bonanza City, Gold Dust, Cornucopia, Mineral City, Oreana, and Copperopolis were names that once flickered into prominence and as quickly vanished into obscurity.

In addition to creating the towns on or near deposits of mineral wealth, the quest for gold and silver resulted in the establishment of supply and outfitting centers located some distance from the mining camps. Sacramento, the first of these towns, and typical of most, served as a jumping-off point and temporary winter residence for miners, as a warehousing and wholesaling center for mining camp merchants, and as a recreation and gambling resort.

Carson City had been laid out a few months before the Nevada rush by Abraham Curry, who skillfully promoted his new settlement as the gateway to the mines. Curry, like General Sutter whose son planned Sacramento, owned the entire site and was thus able to establish a uniform design to guide its mushrooming growth.

The plans of Pierre, South Dakota, and Boise, Idaho, resembled those of Carson City in this respect. Although founded as a railroad town, Pierre owed much of its growth to its role as the starting point for wagonborne freight en route to mining towns in the Black Hills.

Denver, on the other hand, resulted from the almost simultaneous efforts of three townsite companies to seize control of a location rumored to be rich in gold. All three companies used a standardized gridiron pattern, but each town had slightly different dimensions and orientation for its streets, blocks, and lots.

Occasionally, a town combined the functions of mining settlement and supply center as at Helena, Montana. That the supply centers were regarded as more important and more likely to be permanent than the mining towns is indicated by their selection as the state capitals of California, Nevada, Colorado, Idaho, Montana, and South Dakota.

All of these supply centers, and such others as Marysville and Stockton, California, were planned communities; that is, some individual or group determined the town's future pattern and staked it out on the land rather than relying upon spontaneous growth and incremental development. There is nothing particularly surprising about this. By the mid-nineteenth century the planning of towns in America had become a common occurrence, although the functional and aesthetic qualities of their plans left much to be desired.

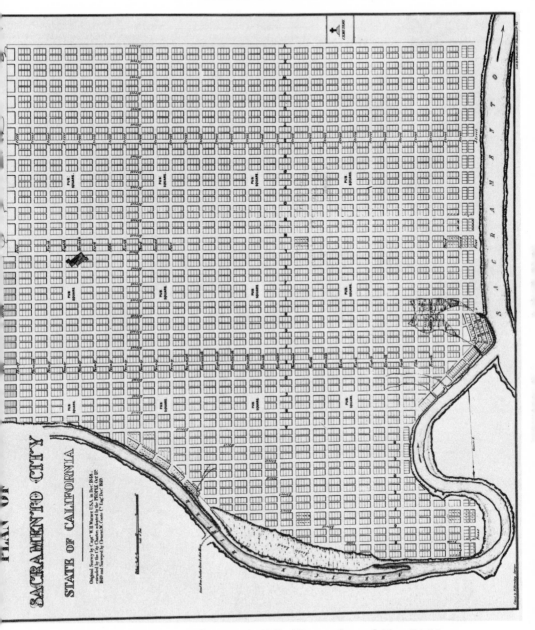

Fig. 1. *Plan of Sacramento, California, in 1849. (Geography and Map Division, Library of Congress.)*

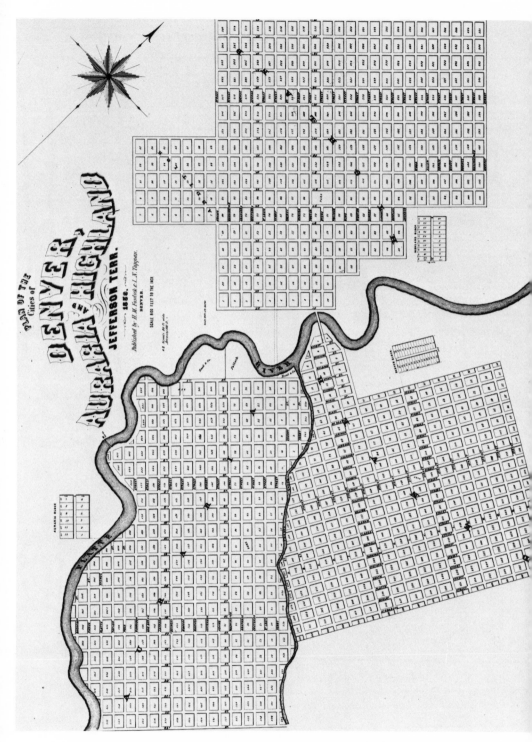

Fig. 2. *Plan of Denver, Colorado, in 1859. (State Historical Society of Colorado, Denver.)*

The supply centers were sufficiently removed from the frantic and seemingly chaotic scramble for land at the mining locations to permit orderly surveying and lot sales. Many persons came to the mining regions not to dig for gold or silver but to make their fortune from real estate speculation in town lots. The attempted creation of towns midway between the mines and the existing frontier of settlement provided an outlet for these townsite promoters. Their method of procedure required that an entire site be platted at one time to provide a supply of lots that might be sold or auctioned.

For every Sacramento that succeeded there must have been several failures. The proprietors of such California paper towns as Tuolumne City, Boston, and New York of the Pacific all planned neatly regular communities, but for one reason or another these towns failed to attract residents and soon were forgotten.

What is startling to find is that in the mining towns themselves urban planning played a considerable role. In California this seems to have been limited to attempts to provide some kind of order in an already established mining camp. In the first mining towns of Nevada and Colorado there are examples of efforts to plan urban growth before a basic town form had fully emerged. Finally, in the later phases of the bonanza West, and with occasional earlier examples, mining towns were often planned and surveyed immediately after the discovery of gold or silver, before the arrival of the vanguard of population.

In his pioneering study of 1885, *Mining Camps: A Study in American Frontier Government,* Charles Shinn did not emphasize the significance of this aspect of western mining towns. Shinn described how groups of miners thrown together in regions lacking civil government organized mining districts, adopted laws governing mineral claims, created provisional towns, and provided for the administration of justice. This impressive response to the need men felt for formal, institutional constraints on human conduct was all the more remarkable because circumstances offered maximum rewards for individual initiative and enterprise.

Shinn, and other more recent scholars, failed to note evidence of planning in some of the earliest mining towns and most of the later ones that would have strengthened his thesis. Documentary records of the period, early cartographic and pictorial material, and the remnants of the towns themselves support the conclusion that urban planning was far from unknown on the western mining frontier.

Few early plats of California mining towns exist, but among those surviving is one of Coloma, the location of Sutter's Mill where James

Marshall discovered gold in 1848. This survey dates from nearly ten years after that event, but the tidy straightness of Main Street, the precisely parallel alignment of Back Street, and its right-angled intersection with High Street may well be of earlier origin. Certainly no one would assert that Coloma represents much of an achievement in urban design, but it is noteworthy that the residents made at least an attempt to establish some kind of physical order—however primitive—in the emerging community.

The records of Sonora are more complete. They reveal that in February 1850 the provisional town council ordered the town surveyed. That this was more than a mere record of existing claims in indicated by the surveyor's report that several buildings encroached on the newly established street lines.

A view of the town published about two years later certainly does not convey much of a sense of order or regularity, but following the town's destruction by fire that same year the citizens appointed a committee empowered to widen streets and lay them off at right angles. It was at that time that Washington Street, the town's main thoroughfare, attained its full width of eighty feet. Even more unusual was the decision of the town council declaring unoccupied lots to be public property. These lots were sold at auction to defray costs of surveying the town and to help support the municipal hospital.

More impressive and better documented is the planning of Virginia City, Nevada. The discovery of the Comstock Lode early in 1859 attracted thousands of miners to the slopes of Mount Davidson. A camp meeting in September resulted in a provisional government, and the following month two surveyors laid out A Street running across the slope, supposedly following the line of the Comstock ledge. This also was more than a survey of existing town lot claims, since early records show that a few miners refused for a time to move their cabins when the survey revealed them to be in the right-of-way of the new street.

As the population swiftly increased, new streets were surveyed parallel to the first. The first detailed view of Virginia City, published in 1861, shows the town as seen from the south and clearly indicates the results of early planning. It was, as Mark Twain observed, a town that "had a slant to it like a roof. Each street was a terrace, and from each to the street below the descent was forty or fifty feet."

In 1865 the town government—by that time operating under an official charter—proudly published its first official map. Many new streets had been planned parallel to those of earlier days. To minimize differences in elevation the main thoroughfares running across the slope were closely spaced and connected by more widely separated short and steep cross streets.

A view in 1868 along C Street, the main business route, shows the degree to which urban order and respectability had been imposed upon this lively mining community. Building and sidewalk lines in fact were as straight and regular as prescribed on the official map.

By 1875 the town reached its peak of prosperity and elegance. Mansions of wealthy mine operators and merchants looked out from lofty sites above A Street. Imposing business blocks, hotels, restaurants, saloons, gambling halls, and retail shops lined both sides of C Street. A group of churches between D and F streets stood as symbols of morality between the upper town and the Chinese quarter and red light district located on the slopes farther down the mountain near the mine entrances and settling ponds. It was a steep climb to the top in Virginia City—both physically and socially. A man's location on the sloping Cartesian grid of the city's streets served as a reliable indicator of his place in society.

Many other Nevada mining towns were also planned using the uninspiring but utilitarian grid pattern: Esmeralda and Aurora in 1860, Washoe in 1861, Austin in 1863, and American City and Mineral City in 1864, among others. Plats of some of these towns are among the townsite surveys of the General Land Office records in the National Archives.

More venturesome—and perhaps because of that fact never carried out—was Adolph Sutro's abortive design for a town at the mouth of the Sutro Tunnel constructed to provide ventilation, drainage, and emergency escape for the miners of the Comstock four miles away. Shown on the plat are four large parks representing an early attempt to introduce facilities for outdoor recreation into a town whose residents would have expected to spend their leisure time in gambling halls, brothels, or saloons.

The early mining communities of Colorado developed about this same time and exhibited many of the same characteristics as these Nevada towns. The first strikes were in the vicinity of Central City where John Gregory found a rich deposit of gold-bearing quartz. The thousands of miners who crowded into the narrow confines of Gregory Gulch certainly had little initial interest in urban planning. Among the regulations adopted for the mining district, only one dealt with an aspect of urban settlement. It provided that "any person may take up, by recording, forty feet front and one hundred deep, for a building lot; but shall not secure the same against being used for mining, if found rich.

FIG. 3. *View of Virginia City, Nevada, in 1875. (Geography and Map Division, Library of Congress.)*

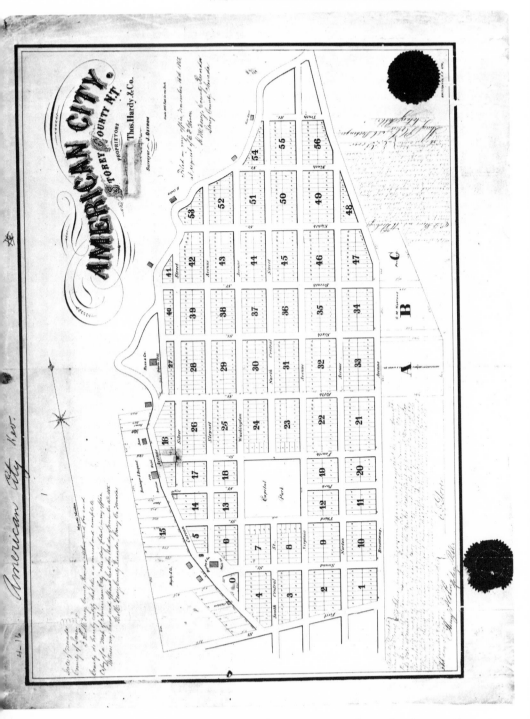

FIG. 4. Plan of American City, Nevada, in 1865. (Records of the Bureau of Land Management, Townsite Surveys, in National Archives Building.)

Should any person work out the ground on which a house stands, he shall secure the house against damage."

Nevertheless, if town lots were to be recorded, there needed to be some reference system, and if lots were to have a "front," streets were required. The first survey and plan may have been made as early as 1860, but the oldest surviving plat is the one drawn by Hal Sayre in 1863. Sayre laid out the first streets following the winding valley floors of the Nevada, Gregory, and Eureka gulches making others at higher elevations parallel to the first. As at Virginia City, these streets were closely spaced because of the steep slopes, and short cross streets were introduced at greater intervals.

A view of Central City in 1873 reveals how the town grew on this simple but functional pattern. By that time the first crude cabins, hastily thrown up by the first miners, had been replaced by more imposing structures. Unhappily, a fire the following year destroyed virtually all of the city portrayed in this view. In the process of reconstruction, the city council continued the earlier tradition of city planning by ordering that Eureka, Lawrence, Main, Gregory, Spring, and High streets be widened.

Idaho Springs had an even more regular plan, a reflection of the relatively level site that George Jackson and his friends surveyed in the summer of 1859 near the place where Jackson had discovered gold a few months earlier. It seems likely that the group anticipated a double financial reward for their activities through the sale of town lots in the valley as well as digging for gold in the hills.

More impressive in its size and setting was Georgetown. George Griffith platted a town there as early as 1860, but it was abandoned because of the difficulty of extracting gold from the peculiar rock of the region. The stubborn ore that yielded gold so reluctantly proved to be mostly silver, and in 1867 a second rush brought a new group of miners to the valley. They employed Charles Hoyt to survey the site, succeeded in capturing the county seat from Idaho Springs, and the following year secured a city charter from the legislature.

A view of the town in 1874 shows more clearly the results of Hoyt's survey. The settlement extended a mile and a half from the foot of Burrell Hill down the half-mile-wide Clear Creek valley. The regularity of Georgetown's grid streets contrasts sharply with the wild, rugged character of the mountainous surroundings. Major portions of this town have been preserved, and the modern visitor can inspect at firsthand the evidence of frontier planning.

In the 1870s another vast silver area was discovered near the head-

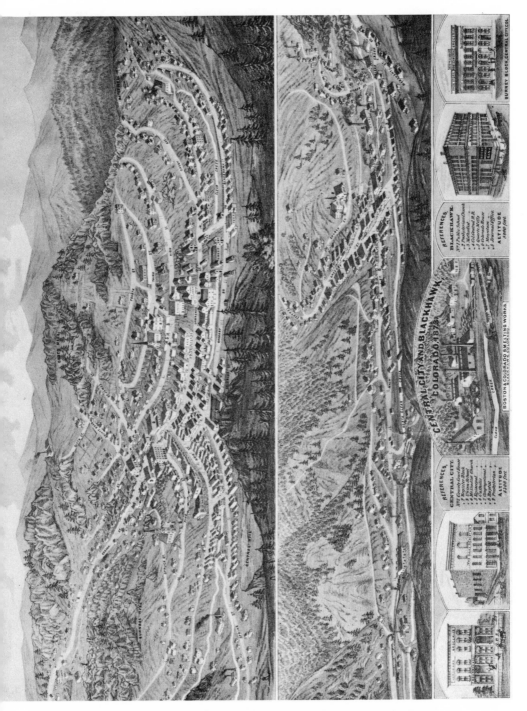

FIG. 5. *View of Central City and Blackhawk, Colorado, in 1873. (Courtesy Amon Carter Museum of Western Art, Fort Worth, Texas.)*

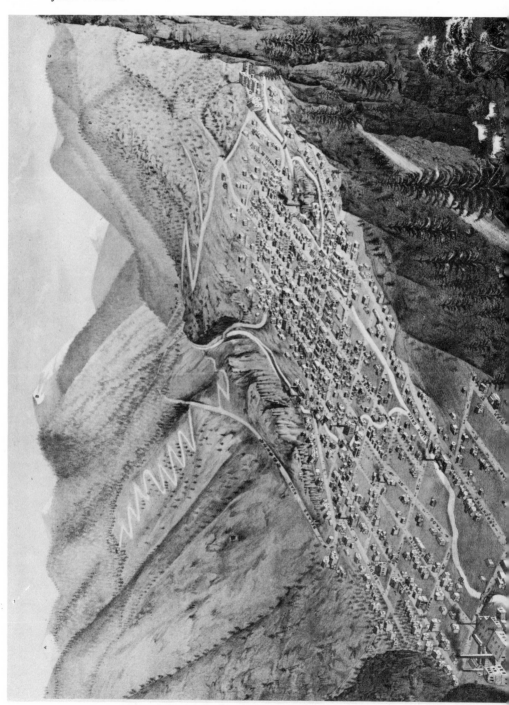

FIG. 6. *View of Georgetown, Colorado, in 1874. (Courtesy Amon Carter Museum of Western Art, Fort Worth, Texas.)*

waters of the Arkansas River. Within two years from the beginning of the rush in 1876 the principal settlement of the area—Leadville—had a population of 5,000. By the end of 1879 that figure tripled. That year the city council passed an ordinance requiring the removal within ten days of any buildings encroaching on the official street lines. One victim of this drastic law was Mayor William James who had unwittingly erected a stable in the bed of a planned street before the surveys had been completed. He promptly demolished the structure. C. E. Wyman, on the other hand, had built his cabin on what was supposed to be a corner lot. It turned out to be located squarely in the middle of Harrison Avenue. Wyman refused to remove his dwelling, and the city government eventually took possession and tore it down.

Such firm enforcement of public regulations would be noteworthy today, and this policy in a town and in an era supposedly characterized by a casual attitude toward law and order is a challenge to some of our beliefs about the nature of frontier society. While the policy and the official plan may not have created a particularly attractive city, it did at least prevent hopeless chaos that surely would have descended upon the community in the absence of any attempt to guide and control the booming expansion of Leadville.

The last of the great mining booms in Colorado produced a series of planned towns around Cripple Creek in the decade of the 1890s. Cripple Creek itself resulted from quick action by two Denver real estate men who had bought the land for ranching some years earlier. When gold was discovered, they hastily gridded off their least valuable 80 acres into streets, blocks, and lots. Adjoining owners of a 140-acre placer claim extended that pattern across their tract. Elsewhere, on the rugged slopes of the golden mountain Victor, Goldfield and several smaller settlements were laid out in similar fashion.

The streets of Cripple Creek rolled and pitched like a ship on a stormy sea. Bennett Avenue, the principal thoroughfare, sloped so steeply from one side to the other that it had to be divided into two terraced lanes, one fifteen feet above the other, supported by a retaining wall. Probably nowhere was rectilinear planning so ill adapted to a site for a city.

The Montana mining rush beginning in 1862 also led to the creation of towns that were planned, along with some that developed more spontaneously and with less order. One month after Henry Edgar and Bill Fairweather discovered gold at Alder Gulch, the Varina Townsite Company filed its survey and claim to the 320 acres of land allowed under federal townsite laws. It was probably that plan, doubtless

Fɪɢ. 7. *Portion of a survey of Leadville, Colorado, and vicinity in 1879, with the addition of railroads and mine shafts to 1910. (Olin Library, Cornell University.)*

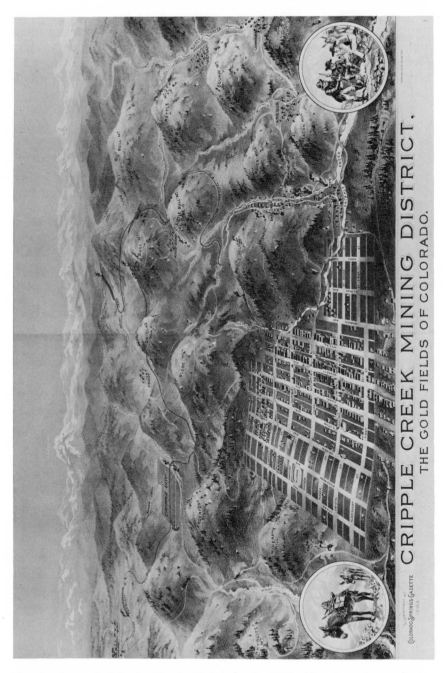

FIG. 8. *View of Cripple Creek, Colorado, in 1894. (Courtesy Amon Carter Museum of Western Art, Fort Worth, Texas.)*

altered to incorporate three parks, three cemetery plots, and a site for the proposed territorial capital, that J. L. Corbett followed when he drew the official plat submitted to the General Land Office in May 1868 by order of the city council of Virginia City. This manuscript plan is decorated with views of the Episcopal church, the proposed capitol, and a photograph of one of the brick buildings on the main street.

E. S. Glover's fine lithograph view, published in 1875, shows that the town had indeed developed along the lines laid down during its first months of existence. Other forms of law and order may have been enforced with some laxity, but those established governing property rights were apparently strictly observed.

The first settlement at Last Chance Gulch, in July 1864, lacked the rectilinear order of Virginia City as miners crowded into the narrow valley to erect tents and cabins wherever they could find space. Here, too, the need for urban planning soon prevailed. The citizens met on October 30, organized a town government, chose the name Helena, elected three commissioners with responsibility to survey the townsite, and, as the minutes of the meeting record, delegated them authority to "make such laws and regulations as may be deemed necessary, to regulate the location and size of lots, streets, alleys, etc."

The official plat of Helena recorded in the United States Land Office early in 1869 reveals the street, block, and lot patterns devised by the commissioners. An earlier lithograph view published in 1865, only one year after the town's founding, shows that the community had followed the commissioners' plan and the regulations adopted to enforce it. Some of the irregularities doubtless reflect occupancy of building sites prior to the adoption of the official plan, while others may have been dictated by topography.

By 1875 the growth pattern of the city was well established. Newly developed sections following the gridiron alignment prescribed by municipal authorities can be seen on E. S. Glover's view published in that year. Helena is not and never was a beautiful community; the rectilinear streets and the hills and valleys are clutched in eternal combat, but the form of the city, for better or for worse, resulted from community direction and control and not from unfettered and unregulated private initiative.

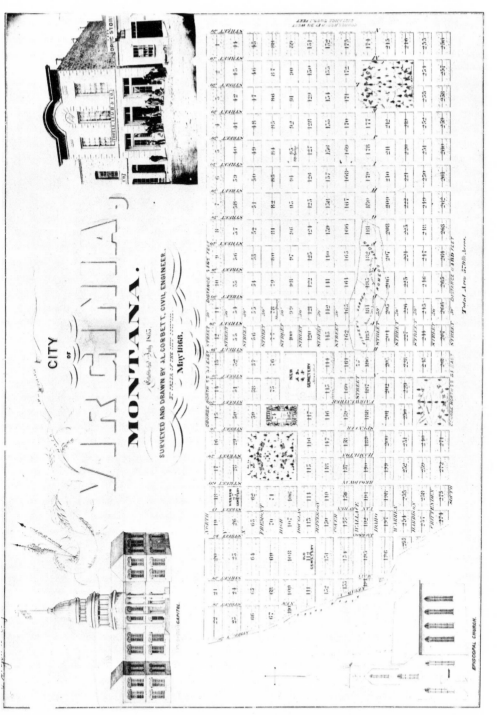

Fig. 9. *Manuscript plan of Virginia City, Montana, in 1868. (Records of the Bureau of Land Management, Townsite Surveys, in National Archives Building.)*

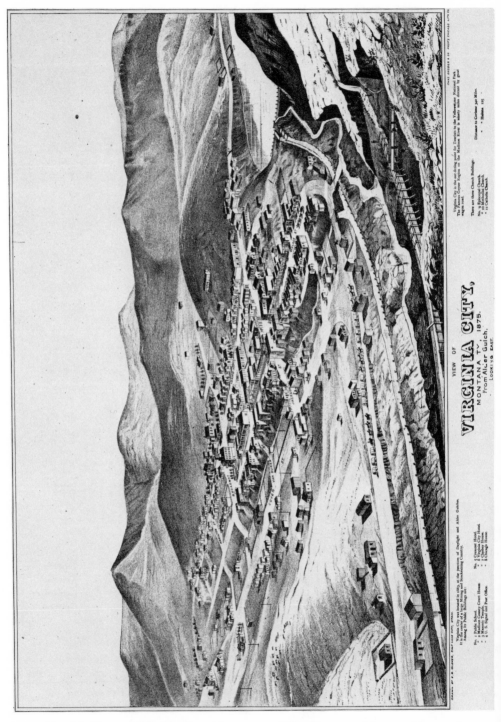

FIG. 10. *View of Virginia City, Montana, in 1875. (Courtesy Montana Historical Society, Helena.)*

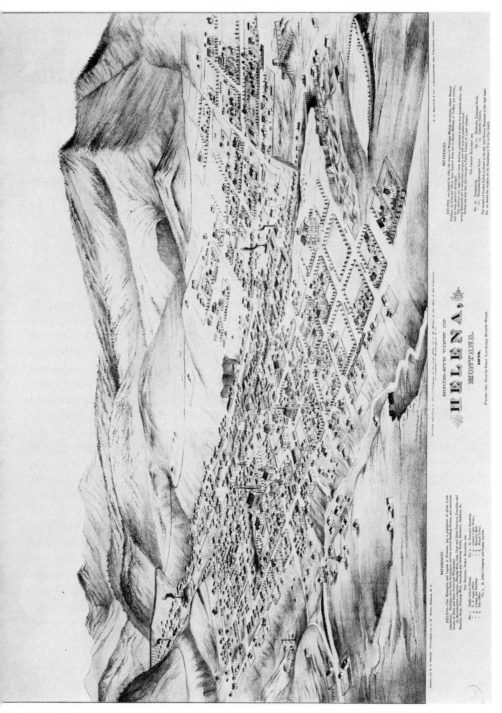

FIG. 11. *View of Helena, Montana, in 1875. (Geography and Map Division, Library of Congress.)*

Settlement on the Public Domain as Reflected in Federal Records Suggested Research Approaches

JANE F. SMITH

Few aspects of American history are more exciting and interesting to scholar and layman alike than the westward moving frontier of American settlement. The significance attributed to this movement by Turner and the chronicling of its details by Paxson, Billington, and others is well known, but the importance of geographical factors in determining the movement's character and extent is too often ignored. The topography of the North American continent was of signal importance from the beginning of English settlement. For more than one hundred fifty years the American colonists were hemmed in at the threshhold of the continent by the great Appalachian barrier stretching some fifteen hundred miles from northern Maine to the hills of Alabama. During the Revolutionary War the embattled colonists "braced themselves against the mountains and fought towards the sea,"[1] but at its conclusion they used the energy released by the successful conflict to rush through the natural breaches in the Appalachian system and, in the first four decades of the nineteenth century, to carry settlement beyond into the Mississippi Valley and the Lake Plains.

This tremendous western surge of pioneer settlement occurred principally, of course, on the public domain—that vast area of land acquired by the United States as it extended its sovereignty over more and more territory. It had been hastened by the policy of the federal government, from the days of the founding fathers, to transfer the lands as rapidly as possible to private ownership.

Requirements of early laws that Indian title be extinguished before lands were surveyed, that the rectangular public land surveys be extended to the public domain before lands were offered for sale, and, after 1800, that they be sold at district land offices, necessitated detailed administrative work and resulted in the creation within the United States Treasury Department of a working bureaucracy, which in 1812 was given bureau status when Congress established the General Land Office. This office was responsible for all aspects of public domain administration except the work of surveying and mapping, which remained the prerogative of surveyors general appointed for each state or territory. In 1836 they too were placed within the General Land Office. That office (the Bureau of Land Management since 1946) has, during its more than one hundred sixty years of existence, transferred most of the public domain to private ownership and, in so doing, created some of the most vitally important federal records extant, recording much of the early history of the exploration, mapping, settlement, and development of the United States from the Appalachian Mountains westward to the Pacific.

Most public land records, leaving aside the Bureau of Land Management's general administrative records, can be classified into four categories: (1) identification records, consisting of field notes and plats of survey, which identify and describe the public lands; (2) status records, consisting of tract books and status plats, which record the ownership and use of public lands and resources; (3) case records (land-entry papers), which document each separate action affecting the public lands and resources; and (4) control records (such as entry lists forwarded by the registers of the different district land offices), copies of patents issued, and proclamations and orders, which provide the legal and administrative basis of rights in or title to public lands and resources. I would like to describe these four categories in somewhat greater detail in the order in which they were listed.

Surveyor's field notes became the first written land records and were the working papers used in preparation of survey plats—the foundation land record by which public lands were and are identified, described, and measured. There are almost thirty thousand cartographic items among holdings in the National Archives relating to basic surveying activities for the period 1785-1946. Among them are manuscript copies of field notes and manuscript plats of the original township surveys in Illinois, Indiana, Iowa, Kansas, Missouri, and Ohio. These begin with plats and field notes of the survey between 1785 and 1787 of the Seven Ranges of Ohio, the first public land surveys conducted, which set the pattern for all that followed. Most of the plats for states farther west and northwest have been retained by the Bureau of Land Management because they are still needed for administrative purposes. Although the various series of field notes and plats differ greatly in detail and usefulness, their descriptions of physical features of the land often constituted, for homesteaders, the best or only guide to the character and value of land available for settlement. The notes include particularly valuable descriptive information about topography, natural vegetation, and potential uses of the land.

In the course of disposing of this surveyed public land, a second class of records—the tract books—were maintained. These ledgers, arranged by township, provide an invaluable record of decisions and actions affecting disposal of each section of the public domain and constitute a geographical index to initial transactions conveying title from the United States government to the first patentee. For each transaction there is a legal description of the land, acreage, price per acre, total cost, name of purchaser, date of sale, receipt numbers and certificate of purchase, name of patentee, and name of the local land office handling the transaction. Many tract books maintained at district land offices in states where the public domain has been exhausted were turned over to some state agency, often the state historical society, when the last district land office was closed, but a duplicate set maintained in the Washington office is complete. Tract books for some sixteen western public land states have been transferred to the General Archives Division at Suitland, Maryland. The Bureau of Land Management retains the remainder. Their value as a settlement record and their research potential for analyses of settlement patterns and other economic and social studies, particularly when used in conjunction with survey plats and related land records, cannot be overemphasized.

Case records, or land-entry papers, accumulated in processing applications for purchase or use of public lands in the thirty public domain states comprise the third important category of land records. Some twenty-seven thousand cubic feet of these case files, dated chiefly between 1800 and 1951, and recording millions of individual transactions, are now in our General Archives Division.

It is difficult to generalize about these records as they range in content from simple applications to purchase, with receipts executed on the spot in the early period, to an elaborate series of applications, proofs, affidavits, and other documents executed over a period of years in later homestead, desert land, and mineral entries. In addition to simple credit- and cash-entry files, the land-entry papers in the National

Archives include records relating to entries based on special conditions of settlement, for example, the Florida, Oregon, and Washington donation files; Virginia and United States bounty-land warrants issued to certain veterans (from the Revolutionary through the Mexican wars) and surrendered to the federal government for public domain land or for script certificates that could be used to purchase tracts of land; homestead entries which frequently include valuable settlement data such as descriptions of houses and other improvements, dates residences were established, number and relationship of family members, citizenship evidence, the nature of crops, and amount of acreage under cultivation; and private land-claim records documenting claims made on the basis of grants or settlement that occurred before the United States acquired sovereignty. There are private land claims in the National Archives relating to land in portions of fifteen states that were granted or settled in this manner during the sovereignty of France, Great Britain, Mexico, and Spain.

The various series of land-entry records before 1908 are arranged alphabetically by state and thereunder by district land office where the entry was made. For each land office there is a separate series for each class of entry. When patents were issued, the volume and page number of the official copy of the patent were noted on the back of the corresponding land-entry file. Chronological access to these entries is provided by "Monthly Abstracts" submitted by registers and receivers of the district land offices. These abstracts of entry, which have been bound into more than fifty-seven hundred volumes, arranged by state and district land office, can be used very profitably in various research studies, such as in analyzing the entries handled in any particular land office in any year or in charting the most active years of settlement in the land district.

The patent or deed file represents, of course, the end product of much activity involving the public domain. The record copies of patents before 1908 were organized in many separate series, corresponding to the land-entry papers themselves. Thus, there were series of patent records for each district land office and for each class of entry made at each land office. Almost twenty-five hundred volumes of these patent records, dated prior to 1908, for public domain land in sixteen western states are now in the General Archives Division of the National Archives.

Although no overall index to entrymen and patentees prior to 1908 was maintained, we do have partial indexes for several series and a consolidated name index for land entries in the states of Alabama, Alaska, Arizona, Florida, Louisiana, Nevada, and Utah. In order to find other land-entry files, it is necessary to know the legal description of the land involved or the approximate date of the entry and the name of the land office through which the entry was made.

The vast body of General Land Office records in the National Archives is amazingly well organized, yet it was not created with economic and sociological research interests of historians or geographers in mind. Scholarly use of these major classes of land records is admittedly complex, but it can be very rewarding if searchers learn to appreciate the close relationship between these major series and the most efficient approach for each specific research problem. In essence, the tract books serve as geographical indexes to the land-entry papers, which in turn become an index to the record copies of patents. It is impossible to locate a specific patent record before 1908 without consulting the appropriate land-entry case file which shows the volume and page number of the patent. Yet specified land cases can often be identified when only a few facts are available. If the approximate date of the entry and the land office involved are known, one can search the chronologically arranged registers' returns or monthly abstracts of entries.

The research potential of these four classes of land records—particularly for various types of quantitative analyses, including certain settlement studies—has been presented by Richard S. Maxwell in his paper on "The Public Land Records of the Federal Government, 1800-1950, and Their Statistical Significance,"[2] and there is no need to mention these suggested research topics here. I do wish to assert and to emphasize, however, that these records and the great quantity of supplemental administrative land records in the National Archives can be used in conjunction with certain records originating with other agencies (now also among our holdings) to trace the advance of settlement on the westward-moving frontier from the Seven Ranges of Ohio to the Pacific Ocean and to study the patterns of settlement and development in any geographical area or the pioneer history of any township in the thirty public land states.

Perhaps the first scholar to fully understand the potential of the federal land records was Joseph Schafer, who, using the phrase "microscopic method applied to history,"[3] asserted more than fifty years ago that the township plats and field notes and the land office tract books could be used to develop "a plat book or atlas" that would give the student of Wisconsin history the "names of first settlers in each section of the state, together with an ocular account of the lands they occupied. . . ."[4] By using basic data provided by the atlas on "how the settlers dealt with the land under varying circumstances and how the land reacted upon the settlers economically and socially," Schafer contended that the historian could undertake "numerous special studies interpretative of Wisconsin and of American history."[5]

Dr. Schafer was, of course, referring primarily to agricultural settlement, but it must not be supposed that all pioneers were farmers—some were miners, others townsmen. The apparent preoccupation of scholars with the agricultural frontier may explain the fact that records among our holdings relating to settlement on mineral lands and the establishment of townsites on the public domain have received far less attention from historians than their content warrants.

While farmers were spreading over the prairies and timbered lands of the Great Lakes states, other settlers moved northwest into the "driftless area" of northwestern Illinois and southwestern Wisconsin. Although offering fewer agricultural opportunities, the outcroppings of rock in this area contained rich veins of lead and other minerals. The 1820s witnessed a great influx into the lead mines of the Fever River region, and by 1830 the thousands of new arrivals, mainly miners, had built Galena at the head of navigation on the river and were already shipping considerable quantities of lead to New Orleans. Others pushed into southwestern Wisconsin and also, in the early 1840s, into the copper-mining lands that opened up on the southern shore of Lake Superior as a result of the well-publicized findings of Douglas Houghton's surveys and the extinguishment of the Chippewa Indian title in 1842-43.

Of particular value in reconstructing the early settlement pattern of these mineral areas is a special collection of records in the National Archives relating to the leasing and operation of lead and copper mines. These records consist chiefly of correspondence and ledgers, originally kept by the United States Superintendent of Mineral Lands in the field offices at Galena, Illinois; Mineral Point, Wisconsin; and Sault Saint Marie, Michigan, which were operated by the Ordnance Bureau of the War Department. The records were transferred to the General Land Office in 1847, when it assumed jurisdiction over all mineral lands. This collection includes, for example, a special tract book of lead land in the Mineral Point District (Wisconsin), a register of suspended entries, and other records that develop the history of early settlement in this area,[6] the significance of which was presented in two articles published in the spring 1969 issue of *Prologue: The Journal of the National Archives*.

Although the General Land Office, from its establishment in 1812, always had responsibility for sale of lands for townsites as well as for other purposes, no really significant townsite legislation was enacted until 1844. Throughout this period, however, the town frontier commanded increasing interest and attention. Indeed, the mania for setting up new towns on the public domain accompanied widespread speculation in farmlands during the 1830s and in part led to the Panic of 1837. Many were little more than paper towns and others disappeared swiftly from the scene.

At least until 1840, the founding and successful development of a town depended primarily upon strategic geographical factors. In this period, before highways and railroads were determinants, only townsites fortunate enough to be located on navigable streams (especially at the head of navigation, like Minneapolis, or at the confluence of two or more streams) or in the vicinity of rich mineral deposits could really hope to boom. New towns also sprang up at Davenport, Dubuque, Burlington, Keokuk, and other terminal points of the Mississippi ferries. On May 23, 1844, Congress finally enacted a townsite law designed to encourage and regulate the settlement of such western townsites and to extend to these towns preemption rights similar to those granted to individual squatters by the Preemption Act of 1841.[7] In implementing this act and later basic legislation of March 2, 1867, and March 3, 1877,[8] the General Land Office created a large quantity of documentation that is of vital importance to the study of town settlement on the westward-moving frontier.

Separate land-entry case files documenting applications for the reservation or purchase of townsites were often set up by the General Land Office after 1844. Townsite files were segregated completely from other land-entry papers after 1880. Totaling over two hundred cubic feet in volume, these files constitute a relatively unexploited source of significant information regarding towns established on the public domain, particularly in the trans-Mississippi region.

Several case files for the Mississippi River port towns may be cited to illustrate the type of settlement data often found in these records. Indeed, they frequently contain correspondence, exhibits, or copies of legal documents that provide illuminating footnotes on the pioneer history of the area. For example, the Galena file contains affidavits and correspondence concerning settlement on the Fever River in 1826 and a copy of an instrument of settlement executed on May 21, 1829, by Amos Farrar, Russell Farnham, and George Davenport regarding property at the portage occupied as one of the earliest trading houses in the area.[9] The much more voluminous Dubuque case file includes correspondence with the register and receiver or the General Land Office commissioner concerning difficulties encountered by early settlers in proving up on their land or protecting it against trespassers, because plats prepared by the surveyor general were unavailable, and letters calling attention to abuses by the commission appointed to lay off the town, particularly in permitting "spurious" preemption rights to be established. There are also letters from J. D. Doty on behalf of the legal representatives of Julian Dubuque and Auguste Chouteau regarding rights of claimants to the tract called Dubuque's Mines, letters to the commissioner dated in 1838 on behalf of mining citizens who cited fraudulent activities of speculators (some of whom merely "ran a fence" around bluff land long worked as mineral ground under permits granted by the United States Superintendent of Mines, claiming it was "enclosed"), and affidavits and other exhibits regarding the laying off of the towns of Ft. Madison, Burlington, Bellview, Peru, and Mineral Point.[10]

As Dr. Schafer employed his microscopic method so effectively in this geographical area, perhaps it would be desirable to develop the pattern of settlement in the township that includes a considerable portion of Galena (Fever River) which was settled in the 1820s. The earliest survey plat that we have for township 28 N, Range 1 W, of the 4th Principal Meridian, is that approved on November 20, 1840, by William Milburn, surveyor of public lands in the states of Illinois and Wisconsin.[11] It provides an excellent starting point for our project because the surveyor entered on the plat the names of pioneers already resident and the location of their houses and fields, and also noted the presence of mineral diggings, furnaces, and timber stands. (See figure) His accompanying field notes identify springs, creeks, and roads and provide more specific information about land diggings, timber, and soil, which he described in several instances as "good fit for cultivation."[12] More precise identification of pioneer settlers can be obtained by an examination of the 1840 census schedules for Jo Daviess County, Illinois, and the relevant tract book pages which also show the type of entry made by each settler. The latter information leads searchers in turn to the land-entry papers and, in appropriate cases, to the bounty-land warrant files and compiled military service records in the National Archives.

It should be noted, of course, that land on the public domain could not even be surveyed and opened for settlement until Indian title was extinguished. Records documenting the negotiation of Indian treaties for this purpose and all other aspects of Indian versus settler frontier problems are in the National Archives among the records of the Bureau

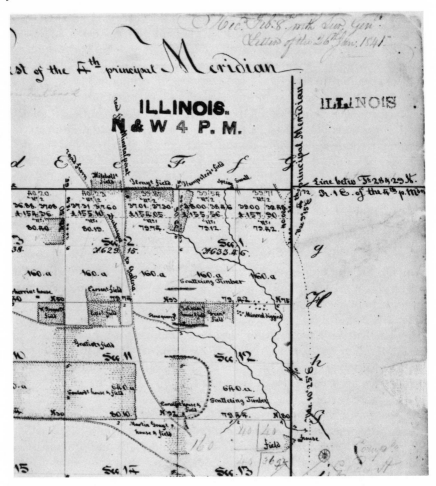

Portion of a survey plat of Galena (Fever River), Illinois, November 20, 1840. (Records of the Bureau of Land Management, Division "E," Headquarters Office Plats, 4th P.M., T 28 N, R 1 W, National Archives Building.)

of Indian Affairs, the Indian Division of the Office of the Secretary of the Interior, and the Office of the Secretary of War.

It is also essential, in analyzing settlement patterns of townships on the public domain, to make effective use of all available postal records since the development of postal service is an integral part of such pioneer history. Of particular importance among the postal holdings are registers of postmasters' appointments, postal route registers, and post office site location reports submitted by postmasters, which provide geographical information to assist the Post Office Department in the preparation of postal maps. Thus, the registers of postmasters' appointments show that on January 15, 1826, Ezekiel Lockwood was serving as first postmaster at Galena, formerly known as Fever River.[13]

Mail route registers in the National Archives, some of which date as early as 1814, can be used to trace the expansion and development of postal service in a particular township from the date the earliest mail-carrying contract was awarded. For each contract the register usually provides such vital data as mail route number, terminals of the route and intervening post office stops, distance between each office on the route, time schedule for the route, name of contractor and amount bid, the way the mail was to be transported, contract changes, and other information. The registers show, for example, that in the 1830s a number of postal routes were already in operation linking Galena and adjoining communities. Among them were route 76A, awarded to Addison Philleo for service once a week from Galena to Prairie du Chien (eighty miles), and route 76C, awarded to the same contractor for service once a week from Galena by way of Gratiot's Grove to Mineral Point (thirty-seven miles).[14] Of particular interest is the register record for postal route 2929 from Galena across the Mississippi River to Dubuque. Awarded to George Ord Karrach for the contract period January 1839 to June 1842, the original proposal stated that the mail was to be carried "15 miles and back twice a week in stages" but made no reference to use of ferry service.[15] It should be noted that one unsuccessful bidder asked $1,200 for service twice a week with the statement that "during high winds" he would "carry the mail and passengers across the Mississippi in yawls."[16]

Geographical site location reports give a legal description of the land on which post offices were located; terminals of the nearest postal routes; and mileage to adjacent post offices, rivers, and creeks. Diagrams and maps that often accompany these reports are especially valuable for the place names they contain. For example, a diagram submitted on July 20, 1865, by the postmaster at Dubuque showed the exact location in sixteen adjoining townships of some twenty-five post offices, most of which were probably discontinued many years ago.[17] Although the reports date generally from the 1870s, those for a particular office occasionally include a site location diagram or other documentation as early as 1837.

Out of the great wealth of materials in the National Archives that can be used in studying pioneer settlement in the trans-Mississippi West and that deserve detailed description, only those documenting a few subject areas of major concern to public domain scholars, i.e., the transportation frontier, the miners' frontier, and the farmers' frontier have been mentioned here.

The wisdom of land-grant railroad policies of the federal government and even the question of overall effectiveness of railroads as agencies of settlement are debatable points with which we need not be concerned, but few will take issue with the assertion that the course of frontier development was drastically changed by the large-scale railroad construction that characterized the third quarter of the nineteenth century. In making the Great Plains and Rocky Mountain regions accessible to settlers for the first time, the network of land-grant railroads and their branches became, in a sense, substitutes for the rivers and streams that had so largely determined patterns of settlement east of the Mississippi. Indeed it is difficult, on the basis of available documentation in the National Archives, to escape the conviction that in the history of the trans-Mississippi West, the study of land settlement and utilization and of railroad development and policy are inseparable parts of the whole.

Although the terms of land grants specifically exempted lands covered by valid homestead or preemption claims, many pioneers who had penetrated the area before the railroad era began soon found their claims in jeopardy. With increasing frequency railroads contested the validity of settlers' claims, especially where surveys had not been made or the settlers had not taken all steps necessary to secure legal claims to the lands they occupied. As land grants to railroads, particularly the proposed transcontinentals, became big business in the 1860s, the basic conflict between early settlers and railroad corporations escalated to such an extent that in 1872 the General Land Office organized a new division, "F," to examine all settlers' claims involving railroad grants, with the exception of conflicts arising from mineral and swamp land claims, and to handle the necessary adjustments. In addition, this division examined all selections by grantees, proposed clear lists for submission to the secretary of the interior for approval, and was responsible for handling the patenting of lands after the lists were approved. Obviously, records documenting these GLO functions are basic to any study of the settler versus railroad struggle, particularly when used in conjunction with the "railroad packages" and other closely related records in the Lands and Railroads Division of the Office of the Secretary of the Interior. For an understanding of the settlement aspects of

300

administration and adjustment of railroad land grants, it is absolutely necessary for the researcher to study these two bodies of records and to understand the relationships between them.

Among the GLO series, of particular value are special files pertaining to some seventy-nine individual land-grant railroads and wagon roads. Comprising about fifty-three feet of material for the period 1829-1935, they include correspondence from registers and receivers, private persons, and railroad company agents concerning implementation of the grants and adjustments of the controversies arising from them. In addition, these files include maps, field notes, appeals by contestants, relinquishments, and deeds. A typical file in this series, that of the Burlington and Missouri Railroad, also includes a map showing the limits of lands selected for the railroad under an act of June 2, 1864; a list of lands in Iowa selected under that act which conflicted with located warrants; and correspondence between settlers and the commissioner of the General Land Office concerning cancellation of certain homestead and land warrant locations.[18]

Holdings in the National Archives also include railroad right-of-way files through the public domain, some sixty-five feet of railroad selection lists, and about one hundred eighty feet of adjustment lists, which are particularly important for settlement studies. For example, the adjustment lists for lands granted to the Burlington and Missouri Railroad in Iowa within the six-, fifteen-, and twenty-mile limits, under the acts of 1856 and 1864, show the location of the grant in terms of a legal land description, the acreage approved under the grant, and the acreage lost to the grant because of prior settlement. Data on the settlers who successfully defended their claims include names of entrymen, dates and types of entry, and the appropriate certificate or warrant numbers.[19] Of obvious significance also are the contested case dockets regarding claims by individual settlers to prior occupancy of land within the railroad grants, 1872-1909, now maintained by the General Archives Division, and the very valuable railroad profiles and maps dealing with railroad rights-of-way and land grants, among the cartographic holdings in the Archives.

The National Archives also has unusually rich and relatively unexploited documentation involving another aspect of settlement on the public domain of the trans-Mississippi West, namely, the miners' frontier of the 1860s and 1870s. In the absence of established federal government policy regarding mineral lands in California and the Rocky Mountains, the miners organized associations and began to regulate their own claims. In part as a result of this not too subtle prodding,

301

Congress in 1866 finally enacted legislation making mineral lands of the public domain, both surveyed and unsurveyed, "free and open to exploration and occupation by all citizens of the United States . . . subject to such regulations as may be prescribed by law, and subject also to the local customs or rules of miners in the several mining districts."[20] The records in the Archives were created, for the most part, in the process of implementing this law and an amendatory act of July 9, 1870.[21] Among the most significant materials are case files for some forty-seven thousand five hundred mineral entries, including applications for patents, citizenship affidavits, powers of attorney, field notes and plats, copies of local rules and customs of mines, abstracts of titles and records of litigation, registers of mining claims (1878-1908), and more than two hundred ten feet of mineral contest dockets now in the General Archives Division.

I do not feel that this brief discussion of National Archives sources for study of settlement on the public domain west of the Mississippi River can be concluded without reiterating the importance of the much neglected townsite files, particularly for studies of the transportation or miners' frontiers. Investors in transportation on the frontier and in mineral lands of the Rocky Mountain region were definitely speculators; so too were most of the town builders who gambled that their choice of location would place them on the projected route of a major railroad or feeder line or near the site of a rich mineral strike. We have over one thousand segregated townsite files for the trans-Mississippi region, including some one hundred twenty-five for Nebraska and Kansas, and approximately two hundred twenty files for the frontier mining states of Idaho, Nevada, and Montana.[22] These files obviously comprise a very rich source of data that would be useful in analytical studies of townsite railroad and mineral speculation. To what extent did projected railroad routes influence the establishment of townsites in Kansas and Nebraska? How many townsites that lost the battle for railroad connections to neighboring communities were able to survive? How many of the one hundred twenty-five townsites established in Montana owed their existence to mining operations, and what percentage of these are now ghost towns that no longer exist even as place names? To what extent do the records reflect the bitter struggle between early settlers holding mining claims and the later arrivals seeking to make entries under the townsite legislation? These questions are, of course, merely suggestive of many interesting studies that could be developed on the basis of research in the townsite and related administrative records.

In the last quarter of the nineteenth century, as it became apparent that agricultural land suitable for settlement on the public domain was almost exhausted, the federal government was compelled to reconsider problems of the arid plains and deserts west of the 100th meridian. The Carey Act, enacted in 1894, was designed to encourage development of state and private irrigation systems but proved to be ineffective. The passage of the landmark Reclamation Act of 1902 soon followed, paving the way for the agricultural conquest of America's last unsettled frontier.

Basic documentation of virtually all aspects of the federal reclamation program is in the National Archives, but this is essentially a twentieth century story—another and final chapter in the saga of American frontier settlement.

NOTES

1. Ellen Churchill Semple, *American History and Its Geographic Conditions*, revised in collaboration with the author by Clarence F. Jones (Cambridge, Mass.: Riverside Press, 1933), p. 58.
2. Paper (preliminary draft) prepared for the Conference on the National Archives and Statistical Research, Washington, D.C., May 1968.
3. Joseph Schafer, "The Microscopic Method Applied to History," *Minnesota History Bulletin* 4 (1921-22): 3-20.
4. Idem, "The Wisconsin Domesday Book," *Wisconsin Magazine of History* 4 (1921-22): 63.
5. Ibid.
6. Records of the General Land Office Relating to Leasing and Operation of Lead and Copper Mines, Record Group 49, Records of the Bureau of Land Management, National Archives Building. (Hereafter records in the National Archives Building are indicated by the symbol NA. The symbol RG is used for record group.)
7. 5 Stat. 657.
8. 14 Stat. 541; 19 Stat. 392.
9. Townsite Case File, Galena, Illinois (T.S. 1), Division "K," RG 49, NA.
10. Townsite Case File, Dubuque, Iowa, ibid. Included are a letter of April 10, 1840, to the president by J. D. Doty; a letter of petition to the commissioner of the General Land Office, May 28, 1838, by a committee on behalf of the people of Dubuque; and a letter from Timothy Davis to the commissioner, December 17, 1838, regarding fraudulent activities of speculators.
11. Manuscript plats of original township surveys, Illinois, Division "E," RG 49, NA.
12. Manuscript copies of Field Notes of Surveys in the state of Illinois— north of the baseline and east and west of the 4th Principal Meridian, vol. 127, p. 163, ibid.

13. Record of Appointment of Postmasters, vol. 4, p. 90, Records of the Post Office Department, RG 28, NA.
14. Route nos. 76A and 76C in Mail Route Register (Addenda), 1830-34 (Ala., Ark., Ill., Ind., Ky., La., Miss., Mo., Tenn.), RG 28, NA.
15. Route no. 2929, 1839-43 (Ill., Ind., Iowa, Mo., Wis.), ibid.
16. Ibid.
17. Reports of Site Locations, Dubuque, Iowa, RG 28, NA.
18. Records relating to Railroad Land Grants, Bundle 1, Burlington and Missouri Railroad, Division "F," RG 49, NA.
19. Adjustment Lists, vol. 183, Burlington and Missouri Railroad, ibid.
20. Act of July 26, 1866, 14 Stat. 251.
21. 16 Stat. 217-18.
22. Townsite Case Files, Division "K," RG 49, NA.

Discussion Summary

The discussion was conducted by *Edward T. Price, Department of Geography, University of Oregon,* chairman of the session on Rural and Urban Settlement. Due to time limitations, the discussion was restricted.

Stanley W. Trimble, Department of Geography, University of Georgia, began the discussion by asking *Terry G. Jordan, Department of Geography, North Texas State University,* why he included canebrakes in his definition of "prairie." "It seems to me," Dr. Trimble continued, "that in a review of eighteenth- and nineteenth-century literature, we find that canebrakes were in fact in great demand by the settlers, whereas this prairie or barren, as you mention, perhaps would be an upland grassland devoid of general tree growth?" Dr. Jordan responded that it was for purposes of generalization but that he recognized "the fundamental differences between the two." He also pointed out that "settlers used the canebrakes as cattle pasture in the early part of the year when the cane was grasslike." At that time of the year cane served "very much the same function" as the prairie. "It shared with the prairie the greater clearing ability; that is, you didn't have to go through the process of cutting down the trees." In conclusion, Dr. Jordan remarked that there were many different types of prairies, each of which "were evaluated differently by the settlers."

Biographical Sketches

JOHN L. ALLEN. Native of Wyoming, educated at University of Wyoming and Clark University (Ph.D., 1969) . . . member of geography faculty of University of Connecticut (1967 to present) . . . research interest in historical geography of the American West in the nineteenth century, the nature of geographical images, and geographical exploration . . . author of *Passage through the Garden: Lewis and Clark and the Image of the American Northwest* (1974) and various articles, including "Geographical Knowledge and American Images of the Louisiana Territory," *Western Historical Quarterly* (1971).

MARTYN J. BOWDEN. Native of England, educated at London University, University of Nebraska, and University of California (Ph.D., 1967) . . . member of geography faculties of Dartmouth College (1963-64) and Clark University (1964 to present) . . . secretary of the Eastern Historical Geography Association . . . founding editor of the Historical Geography Newsletter . . . research interest in historical perception (of the American West) and historical urban geography . . . coeditor of *Geographies of the Mind* (forthcoming) and author of "Growth of Central Districts of Large Cities," *The New Urban History* (forthcoming), and "The Great American Desert and the American Frontier," *Anonymous Americans* (1972).

FRANKLIN W. BURCH. Native of Minnesota, educated at Saint John's University, University of Notre Dame, and The Catholic University of America (Ph.D., 1965) . . . taught at Air Force Weather Observer School (1945-46) and member of history faculty of LaSalle College (1955-57) . . . member of the staff of the National Archives (1958-66, 1973 to present) . . . state archivist of Minnesota (1966-73) . . . specialist in archives administration and records appraisal . . . author of *Alaska's Railroad Frontier: Railroads and Federal Development Policy, 1898-1915* (1965) and archival finding aids.

ANDREW HILL CLARK. Native of Canada, educated at Brandon College of McMaster University, University of Toronto, and University of California at Berkeley (Ph.D., 1944) . . . geographer, Office of Strategic Services and United States Department of State (1944-46) . . . member of geography faculties of Canterbury University, Christchurch, New Zealand; Johns Hopkins and Rutgers Universities; and University of Wisconsin, Madison (1951 to present) . . . Vernor Clifford Finch Research Professor of Geography, University of Wisconsin, Madison (from 1966) . . . recipient of numerous awards and honors, including Honorary President of the Association of American Geographers (1961-62); citation by Beveridge Award Committee, American Historical Association, for best historical work on Canada (1968); Guggenheim Fellowship (1961-62); visiting professor at University of Dundee (1971-72); and the annual single Award for

Scholarly Distinction in Geography by Canadian Association of Geographers (1974) . . . research interest in cultural and historical geography of areas of European settlement . . . editor of *Monograph Series*, Association of American Geographers (1957-63); Historical Geography of North American Series, Oxford University Press (1971 to present); and coeditor of the *Journal of Historical Geography* (from 1974) . . . author of numerous books and articles, including *Three Centuries and the Island: A Historical Geography of Settlement and Agriculture in Prince Edward Island, Canada* (1959); *Acadia: The Geography of Early Nova Scotia to 1760* (1968); and "Historical Geography in North America," *Progress in Historical Geography* (1972).

ROBERT L. CLARKE. Native of Florida, educated at Bethune-Cookman College, Saint Augustine College, and University of Wisconsin (M.A., 1948) . . . member of history faculty of Virginia State College, Petersburg (1950-70) . . . specialist in Afro-American History, National Archives (from 1970) . . . director of the National Archives Conference on Federal Archives as Sources for Research on Afro-Americans (1973) . . . fellow, Cooperative Program in the Humanities . . . author of articles in *Florida Historical Quarterly* and *Journal of Southern History*.

LOUIS DE VORSEY, JR. Native of New Jersey, educated at Montclair State College, Indiana University, Stockholm University, and University of London (Ph.D., 1965) . . . member of geography faculties of East Carolina University, University of North Carolina (1965-67), and University of Georgia (1967 to present) . . . Editorial Board, *Southeastern Geographer* . . . author of books and articles, including *The Indian Boundary in the Southern Colonies, 1763-1775* (1966); *De Brahm's Report of the General Survey in the Southern District of North America* (1971); and "A Background to Surveying and Mapping at the Time of the American Revolution: An Essay on the State of the Art," *The American Revolution, 1775-1783: An Atlas of Eighteenth Century Maps and Charts* (1972)

RALPH E. EHRENBERG. Native of Minnesota, educated at University of Minnesota (M.A., 1968) . . . cartographer, Aeronautical Chart and Information Center (1964-66) . . . member of the staff of the National Archives (1966 to present) . . . director, Cartographic Archives Division (from 1972) . . . research interest in geographical exploration and history of cartography . . . fellow, Council on Library Resources (1972-73) . . . author of articles and research aids, including "Nicholas King: First Surveyor of the City of Washington, 1803-1812," *Records of the Columbia Historical Society* (1969-70), and *Cartographic Records in the National Archives of the United States Useful for Urban Studies* (1973).

MEYER H. FISHBEIN. Native of New York, educated at American University (M.A., 1954) . . . member of the staff of the National Archives (1940-43, 1947 to present); chief, Business Economics Branch (1957-61); senior records appraisal specialist (1962-68); director, Records Appraisal Staff (1968 to present) . . . chief records analyst, New York State Banking Department (1946-47) . . . fellow, Society of American Archivists . . . director, Conference on the National Archives and Statistical Research (1968) . . . editor of *The National Archives and Statistical Research* (1973) and articles and archival inventories, including *Early Business Statistical Operations of the Federal Government* (1958) and *The Censuses of Manufactures: 1810-1890* (1963).

HERMAN R. FRIIS. Native of California, educated at University of California at Los Angeles, Imperial University of Tokyo, and University of California, Berkeley (M.A., 1934), with additional work at University of Wisconsin . . . geographer and archivist, National Archives (1938-41, 1946 to present); director, Center for Polar Archives (from 1967) . . . participant in two antarctic expeditions as official guest of the commander of the United States Naval Support Force Antarctica and Operation Deepfreeze (1960), and as United States Exchange Scientist with the Japanese Antarctic Research Expedition (1969-70) . . . official United States delegate to the Tenth Pacific Science Congress held at the University of Hawaii (1961), the Twentieth International Geographical Congress held in London (1964), and the First Congress on the History of the Science of Oceanography held in Monaco (1966) . . . recipient of various awards, including the Outstanding Achievement Award of the Association of American Geographers (1965) and the Antarctic Medal and Citation by the assistant secretary of the navy (1965) . . . fellow, Society of American Archivists (1960) . . . author and editor of more than one hundred books, articles, and maps on the history of cartography, exploration, and historical geography, including *A Series of Population Maps of the Colonies and the United States, 1625-1790* (1941, revised 1968); *A History of Geographical Exploration of the Pacific Basin* (1967); and, with Martin P. Claussen, *American and Foreign Maps Published by the United States Congress, 1789-1861: Historical Catalog and Index* (forthcoming).

SAM B. HILLIARD. Native of Georgia, educated at the University of Georgia and University of Wisconsin (Ph.D., 1966) . . . member of geography faculties of University of Wisconsin-Milwaukee, Southern Illinois University, and Louisiana State University (1971 to present) . . . research interests in historical geography of the United States, with emphasis on agriculture and the South . . . author of *Hog Meat and Hoecake; Food Supply in the Old South 1840-1850* (1972) and articles in the *Proceedings of the American Philosophical Society* and *Annals of the Association of American Geographers.*

JOHN A. JAKLE. Native of Indiana, educated at Western Michigan University, Southern Illinois University, and Indiana University (Ph.D., 1967) . . . member of geography faculties of University of Maine, Western Michigan University, and University of Illinois (1967 to date) . . . recipient of National Science Foundation grant in Education in Science (1970) . . . research interest in historical and social geography, particularly the human cognition of historic landscapes and historic area preservation as a process of environmental management . . . member of Illinois Historic Sites Advisory Council . . . author of books and articles, including *The Spatial Dimensions of Social Organization: A Selected Bibliography for Urban Social Geography* (1970); "Time, Space, and the Geographic Past: A Prospectus for Historical Geography," *American Historical Review* (1971); and *Images of the Ohio Valley: Historical Landscapes in Geographical Perspective* (forthcoming).

ROBERT L. JANISKEE. Native of Michigan, educated at Western Michigan University and University of Illinois (Ph.D., 1974) . . . member of geography faculty of University of South Carolina (1972 to present) . . . research interests in environmental perception, behavioral geography, and recreational geography.

HILDEGARD BINDER JOHNSON. Native of Germany, educated at Universität Innsbruck, Universität Rostock, Universität Marburg, and Universität Berlin (Ph.D., 1933) . . . tutor at Bromley Public High School for Girls, Kent, England (1934-35) . . . member of geography faculty of Macalester College (1947 to present) . . . editor of *Minnesota Geographer* (1950-61) . . . president, Minnesota Council for Social Studies (1958-60) . . . awards include citation by Association of American Geographers for meritorious contribution to the field of geography (1958) and Thomas Jefferson Award from the Robert Earll McConnell Foundation, College of William and Mary (1971) . . . research interests in historical geography and historical cartography . . . author of more than sixty books and articles on cartography, geography, history, sociology, and conservation, including "The Distribution of the German Pioneer Population in Minnesota," *Rural Sociology* (1941), "Zur historischen und rechtlichen Problematick von Grenze und Flussgebiet in Nordamerika," *Forschungen zu Staat and Verfassung* (1958), and *Carta Marina, 1525* (1963).

TERRY G. JORDAN. Native of Texas, educated at Southern Methodist, University of Texas, and University of Wisconsin (Ph.D., 1965) . . . member of geography faculties of Arizona State University and North Texas State University (1969 to present) . . . recipient of Woodrow Wilson Fellowship and Southern Fellowships Foundation Fellowship . . . research interest in the cultural-historical geography of Texas, with special interest in ethnic groups, folklore, and cultural landscape . . . author of books, articles, and maps, including *German Seed in Texas Soil: Immigrant Farmers in Nineteenth Century Texas* (1967) and "[Map of] Population Origin Groups in Rural Texas," *Annals of the Association of American Geographers* (1970).

D. W. MEINIG. Native of Washington, educated at Georgetown University and University of Washington (Ph.D., 1953) . . . member of geography faculties of University of Utah and Syracuse University . . . Maxwell Professor of Geography, Syracuse University . . . research interests in the American West, American culture, nineteenth-century colonizations, and culture area concepts . . . author of numerous books and articles, including "The Mormon Culture Region," *Annals of the Association of American Geographers* (1965); *The Great Columbia Plain* (1968); *Imperial Texas* (1969); *Southwest* (1971); and "American Wests," *Annals of the Association of American Geographers* (1972).

H. ROY MERRENS. Native of England; educated at University College, London; University of Maryland; and University of Wisconsin (Ph.D., 1962) . . . member of geography faculties of Rutgers University; University of Wisconsin; San Fernando Valley State College; and York University, Ontario (1968 to date) . . . recipient of Fulbright Travel Award (1955-57), National Science Foundation Institutional Awards (1962-65), and Guggenheim Fellowship (1966-67) . . . research interest in eighteenth-century geography of the southern colonies

. . . author of books, articles, and maps, including *Colonial North Carolina in the Eighteenth Century: A Study in Historical Geography* (1964); "Historical Geography and Early American History," *William and Mary Quarterly* (1965); and the *Colonial South Carolina Scene: Contemporary Views, 1697-1774* (forthcoming).

WILLIAM D. PATTISON. Native of Indiana, educated at the University of Chicago (Ph.D., 1957) . . . member of geography faculties of University College, London; University of California, Los Angeles; San Fernando Valley State College; and University of Chicago . . . author of *Beginnings of the American Rectangular Land Survey System, 1784-1800* (1957; reprinted, 1964) and various articles, including "Use of the United States Public Land Survey Plats and Notes as Descriptive Sources," *Professional Geographer* (1956), and "The Four Traditions of Geography," *Journal of Geography* (1964).

JOHN W. REPS. Native of Missouri, educated at Dartmouth College, Cornell University (Master of Regional Planning, 1947), University of Liverpool, and London School of Economics . . . planning aide, United States National Resources Planning Board (1942) . . . planning director, Broome County, New York Planning Board (1947-50) . . . member of city and regional planning faculty of Cornell University (1948 to present) . . . recipient of Guggenheim Fellowship (1958), American Institute of Architects Foundation Scholarship (1965), Fulbright Research Fellowship (1965-66) . . . research interests in history of American planning . . . author of many books and articles, including *The Making of Urban America: A History of City Planning in the United States* (1965), *Monumental Washington: The Planning and Development of the Capital Center* (1967), *Town Planning in Frontier America* (1969), and *Tidewater Towns: City Planning in Colonial Virginia* (1971).

JAMES B. RHOADS. Native of Iowa, educated at University of California at Berkeley and The American University (Ph.D., 1965) . . . member of the staff of the National Archives (1952 to present); archivist of the United States (from 1968) . . . serves *ex officio* as chairman of the National Historical Publications Commission and The Archives Advisory Council . . . member of Board of Trustees for the Woodrow Wilson International Center for Scholars, and Federal Council on Arts and Humanities . . . vice president, International Council on Archives . . . fellow and president, Society of American Archivists . . . contributor of articles to archival and historical publications.

JANE F. SMITH. Native of Virginia, educated at Mary Baldwin College, University of Wisconsin (M.A., 1938), and The American University . . . member of the staff of the National Archives (1942 to present)); director, Civil Archives Division (from 1971) . . . director, National Archives Conference on Research in the History of Indian-White Relations (1972) . . . fellow, Society of American Archivists . . . subject specialist in frontier and settlement history . . . editor, *The National Archives and Research in the History of Indian-White Relations* (forthcoming) and various articles, including "The Use of Federal Records in Writing Local History: A Case Study," *Prologue: The Journal of the National Archives* (1969), and "Commentary [Panel on Land, Agriculture, Fisheries, and Mines]," *The National Archives and Statistical Research* (1973).

PETER O. WACKER. Native of New Jersey, educated at Montclair State College, New Jersey, and Louisiana State University (Ph.D., 1966) . . . member of geography faculties of Louisiana State University and Rutgers University (1964 to present) . . . recipient of New Jersey Teachers of English Author Award (1968) and Guggenheim Fellowship (1971-72) . . . fellow, New Jersey Historical Society . . . research interest in the historical and cultural geography of New Jersey . . . author of books and articles, including *The Musconetcong Valley of New Jersey* (1969), which received a Certificate of Commendation from the American Council for State and Local History, and *A Cultural Geography of Pre-Industrial New Jersey*, vol. 1 (forthcoming).

DAVID WARD. Native of England, educated at University of Leeds and University of Wisconsin (Ph.D., 1963) . . . member of geography faculties of University of Leeds, Carleton University (Canada), University of British Columbia (1964-66), and University of Wisconsin (1966 to present) . . . recipient of Guggenheim Fellowship (1970-71) . . . research interests in the historical geography of the industrial revolution and nineteenth-century urbanization . . . author of *Cities and Immigrants: A Geography of Change in Nineteenth Century America* (1971) and articles in *Annals of the Association of American Geographers, Economic Geography, Geographical Analysis,* and other journals.

312

Appendices

Bibliography to Resources on Historical Geography in the National Archives

RALPH E. EHRENBERG

Many of the records of the federal government that comprise the national archives are inherently geographic in nature. They record and document in words and graphics the steady westward movement and settlement of diverse geographic regions by people of various social and economic backgrounds. These records also reveal the participation of the federal government in this movement and its attempt to hold the national experiment together by an integrated system of transportation routes and communication lines. Following the Civil War, the federal government's concern with inventorying, classifying, and measuring national resources (human and natural) likewise created records that should be of interest to geographers.

Almost seventy years ago Albert Demangeon described and analyzed the resources of the Archives Nationales in Paris for French geographers.[1] American geographers still await their Demangeon. Until the time that a comprehensive guide can be prepared, geographers may find this bibliography useful. Its purpose is to list selected publications and issuances pertaining to original records in the National Archives and Records Service that have potential research value for historical geographers. While the records of NARS are virtually worldwide in their geographical scope, this bibliography is limited to the United States. The time period covered is about 1775 to 1950.

Since its establishment nearly forty years ago, the staff of the National Archives and interested scholars from the academic community have prepared a variety of finding aids to the records, differing greatly in format and quality. There are, generally, four main categories of finding aids:

(1) *Resource Papers*

These include (a) Reference Information Papers and Reference Information Circulars issued by the National Archives and Records Service, and (b) articles prepared by academic researchers and published in scholarly journals. Resource papers are usually subject- or area-oriented.

(2) *Letterpress Publications*

These include the various guides, inventories, and special lists that form the backbone of any archives publication program. They range from narrative descriptions of individual records, such as maps, to collective descriptions of large homogeneous series and record groups.

(3) *Internal Issuances*

Internal issuances in the National Archives include preliminary checklists; preliminary inventories, supplements to checklists, or inventories reproduced by the former Office of Military Archives; and finding aids—usually preliminary inventories—reproduced by the former Office of Civil Archives. They were produced primarily for internal use in the National Archives and are not distributed as National Archives publications. Electrostatic copies, however, may be obtained for a fee. Although many of these are in draft form and others have become somewhat outdated, they are nevertheless useful research tools that are suggestive as well as informative.

(4) *Microfilm Pamphlets*

The National Archives has been microfilming selected groups of records as a form of publication since 1940. These publications "serve to bridge the gap between the costly printed source materials and the great mass of unpublished documents."[2] For many microfilm publications, accompanying letterpress pamphlets have been prepared that reproduce title pages and introductory materials filmed with the records. In addition, these microfilm pamphlets include indexes or lists, roll-by-roll descriptions, and pricelists.

Resource papers, letterpress publications, and microfilm pamphlets published by the National Archives can be obtained by writing to the Publication Sales Branch (NEPS), National Archives and Records Service (GSA), Washington, D.C., 20408, or to the appropriate regional archives.[3] Electrostatic copies of internal issuances can be obtained for a fee from the Printed Documents Division (NNHL).

For ease of reference, the format of this bibliography generally follows Douglas R. McManis's *Historical Geography of the United States: A Bibliography*.[4] The basic guide to the resources in the National Archives is Frank B. Evans, "The National Archives and Records Service and Its Research Resources —A Select Bibliography."[5] This is supplemented by "Publications of the National Archives and Records Service," published quarterly in *Prologue: The Journal of the National Archives*, and the "Bibliography: Selected Writings on Archives, Current Records, and Historical Manuscripts," published each July in the *American Archivist*. Recent National Archives accessions are also described quarterly in *Prologue* and the *American Archivist*. For those historical geographers who have not used archival resources, Philip C. Brooks's *Research in Archives: The Use of Unpublished Primary Sources*, will prove useful.[6] Brooks, past director of the Harry S. Truman Library, was associated with the National Archives for more than thirty years. Geographers may also profit from Samuel P. Hays, "The Use of Archives for Historical Statistical Inquiry,"[7] and Oscar E. Anderson, "The Use of Archives in Historical Research."[8]

The place of publication of references listed in this bibliography, unless otherwise indicated, is Washington, D.C. Frequently cited periodicals, serials, and organizations are designated with the following abbreviations and symbols:

AA   *American Archivist*
AAAG   *Annals of the Association of American Geographers*
AH   *Agricultural History*
FRC   Federal Records Center, NARS
NA   National Archives
NARS   National Archives and Records Service
NC   Finding Aid Reproduced by the Office of Civil Archives
NM   Finding Aid Reproduced by the Office of Military Archives
PAM   Pamphlet Accompanying Microcopy
PC   Preliminary Checklist
PDM   Pamphlet Describing Microcopy
PG   *Professional Geographer*
PI   Preliminary Inventory
Prologue *Prologue: The Journal of the National Archives*
RIC   Reference Information Circular
RIP   Reference Information Paper
SL   Special List

NOTES

1. Albert Demangeon, *Les Sources de la Géographie de la France aux Archives Nationales* (Paris: Société Nouvelle de Librarie et d'Edition, 1905), 120 pp.
2. U.S., National Archives and Records Service, *List of National Archives Microfilm Publications* (Washington, D.C., 1968), p. xi.
3. The regional federal archives are located in Atlanta, Boston, Chicago, Dayton, Denver, Fort Worth, Kansas City, Los Angeles, New York, Philadelphia, Saint Louis, San Francisco, Seattle, and Washington. Their addresses are listed on the back cover of each issue of *Prologue: The Journal of the National Archives.*
4. Douglas R. McManis, *Historical Geography of the United States: A Bibliography—Excluding Alaska and Hawaii* (Ypsilanti, Michigan: Eastern Michigan University, 1965), 249 pp.
5. Frank B. Evans, "The National Archives and Records Service and Its Research Resources—A Select Bibliography," *Prologue: The Journal of the National Archives* 3 (Fall 1971): 88-112.
6. Philip C. Brooks, *Research in Archives: The Use of Unpublished Primary Sources* (Chicago and London: University of Chicago Press, 1969), 127 pp.
7. Samuel P. Hays, "The Use of Archives for Historical Statistical Inquiry," *Prologue: The Journal of the National Archives* 1 (Fall 1969): 7-15. Also published in NA, *The National Archives and Statistical Research,* ed. Meyer H. Fishbein, National Archives Conferences (Athens: Ohio University Press, 1973), 2:60-71.
8. Oscar E. Anderson, "The Use of Archives in Historical Research," *Research Methods in Librarianship: Historical and Bibliographical Methods in Library Research,* ed. Rolland E. Stevens (Urbana: University of Illinois, Graduate School of Library Science, 1971), pp. 42-50.

I. UNITED STATES

General

Crawford, William R. "Sociological Research in the National Archives." *American Sociological Review* 6 (April 1941): 203-16. Abstract of a report prepared for the Social Science Research Council by the Committee on the Control of Social Science Data.

Lewinson, Paul. "The Industrial Records Division of the National Archives: Economics, Welfare, and Science in United States History." NA Accessions no. 55 (1960), pp. 1-7. A brief analysis of the holdings of the Industrial Records Division, which became part of the Civil Archives Division in 1971. It deals chiefly with the following subjects: business and industry, transportation, communications, science, and welfare (housing, education, and health).

Muntz, A. Philip. "Federal Cartographic Archives: A Profile." *Prologue* 1 (Spring 1969): 3-7. A brief description of the functions and holdings of the Cartographic Archives Division of the National Archives.

NA. *Catalog of National Archives Microfilm Publications.* 1974. 184 p. Lists more than twenty-one hundred microfilm publications in the fields of American, European, Far Eastern, African, and Latin American history.

————. *Civil War Maps in the National Archives.* 1964. 127 p. Describes 8,000 manuscript and annotated published maps prepared by federal and confederate surveyors and cartographers showing communication and transportation systems, terrain, land use, place names, and sometimes names of individual landowners.

————. *Descriptive Commentaries from the Medical Histories of Posts.* PDM no. 903. 1973. 11 p. The descriptive commentaries, dating from 1868 to 1913, prepared by the senior medical officer of each American post, contain monthly reports on conditions that affected the health of the troops. These included physical condition of the post; geology, botany, and zoology of the locality; and miscellaneous matters such as water supply and ethnology.

————. *Economic and Social Data among Pre-Federal Records.* By Kathryn M. Murphy. RIP no. 58. 1973. 10 p. Covers the period 1774 to 1789.

————. *Guide to Cartographic Records in the National Archives.* 1971. 444 p. General description of more than 1.6 million maps and charts in the National Archives dating from ca. 1760 to 1966.

————. *Guide to the Ford Film Collection in the National Archives.* By Mayfield Bray. 1970. 118 p. One of the first producers of nonnewsreel educational film, Henry Ford's motion picture department was active from 1914 to the early 1940s. Of special interest are films on conservation and agricultural, industrial, and regional geography. Under the heading industrial geography are films on cotton milling (1920-22), ice harvesting (1916), iron and steel processing (1920), lumbering (1917-22), meatpacking (1919-22), and coal mining (1916-22).

_____. *Guide to the National Archives of the United States.* 1974. 884 p. The basic reference tool to all official records of the United States government.

_____. *List of Selected Maps of States and Territories.* By Janet L. Hargett. SL no. 29. 1971. 113 p. Describes approximately nine hundred maps selected from holdings of the Cartographic Archives Division. The maps date from the late eighteenth century to 1920.

_____. *Motion Pictures in the Audiovisual Archives Division of the National Archives.* By Mayfield S. Bray and William T. Murphy. Prepared for the National Archives Conference on the Use of Audiovisual Archives as Original Source Materials. 1972. 34 p. Describes over sixty thousand reels of edited and unedited educational, training, and historical motion pictures dating from 1894 to the present. They touch on such topics as agriculture, American Indians, conservation, westward expansion, industry, mining, and reclamation and its impact upon communities.

_____. *The National Archives and Statistical Research,* edited by Meyer H. Fishbein. National Archives Conferences, vol. 2. Athens: Ohio University Press, 1973. 225 p. The proceedings of the second scholarly conference sponsored by the National Archives examines selected statistical records and "how they can be used by economists, historians, geographers, political scientists, sociologists, and statisticians."

_____. *Pre-Federal Maps in the National Archives: An Annotated List.* By Patrick D. McLaughlin. SL 26. 1971. 42 p. Describes approximately two hundred maps dating from 1588 to 1790.

_____. *Sound Recordings in the Audiovisual Archives Division of the National Archives.* By Mayfield S. Bray and Leslie C. Waffen. Preliminary Draft prepared for the National Archives Conference on the Use of Audio-visual Archives as Original Source Materials. 1972. 30 p. Of potential interest to historical geographers are recordings on the history and development of federal agencies involved in geographical work ("Uncle Sam Calling-Story of the 1940 Census," activities of the General Land Office and the Geological Survey, and development of the Rural Electrification Administration and its impact upon agriculture); recordings pertaining to geographical topics (reclamation of land through irrigation, dust bowl migration, and conservation of forests and lumber); recordings of topics closely related to historical geography (history of agriculture in the United States); and special subjects (recordings of the proceedings of the Conference on the National Archives and Research in Historical Geography, November 8-9, 1971).

_____. *Still Pictures in the Audiovisual Archives Division of the National Archives.* By Mayfield S. Bray. Preliminary Draft prepared for the National Archives Conference on the Use of Audiovisual Archives as Original Source Materials. 1972. 48 p. "There are now more than 5 million still picture items in the Audiovisual Archives Division, including artworks, photographs of artworks, posters, and photographs dating from the seventeenth century to the present. In addition to documenting activities of 125 Federal agencies, they illustrate the social, economic, cultural, political, and diplomatic history of America from the earliest colonial times to the present."

————. *The Territorial Papers of the United States.* PDM no. 721. 1972. 46 p. "The Territorial Papers of the United States consist of the official records of those Federal territories which ultimately became States of the Union. In 1925 Congress first authorized the Secretary of State to cause to be collected, transcribed, arranged, and edited the papers relating to the territories which are found in the archives in Washington. . . . The first volumes of the series were published in 1934, and the project continued, first in the Department of State and after 1950 in the National Archives." This microfilm publication reproduces the first twenty-six volumes of *The Territorial Papers of the United States.*

Pinkett, Harold T. "Records in the National Archives as Sources for Research in the Social Sciences." *Social Studies* 43 (April 1952): 147-51. In this brief treatment of an important topic, a senior archivist of the National Archives calls attention to some of the most pertinent material useful for social science research.

Pumphrey, Lowell M. "Material in the National Archives of Special Interest for Economists." *American Economic Review* 31 (June 1941): 344-45. Abstract of a report prepared for the Social Science Research Council by the Committee on the Control of Social Science Data. A copy of the full report is available in the National Archives Library.

Smith, Jane F. "Commentary [Panel on Land, Agriculture, Fisheries, and Mines]." In *The National Archives and Statistical Research,* edited by Meyer H. Fishbein. National Archives Conferences, 2:168-77. Athens: Ohio University Press, 1973. Emphasizes pertinent unpublished statistical sources in the National Archives prepared by the Department of Agriculture and Interior.

Tucker, Sara Jones. "Archival Materials for the Anthropologist in the National Archives." *American Anthropologist* 43 (October 1941): 617-44. Out of date but useful as a general guide to important series of social records.

Exploration and Settlement

Friis, Herman R. "A Brief Review of the Development and Status of Geographical and Cartographical Activities of the United States Government: 1776-1818." *Imago Mundi* 19 (1965): 68-80. By a distinguished archivist-geographer whose knowledge of federal geographical and cartographic activities is unsurpassed.

————. "Highlights of the First Hundred Years of Surveying and Mapping of the United States by the Federal Government, 1775-1880." *Surveying and Mapping* 18 (1958): 186-206. Includes reproductions of many important manuscript maps from the National Archives.

Harrison, Robert W. "Public Land Records of the Federal Government." *Mississippi Valley Historical Review* 41 (September 1954): 277-88. Excellent analysis of the several classes of public land records and the types of information they contain.

NA. *Aerial Photographs in the National Archives.* By Charles E. Taylor and Richard E. Spurr. SL no. 25. 1973. 106 p. This list describes aerial survey photographs taken by the Agricultural Stabilization and Conservation Service, the Soil Conservation Service, the Forest Service, the Geological Survey, and the Bureau of Reclamation, from ca. 1934 to 1943. The photographs cover more than 85 percent of the contiguous land area of the United States.

————. *Geographical Exploration and Mapping in the Nineteenth Century: A Survey of the Records in the National Archives.* By Ralph E. Ehrenberg. RIP no. 66. 1973. 22 p. Briefly describes records of major federal mapping and surveying agencies and their research potential.

————. *Geographical Exploration and Topographic Mapping by the United States Government, 1777-1952; An Exhibit Catalog.* 1952. Reprint ed. 1971. 52 p. The material on geographical exploration was selected "with the idea of illustrating both the scope of Government explorations and the wealth of information on climate, demography, vegetation, soil, physiography, natural resources, transport facilities, and land use to be found in the journals, reports, maps, drawings, and other mediums of expression by which the expeditions recorded their discoveries."

————. *Historical Information Relating to Military Posts and Other Installations, ca. 1700-1900.* PDM no. 661. 1972. 7 p. The microfilm publication described by PDM no. 661 reproduces the twenty-seven-volume "Outline Index of Military Forts and Stations," which was compiled and maintained by the Adjutant General's Office. The AGO was responsible for the supervision of tracts of land from the public domain for military purposes. In addition to information on permanent and temporary United States Army posts, there are entries on colonial frontier forts, confederate forts, fortified Indian towns, civilian and fur company blockhouses, "Indian Trading Houses," as well as entries for British, French, Spanish, and Dutch installations within the present boundaries of the United States. Indispensable source material for the study of military geography of the United States and its impact upon settlement.

————. *Index to General Land Office Abandoned Military Reservations Files, 1822-1937.* By Arthur Hecht and Lester W. Smith. Index no. 1. 1945. Photoprocessed. 28 p. The General Land Office was involved in the creation and disposal of military reservations from the public domain. More than four hundred dossiers were prepared pertaining to military reservations. The dossiers generally include correspondence, maps, and plats.

————. *Letters Sent by the General Land Office to Surveyors General, 1796-1901.* PAM no. 27. 1964. 4 p. Pertains to the general administration of public lands. Related records are described in *Miscellaneous Letters Sent by the General Land Office, 1796-1889.* (PAM no. 25, 1965, 10 pp.); *Letters Received by the Secretary of the Treasury Relating to Public Lands, 1831-1849* (PAM no. 726, 1971, 5 pp.); *Letters Sent by the Secretary of the Treasury Relating to Public Lands ("N" Series), 1801-1878.* (PAM no. 733, 1970, 4 pp).

————. *Letters Sent by the Land and Railroad Division of the Office of the Secretary of the Interior, 1849-1904.* PAM no. 620. 1966. 19 p. "The letters relate to such subjects as legislation and appropriations, land surveys, the disposal of public lands as provided by the Homestead Act and other laws, disputed entries, withdrawal of lands from entry and establishment of forests and other reserves, military reservations, railroad land grants and rights-of-way, land grants to the States, Indian lands, private land claims, depredations on the public domain (especially of timber), townsites, geological surveys, reclamation and irrigation, establishment and discontinuance of land offices."

――――. *Letters Sent by the Topographical Bureau of the War Department and by Successor Divisions in the Office of the Chief of Engineers, 1829-70.* PAM no. 66. 1965. 4 p. The Topographical Bureau was responsible for geographical exploration and surveys pertaining to internal improvements. Records of the bureau pertain to canal and railroad routes; international, state, territorial, and Indian reservation boundaries; surveys of the coast and the Great Lakes; and the exploration of the West. Series of related records have been reproduced as separate microfilm publications. These are *Registers of Letters Received by the Topographical Bureau of the War Department, 1824-1866* (PAM no. 505, 1964, 4 pp.); and *Letters Received by the Topographical Bureau of the War Department, 1824-1865* (PAM no. 506, 1965, 8 pp). A series of internal improvement maps are described by W. L. G. Joerg, "The Internal Improvement Maps (1825-1835) in the National Archives," *AAAG* 28 (1938): 52-53.

――――. *List of Cartographic Records of the Bureau of Indian Affairs.* By Laura E. Kelsay. SL no. 13. 1954. 127 p. Describes about fifteen thousand maps of the Bureau's Central Map File (early 1800s to 1939) and Irrigation Division (1872-1943). The maps show exploration routes, tribal lands, Indian cessions and reservations, military reservations, boundary lines, private land grants, railroad grants, allotments to individual Indians, homestead claims, school lands, church lands, national forests and parks, townships, townsites, farming and grazing districts, mineral lands, irrigation projects, and rights-of-way through Indian lands of railroads, pipelines, telephone and telegraph lines, highways, electric transmission lines, canals, and irrigation ditches.

――――. *List of Cartographic Records of the General Land Office.* By Laura E. Kelsay. SL no. 19. 1964. 202 p. The maps of the General Land Office, dating from 1790 to 1946, pertain largely to the progress of land surveys and the disposal of lands in the public land states and territories.

――――. *List of Documents concerning the Negotiation of Ratified Indian Treaties, 1801-1869.* By John H. Martin. SL no. 6. 1949. 175 p.

――――. *Preliminary Checklist of the Classified Files of the Division of Territories and Island Possessions, Department of Interior.* By Kenneth Munden. PC no. 7. 1943. 65 p. Photoprocessed. Divided into two parts: territories and island possessions (Alaska, Arizona, Guam, Hawaii, New Mexico, Oklahoma, Philippine Islands, Puerto Rico, Samoa, and Antarctica) and the Alaska railroad. Records date, generally, from 1907 to 1934.

――――. *Preliminary Inventory of the Land-Entry Papers of the General Land Office.* By Harry P. Yoshpe and Philip P. Brower. PI no. 22. 1949. Describes vital documents on disposal of the public domain not available elsewhere, including material on military bounty-land warrants, Indian scrip (Chippewa, Choctaw, and Sioux), private land claims, forest reserves, and mineral claims.

──────. *Public Land Records of the Federal Government, 1800-1950, and Their Statistical Significance.* By Richard S. Maxwell. RIP no. 57. 1973. 18 p. Evaluation of the research potential of basic land settlement records of the public land states, by a veteran archivist.

──────. *Records of the Coast and Geodetic Survey.* By Nathan Reingold. PI no. 105. 1958. 83 p. The records date from 1807, when Congress authorized a systematic survey of the coasts. Although primarily scientific in content, the Coast and Geodetic Survey records often provide accurate descriptions of particular localities. They are also valuable for the determination of old land-title boundaries along the coasts.

──────. *Records of the National Park Service.* By Edward E. Hill. PI no. 166. 1966. 52 p. The records described include material on national parks (1872-1966), the National Capital Region, the Potomac [Canal] Company (1785-1828), and the Chesapeake and Ohio Canal Company (1828-1938).

──────. *Records of the Public Works Administration.* By L. Evans Walker. PI no. 125. 1960. 32 p. Records of the PWA provide basic documentation pertaining to national planning and its impact upon the geography of the United States, beginning 1933.

──────. *Records Relating to International Boundaries.* By Daniel T. Goggin. PI no. 170. 1968. 98 p. The State Department's official file of international boundaries of the United States. Includes cartographic and technical, as well as political and geographical, material.

Pattison, William D. "Use of the U.S. Public Land Survey Plats and Notes as Descriptive Sources." PG 8 (January 1956): 10-14. Analysis of the geographical research potential of the General Land Office township plats and field notes.

Smith, Clifford Neal. *Federal Land Series: A Calendar of Archival Materials on the Land Patents Issued by the United States Government, with Subject, Tract, and Name Indexes.* 2 vols. Chicago: American Library Association, 1972-73. The first attempt to calendar and index manuscript source material on land grants of the United States, which are located in the National Archives and various state archives and historical collections. Among the records in NARS that have been or will be included are the early files of the United States Treasury, the United States Department of State, and the General Land Office. Thus far, two volumes have been completed: volume 1, *1788-1810,* 1972, 338 pp., and volume 2, *Federal Bounty-Land Warrants of the American Revolution, 1799-1835,* 1973, 391 pp.

Population Characteristics

GENERAL

Barrows, Robert G. "The Manuscript Federal Census: Source for a 'New' Local History." *Indiana Magazine of History* 69 (September 1973): 181-92. By "New Local History," the author means social history, with a particular emphasis on common people. Discusses the imperfections and shortcomings of census schedules as well as their potential research value.

Franklin, W. Neil. "Availability of Federal Census Schedules in the States." *National Genealogical Society Quarterly* 50 (March 1962): 19-25.

Hazel, Joseph A. "Semimicrostudies of Counties from the Manuscripts of the Census of 1860." PG 17 (July 1965): 15-19.

Hill, Joseph A. "The Historical Value of the Census Records." *Annual Report of the American Historical Association for the Year 1908.* 2 vols. 1909. 1:197-208.

Howerton, Joseph B. "The Resources of the National Archives for Ethnic Research." *Immigration History Newsletter* 5, no. 2 (November 1973): 1-7.

Lathrop, Barnes F. "History From the Census Returns." *Southwestern Historical Quarterly* 51 (April 1948): 293-312. A good description and evaluation of the manuscript census schedules with illustrations of pages from the census of 1850. Includes both population and nonpopulation schedules.

Muntz, Philip A. "Sources in the National Archives Relating to Vital Statistics, Public Opinion, and Population Data." In *The National Archives and Statistical Research,* edited by Meyer H. Fishbein. National Archives Conferences, 2:86-92. Athens: Ohio University Press, 1973. General introduction by the codirector of the Conference on National Archives and Historical Geography.

NA. *Cartographic Records of the Bureau of the Census.* By James Berton Rhoads and Charlotte M. Ashby. PI no. 103. 1958. 108 p. Includes a list of maps of enumeration districts for each census from 1880 to 1940 and written descriptions of enumeration district boundaries for each census from 1850 to 1940. The written descriptions include population data and often other statistical information for each enumeration district. A revised edition, which will include the censuses of 1950 and 1960, is in preparation.

————. *Federal Census Schedules, 1850-80: Primary Sources for Historical Research.* By Carmen R. Delle Donne. RIP no. 67. 1973. 29 p. Prepared for the Conference on the National Archives and Research in Historical Geography. An excellent introductory analysis.

————. *Federal Population Censuses, 1790-1890: A Catalog of Microfilm Copies of the Schedules.* Publication no. 71-3. 1973. 90 p. The schedules provide basic population statistical data including age, sex, and race. From 1850 onward, occupation and place of birth is included.

————. *Federal Population and Mortality Census Schedules, 1790-1890, in the National Archives and the States: Outline of a Lecture on Their Availability, Content, and Use.* By W. Neil Franklin. SL no. 24. 1971. 89 p. Prepared initially as a lecture for the annual Institute of Genealogical Research cosponsored by NARS and The American University. Section 2 includes a list of institutions in the United States that have copies of federal population and mortality census schedules for 1800-1890. Section 3 briefly describes the content of the schedules. Section 4 consists of a comprehensive annotated bibliography of published and unpublished finding aids relating to census schedules.

———. *Guide to Genealogical Records in the National Archives.* By Meredith B. Colket, Jr., and Frank E. Bridgers. Publication no. 64-8. 1964. 145 p. Useful sections on population and mortality census schedules, passenger arrival lists, bounty-land warrant application records, land-entry records for the public land states, and records relating to native Americans.

———. *Passenger Lists of Vessels Arriving at Baltimore, 1820-1891.* PDM no. 255. 1973. 6 p. Related microcopy publication pamphlets are *Index to Passenger Lists of Vessels Arriving at Baltimore (Federal Passenger Lists), 1820-1897* (PAM no. 327, 1970, 8 pp.); *Index to Passenger Lists of Vessels Arriving at Baltimore (City Passenger Lists), 1833-1866* (PAM no. 326, 1970, 7 pp.); and *Quarterly Abstracts of Passenger Lists of Vessels Arriving at Baltimore, 1820-1869* (PAM no. 596, 1970, 4 pp.).

———. *Passenger Lists of Vessels Arriving at Boston, 1820-1891.* PAM no. 277. 1970. 7 p. An accompanying card index was prepared by the Work Projects Administration between 1935-37 and is described in microcopy publication pamphlet *Index to Passenger Lists of Vessels Arriving at Boston, 1848-1891* (PAM no. 265, 1969, 8 pp.). The cards provide information on name, age, sex, arrival date, occupation, birthplace, country of citizenship, last place of residency, mental and physical health, and state destination.

———. *Passenger Lists of Vessels Arriving at New Orleans, 1820-1902.* PAM no. 259. 1969. 6 p. A related microcopy pamphlet is *Quarterly Abstracts of Passenger Lists of Vessels Arriving at New Orleans, 1820-1875* (PAM no. 272, 1969, 4 pp.).

———. *Passenger Lists of Vessels Arriving at New York, 1820-97.* PAM no. 237. 1962. 20 p. The records reproduced on this microfilm publication (675 rolls) are the original passenger lists submitted by masters of vessels to the Collector of Customs at New York. An alphabetical card index to the names on the passenger lists arriving at the Port of New York is also available (PAM no. 261, 1964, 5 pp.).

———. *Passenger Lists of Vessels Arriving at Philadelphia, 1800-1882.* PDM no. 425. 1971. 7 p. Passenger lists prior to 1820 include only the passenger's name and quantity of baggage. An accompanying index, arranged alphabetically by surname of passenger and containing over half a million entries, is available (PAM no. 360, 1964, 4 pp.).

———. *Population Data in Passport and Other Records of the Department of State.* By Mark G. Eckhoff. RIP no. 47. 1973. 7 p. Includes a description of vital statistical records comprising reports of births, marriages, and deaths of United States citizens abroad, 1792-1944.

———. *Population Schedules, 1800-1870. Volume Index to Counties and Major Cities.* SL no. 8. 1951. 217 p. "This is an index to the bound volumes of population schedules of the United States in the National Archives. . . . The index shows for each county the earliest decennial census (except 1790) for which the National Archives has schedules."

———. *Records of the Bureau of the Census.* By Katherine H. Davidson and

Charlotte M. Ashby. PI no. 161. 1964. 141 p. Includes an administrative history of census-taking and a description of the population schedules, 1790-1950.

_____. *Records of the Federal Writers' Project, Work Project Administration, 1935-44.* By Katherine H. Davidson. PI no. 57. 1953. 15 p. Includes descriptions of records pertaining to ethnic studies during the 1930s.

_____. *A Supplemental Index to Passenger Lists of Vessels Arriving at Atlantic and Gulf Coast Ports (Excluding New York), 1820-1874.* PAM no. 334. 1969. 8 p. This index supplements other separate indexes in the National Archives on passenger lists of vessels arriving at the following ports: Baltimore, Boston, New Bedford, New Orleans, and Philadelphia.

AFRO-AMERICAN

Lewinson, Paul. *A Guide to Documents in the National Archives for Negro Studies.* American Council of Learned Societies. Committee on Negro Studies. Publication no. 1. 1947. 28 p. The first two sections are useful to researchers in nineteenth-century historical geography. Section A briefly describes records relating to slavery, the slave trade, and African colonization of freed slaves to 1861. Section B lists material pertaining to colonization and reconstruction from 1861, including the confiscation and distribution of land to former slaves and aspects of the plantation economy.

McConnell, Roland C. "Importance of Records in the National Archives on the History of the Negro." *Journal of Negro History* 34 (April 1949): 135-52. Suggestive rather than exhaustive treatment that emphasizes "the fact that practically every aspect of Federal-Negro relationship has been recorded and the records, in many cases . . . are in the National Archives and are available."

Mock, James R. "The National Archives with Respect to the Records of the Negro." *Journal of Negro History* 23 (January 1938): 49-56. Superseded by Lewinson and McConnell, above. Interesting because it is one of the first articles to describe a portion of the holdings of the National Archives.

NA. *Audiovisual Records in the National Archives Relating to Black History.* By Leslie Waffen, Nancy Malan, and Charles Thomas. Preliminary Draft prepared for the Fifty-Sixth Annual Meeting of the Association for the Study of Negro Life and History, October 1971. Revised, July 1972. 12 p. "This paper is not intended as an exhaustive survey of all audiovisual records in the National Archives relating to black history. Its purpose is, however, to present a representative selection to indicate the breadth and scope of materials available for study and to suggest areas for concentrated research."

_____. *Black Studies: Select Catalog of National Archives and Records Service Microfilm Publications.* 1973. 71 p. "This catalog is designed to acquaint researchers with the more important material available within the National Archives and Records Service microfilm program relating to the history of American Blacks."

_____. *Data Relating to Negro Military Personnel in the Nineteenth Century.* By Aloha P. South. RIP no. 63. 1973. 8 p.

————. *List of Free Black Heads of Families in the First Census of the United States 1790.* By Debra L. Newman. SL no. 34. 1973. 44 p. Lists names of the black heads of families and the number of persons in each family but does not give their geographical location.

————. *Nineteenth-Century Puerto Rican Immigration and Slave Data.* By George S. Ulibarri. RIP no. 64. 1973. 9 p.

————. *Records of the Office of the Secretary of the Interior Relating to the Suppression of the African Slave Trade and Negro Colonization, 1854-72.* PAM no. 160. 1961. 16 p.

————. *Tabular Analysis of the Records of the U.S. Colored Troops and Their Predecessor Units in the National Archives of the United States.* By Joseph B. Ross. SL no. 33. 1973. 27 p. Particularly useful to geographers and other social scientists are the regimental descriptive books of the Civil War period. These include, in tabular form, enlistee's age; height; complexion; location of birth by town, country, and state; and occupation at time of enlistment.

Pinkett, Harold T. "Recent Federal Archives as Sources for Negro History." *Negro History Bulletin* 30 (December 1967): 14-17. Treats selected records dating from the 1930s dealing with "economic and social aspects of American life greatly affecting Negroes."

ASIAN AMERICAN

NA. *Statistics and Statistical Materials in the Records of the War Relocation Authority.* By James Paulauskas. Preliminary Draft prepared for the Conference on the National Archives and Statistical Research. 1968. 6 p. Photoprocessed. The WRA was established by Executive Order No. 9102, March 18, 1942, "to develop and operate a program for the removal, relocation, maintenance, and supervision of all persons of Japanese descent." Data on over one hundred sixty thousand evacuees were kept in individual case files. This data includes names of parents and their countries of birth, father's occupation, education, public assistance, height, weight, family number, sex, race, and spouse's race, birthdate, age, birthplace, language spoken, occupation, employment history, and religion.

EUROPEAN AMERICAN

Calkin, Homer L. "The United States Government and the Irish: A Bibliographical Study of Research Materials in the U.S. National Archives." *Irish Historical Studies* 9 (March 1954): 28-54. Particularly good on Irish immigration.

Reingold, Nathan. "Resources on American Jewish History in the National Archives," *American Jewish Historical Society,* Publication no. 47 (June 1958): 186-95.

NATIVE AMERICAN

Litton, Gaston. "The Resources of the National Archives for the Study of the

American Indian." *Ethnohistory* 2 (Summer 1955): 191-208. A good general introduction.

NA. *The American Indian. Select Catalog of National Archives Microfilm Publications.* 1972. 50 p. "This select catalog lists the records published on microfilm by the National Archives and Records Service that relate directly to Indians, to the formation and enforcement of Federal Indian policy, and to the personnel that created or enforced that policy."

_____. *Audiovisual Records Relating to Indians, in the National Archives.* By Joe Doan Thomas. Preliminary Draft prepared for the National Archives Conference on Research in the History of Indian-White Relations. 1972. 17 p. Photoprocessed. A description of 11,000 still pictures, 300 sound recordings, and 125 reels of motion picture film pertaining to the American Indian.

_____. *Indian Census Rolls, 1885-1940.* PAM no. 595. 1967. 34 p. "These census rolls were usually submitted each year by agents or superintendents in charge of Indian reservations as required by an act of Congress of July 4, 1884. The information given in the rolls varies to some extent; but usually given are the English and/or Indian name of the person, roll numbers, age or date of birth, sex, and relationship to head of family."

_____. *Records of the Bureau of Indian Affairs.* By Edward E. Hill. PI no. 163. 2 vols. 1965. 459 p. Volume 1 includes descriptions of records of Indian trade and the factory system, Indian removal, land allotments, and enrollment and census material. Volume 2 consists of the field office records, particularly superintendencies and agencies. Selected records have been microfilmed: *Records of the Central Superintendency of Indian Affairs* (PAM no. 856, 1973, 23 pp.); *Letters Sent by the Indian Division of the Office of the Secretary of the Interior, 1849-1903* (PAM no. 606, 1965, 8 pp.); *Letters Received by the Office of Indian Affairs, 1824-80* (PAM no. 234, 1966, 72 pp.); and *Selected Classes of Letters Received by the Indian Dvision of the Office of the Secretary of the Interior, 1849-1880* (PAM no. 825, 1972, 4pp.).

_____. *Records of the Cherokee Indian Agency in Tennessee, 1801-35.* PAM no. 208, 1953. 7 p. Among the subjects dealt with by the records reproduced on this microcopy are the economic and social conditions of the Cherokees, trade, travel through Cherokee country, unauthorized settlement on Indian land, and the Cherokee migration westward. Pertinent enrollment records are described in *Records Relating to Enrollment of Eastern Cherokee. By Guion Miller, 1908-1910* (PAM no. 685, 1967, 4 pp.).

_____. *Report Books of the Office of Indian Affairs, 1838-1885.* PAM no. 348. 1964. 5 p. The records reproduced in this microfilm publication (fifty-three rolls) relate to every aspect of the administration of Indian affairs, including establishment of reservations, appraisement and sale of land, allotments, schools, agriculture, location of agencies, and the purchase and transportation of supplies.

_____. *Special Files of the Office of Indian Affairs, 1807-1904.* PAM no. 574. 1965. 34 p. Among the Special Files are correspondence and reports on Indian emigration, Cherokee slaves, trade with Indians, Indian agriculture, and boundary surveys.

————. *Vital Statistics in the National Archives Relating to the American Indian.* By Carmelita S. Ryan. RIP no. 61. 1973. 13 p. Prepared for the National Archives Conference on Statistical Research. An excellent summary.

Agriculture

Edwards, Everett E. "Agricultural Records: Their Nature and Value for Research." *AH* 13 (January 1939): 1-12. General introduction to agricultural records by a noted historian in the Bureau of Agricultural Economics, United States Department of Agriculture. The National Archives is mentioned only briefly.

Guthrie, Chester L. "The United States Grain Corporation Records in the National Archives." *AH* 12 (October 1938): 347-54. The records of the Grain Corporation provide statistical data on mill products, elevators and mills, and the movement of grains during World War II and the early 1920s. These records are described in greater detail in *Preliminary Inventory of the Records of the United States Grain Corporation,* compiled by Philip R. Ward and Carolyn K. Fagan (NC no. 143, 1966, 32 pp.).

Kahn, Herman. "Records in the National Archives Relating to the Range Cattle Industry, 1865-1895." *AH* 20 (July 1946): 187-90. Touches on a variety of related topics such as cattle smuggling across international boundaries; export trade in beef; political activities of cattlemen; political, economic, and social conditions in the Rocky Mountain territories; free grazing on the public domain; illegal fencing on the public domain; quarantine legislation; illegal entry on Indian lands; beef production; and transportation of beef.

Kulsrud, Carl J. "The Archival Records of the Agricultural Adjustment Program." *AH* 22 (July 1948): 197-204. Traces the administrative history of the Agricultural Adjustment Program, which was designed to place agriculture on a basis of economic equality with industry during the 1930s, and appraises the records created by the agencies that operated the program.

NA. *Cartographic Records of the Bureau of Agricultural Economics.* By William J. Heynen. SL no. 28. 1971. 110 p. These records pertain primarily to agricultural geography for the period 1902-53 but several series are broader in scope. The maps prepared by the Division of Agricultural History and Geography show distribution of farms, slaves, crops, livestock, and rural population for various periods during the nineteenth and early twentieth centuries. Two other series of interest describe the cartographic works of O. E. Baker and F. J. Marschner.

————. *Preliminary Checklist of the Records of the Office of the Secretary of Agriculture, 1839-1943.* By Guy A. Lee, Max Levin, and Lois Bell Miller. PC no. 19. 1945. 101 p. Summarized in Guy A. Lee, "The General Records of the United States Department of Agriculture in the National Archives." *AH* 19 (October 1945): 242-49.

_____. *Preliminary Checklist of Reports Received by the Office of Foreign Agricultural Relations, Department of Agriculture.* By Lois Bell Miller. PC no. 8. 1943. 52 p. Photoprocessed. The records described consist of agricultural reports, 1903-38; forestry and forest products reports, 1901-41; and cables, 1922-39. These records originated with American consular officials, agricultural trade commissions, agricultural attaches, and special agents. They include information on agricultural production, market trends, prices, consumption, and trade.

_____. *Preliminary Inventory of the Records of the United States Sugar Equalization Board, Inc.* By Forrest R. Holdcamper. NC no. 72. 1964. 7 p. A World War I agency. Entries 18-23 briefly describe the records of the Statistical Department of the Board pertaining to sugar production and trade.

_____. *Records of the Bureau of Agricultural Economics.* By Vivian Wiser. PI no. 104. 1958. 212 p. Covers the period 1896-1953. Particularly important are the records of the Divisions of Farm Population and Rural Life, Land Economics, Marketing and Transportation Research, and Statistical and Historical Research.

_____. *Subject-Numeric Headings of Correspondence Files of the Office of the Secretary of Agriculture, 1906-56.* By Harold T. Pinkett, Charles E. Neal, and Monroe A. Bethea. NC no. 14. 1962. 157 p. Photoprocessed.

Pinkett, Harold T. "The Archival Product of a Century of Federal Assistance to Agriculture." *American Historical Review* 69 (April 1964): 689-706. A brief but thorough survey of the records produced by various federal agencies that aided and influenced the development of American agriculture from 1862 to World War II and their research potential.

_____. "Early Records of the United States Department of Agriculture." *AA* 25 (October 1962): 407-16. Examines the reasons for the lack of early records of the Department of Agriculture (1862-92)—"a scantiness perhaps unparalleled in the archival history of major Federal agencies"—and suggests that the loss of these early records was partially offset by the department's published monthly and annual reports and by the preservation of a few papers of its early administrators and scientists by state and private organizations.

_____. "Records of the First Century of Interest of the United States Government in Plant Industries." *AH* 29 (January 1955): 38-45. A review of the records of an industry that played an important role in the economic growth of the United States.

Trade and Commerce

Fishbein, Meyer H. "Business History Resources in the National Archives." *Business History Review* 38 (Summer 1964): 232-57. The bulk of the records described date from 1900-1939, but numerous references to nineteenth-century business history are included. The most important section for historical geographers is "Business Promotion and Regulations." It includes separate, brief descriptions of records pertaining to transportation, communication, and mining.

————. "Early Business Statistical Operations of the Federal Government." *National Archives Accession* 54 (1958): 1-29. Reprinted as RIP no. 51. 1973. 35 p. Business statistics, as defined in this paper, pertain to "the collection, tabulation, and analysis of quantitative data about enterprises engaged in selling goods or services for profit." Covers period 1745 to 1890.

Holdcamper, Forrest R. "Registers, Enrollments and Licenses in the National Archives." *American Neptune* 1 (July 1941): 275-94. A discussion of nineteenth-century American shipping records originally in the custody of the Bureau of Marine Inspection and Navigation. For a listing of merchant vessels for a specific port, see the voluminous two-volume work, *List of American-Flag Merchant Vessels that Received Certificates of Enrollment or Registry at the Port of New York, 1789-1867,* compiled by Kenneth R. Hall (SL no. 22, 2 vols., 1968). Lists the tonnage, year, and place of construction for more than twenty-six thousand vessels.

Lambert, Robert S. "Income-Tax Records as Sources for Economic History." *AA* 24 (July 1961): 341-44. Illustrates the value of income tax records to the study of natural resources industries such as the logging industry. Although corporate tax returns are currently retained by the IRS, NARS and the IRS are considering whether or not it will be possible to transfer a statistically derived sample of these returns to NARS.

NA. *Commerce Data among State Department Records.* By Milton O. Gustafson. RIP no. 53. 1973. 8 p. Discusses reports on commercial and economic subjects submitted by United States consular officials assigned to foreign countries.

————. *Corporation Assessment Lists, 1909-1915.* PAM no. 667. 1967. 9 p. The lists show names and addresses of corporations, type of business, and kind and amount of tax. Arranged by state.

————. *General Correspondence of the Office of the Secretary of Commerce, 1929-1933.* PDM no. 838. 1972. 4 p. In addition to routine administrative matters, the records described provide important documentation on the economic depression and the activities of business, public works, mining, railroads, trade, and building construction.

————. *Internal Revenue Assessment Lists.* PAM, various numbers. 1969-73. Prepared during the Civil War, the assessment lists are divided into three basic categories: annual, monthly, and special. The annual lists provide information on trades and occupations and the monthly lists provide information on manufactured products "ranging from ale to zing," transportation companies, and sales on slaughtered cattle, hogs, and sheep. The following assessment lists have been microfilmed and accompanying descriptive pamphlets have been prepared: Alabama, 1865-1866 (PAM no. 754, 1969, 7 pp.); Arkansas, 1865-1866 (PAM no. 755, 1969, 7 pp.); California, 1862-1866 (PAM no. 756. 1969, 8 pp.); Colorado Territory, 1862-1866 (PAM no. 757, 1969, 4 pp.); Connecticut, 1862-1866 (PAM no. 758, 1969, 7 pp.); Delaware, 1862-1866 (PAM no. 759, 1969, 5 pp.); District of Columbia, 1862-1866 (PAM no. 760, 1969, 5 pp.); Florida, 1865-1866 (PAM no. 761, 1969, 3 pp.); Georgia, 1865-1866 (PAM no. 762, 1969, 10 pp.); Idaho Territory, 1865-1866 (PAM no. 763 1969, 3 pp.);

Illinois, 1862-1866 (PAM no. 764, 1970, 11 pp.); Indiana, 1862-1866 (PDM no. 765, 1971, 11 pp.); Iowa, 1862-1866 (PDM no. 766, 1973, 8 pp.); Kentucky, 1862-1866 (PDM no. 768, 1972, 18 pp.); Louisiana, 1863-1866 (PDM no. 769, 1972, 7 pp.); Maine, 1862-1866 (PDM no. 770, 1972, 7 pp.); Maryland, 1862-1866 (PDM no. 771, 1973, 6 pp.); South Carolina, 1864-1866 (PDM no. 789, 1973, 7 pp.); Virginia, 1862-1866 (PDM no. 793, 1973, 19 pp.); West Virginia, 1862-1866 (PDM 795, 1973, 11 pp.).

————. *Major Quantitative Sources among the Foreign Service Post Records of the Department of State, 1789-1935.* By R. L. Heise. Preliminary Draft prepared for the Conference on the National Archives and Statistical Research, May 1968. 5 p. Includes a brief discussion of sources relating to trade and commerce in post records.

————. *Major Sources in Customs Bureau Records for Statistical Data on Exports and Imports of the United States to 1900.* By Jerome Finster. RIP no. 49. 1973. 13 p. "This paper describes four species of records . . . that may be large enough for statistical exploitation. These types of records are foreign outward (export) manifests, foreign inward (import) manifests, entries for imports, and impost books."

————. *Materials in the National Archives Containing Statistical Data on Economic Subjects, 1910-44.* By Guy A. Lee. RIC no. 33. 1945. 17 p. Identifies a variety of pertinent records on agriculture, manufacturing, transportation, trade, housing, commerce, and mining.

————. *Materials in the National Archives Relating to Food Production and Distribution, 1917-40.* RIC no. 17. 1943. 13 p.

————. *Preliminary Inventory of the Records of the Bureau of Customs.* By Forrest R. Holdcamper. NC no. 154. 1968. 215 p. In a suggestive article on the research value of the customhouse records in Massachusetts, Samuel E. Morison has described these records "as the most important existing source for commerce, fishing, shipping and shipbuilding" (*Proceedings of the Massachusetts Historical Society* 54 [1920-21]: 324-31). They also include material relating to slave trade. The period covered is from 1789 to 1900.

————. *Preliminary Inventory of the Records of Former Russian Agencies: Records of the Russian-American Company.* By Daniel T. Goggin. NC no. 40. 1963. 4 p. The Russian-American Company, established by Czar Paul I in 1799, was granted a trade monopoly in Russian North America and held complete political control of the area until 1867. The records described in this inventory include correspondence relating to Indians, fur prices, transportation, prices of supplies, equipment for exploring and trading expeditions, and agriculture (1818-67); logs of company ships (1850- 67); and the journals of Lt. Lavrentii A. Zagoskin's overland exploration to the Lower Yukon basin and the southwestern mainland of Alaska (1842-44) and Capt. N. Arkhimandritov's explorations on Kodiak Island, Norton Sound, and Pribilof Islands (1860-64). The records are almost all in Russian and are available on microfilm (PDM no. 11, 1971, 195 pp.).

————. *Records of the Federal Trade Commission.* By Estelle Rebec. SL no. 7.

1948. 7 p. The records of the Economic Division (1915-38) consist of investigations relating to diverse economic matters, including agricultural incomes, chainstores, dairy products, power and gas utilities, coal, meat, and cooperate marketing.

————. *Records of the United States Shipping Board.* By Forrest R. Holdcamper. PI no. 97. 1956. 164 p. Established in 1917 to regulate "carriers by water, for developing a naval auxiliary, and for expanding the development of the United States merchant marine." Geographers will find the records of the Statistical Department (1919-35) particularly helpful.

————. *Statistical Data on the National Wealth and Money Supply To Be Derived from Internal Revenue Records.* By Hope K. Holdcamper. RIP no. 55. 1973. 5 p. A description of internal revenue assessment lists on goods and land dating back to 1798.

Pumphrey, Lowell J. "Materials in the National Archives of Especial Interest for Economists." *American Economic Review* 31 (June 1941): 344-45. Cursory and generally out of date.

Stark, Marie Charlotte. "Materials for Research in the Files of International Claims Commissions." *American Neptune* 3 (January 1943): 48-54. Describes various kinds of records relating to shipping and commerce.

Manufacture and Industry

Fishbein, Meyer H. "The Censuses of Manufactures, 1810-1890." *NA Accessions* 57 (June 1963): 1-20. Reprinted as RIP no. 50. 1973. 31 p. The censuses are "examined in terms of the professional qualifications of their authors, the adequacy of the procedures used in gathering data, and the contents of the reports."

Krauskopf, Robert W. "Commentary [Panel on Manufactures]." In *The National Archives and Statistical Research,* edited by Meyer H. Fishbein. National Archives Conferences, 2:137-42. Athens: Ohio University Press, 1973. Brief discussion of selected records in the National Archives relating to manufacturing.

NA. *Materials in the National Archives Relating to the Basic Iron, Steel, and Tin Industries.* RIC no. 23. 1943. 7 p. Limited to the period 1900-1936.

————. *Materials in the National Archives Relating to Labor Migration during the First World War and Post-War Period.* RIC no. 15. 1943. 5 p. An exploratory survey covering the period 1917-20.

Porter, Patrick G. "Source Material for Economic History: Records of the Bureau of Corporations." *Prologue* 2 (Spring 1970): 31-33. The bureau, which spanned the years 1903-14, was established to investigate and publish reports on the operations of interstate corporations. Noteworthy are the records of investigations which were never published. They include printed questionnaires and transcripts of interviews, along with corporate annual reports and trade association publications, relating to American manufactures and distributors. The bureau was succeeded by the Federal Trade Commission.

Transportation and Communication

NA. *Cartographic Records of the Office of the Secretary of the Interior.* By Laura E. Kelsay. PI no. 81. 1955. 11 p. Includes descriptions of cartographic records of Pacific Railroad surveys transferred from the War Department's Office of Exploration and Surveys and cartographic records of the Pacific Wagon Road Office.

————. *Material in the National Archives Relating to Transportation.* RIC no. 36. 1948. 40 p. Although out of date, this publication nevertheless provides the researcher with a good introduction to archival sources relating to transportation. Section 1 includes a brief description of each record group in which there is significant material on the subject. Section 2 consists of a list of record groups by number only, arranged under nineteen broad fields of transportation such as domestic shipping, highways, local transportation, and so forth.

————. *Records of the Bureau of Public Roads.* By Truman R. Strobridge. PI no. 134. 1962. 34 p. These records cover the period from 1893 to 1950.

————. *Records of the Commissioner of Railroads.* By Marion M. Johnson. PI no. 158. 1964. 18 p. Covers period 1861-1904. The records of the commissioner include annual reports of forty government- and state-aided railroads; information concerning the number of passengers and amount of freight carried; and reports of amount of land sold to actual settlers. Recent data on railroads are described in *Preliminary Inventory of the Records of the U.S. Railroad Administration, 1917-1945,* compiled by Charles Zaid (NC no. 9, 1962, 31 pp.).

————. *Records of the Post Office Department.* Compiled by Arthur Hecht, Frank J. Nivert, Fred W. Warriner, Jr., and Charlotte M. Ashby. Revised by Forrest R. Holdcamper. PI no. 168. 1967. 54 p. The official records date from 1786. Also includes the journal of Hugh Finlay who was appointed surveyor of the Post Roads on the Continent of North America by the British postmaster general in 1772. Appendixes 4 and 5 include a list of post route maps dating from 1855.

————. *Select List of Titles in the Bureau of Public Roads Highway Transport File (Prints).* By Susan Kay Parker and Sodie S. Mittman. NC no. 137. 1965. 21 p. Photoprocessed. Includes a list of general subject file photographs, and a list of photographs of historical roads and trails, 1900-1953.

————. *Transportation in Nineteenth-Century America: A Survey of the Cartographic Records in the National Archives of the United States.* By Patrick D. McLaughlin. RIP no. 65. 1973. 15 p. Includes a general description of manuscript internal improvement maps from the records of the United States Senate. The latter are also described by W. L. G. Joerg, "The Internal Improvement Maps (1825-1835) in the National Archives." *AAAG* 28 (1938): 52-53.

————. *The Valuation Records of the Interstate Commerce Commission as a Source of Statistical Data Relating to American Railroads during the Nineteenth Century*. By Joseph B. Howerton. RIP no. 56. 1973. 36 p. The Interstate Commerce Commission investigated the financing and inventoried the property of American railroads beginning in 1913. This program came to be called the "valuation." "The purpose of this paper is to point out the location of nineteenth-century information among the mass of valuation records still in existence, describe the material, and make some tentative evaluation of it as a source of statistical data for historical research."

Urban Developments

NA. *Cartographic Records of the Federal Housing Administration*. By Charlotte Munchmeyer. PI no. 45. 1952. 57 p. Statistical, geographical, and cartographic studies of 361 American cities undertaken during the 1930s. Basic documentation that has generally been overlooked by historical geographers.

————. *Cartographic Records in the National Archives of the United States Useful for Urban Studies*. By Ralph E. Ehrenberg. RIP no. 68. 1973. 14 p. Examines city plans compiled and collected by various federal agencies; enumeration district maps and descriptions prepared by the Census Bureau, 1880-1950; real property surveys undertaken by the Federal Housing Administration during the 1930s; and aerial survey photographs taken by the Soil Conservation Service from 1937 to 1942.

————. *Index to Records of the General Land Office in the National Archives Relating to Town Sites and Other Areas Classified as "Sites," 1855-1925*. By Arthur Hecht. 1945. Photoprocessed. Townsite case files may include correspondence, "declaratory statements," descriptions of the sites, affidavits, legal proofs and transcripts of proceedings and hearings, maps and plats, newspaper clippings, notices of appeal, and photographs.

————. *The National Archives and Urban Research*, edited by Jerome Finster. National Archives Conferences, vol. 6. Athens: Ohio University Press, 1974. The proceedings of the sixth scholarly conference sponsored by the National Archives and Records Service. The following articles, prepared by NARS staff members, are particularly pertinent: William E. Lind, "A General View of Urban Population Research Possibilities in the National Archives;" Jerome Finster, "Some Aspects of Urban Housing Records in the National Archives;" Leonard Rapport, "Urban Transportation Records in the National Archives;" and Joseph B. Howerton, "Federal Assistance to Cities, 1900-1930."

————. *Photographs of the American City: Select Audiovisual Records*. N.d. 15 p. "The selection of photographs listed in this publication depicts the city, its development, and its people and their way of life from the early nineteenth century to recent times. They were selected for their aesthetic quality and historical relevance to the development of urban America and are classified under the following headings: Artists' Conceptions of Nineteenth-Century Cities, Skylines and Streets, City Life, Urban Transportation, the City in Turmoil, and Twentieth-Century Art Reflecting Urban Themes."

————. *Reports of the National Resources Planning Board, 1936-1943.* PDM no. 120. 1972. 3 p. Particularly interesting are the selected reports of the Research Committee on Urbanism, one of the NRPB technical committees. Organized in 1935, it was "assigned responsibility for assessing the role of the Urban Community in the national economy."

Natural Resources and Climatology

Collier, Clyde M. "The Archivist and Weather Records." *AA* 26 (October 1963): 477-85. The author was archivist of the National Weather Records Center, Asheville, North Carolina.

NA. *Alaska File of the Secretary of the Treasury, 1868-1903.* PAM no. 720. 1968. 5 p. Relates to fur sealing and salmon fisheries.

————. *Central Office Records of the National Resources Planning Board.* By Virgil E. Baugh. PI no. 50. 1953. 66 p. The NRPB was established during the 1930s to prepare "a program and plan of procedure dealing with the physical, social, governmental, and economic aspects of public policies for the development and use of land, water and other national resources."

————. *Journal and Report of James Leander Cathcart and James Hutton, Agents Appointed by the Secretary of the Navy to Survey Timber Resources between the Mermentau and Mobile Rivers, November 1817-May 1819, with an Appendix Consisting of Copies of Letters Received and Sent.* PDM no. 8. 1972. 2 p.

————. *Letters Sent by the United States Geological Survey, 1869-1895.* PAM no. 152. 1965. 4 p. The records of the USGS, which was established in 1879, and its predecessors (the Hayden, Powell, Wheeler, and King surveys) are of value not only for the history of geology but also for the history of mining, irrigation, land use, and conservation. Related microcopy publications are described in *Letters Received by the United States Geological Survey, 1879-1901* (PAM no. 590, 1965, 8 pp.); *Registers of Letters Received by the United States Geological Survey, 1879-1901* (PAM no. 157, 1965, 4 pp.); *Letters Received by John Wesley Powell, Director of the Geographical and Geological Survey of the Rocky Mountain Region, 1869-79* (PAM no. 156, 1965, 8 pp.); *Records of the Geological Exploration of the Fortieth Parallel ("King Survey"), 1867-81* (PAM no. 622, 1965, 4 pp.); and *Records of the Geological and Geographical Survey of the Territories ("Hayden Survey"), 1867-79* (PAM no. 623, 1966, 4 pp.).

————. *Materials in the National Archives Relating to Rubber.* RIC no. 29. 1944. 15 p. Covers the period 1896-1942.

————. *Preliminary Checklist of the Records of the Joint Information Board on Mineral and Derivatives.* By Albert Whimpey. PC [no. 4]. 1943. 19 p. Photo-processed. The Mineral Subject File consists of reports, memorandums, and statistics on mineral resources, supplies, imports and exports, and other data, 1917-19.

————. *Preliminary Inventory of Operational and Miscellaneous Meteorological Records of the Weather Bureau.* By Helen T. Finneran. NC no. 3. Revised,

1965. 38 p. Describes and lists meteorological correspondence of the Smithsonian Institution, 1847-67, the Signal Office, 1870-93, and the Weather Bureau, 1894-1942; records of surface land observations, 1819-1941; marine observations, 1842-1930; diaries, journals, and miscellaneous papers containing meterological data, 1792-1916; and records of polar expeditions, 1881-1923. The main body of related records for the period 1819 to 1892 is described in *List of Climatological Records in the National Archives* (SL no. 1, 1942, 160 pp.) and, from 1892 to 1938, in *Climatological and Hydrological Records of the Weather Bureau* (PI no. 38, 1952, 76 pp.).

———. *Preliminary Inventory of the Records of the Fish and Wildlife Service.* By Edward E. Hill. NC no. 114. 1965. 28 p. Among the many activities of the predecessors of the Fish and Wildlife Service were the collection of statistics concerning commercial fisheries and responsibility for regulation of the Alaskan fishery and fur seal industries. Records described date from 1868 to 1940.

———. *Statistical Records concerning National Forest Timber Sales, 1908-37.* By Harold T. Pinkett. RIP no. 60. 1973. 7 p.

Pinkett, Harold T. "Forest Service Records as Research Material." *Forest History* 13 (January 1970): 19-29. General introduction. For a comprehensive treatment, see *Preliminary Inventory of the Records of the Forest Service,* compiled by Harold T. Pinkett, revised by Terry W. Good (PI no. 18, 1969, 23 pp.), and *Preliminary Inventory of the Cartographic Records of the Forest Service,* compiled by Charlotte M. Ashby (PI no. 167, 1967, 71 pp.).

———. "Records of Research Units of the United States Forest Service in the National Archives." *Journal of Forestry* 15 (April 1947): 272-75. Describes the records of the Research Compilation File, 1897-1936, which "served as a source of information on all phases of forest management, description, history, and economics;" the Project File of the Forest Products Laboratory, 1917-35; the Copeland Report Data, 1932-33, which "discussed the whole question of public forest policy and the coordinated federal and state action necessary to promote the most efficient use of forest resources for the general welfare;" and the Forest Taxation Inquiry Records, 1926-37, which reveals forest land types, acreage, and value of forest products.

II. REGIONAL

Southern

FRC, Atlanta. Archives Branch. *Research Opportunities.* Atlanta, 1967. 7 p. Brochure describing archival records in the Atlanta Federal Records Center. The records date from 1716 and include colonial and confederation records pertaining to the Acts of Trade and Navigation (1716-63), customs records (1803-1962), and records of activities of the Eastern Band of Cherokees (1886-1961).

Friis, Herman R. "Highlights of the Geographical and Cartographical Activities

of the Federal Government in the Southeastern United States, 1776-1864."
Southeastern Geographer 6 (1966): 41-57. Excellent survey.

NA. *Housing Records in the National Archives for Nashville and Atlanta.* By
Katherine H. Davidson. Preliminary Draft prepared for the Conference on the
National Archives and Urban Research. 1970. 20 p. Based on records prepared
during the Great Depression. Includes a good bibliography of pertinent finding aids.

———. *Journal of Charles Mason during the Survey of the Mason and Dixon
Line, November 15, 1763-September 11, 1768.* PDM no. 86. 1972. 2 p.

———. *The Southeast during the Civil War: Selected War Department Records
in the National Archives of the United States.* By Dale E. Floyd. RIP no. 69.
1973. 8 p. "This paper describes certain records in the National Archives of the
United States that can be used in studying the historical geography of the
Southeastern States during the Civil War."

———. *Statistical Records of the Bureau of Refugees, Freedmen, and Abandoned
Lands.* By Elaine C. Everly. RIP no. 48. 1973. 9 p. The records of the bureau include important material on Americans of African descent during the post-
Civil War period. Of particular interest to geographers are the monthly ration-
issue reports, which include, by district, the number of Blacks who received
rations, land reports, school reports, and reports of sick and wounded. More
detailed is the *Preliminary Checklist of the Records of the Bureau of Refugees,
Freedmen, and Abandoned Lands, 1865-1872,* compiled by Elizabeth Bethel,
Sara Dunlap, and Lucille Pendell. (PC no. 46, n.d., 64 pp.).

Western

FRC, Denver. Archives Branch. *Preliminary Guide to the Research Records in
the Denver Federal Records Center.* By Robert Svenningsen. Denver, 1969.
46 p. Contains descriptions of archival records in the Archives Branch of the
Denver Federal Records Center that were created by federal agencies in
Arizona, Colorado, New Mexico, Utah, and Wyoming.

———. Archives Branch. *Preliminary Inventory of the Records of the Mescalero
Indian Agency.* By Robert Svenningsen. Denver, 1971. 14 p. Records include
statistical summaries and reports pertaining to tribal population, sources of
income, value and types of crops produced, logging, disease, and employment.

FRC, Kansas City. Archives Branch. *Preliminary Inventory of the Records of the
Potawatomi Indian Agency, Bureau of Indian Affairs.* By Harry Svanda. Kansas City, 1965. 25 p.

———. Archives Branch. *Preliminary Inventory of the Records of the Winnebago Indian Agency, Bureau of Indian Affairs.* By Harry Svanda. Kansas City,
1965. 27 p.

FRC, Los Angeles. Archives Branch. *Preliminary Inventory of the Records of the
Arizona Territorial Court in the Los Angeles Federal Records Center.* By Norman E. Tutorow. Los Angeles, 1970. 60 p. The naturalization petitions and

certificates of citizenship are useful for the study of Chinese and Mexican immigration.

_____. Archives Branch. *Preliminary Inventory of the Records of the Bureau of Customs in the Los Angeles Federal Records Center.* By Norman E. Tutorow. Los Angeles, 1970. 49 p. Describes records of the following customs offices: Los Angeles (1877-1954), San Pedro (1873-1961), and San Diego (1875-1955).

_____. Archives Branch. *Preliminary Inventory of the Records of the Bureau of Land Management.* Compiled by Gilbert Dorame. Los Angeles, 1966. 83 p. The records described here were created or received in land offices and other field activities in Los Angeles, California (1853-1961), and Arizona (1860-1960).

FRC, San Francisco. Archives Branch. *Preliminary Inventory of the Records of the Bureau of Indian Affairs, Northern California and Nevada Agencies.* Compiled by Thomas W. Wadlow and Arthur R. Abel. Revised by Arthur R. Abel. San Francisco, 1966. 27 p.

_____. Archives Branch. *Preliminary Inventory of the Records of the Bureau of Land Management, Northern California and Nevada, 1861-1968.* Compiled by John P. Heard. San Francisco, 1970. 60 p.

_____. Archives Branch. *Preliminary Inventory of the Records of the District Director of Customs, San Francisco District, and of the Ports of Eureka and Monterey, 1848-1968.* Compiled by Arthur R. Abel. San Francisco, 1969. 24 p.

FRC, Seattle. Archives Branch. *Preliminary Inventory of the Records of the Bureau of Indian Affairs, Northern Cheyenne Indian Agency.* By Elmer W. Lindgard. Seattle, 1969. 3 p.

_____. Archives Branch. *Preliminary Inventory of the Records of the Bureau of Indian Affairs, Warm Springs Agency Records, 1861-1925.* By Elmer W. Lindgard. Seattle, 1968. 4 p.

Heard, John P. "Resource for Historians: Records of the Bureau of Land Management in California and Nevada." *Forest History* 12 (July 1968): 20-26. A good description of the BLM records housed in the San Francisco Federal Records Center. Of special interest to historical geographers are the original township surveys, land-entry records (oil and gas, desert lands, minerals, homesteads, public sales, rights-of-way, and recreation and public purposes), and tract books. The records date from 1861.

Jackson, W. Turrentine. "Dakota Territorial Papers in the Department of Interior Archives." *North Dakota Historical Quarterly* 9 (July 1944): 209-20.

_____. "Materials for Western History in the Department of the Interior Archives." *Mississippi Valley Historical Review* 35 (June 1948): 61-76. "The National Archives still remains the greatest depository of unused sources on the history of the Great Plains and Far West. Manuscripts for research in the field of history and related social studies have hardly been touched."

_____. "Territorial Papers in the Department of the Interior Archives, 1873-1890:

Washington, Idaho, and Montana." *Pacific Northwest Quarterly* 35 (October 1944): 323-41.

Joerg, W. L. G. "The Lafora Map of the Frontier of New Spain in 1766-67 in the National Archives: A Preliminary Examination." *Proceedings of the Eighth American Scientific Congress Held in Washington, May 10-18*, vol. 9 (1943), pp. 65-66. The earliest manuscript map in the National Archives.

Meany, Edmond J., Jr. "Food Administration Papers for Washington, Oregon, and Idaho Deposited in the National Archives." *Pacific Northwest Quarterly* 29 (October 1938): 373-82.

NA. *Federal Exploration of the American West before 1880*. 1963. 31 p. An exhibit catalog.

————. *Interior Department Territorial Papers: Dakota, 1863-1889*. PAM no. 310. 1963. 4 p.

————. *Letter Book of the Arkansas Trading House, 1805-1810*. PDM no. 142. 1972. 2 p. "The Arkansas factory was located at Arkansas Post on the Arkansas River in Louisiana Territory. . . . In addition to documenting the trading business at the Arkansas factory, the letter book also contains information about the physical plant, the kind of goods on hand, the shipment of goods, competition from private traders, and conditions among the Indians. Information about the rivers, climate, and general topography of the region is also contained in the letter book."

————. *List of Photographs of Irrigation Projects of the Bureau of Reclamation*. By Emma B. Haas, Anne Harris Henry, and Thomas W. Ray. SL no. 15. 1959. 33 p. "The photographic records covered by this Special List were made to serve the following purposes: (1) to document the historical development and engineering progress of the irrigation projects; (2) to record pictorially the benefits brought to the millions of acres that were irrigated; (3) to publicize the lands available for sale; and (4) to advertise the merits of extensive irrigation." The prints were made from 1902 through 1936 and cover most of the western states.

————. *Records of the Bureau of Reclamation*. By Edward E. Hill. PI no. 109. 1958. 27 p. Coverage is from 1902-1958.

————. *Records of the Tenth Military Department, 1846-51*. PAM no. 210. 1955. 3 p. The Tenth Military Department had jurisdiction over Oregon Territory and California. These records include Treasury Department circulars relating to correspondence on subjects such as trade, Indian affairs, and exploration.

————. *The Territorial Papers of the United States: The Territory of Wisconsin, 1836-1848 (a Microfilm Supplement)*. PDM no. 236. 1971. 37 p. This issuance supplements *The Territorial Papers of the United States* volumes in letterpress. It describes 122 rolls of microfilm of selected textual and cartographic records from twenty-six record groups relating to all functions of government in Wisconsin Territory, especially public lands, Indians, commerce, and military activity.

Odgers, Charlotte H. "Federal Government Maps Relating to Pacific Northwest History." *Pacific Northwest Quarterly* 38 (July 1947): 261-72. Describes selected maps of the Pacific Northwest in the National Archives of the United States, copies of which have been deposited in the University of Washington and the State College of Washington. These maps pertain to "the distribution of Indian tribes and reservations, the reconnaissance work done by the United States Army, the location of military roads and railway land grants, the progress of public land surveys, and the changing network of postal routes."

Schusky, Mary Sue, and Schusky, Ernest L. "A Center of Primary Sources for Plains Indian History." *Plains Anthropologist: Journal of the Plains Conference* (1970), pp. 104-8. A brief discussion of archival sources relating to Plains Indians found in the federal records centers at Kansas City, Fort Worth, and Denver. It is followed by an analysis of the kinds of material available for the Lower Brule reservation.

Strong, Dennis F. "Sources for Pacific Northwest History: The Federal Records Center in Seattle." *Pacific Northwest Quarterly* 49 (January 1958): 19-20.

Svenningsen, Robert. "Genealogical Records in the Denver Federal Archives and Records Center." *Journal of the Utah Genealogical Association* 2 (June 1973): 43-50.

Swadesh, Frances L. "Analysis of Records of the Southern Ute Agency, 1877 through 1952: National Archives RG 75, in the Federal Records Center, Denver, Colorado." In *Ethnohistorical Bibliography of the Ute Indians of Colorado*, by Omer C. Stewart, app. A, pp. 61-71. Boulder: University of Colorado Press, 1971.

Tutorow, Norman E. "Source Materials for Historical Research in the Los Angeles Federal Records Center." *Southern California Quarterly* 53 (December 1971): 333-44. The records date from 1853 and "are an invaluable research source for scholars studying local, state, regional, or national history, particularly as it involves the federal government."

Tutorow, Norman E., and Abel, Arthur R. "Western and Territorial Research Opportunities in Trans-Mississippi Federal Records Centers." *Pacific Historical Review* 40 (November 1971): 501-18. Excellent overview of holdings in the following regional federal archives: Kansas City, Denver, San Francisco, Los Angeles, and Seattle.

III. STATES

Alaska

Frederick, Robert A. "Caches of Alaskana: Library and Archival Sources of Alaskan History." *Alaska Review* 2, no. 3 (Fall and Winter 1966-67): 39-79. Pages 50 to 58 include a list of sample series of records and individual documents and maps to be described in the forthcoming NARS publication, *Guide to Materials on Alaska in the National Archives*.

NA. *Interior Department Territorial Papers: Alaska, 1869-1911.* PAM no. 430. 1964. 8 p. These papers pertain to the exploration and settlement of Alaska.

―――――. *Materials in the National Archives Relating to Alaska.* RIC no. 6. 1942. 10 p. Cursory and incomplete list. Arranged alphabetically by name of the federal agency or bureau that created the records.

Arizona

NA. *Interior Department Territorial Papers: Arizona, 1868-1913.* PAM no. 429. 1963. 5 p.

―――――. *Records of the Arizona Superintendency of Indian Affairs, 1863-1873.* PAM no. 734. N.d. 7 p. The records relate to all aspects of the Arizona Superintendency.

―――――. *State Department Territorial Papers: Arizona, 1864-72.* PAM no. 342. 1961. 2 p. The papers described are primarily letters and reports sent by the governor or the secretary of the territory to the secretary of state. While most of the papers are administrative in nature, some pertain to mining and supply routes.

California

NA. *Letters Sent by the Governors and by the Secretary of State of California, March 1, 1847-September 23, 1848.* PAM no. 182. 1957. 2 p. The correspondence touches on such subjects as trade, Indian affairs, the collection of customs, claims, and the discovery of gold.

―――――. *Military Development and Urban Growth in the San Francisco Bay Area prior to World War II.* By William H. Cunliffe. Preliminary Draft prepared for the Conference on the National Archives and Urban Research. 1970. 31 p.

―――――. *Records in the National Archives Relating to Public Works in the City of Sacramento.* By Edward E. Hill. Preliminary Draft prepared for the Conference on the National Archives and Urban Research. 1970. 20 p. Emphasizes projects of the Department of Interior Bureau of Reclamation, and navigation and flood control projects of the Army Corps of Engineers.

―――――. *Selected Records of the Departments of the Treasury and Commerce Relating to the Economic Development of San Francisco, 1847-1967.* By William F. Sherman. Preliminary Draft prepared for the Conference on the National Archives and Urban Research. 1970. 9 p.

Colorado

NA. *Schedules of the Colorado State Census of 1885.* PAM no. 158. 1965. 4 p.

―――――. *State Department Territorial Papers: Colorado, 1859-74.* PAM no. 3. 1954. 23 p. Primarily administrative in character, but some of the records describe conditions of the territory. Particularly interesting is a report and maps by the geographically minded Governor William Gilpin to Secretary of State Seward, based on explorations conducted in the summer of 1861.

District of Columbia

Bethel, Elizabeth. "Material in the National Archives Relating to the Early History of the District of Columbia." *Records of the Columbia Historical Society* 42/43 (1940-41): 169-87. Useful but dated survey of selected textual and cartographic records.

NA. *Preliminary Inventory of the Records of the United States District Courts for the District of Columbia.* By Janet Weinert. NC no. 2. 1962. 15 p. Pertinent series are slavery records, 1821-63, and probate records, 1799-1905. The latter includes inventories and sales and reports of appraisers on goods, chattel, and personal estates.

_____. *Records of the City of Georgetown (D.C.), 1800-1879.* PAM no. 605. 1965. 4 p. "The volumes reproduced consist mainly of tax assessment records and include journals, ledgers, and related volumes of various Georgetown municipal offices."

_____. *Urban Housing and Rental Data in the Records of the Rent Commission of the District of Columbia.* By Kathryn M. Murphy. Preliminary Draft prepared for the Conference on the National Archives and Urban Research. 1970. 10 p. The District of Columbia was chosen to illustrate the "sources of information about urban housing conditions that may be found in the files of a rent-control agency." Covers period 1919-25.

Florida

Drewry, Elizabeth B. "Materials in the National Archives Relating to Florida, 1839-1870." *Florida Historical Quarterly* 23 (October 1944): 97-115. A survey of pertinent series among the records of the Departments of State and War, the Office of Indian Affairs, the General Land Office, and the United States Senate. The author points out that "Florida, more than many states, is well represented in the Federal archives [because of] the circumstances of her relations with the United States while yet a province of Spain, of her existence as a territory of the United States for almost a quarter of a century, and of her participation in the Civil War."

NA. *Schedules of the Florida State Census of 1885.* PDM no. 845. 1971. 3 p. Consists of four general schedules: population, agriculture, manufactures, and mortality.

Georgia

NA. *Letter Book of the Creek Trading House, 1795-1816.* PDM no. 4. 1973. 3 p. The factory for Creek Indians, which operated longer than any other government trading house, was located at various sites in southern Georgia. "In addition to documenting the regular trading business at the factory, the letter book also contains information about the kinds of goods needed for the trade, shipment of trade goods and peltry, competition with private traders, relations with the military, and conditions among the Indians."

Idaho

NA. *Interior Department Territorial Papers: Idaho, 1864-90.* PAM no. 191. 1956. 2 p.

———. *Records of the Idaho Superintendency of Indian Affairs, 1863-1870.* PDM no. 832. 1972. 7 p. The records described consist mainly of the superintendent's correspondence. It relates to all aspects of Indian affairs within the Idaho Superintendency, including treaties, land surveys, location and establishment of reservations, and trade.

Illinois

NA. *Records in the National Archives Relating to Transportation in Chicago.* By George S. Ulibarri. Preliminary Draft prepared for the Conference on the National Archives and Urban Research. 1970. 14 p.

———. *Some Sources of Federal Documentation of Minority Groups in Chicago.* By Joseph B. Howerton. Preliminary Draft prepared for the Conference on the National Archives and Urban Research. 1970. 24 p. Interesting analysis of data pertaining to native Americans and other minorities in the nineteenth-century city and employment and housing during the twentieth century.

Indiana

FRC, Chicago. Archives Branch. *Preliminary Inventory Records of the United States Courts for the District of Indiana.* By Warren B. Griffen. Chicago, 1967. 32 p. Potentially valuable are the railroad record books (1879-83) and bankruptcy records reflecting business or economic decline (1867-1956).

Iowa

NA. *Cartographic Records Relating to the Territory of Iowa, 1838-46.* By Laura E. Kelsay and Frederick W. Pernell. SL no. 27. 1971. 27 p. With a few exceptions all of the maps described were prepared by or for agencies of the federal government.

Massachusetts

NA. *Records in the National Archives Relating to Immigration to Boston.* By Carmelita S. Ryan. Preliminary Draft prepared for the Conference on the National Archives and Urban Research. 1970. 18 p. Discusses passenger lists (1820-1943), naturalization records, and the Massachusetts Federal Writers Project's unpublished materials pertaining to immigration.

Michigan

NA. *City in Crisis: The Impact of Depression on Detroit, Michigan, as Re-*

flected in Records of the Federal Relief Agencies. By Robert M. Kvasnicka. Preliminary Draft prepared for the Conference on the National Archives and Urban Research. 1970. 30 p. Good bibliography.

Minnesota

Ehrenberg, Ralph E. "Cartographic Records on the Red River Region in the National Archives." *Red River Valley Historian* 2, no. 3 (Autumn 1968): 5-7. Primary emphasis is on nineteenth-century exploration and settlement.

NA. *Records of the Minnesota Superintendency of Indian Affairs, 1849-1856*. PDM no. 842. 1971. 8 p.

Smith, G. Hubert. "Some Sources for Northwest History: The Archives of Military Posts." *Minnesota History* 22 (1941): 297-301. The author uses official records of Fort Ridgely, now in the National Archives, as illustrative of the value of post records in historical research. Copies of these post documents are available on microfilm at the Minnesota Historical Society.

Missouri

McCain, William D. "The Papers of the Food Administration for Missouri, 1917-1919, in the National Archives." *Missouri Historical Review* 32 (October 1937): 56-61. A World War I agency established to control the supply and distribution of food production and fuel. Useful for studying the industrial and commercial development of the state and the economic life of its inhabitants.

Montana

NA. *Interior Department Territorial Papers: Montana, 1867-89*. PAM no. 192. 1956. 2 p.

———. *Records of the Montana Superintendency of Indian Affairs, 1867-1873*. PDM no. 833. 1972. 7 p. Topics covered include Indian emigration and subsistence, location of agencies, trade, and transportation of goods and supplies.

———. *Records of the Office of the Secretary of the Interior Relating to the Yellowstone National Park, 1872-1886*. PDM no. 62. 1973. 5 p.

———. *State Department Territorial Papers: Montana, 1864-72*. PAM no. 356. 1961. 3 p. Among the subjects covered are mining and railroads.

Nebraska

NA. *Schedules of the Nebraska State Census of 1885*. PAM no. 352. 1961. 3 p. Includes four general schedules: population, agriculture, manufactures, and mortality.

———. *State Department Territorial Papers: Nebraska, 1854-67*. PAM no. 228. 1955. 2 p. The papers consist primarily of correspondence on a variety of subjects, including internal improvements such as the construction of wagon roads and railroads.

345

Nevada

Campbell, Ann. "In Nineteenth-Century Nevada: Federal Records as Sources for Local History." *Nevada Historical Society Quarterly.* Forthcoming.

NA. *Records of the Nevada Superintendency of Indian Affairs, 1869-1870.* PDM no. 837. 1972. 6 p.

New Hampshire

Owens, James K. "Federal Court Records of New Hampshire." *Historical New Hampshire* 25 (Fall 1970): 37-40. The court records, housed at the Federal Records Center, Waltham, Massachusetts, contain material on land speculation and settlement, maritime and inland trade, and immigration and naturalization, 1789-1945.

New Mexico

Lounsbury, Ralph G. "Materials in the National Archives for the History of New Mexico before 1848." *New Mexico Historical Review* 21 (July 1946): 247-56. Survey of records relating to exploration, boundaries, consular representation, claims, communications, and military affairs. At the time this article was written, the extensive records of the Bureau of Indian Affairs and the General Land Office had not yet been transferred to the National Archives.

NA. *Despatches from United States Consuls at Santa Fe, 1830-1846.* PAM no. 199. 1965. 3 p.

―――. *Interior Department Territorial Papers: New Mexico, 1851-1914.* PAM no. 364. 1962. 6 p. The Subject Classified Files pertain to investigations of land transactions of lumber and mining companies, 1907-13, and correspondence relating to inspection of coal mines, 1892-1907.

―――. *Schedules of the New Mexico Territory Census of 1885.* PDM no. 846. 1972. 3 p. Four general schedules are included: population, agriculture, manufactures, and mortality.

North Carolina

McConnell, Roland C. "Records in the National Archives Pertaining to the History of North Carolina." *North Carolina Historical Review* 25 (July 1948): 318-40.

NA. *List of North Carolina Land Grants in Tennessee, 1778-1791.* PDM no. 68. 1972. 3 p.

Ohio

NA. *Letters Received by the Secretary of the Treasury and the Commissioner of the General Land Office from the Surveyor General of the Territory Northwest of the River Ohio, 1797-1849.* PAM no. 478. 1965. 3 p. The surveyor general was responsible for surveying the boundaries and subdivisions of the territory; surveying lands acquired under the provisions of the Treaty of

Greenville, August 3, 1795; and general administrative duties. Related records are described in *Letters Sent by the Surveyor General of the Territory Northwest of the River Ohio, 1797-1854* (PDM no. 477, 1972, 3 pp.); *Letters Received by the Surveyor General of the Territory Northwest of the River Ohio, 1797-1856* (PAM no. 479, 1964, 3 pp.); and *State Department Territorial Papers: Territory Northwest of the River Ohio, 1781-1801* (PDM no. 470, 1972, 2 pp.).

_____. *U.S. Revolutionary War Bounty-Land Warrants Used in the U.S. Military District of Ohio and Related Papers (Acts of 1788, 1803, 1806).* PDM no. 829. 1972. 8 p. A warrant normally shows the date of issuance, name and rank of the veteran, state from which he enlisted, and name of the heir or assignee. The second series (acts of 1803, 1806) is accompanied by a certificate indicating where, in the United States Military District of Ohio, the bounty land was located.

Oklahoma

Murphy, Kathryn M. "Oklahoma History and the National Archives." *Chronicles of Oklahoma* 30 (Spring 1952): 105-20. A discussion of the functions of the National Archives is followed by a brief survey of selected records.

Oregon

NA. *Abstracts of Oregon Donation Land Claims, 1852-1903.* PAM no. 145. 1955. 2 p. "Donation claims" were claims to grants based upon settlement of a particular tract prior to surveying.

Pennsylvania

Connor, R. D. W. "The National Archives and Pennsylvania History." *Pennsylvania History* 7 (April 1940): 63-78. General introduction by the first archivist of the United States.

NA. *United States Direct Tax of 1798: Tax List for the State of Pennsylvania.* PAM no. 372. 1963. 21 p. Tax lists include information on lands, lots, wharves, slaves, and dwelling houses (location, dimensions, construction materials, number of stories, number and dimensions of windows, and names of owners or occupants).

Wood, Richard G. "Research Materials in the National Archives Pertaining to Pennsylvania." *Pennsylvania Magazine of History and Biography* 69 (April 1945): 89-102. Includes examples of pre-federal and federal records. For the federal period, emphasis is on economic and social materials (notably the "Old Loans" records, which illustrate the financial affects of federal government actions, 1790-1840), nonpopulation schedules, and customs records.

South Carolina

Dickson, Maxcy R. "Sources for South Carolina History in the Nation's Capital." *Proceedings of the South Carolina Historical Association* (1942), pp. 50-54.

347

Texas

Evans, Luther H. "Texana in the Nation's Capital." *Southwestern Historical Quarterly* 50 (October 1946): 220-35. Major stress on Library of Congress, but briefly describes records in NARS for the period after 1845.

Lounsbury, Ralph G. "Early Texas and the National Archives." *Southwestern Historical Quarterly* 46 (January 1943): 203-13. A general survey of selected records. Limited to the formative period prior to annexation in December 1845.

Utah

NA. *Interior Department Territorial Papers: Utah, 1850-1902.* PAM no. 428. 1963. 4 p.

————. *Records of the Utah Superintendency of Indian Affairs, 1853-1870.* PDM no. 834. 1972. 7 p.

————. *State Department Territorial Papers: Utah, 1853-73.* PAM no. 12. 1965. 4 p.

Vermont

Franklin, W. Neil. "Materials in the National Archives Relating to Vermont." *Vermont History* 27 (July 1959): 240-55. A selective rather than comprehensive description by a long-time staff member of NARS.

Gorham, Alan. "Federal Court Records Pertaining to Vermont Sources for Study." *Vermont History* 36 (1968): 142-43. Brief notice of federal court records in the Waltham, Massachusetts, Federal Records Center, administered by NARS.

Putnam, Herbert E. "Vermont Population Trends—1790 to 1930—as Revealed in the Census Reports." *Vermont History* (March 1941): 14-26.

Virginia

Gondos, Victor, Jr., and Gondos, Dorothy. "Materials in the National Archives Relating to Alexandria, Virginia." *Virginia Magazine of History and Biography* 57 (October 1949): 421-32. Early federal period. The largest single group of records pertaining to maritime matters attests to Alexandria's role as an important port.

Washington

FRC, Seattle. Archives Branch. *Preliminary Inventory of the Records of the Seattle District Corps of Engineers.* By Elmer W. Lindgard. Seattle, 1968. 4 p. Records described relate to river and harbor improvements in Washington, 1894-1940, and meteorological records, 1912-21.

NA. *Abstracts of Washington Donation Land Claims, 1855-1902.* PAM no. 203.

1956. 3 p. "Donation claims" were claims to grants based upon settlements of a particular tract prior to surveying.

_____. *Records of the Collectors of Customs, Puget Sound District, in the Federal Records Center, Seattle, Washington.* By Elmer W. Lindgard. PI no. 122. 1960. 18 p. Covers the period 1851-1913. Useful for the study of import duties and Chinese migration.

Wisconsin

FRC, Chicago. Archives Branch. *Preliminary Inventory of the United States Court for the District of Wisconsin.* By Roger Hilgenbrink. Chicago, 1968. 25 p. Historical geographers will find the immigration and naturalization records useful.

Friis, Herman R. "The David Dale Owen Map of Southwestern Wisconsin." *Prologue* 1 (Spring 1969): 9-28. Based on detailed township plats prepared by Owen in the mid-1830s.

NA. *The Territorial Papers of the United States: The Territory of Wisconsin, 1836-1848 (a Microfilm Supplement).* PDM no. 236. 1971. 37 p. A supplement to *The Territorial Papers of the United States,* volumes in letterpress. Selected from twenty-four record groups and filmed on 122 rolls of microfilm, the records provide indispensable documentation for the early settlement of Wisconsin Territory. Rolls 121 and 122 are of cartographic records. PDM 236 includes a five-page index to proper names and subjects of the cartographic records. A full description of the maps can be found in *Cartographic Records Relating to the Territory of Wisconsin, 1836-1848,* compiled by Laura E. Kelsay and Charlotte M. Ashby (SL no. 23, 1970, 41 pp.).

Smith, Jane F. "The Use of Federal Records in Writing Local History: A Case Study." *Prologue* 1 (Spring 1969): 29-51. This article could also have been titled, "The Use of Federal Records in Writing Local Historical Geography." Based on land office records for Wisconsin.

Wyoming

Jackson, W. Turrentine. "Territorial Papers of Wyoming in the National Archives." *Annals of Wyoming* 16 (January 1944): 45-55.

NA. *Interior Department Territorial Papers: Wyoming, 1870-90.* PAM no. 204. 1956. 2 p.

National Archives Resource Papers

The following list of resource papers was distributed at the Conference on the National Archives and Research in Historical Geography to acquaint researchers with some of the records in the National Archives pertaining to historical geography. Those that have been published as National Archives reference information papers can be obtained without charge by writing to the Publications Sales Branch (NEPS), National Archives and Records Service (GSA), Washington, D.C., 20408. Those that have not been published can be obtained, without charge, by writing to the Cartographic Archives Division (NNS), National Archives and Records Service (GSA), Washington, D.C., 20408.

Federal Census Schedules, 1850-80: Primary Sources for Historical Research, National Archives Reference Information Paper No. 67, by Carmen R. Delle Donne (Washington, 1973).

"Textual Records of the Geological Survey in the National Archives: A Summary View," by Charles E. Dewing.

Geographical Exploration and Mapping in the Nineteenth Century: A Survey of the Records in the National Archives, National Archives Reference Information Paper No. 66, by Ralph E. Ehrenberg (Washington, 1973).

The Southeast during the Civil War: Selected War Department Records in the National Archives. National Archives Reference Information Paper No. 69, by Dale E. Floyd. (Washington, 1973).

Records and Policies of the Post Office Department Relating to Place-Names, by Arthur Hecht and William J. Heynen (forthcoming).

Pre-1930 Agricultural and Related Maps in the National Archives, by William J. Heynen (forthcoming).

"Whaling Logs in the Maury Log Collection: A Resource for Geographical Research," by Joseph B. Howerton.

Cartographic Records in the National Archives Relating to Indians in the United States, by Laura E. Kelsay (forthcoming).

Transportation in Nineteenth-Century America: A Survey of the Cartographic Records in the National Archives of the United States, Reference Information Paper No. 65, by Patrick D. McLaughlin (Washington, 1973).

"Land Use U.S.A.: An Archival Profile," by Harold T. Pinkett.

Index

Acts of Trade and Navigation: records of, 337

Adams, Herbert B.: 238

Aerial photography: records of, 320-21

Afro-American: population, 23-83; records of, 326-27, 338, 343, 347; slaves in British Army, 173-74

Agriculture: 118-19; records of, 318-20, 329-30, 332

Agriculture Department, U.S.: 7; records of, 322, 329-30, 337

Alaska: records of, 321-42

Alaska Railroad: 215, 219; records of, 322

Allen, John L.: 103-11, 163, 307

Allen, Paul: 141

American Indian: *See* Native Americans

American Military Pocket Atlas: 98

American Philosophical Society: 164, 225

Andrews, Charles M.: 238

Archives: derivation of word, 9; earliest, xiii; geography and, xiii; quantitative data in, 222. *See also* National Archives

Archives Nationales (Paris): 315

Arizona (state): mining towns in, 272; records of, 322, 338-39; Tombstone, 272

Arizona (territory): 342

Arkansas: 331; land surveys in, 121; mining towns in, 272; records of, 322, 338-39

Arkansas River: 111, 283

Arkansas Trading House: 340

Arkhimandritov, Capt. N.: 332

Army Corps of Engineers, U.S.: 7

Arrowsmith, Aaron: 105, 107, 112

Atlantic seaboard: colonial settlement of, 235-42

Audiovisual Archives Division, National Archives: 8, 319

Austin, Stephen F.: 250

Austin Colony, Texas: settlement of, 250-52

Baker, Alan: 87

Baker, O. E.: 329

Barrows, Harlan: 244

Beef trade: in New Orleans, 206-7, 211-12; export, records of, 329

Bell, John R.: 147

Bennett, Hugh: 119

Berkeley school of cultural historical geographers: 17-18

Biddle, Nicholas: 140

Bidwell, Percy: 244

Billington, Ray Allan: 244, 290

Black population: *See* Afro-American population

Borchert, John: 128

Bougainville, Louis Antoine de: 96

Boundary lines: in surveys, 118; international, records of, 323

Bowden, Martyn J.: 169-90, 229-30, 307

Bowen, Emanuel: 88

Brahm, William Gerard de: *See* De Brahm, William Gerard

Bridenbaugh, Carl: 235-36

351

British archives: source material in, 18
British army: black slaves in during Revolution, 73-74
British East Florida: De Brahm surveys of (1765-71), 87-99
Brooks, Philip C.: 316
Brown, Ralph H.: 3, 114, 236
Brush, John: 229
Burch, Franklin W.: 215-23, 307
Bureau of Agricultural Economics, U.S.: records of, 329-30
Bureau of the Census, U.S.: records of, 324, 335
Bureau of Corporations, U.S.: 333-34
Bureau of Indian Affairs, U.S.: 297-98; records of, 322, 327-28, 338-39
Bureau of Land Management, U.S.: 291-92, 339
Bureau of Marine Inspection and Navigation, U.S.: 216
Bureau of Public Roads, U.S.: 216, 334
Bureau of Reclamation, U.S.: 340
Bureau of the Census, U.S.: records of, 324, 335
Burlington and Missouri Railroad: 301
Burlington Railroad Land Office: 123
Burnet, William: 39

Cadastral system: in land surveys, 119
Calhoun, John C.: 145
California: Coloma, 276; Columbia, 271; Downieville, 271; Eureka, 339; gold discovery in, 271, 275-76; Grass Valley, 271; Jackson, 271; Lake Bigler, 150-53; Los Angeles, 359; Marysville, 272; mining towns in, 271, 275; Monterey, 339; Mormon Bar, 271; records of, 331, 339-40, 342; Sacramento, 273-342; San Diego, 339; San Francisco, 170-92, 339, 342; San Pedro, 339; Sonora, 271, 276; Stockton, 272; Sutter's Mill, 275
Campbell, A. H.: 150-52
Canada: Black settlements in New Brunswick, 74-77; Saint Johns River, 93; Saint Lawrence River, 90, 216
Canadian survey: township lines in, 121-26
Canebrakes: See Texas, canebrakes
Cappon, Lester J.: 160
Carey Act (1894): 303
Cartographic Archives Division, National Archives: 6, 157
Cathcart, James Leander: 336
Cedar Rapids and Missouri River Railroad Company: 125
Census (states): See names of individual states

Census (U.S.): of 1726, 35-39, 67; of 1772-73, 40, 69; of 1790, 42; of 1810 and 1820, 226; of 1850, 324; of 1860, 59, 72, 324; industrial, 226; manufactures, 333; records of, 323-28, 350
Central Business District: mobility in, 169-90
Charlevoix, Pierre Francois Xavier de: 96
Cherokee Indians: records of, 328-29, 337
Cheyenne Indian Agency: records of, 339
Chippewa Indians: 295; records of, 322
Choctaw Indians: records of, 322
Chouteau, Auguste: 297
Cities: ethnic division of labor in, 258-69; immigrant families in, 260; Irish-German ghettos in, 262; mid-nineteenth-century patterns of immigration in, 261-62; settlement of, 233-303. See also Settlement sites; Townsites; and names of specific cities or states
Civil Aeronautics Board: 215
Civil War: records of compared with those of Revolutionary War, 81
Clark, Andrew Hill: 4, 9-17, 83, 87, 307
Clark, George Rogers: 164
Clark, William: 105, 140, 164
Clarke, Robert L.: 73-83, 308
Clawson, Marian: 119
Climatology: records relating to, 336-37, 348
Coast and Geodetic Survey, U.S.: 119; records of, 323
Colonial America: neglect of geography of, 236
Colonial Atlantic seaboard: settlement of, 235-42
Colorado (state): Blackhawk, 271; Central City, 271, 280; Cripple Creek, 271, 283; Denver, 272, 274; Georgetown, 271, 280; Gregory Gulch, 277; Idaho Springs, 271, 280; Leadville, 271, 283, 284; mining towns in, 271-72, 277-78; records of, 331, 338, 342
Colorado (territory): records of, 342-43
Colorado River, Tex.: 109, 111, 245, 250
Columbia River: 107
Commerce: and industry, 167-232; trade and, records relating to, 330-32
Commerce Department, U.S.: 224
Commissioner of Railroads: 216
Communication: transportation and, 334-35
Comstock Lode, discovery of: 276
Comte, Auguste: 12
Congress, U.S.: Constitution and, 225, 228; National Archives and, 228

Connecticut: Academy of Arts and Sciences, 225; colonial settlements in, 239; records of, 331; settlement of Wethersfield, 239
Conservation: records on, 318, 319
Constitution, U.S.: 225, 228
Continental Congress: Jefferson committee, 132
Conzen, Michael P.: 231
Cook, James: 164
Corbett, J. L.: 286
Corn: in Texas prairies, 252-53
Corn and meat trade: New Orleans, 208-9, 212-13
Coues, Elliott: 141
Coulter, John: 111
Covered bridges: 193-200
Creek Indians: 343
Creole slaves: fertility rate of, 81
Cultural historical geographers: Berkeley school of, 17-18
Cumming, William P.: 91
Customs Bureau, U.S.: records of, 332, 339

Dakota Territory: records of, 339-40
Dartmouth, William Legge: earl of, 97
De Brahm, Ferdinand: 93
De Brahm, William Gerard: 87-99, 164
Delaware: records of, 331
Delle Donne, Carmen: 82
Demangeon, Albert: 315
Department of State, U.S.: records of, 323
Des Barres, Joseph Frederick Wallet: 98
De Ulloa, Antonio de: 96
De Vorsey, Louis, Jr.: 87-99, 160-61, 164 308
De Witt, Simeon: 163
District of Columbia: records of, 331, 343
Donaldson, Thomas: 120ˉ
Drouillard, George: 111, 113
Dutch West India Company: 27

Earle, Carville: 238
Eastin, Roy B.: 218
École des Chartes: 222
Ecological balance: concern with, 13
Economic subjects: records on, 318, 320, 332-33
Edwards, Clinton R.: 164
Ehrenberg, Ralph E.: 140, 308, 315-49
Ellicott, Andrew: 98
Environment, deterioration of: 13
Ethnic differentiation: population turnover and, 259
Ethnic division of labor: 258-69
Ethnic groups: records relating to, 324, 326-27, 339

Ethnology: 318, 320
Evans, Frank B.: 316
Exploration: *See* Geographical exploration
Exports and imports: statistical data in, 332

Federal Aviation Administration: 215
Federal Coordinator of Transportation: 215
Federal Housing Administration: 335
Federal land survey system: 122-23
Federal Maritime Commission: 216
Federal Trade Commission: 224; records on, 332, 334
Fertility rates: among Creole slaves, 81-82
Fish and Wildlife Service, U.S.: records of, 337
Fishbein, Meyer H.: 224-28, 308-9
Fisheries: records on, 320, 336-37
Florida: De Brahm surveys of, 87-99; Keys, 93; records of, 331, 343; Saint Augustine, 93, 164; Saint Marys River, 93
Fogel, Robert: 228
Food production: records on 332, 345. *See also* Agriculture
Foodstuffs: in antebellum regional trade, 204-5
Ford, Amelia Clearly: 162
Ford, Henry: 318
Foreign Service post records: 332
Forest and Recreation Districts, U.S.: 230
Forest products: records of, 330, 336-37
Forest Service, U.S.: 337
France: historical geography in, 222, 315
Frémont, Jessica Benton: 144, 149
Frémont, John C.: 144, 148
French and Indian War: 15
Friis, Herman: 6, 139-56, 160, 236, 309
Frontier process: importance of geographical factors on, 290
Fuller, Harlin M.: 144, 147

Gallatin, Albert: 106-7, 140
Galpin, C. J.: 216
Gates, Paul: 161
General Archives Division, National Archives: 292-93. *See also* National Archives
General Land Office, U.S.: 6, 136, 155-56, 220, 277, 286, 291, 295, 300; establishment of, 395-96; file organization in, 294; land-grant railroad and wagon road records in, 301; plats of, 123; records of, 320-23, 335; townsite files of, 296
General Services Administration, U.S.: 5
Geographers: as environmental determinists, 14; historical, 14-18, 193-94;

methods and purposes of, 10; problems faced by, 17-18. *See also* Historical geographers

Geographical exploration: 85-165; records of, 320-23, 337-38, 340, 350

Geography: as scholarly discipline, 19

Geological Survey, U.S.: 336, 350

Georgia: Atlanta, 338; records of, 331, 343-44; royal colony, 90; Savannah, 77-80; Savannah River, 91

German-Irish ghettos: mid-nineteenth century, 262

Ghettos: black, in Newark, N.J., 62; Irish-American, in New York City, 262

Gilpin, William: 343

Glacken, Clarence: 114

Glover, E. S.: 286

Gold: discovery of, 271, 276

Gold and silver towns: rise of, 271-72

Grain Corporation, U.S.: records of, 329

Grasslands: as pastures, 253; as pioneer settlement sites, 244; tree growth on, 305. *See also* Prairie

Great Britain: territory of in North America, 88-89

Great Lakes-St. Lawrence-Mohawk trade route: 205

Great Plains: nineteenth-century perception of, 21

Guadalupe Largo: survey of, 150-52, 159

Gulf-Atlantic trade route: 203

Gunter, Edmund: 119

Habersham, James: 91

Haefner, Harold: 125

Hafen, LeRoy R.: 144, 147

Hague, Arnold: 141

Harley, Brian: 88

Harvard University: 98

Hays, Samuel P.: 316

Heimatkunde: in undergraduate instruction, 26

Higman, Barry: 81

Hilliard, Sam B.: 202-13, 229, 309

Historians: epistemological considerations and, 17

Historical geographers: areas of interest to, 14-16; cultural, 17-18; in decision-making councils, 194; distinguishing characteristics of, 14; methodology of, 10; orientation of, 193; research and, 194

Historical geography: colonial America, 236; common forum for, xiv; France, 222-23; original and published sources in, 139-56, 315-49

Historic landscapes: geographical environ-

ment and, 194; management of, 193-200; user-perception research in, 197-98

History: literature of, 11; philosophy and methodology of, 19; poetry and, 19; research in, 17, 18

Holland, Samuel: 89, 100

Homestead Act (1862): 321

Homestead claims: pioneer settlements and, 300

Homestead property: land surveys and, 124

Houghton, Douglas: 295

Hoyt, Charles: 280

Hudson-Mohawk lowland trade route: 203

Hutchins, Thomas: 160

Hutchins, William: 163

Hutton, James: 336

Idaho (state): Boise, 272; mining towns in, 272; records of, 331, 340, 344

Idaho (territory): 340, 344

Illinois: Chicago, 344; Galena, 296-99; (Fever River) records of, 332, 344

Immigration: Chinese, 339, 349; ethnic division of labor and, 260; mid-nineteenth-century patterns of, 261-62; records of, 324, 339, 344, 346

Income tax records: 331

Indiana: Billie Creek Village, 196; Parke County, covered bridges in, 194-95; records of, 332, 344

Indians: *See* Native Americans

Industrial census: 226

Industrial geography: records of, 318-19

Industry: and commerce, 167-232; manufacture and, records relating to, 333-34

Initial occupance: concept of, 136

Inland Waterways Corporation, U.S.: 215

Innes, Frank C.: 81, 161

Interior Department, U.S.: 232; Lands and Railroads, Division of, 300

Internal improvements: 216; records of, 334

Internal Revenue assessment tests: 331

International Geographical Congress: 88

Interregional trade: foodstuffs in, 204-5; New Orleans food trade and, 205-9; pre-Civil War, 202-13

Interstate Commerce Act: 228

Interstate Commerce Commission, U.S.: 215, 217-18, 224; records of, 335

Iowa (state): Burlington, 296; Davenport, 296; Dubuque, 296, 299; Keokuk, 296; records of, 332; squatters in, 116

Iowa (territory): 344

Iowa/Minnesota boundary: road system at, 127

Irish-German ghettos: in American cities, 262
Irrigation projects: of Bureau of Reclamation, 340
Isaac, Rhys: 240

Jackson, Donald: 144, 148-49
Jackson, George: 280
Jakle, John A.: 193-200, 230, 309
James, Preston: 164
Jamestown, Va.: settlement at, 242
Janiskee, Robert L.: 193-200, 310
Japanese jori system: 115, 119
Jean, Dennis: 162
Jefferson, Thomas: 103-11, 158, 163; correspondence with scientists, 105; exploring expeditions authorized by, 140; influence on Lewis and Clark expedition, 110; land ordinance and, 132-34, 138, 162; letter to Michaux, 105; on Missouri River geography, 106; on Northwest Passage, 103; on roads and property boundaries, 138. *See also* Continental Congress
Jennings, Peter: 77
Joerg, W. L. G.: 6, 159
Johnson, Hildegard Binder: 131, 160-62, 310
Jordan, Terry G.: 244-55, 305, 310
Jori system, Japan: 115, 119

Kalm, Pehr: 21
Kentucky: records of, 332
King, Nicholas: 104, 107, 140-44, 158
Kniffen, Fred: 136
Knights, Peter: 170
Kovacik, Charles: 82

Labor Department, U.S.: 224
Land Act (1796): 118, 134, 138
Land disposal: congressional attitude toward, 138
Land-grant railroad policies: 300
Land Office Records: 6-7
Land Ordinance of 1785: 134
Land records: 291-93
Landscape: historic. *See* Historic landscapes
Landscape design: rectilinear partitioning and, 135-37
Land surveys: cadastral system in, 116-19; first public, 291; forty-acre units in, 123, 128; Indian titles in, 123, 130; principal meridians in, 122-23; rectangularity in, 119, 128-29, 131-37. *See also* Surveys; Public lands; Township surveys

Land use: 350
Land-Water Conservation Act: 232
Ledyard, John: 111, 163, 165
Lee, Charles E.: 231-32
Lemon, James: 238
Levine, Jonathan: 81
Lewis, Meriwether: 105, 107, 109, 140, 164
Lewis, Peirce: 82-83, 230-31
Lewis and Clark Expedition: 103, 105-6, 113, 140, 157, 164
Library of Congress: 163; Geography and Maps Division, 107
Locke, John: 161
Log culture complex, Texas: 247-48
Long, Stephen Harriman: 141, 144-47, 158
Louisiana: Lake Pontchartrain, 229; New Orleans, 204-13, 325; records of, 352
Louisiana Purchase: 140
Lowenthal, David: 231

McGregor Western Railroad Company: 124
Mackenzie, Alexander: 105
McManis, Douglas R.: 229, 316
Main, Jackson: 14
Maine: records of, 332
Mandan villages: 110, 140
Manufactures: 332; and industry, 333-34
Manual of Surveying Instruction: 128
Map(s) by: Aaron Arrowsmith, 105, 107-10; Emanuel Bowen, 88-89; Bureau of Indian Affairs, 322; William Gerard De Brahm, 95-97; Joseph Des Barres, 98; William Clark, 111; George Drouillard, 111; Federal Housing Administration, 335; Forest Service, 337; General Land Office, 33; Nicholas King, 104, 141-44; Nicholas de LaFora, 340; Stephen H. Long, 144-47; John Mitchell, 107; David Dale Owen, 349
Maps in the National Archives on: agriculture, 350; Civil War, 318; internal improvements, 334; Iowa Territory, 344; Native Americans, 350; post routes, 299; pre-federal period, 319; Red River of the North, 345; states and territories, 319; urban areas, 335; Wisconsin Territory, 349
Maritime Administration, U.S.: 216
Maritime Labor Board, U.S.: 216
Marschner, F. J.: 329
Marx, Karl: 10, 12
Maryland: records of, 332; Baltimore, 325
Massachusetts: Boston, 325, 344; colonial settlements in, 239; Northampton, 169; records of, 344

New Mexico (state): mining towns in, 272; records of, 322, 338, 346
New Mexico (territory): 346
New Orleans: in interregional trade, 204-13
New Spain: Lafora map of, 340
New York: Rochester, 169; New York, 264-69, 325
New York City: ethnic division of labor in, 259-69; German households in (1860), 265-68; Irish and German employment in (1860), 266-68; Irish households in (1860), 265-68; wards of, 264
North America: Arrowsmith map of (1802), 105, 107; British control in, 88-89
North Carolina: colonial settlements of, 241; records of, 346
North Dakota: townships in, 121
Northern Pacific Railroad: 216
Northwest Ordinance (1787): 132
Northwest Passage: Missouri River and, 103
Nootka Sound: 105

Office of Price Administration, U.S.: 224
Ohio: records of, 346-47; Seven Ranges, 291, 294
Oklahoma: records of, 322, 347
Ordinance of 1785: 116, 118. *See also* Northwest Ordinance
Ordnance Bureau, U.S.: 295
Oregan River: 105
Oregon: mining towns in, 272; records of, 340, 347
Owen, David Dale: survey by, 154-56, 159

Pacific Northwest Coast: reconnaissance of, 164
Pacific Ocean: Northwest Passage to, 103
Pacific Railroad Surveys: 159
Panic of 1837: 296
Pappus of Alexandria: 115
Parke, John G.: 150-51, 159
Parke County, Indiana: covered bridges in, 194-95; historical management of, 199; user-perception study in, 197-99
Parke County Historical Society: 196
Parker, Joel: 238
Passage to India: Jefferson and, 103-11
Patent or deed files: National Archives, 293
Pattison, William D.: 131-37, 160, 162-63, 311
Pederson, Eldor: 162
Pennsylvania: Philadelphia, 325; records of, 347

Pike, Zebulon: 111
Pioneer settlements: following Revolutionary War, 290-91; grasslands and, 244-45; in trans-Mississippi West, 300; land-grant railroads and, 300
Place persistence: 176; decennial rates for, 189. *See also* San Francisco
Plantations: *See* Rhode Island; Virginia
Polar exploration: 337
Popper, Karl: 13
Population: Colonial America, 236; mobility, in inner city, 169-90; records relating to, 321, 323-29, 348
Population turnover: ethnic differentiation in, 259. *See also* Afro-American population
Pork trade, New Orleans: 206-7
Post, Jeremiah: 160
Postal maps: 299
Post Office Department, U.S.: 7, 299; records of, 250, 334
Potawatomi Indian Agency: records of, 338
Potomac River: in British East Florida surveys, 89
Powell, John Wesley: 336
Powell, Sumner C.: 239-40
Prairie: avoidance of as settlement sites, 244; burning of, 253; as potential croplands, 249; types of in Texas, 245-46, 305
Price, Edward T.: 305
Prince, Hugh C.: 217
Progressive Era: 220
Public domain: settlement on, 290-303
Public land records: classification of, 291; records of, 320-23
Public lands: first surveys of, 291-92
Public Works Administration, U.S.: records of, 323
Purcell, Joseph: 93

Railroad Administration, U.S.: 334
Railroad routes: records of, 322; townsite choice and, 302. *See also* Transportation
Randall, Richard: 161
Rand McNally & Company: 161
Range cattle industry: 329
Raup, Hallock F.: 160
Reclamation Act (1902): 303; records on, 319
Reconstruction Finance Corporation, U.S.: 224
Rectangular Land Survey System: 131-37
Red River: 245; early settlements along, 249-51
Regional archives: 337-41
Reps, John W.: 271-89, 311

Research: opportunities for, 10-11; records in relation to, 218-20

Resource papers: in National Archives, 315

Revolutionary War: Clinton materials in, 14; De Brahm survey and, 94, 97-98; definitive work on, 12; nineteenth-century population studies on, 78; pioneer settlements following, 290-91; records of compared with those of Civil War, 81; slaves in British Army during, 73-74

Rhoads, James B.: 4-9, 311

Rhode Island: colonial settlements in, 239; plantations, 239

Rio des los Apostolos: 109

Rio Grande: 109, 111

Ristow, Walter W.: 163

Roads: See Transportation

Rocky Mountain fur trade: 111

Rolvaag, O. E.: 127

Roman Centuriation cadastral survey: 119

Romans, Bernard: 93, 98, 101

Rural and urban settlement: 233-303. See also Mining towns; Settlement sites; Townsites

Rural Electrification Administration, U.S.: 319

Russian-American Company: records of, 332

Sabine River: 252

Saint Johns River: 93

Saint Lawrence Seaway Development Corp.: 216

Saint Lawrence Valley: cartography in, 90

Saint Marys River, Florida: 93

San Francisco, Calif.: apparel-shopping activity group in, 185-87; banking activity group changes in, 175; bank locations in, 186; building changes vs. medical activities in, 180-82; Central District in, 170-76, 189; dry goods and clothing store locations in, 188; functional-structure changes in buildings of, 182; garment district changes in, 172, 178-79; leapfrogging of districts in, 183-85, 190, 192; locational changes of theatrical district in, 184; medical group activities in, 173, 180-82; movie district in, 184-85, 191; new establishments in, 190; place-persistent establishments in, 170-71; regional-persistent establishments in, 170-71; theater district locational changes in, 174, 183-84, 191

Sauer, Carl: 6-7, 244

Savannah River: settlements on, 91

Sayre, Hal: 280

Schafer, Joseph: 294-95, 297

Schellenberg, T. R.: 218-19

Schmeckebier, Lawrence F.: 218-19

Schmidt, Louis B.: 202-3

Schretter, Howard: 161

Scofield, Edna: 238

Settlement: records relating to, 320-23. See also Pioneer settlements; Settlement sites

Settlement sites: choice of in frontier Texas, 244-55; colonial Atlantic seaboard, 235-42; grasslands or prairies as, 244-46, 249; vegetational perception and, 244-55. See also Mining towns; Townsites

Seven Ranges (Ohio): 291, 294

Shinn, Charles: 275

Shipbuilding Stabilization Committee, U.S.: 216

Shipping Board, U.S.: 216, 333

Simpson, James Hervey: 150

Sioux Indians: records of, 322

Slavery: 75; abolition of in New Jersey, 26, 34; slave ship, manifests for (1794, 1850): 77-80. See also Afro-American population, southern slave plantations

Smith, Buckingham: 99

Smith, Jane F.: 290-304, 311

Snake River: 111

Sobel, Joel: 229

Social Science Research Council: 10, 318

Social subjects: records of, 318, 320

Soil Conservation Service, U.S.: 119, 128, 335

Sorokin, Pitirim: 12, 19

South Carolina: records of, 332, 347

South Dakota: Crook City, 272; Deadwood, 272; Lead, 272; mining towns in, 272; Pierre, 272

Southwest: major rivers of, 109

"Spatial:" as jargon word, 15, 20

Spence, Mary Lee: 144, 148-49

Squatter's township plan: 117

State Department, U.S.: 218

Superintendent of Mineral Lands, U.S.: 295

Supreme Court, U.S.: 225

Surveys: 85-129; cadastral system, 116-19; first for public lands, 291; forty-acre units in, 123, 128; historical development of as principle of order, 114, 129; Mason and Dixon Line, 338; planning of towns, 120-21; records of, 320-23, 336-38; section lines, 115-16

Sutro, Adolph: 277

Swift, William H.: 141, 144, 146-47
SYMAP Program, Harvard Laboratory for Computer Graphics: 59

Tennessee: Fort Loudon, 101; Nashville, 338; records of, 328, 346
Territoriality: geographic interest in, 20; as jargon word, 15
Territories (U.S.): records of, 320, 322, 339-40
Texas: Anglo-American pioneers in, 245, 249-50; Austin Colony, 250-52; Bailey's Prairie, 250; Bean's Prairie, 252; Blackland Prairie, 253; Brazos River, 245, 250; canebrakes, 247, 252, 305; Caney Creek, 247; Craft's Prairie, 252; forest clearance in, 249; forest-prairie mosaic in, 246; frontier settlement sites in, 244-55; grasslands in, 245-55; grazing areas in, 248; Hemphill's Prairie, 252; Jones Prairie, 253; Jonesborough, 250; log culture complex in, 247-48; Montgomery Prairie, 252; Pecan Point, 250; records of, 348; Robertson Colony, 252; small prairies in Eastern woodlands of, 254; timber in, 247; Wallace Prairie, 252; Webber's Prairie, 250; weed prairies in, 247
Thernstrom, Stephan: 170
Thrower, Norman: 136, 161
Thwaites, Reuben Gold: 141, 144
Towns: bonanza, in West, 271-89; rise of, 233-303. See also Settlement sites; Townsites
Township plan: creation of, 115; five-acre blocks in, 129; squatters, 116-17
Township roads: maintenance of by county, 125
Township surveys: 122-24, 130
Townsite files: extent of in National Archives, 302, 335
Townsites: 40-acre multiples in, 120, 124; by states, 120; records of, 322. See also Mining towns; Settlement sites
Toynbee, Arnold: 12
Tract books: surveys and, 292
Trade: Federal trading houses, 340, 343; records of, 329-30, 332, 337; Rocky Mountain, 111; routes of, 203, 205. See also Interregional trade; names of individual agricultural products
Transportation: Chicago, 344; commerce and, 167-232; nation-building role of, 215-16; records on, 331-32, 334-35, 340, 344, 350

Transportation and Communications Service, U.S.: 216
Transportation Department, U.S.: 220
Transportation research: design of, 215-23
Treasury Department, U.S.: 226, 291
Treat, Jackson Payson: 119
Trewartha, Glenn: 238
Trimble, Stanley W.: 305
Trindell, Roger T.: 163
Trinity River: 245, 252
Tunnard, Christopher: 127
Turner, Frederick Jackson: 162, 244, 290
Twain, Mark: 276

United States Land Office: 286. See also General Land Office
United States Land Survey: as principle of order, 114-29
Urban and rural settlements: 233-303. See also Settlement sites; names of specific cities
Urban development: records of, 335-38
Urban Mass Transit Administration, U.S.: 216
Urban planning: mining frontier and, 271-76
Urlsperger, Samuel: 90-92
User-perception research: in historic landscape management, 197-99
Utah (state): mining towns in, 272; records of, 338
Utah (territory): mapping of, 150; records of, 348

Valuation case files: in ICC series, 227
Vegetational perception: in Texas frontier settlement site choice, 244-55
Vermont: records of, 348
Virginia: Alexandria, 348; plantations and estates, settlement of, 240-41; records of, 240-41, 332, 348

Wacker, Peter O.: 25-67, 81-82, 312
Wallace, William H.: 162
Ward, David: 258-69, 312
War Department, U.S.: 140, 295
Warkentin, John: 21
War of 1812: 83
War Relocation Authority, U.S.: 327
War Shipping Administration, U.S.: 216
Washington (state): mining towns in, 272; records of, 340, 348
Washington (territory): 339-40
Weather Bureau, U.S.: 336-37
Webb, Walter Prescott: 244, 249

Western mining frontier: urban planning on, 271-89
Western territory: township system in, 115
West Virginia: records of, 332
Wheat trade: in New Orleans, 209, 213
Willamette River: 113
Williamson, Hugh: 132, 162
Winnebago Indian Agency: records of, 338
Wisconsin (state): forest-prairie relationship in settlement of, 155; records of, 349
Wisconsin (territory): 340; 349

Wright, John K.: 16
Wyoming (state): mining towns in, 272; records of, 338
Wyoming (territory): 349

Yellowstone River: 110-11
Yonge, Henry: 92
Young, J. J.: 153

Zelinsky, Wilbur: 25, 81